THE WAYS OF WISDOM

THE WAYS OF WISDOM

Towards a Global, Postsecular, *Convivencia* Theology

Anthony Mansueto

☙PICKWICK *Publications* • Eugene, Oregon

THE WAYS OF WISDOM
Towards a Global, Postsecular, *Convivencia* Theology

Copyright © 2016 Anthony Mansueto. All rights reserved. Except for brief quotations in critical publications or reviews, no part of this book may be reproduced in any manner without prior written permission from the publisher. Write: Permissions, Wipf and Stock Publishers, 199 W. 8th Ave., Suite 3, Eugene, OR 97401.

Pickwick Publications
An Imprint of Wipf and Stock Publishers
199 W. 8th Ave., Suite 3
Eugene, OR 97401

www.wipfandstock.com

PAPERBACK ISBN: 978-1-4982-0026-4
HARDCOVER ISBN: 978-1-4982-8717-3

Cataloguing-in-Publication data:

Mansueto, Anthony E.

The ways of wisdom : towards a global, postsecular, convivencia theology / Anthony Mansueto.

viii + 288 pp. ; 23 cm. Includes bibliographical references.

ISBN 978-1-4982-0026-4 (paperback) | ISBN 978-1-4982-8717-3 (hardback)

1. Metaphysics. 2. Philosophy, Modern. 3. Theology. I. Title.

BR118 .M34 2016

Manufactured in the U.S.A.   03/15/16

This work is dedicated to Maria Coeli and Simon Harry Mansueto, who helped me understand, at long last, the nature of relational, transformative generativity.

Contents

1 The Desire to Be God · 1

2 Theology *Is* Intercultural Engagement · 27

3 Being and Dependent Origination · 56

4 The Way of Justice and Liberation · 94

5 The Way of Harmony · 139

6 God's Work of Redemption · 155

7 The Engine of Divinity · 186

8 The Solution to the Riddle of History · 208

9 The Way of Ways · 240

Bibliography · 275

1

The Desire to Be God

The Quest

Humanity is the desire to be God (Sartre, Jean Paul. *Being and Nothingness*, 1943/1993: 556). Being finite, we are aware of the infinite and seek *to be* without limit. Being contingent, dependent on other beings for our existence, we seek the power of *Being as such* and seek it absolutely. It is this *Being* that, as something set apart, because we seek it but do not have it, we call the *sacred*. It is the condition for and horizon of any possible world we might inhabit, apart from which such worlds are groundless and lack meaning.

The mere fact that we *seek Being* does not, to be sure, imply that such Being *is*. But it does mean that the struggle for existence that we share with everything else in the material universe, whether extended, elemental, mineral, vegetable, or animal, takes on a new dimension. We seek Being not just *objectively*, in the form of our own survival and reproduction, but *subjectively* as an autonomous generative power. And we suffer from its absence. Our very existence is a longing for Being which is, in the end, insatiable. And everything that we do, no matter how mundane, is infused with this longing. Everything we do is not just an encounter with, but a reaching for, the sacred.

Human beings, furthermore, have a definite strategy for seeking Being, both objectively, as their own survival and reproduction, and subjectively, as an object of knowledge and desire. Some things, such as mathematical objects, exist only *in potentia,* as categories defined by operations on and relations between hypothetical elements which are, in turn, defined by these operations and relations. Some *mathematicals*, in turn, exhibit properties, such as dimension and extension, which make more complex forms of organization possible, giving rise to fundamental forces governed by mathematical laws, and to *elements* and *compounds* formed in accord with these laws. Some *elements* and compounds, which we call *minerals*, seek Being by exploiting the Boltzman Order Principle or some other thermodynamic law to conserve, however temporarily, their form. More complex compounds (*plants*) seek Being by nutrition, growth, and reproduction, or by sensation and locomotion (*animals*). But we humans seek Being by cultivating the ecosystems we inhabit in order to make higher, more complex forms of being possible. Our encounter with the sacred is, in other words, from the very beginning, an encounter with ourselves as *laboring being*.[1]

Human history is fundamentally the history of our search for Being, and of the distinct *ways* of being human to which it has given rise. Seeking *to be*, we proliferate throughout diverse ecosystems, create increasingly complex technologies, centralize and allocate resources for production, build and exercise power, and create imaginative, conceptual, and transconceptual artifacts which articulate and embody our quest and its specific forms.

In the beginning, human beings sought *to be* by means of hunting, gathering, and cultivation: by participating in the cycles of death and life and nurturing the organized and meaningful *cosmos* into which they had been born. The universe was transparent to its ground and all acts were understood as sacred: as a participation in Being. At the same time, the boundary between contingent and necessary Being, finite and Infinite, was recognized as impermeable. While human beings might *participate* in Being more fully than minerals, plants, and animals, there was no question of becoming divine, however much we might want to. Indeed, the divine properly understood, while ever present as ground and aim, was rarely if ever fully thematized as such. The divine was our Mother, a womb from which we only ever partly emerged.

---

1. It was ironically Marx who, in extending Feuerbach's critique of religion, first established *scientifically* the specific quality of human spirituality (Marx 1844/1978, 1846/1978) as *labor* or what we prefer to call *relational transformative generativity*.

> Men can be distinguished from animals by consciousness, by religion or anything else you like. They themselves begin to distinguish themselves from animals as soon as they begin to produce their means of subsistence, a step which is conditioned by their physical organisation. By producing their means of subsistence men are indirectly producing their actual material life (Marx 1846/1978).

This should not, to be sure, be understood to exclude the other characterizations of the sacred which define the sociology of religion. Because labor always and only involves collaboration, it is also always social, the activity of a supraindividual collective reality (Durkheim 1911/1964). The *sacred* is thus the *social*. And because labor is always already an intellectual act, consciously ordered to an end, it is also always constitutively *meaningful* (Weber 1921/1968). The *sacred* is the ground and horizon of any possible meaning.

Being aware of *Being as such*, however dimly, we could never be satisfied with mere participation. At first, to be sure, we had no choice. But eventually metal technologies made it possible to enslave and instrumentalize others and live off their labor (Childe 1851, Lenski 1981), and so to imagine ourselves as ends rather than means, as indeed *the* end itself which we sought, as *Being as such*. We became as gods, recipients of great public liturgies centered around the sacrifice of the human: where not literally, then figuratively, as the human labor which makes life possible.

The conquest and sacrifice of the human was also, always, the conquest and sacrifice of the feminine. This is not because women have no drive to conquer or lack the ability. It is, rather, that women found themselves bound by their own generative power to the bearing and rearing of children (Firestone 1970/2003). On the one hand they already participate in *Being* to a higher degree than men (through childbearing), and perhaps saw less reason to conquer and exploit the generative power of another. And they would have felt more immediately the loss of authentic generativity which conquest implied. It was there in the face of the children they would have had to abandon to go off to war. On the other hand they soon found themselves the object rather than the subjects of the new *way* of conquest and exploitation. The advent of warfare as a strategy for economic development—and deification—was the world historical defeat of the female sex (Engels 1884/1948).

It could not have been otherwise. Had we not made war there would likely have been no significant organization above the village level, and certainly nothing beyond the pre-urban ritual centers at places like Chaco, Stonehenge, and Gobekli Tepe. And besides, we are the *desire to be God*. Thus was born the *way* of the Master, the *sacral monarchic way of conquest, exploitation, and sacrifice*. This was the first manifestation of what we are calling the *Saeculum*, the attempt to achieve divinity, or at least transcend finitude and/or contingency, by means of instrumentalizing others.

Conquest gave birth to the first urban civilizations—Mesopotamia, Egypt, the Huang He, and (with some differences) the Indus Valley, a world of warlords and walled cities and pyramids of sacrifice. We thought ourselves great *ba'alim*, lords and masters. But we were not. Lord Death was our master then and we were *his* slaves. Conquest itself creates nothing, and the conquered are never particularly creative. And being finite and contingent, all that is old eventually disintegrates, decays, and dies. It should thus come as no surprise that throughout the Afro-Eurasian "Old World" where it was born, this *way* suddenly collapsed sometime around the end of the Bronze Age, between 1200 and 1000 BCE, giving humanity a chance for a new beginning.

That new beginning took the form of what Karl Jaspers (Jaspers 1953) has called the Axial Age—the period which gave birth to Judaism, Hellenism, Hinduism, Buddhism, Taoism, and Confucianism. Over a period of about six hundred years (800-200 BCE), in each of the principal centers of Afro-Eurasian civilization, specialized agriculture and crafts production and petty commodity production transformed humanity's *way* of being. Comparative advantage based on ecological niche and human value-added rooted in *techne* now competed with conquest as strategies for growth and development. The emergence of first regional and then global trade networks brought competing *ways* into contact with each other, rendering meaning problematic for the first time. Humanity found itself in a world of formal relations (the market) which created the basis in experience for formal abstraction, the rise of abstract mathematics, and ultimately of philosophy. Image and story give way, at least partly, to concept and argument. Those formerly bound to serve the aristocracy of warlords and priests began to struggle for the right to enjoy the fruits of their labor, to govern themselves, to participate fully in both deliberation around questions of meaning and value and to claim for themselves the *theosis* (deification) which was previously reserved for the aristocracy.

This is the point of origin of the three great *ways* of which what are ordinarily called the "world religions" are ultimately variations: *the way of liberation and justice* (Judaism, Christianity, and Islam), *the way of the search for Being* (including Hellenism, Hinduism, Buddhism, the Jaina tradition, and their peripheries), and *the way of harmony* (Taoism, Confucianism, and perhaps some other Chinese traditions). The first of these we can call *the way of the Slave* proper, of those who, defeated by the warlord, are reduced to pure labor power, and discover therein the power of Being as such (Hegel 1807/1993), something which gives them the vantage point of Being prior to any dialectical ascent. The second two, the *way of the search for being* and *the way of harmony*, we call *clerical* ways because reflect more nearly the perspective of *intelligentsias* which, in the wake of the late Bronze Age collapse and the failure of the sacral monarchic project, and even more so with the development of petty commodity production, sought to develop new strategies for *theosis* which did not fall into the trap of the Master, or for living in harmony with a universe in and from which *theosis* was impossible.

What these great axial ways did *not* call into question, at least not radically or consistently enough to make a difference, was the patriarchal expropriation of female generative power. Even when born of a peasant revolt, like ancient Israel (Gottwald 1979), one led in part by women (Judges 5), and even when devoted to the *Magna Mater, Prajnaparamita, Tara,* the *Mahavidya,* or *Guan Yin* (Stone 1976) the emerging axial ways remained overwhelmingly attempts by men to liberate men. This left more of the old sacral monarchic dynamic intact than anyone understood or imagined.

And with the underlying dynamic of patriarchal expropriation intact, it should thus come as no surprise that new empires arose—the Hellenistic and Roman, the Mauryan and the Qin being the most important—which exploited not so much direct production, but rather the global trade in luxury goods (silk, spices, porcelain, wine, oil, slaves, and precious metals). known as the great *Silk Road*. This strategy proved far more effective than the earlier sacral monarchic project and resulted in empires large and powerful enough to imagine themselves as global in character. Though none were really more than regional hegemons, they were fare more powerful than their Bronze Age predecessors. Where the *ba'alim* had proven vulnerable to relatively small scale revolts by poorly armed marginalized peasant communities of the sort which brought Israel into being (Gottwald 1979) or to the combination of ecodemographic collapse and the withdrawal of villages back into subsistence agriculture which is the most likely explanation for the sudden "disappearance" of so many early proturban and urban civilizations around the planet, the great Iron Age empires, while they might periodically lose some territory to an uprising like that of Maccabees, were ultimately beyond the reach of most revolutionary popular forces, except where these forces were themselves (like emerging Islam or the Chinese peasant revolts which created new dynasties) emerging *Imperia*. This is why it seemed to many Silk Road Era critics of *Empire* that they were struggling not with human beings but rather *directly* with angelic/demonic/asuric "powers and principalities" of which the earthly *Imperia* were simply agents (Eph 6:12). This was the second manifestation of the *Saeculum*.

Sometimes these empires attempted to repress the axial traditions, as in the case of the Qin (Collins 1998) or early Roman responses to Judaism and Christianity. Ultimately, however, the new empires co-opted them and used them as forms of legitimation. This in turn meant that the fundamentally exploitative character of these empires was softened and transformed, sometimes very significantly, by the influence of the axial project (the Tang and the Song, the Mauryans, and the Abbasids and Fatimids are probably the best examples in this regard) (Mansueto 2010a). The result was the protracted war of position between competing *ways* of being human that we often identify as the Middle Ages, though it is, more properly characterized as the great Silk Road Era (200 BCE-1800 CE).

During this period the great Axial *ways* worked out their own internal implications and contradictions. For the *way of justice and liberation* this meant ascertaining what *justice* might mean in a world of resurgent empire. Could *Empire* be defeated as it was in the Late Bronze Age, and a new era of justice and peace ushered in (Jewish Messianism, including earliest Christianity and then later Islam)? Or was empire inevitable, at least for the foreseeable future? If so, how could the just act effectively at the margins to catalyze struggles for justice (Pharisaism and Rabbinic Judaism)? Or was the struggle for justice more a spiritual than a political discipline, something which stretches us beyond the merely human, towards the divine (most later Christianity)? For the *way of the search for Being* this meant asking whether or not dialectics terminate in a first principle in terms of which the universe can be explained and human action ordered (Hellenism and most Hinduisms) or, rather, in a recognition of that *everything* is empty of inherent existence and dependent on everything else (Buddhism). For the *way of harmony* this meant determining whether or not the *way* itself could be captured in language and in law (Confucianism), or whether or not this was itself the point of origin or all forms of oppression (Taoism).

But the axial *ways* also engaged each other, not yet globally, but piecemeal, along the intercivilizational frontiers crossed by the Silk Road. Hellenism engaged Judaism and its offspring, Christianity and Islam. Buddhism, which was born in India, found its most complex expressions in Southeast Asia, China, and the Himalayan Plateau. And an Islam already transformed by its interaction with Hellenism engaged the complex of ways which we now (perhaps incorrectly or at least anachronistically) call Hinduism along a broad frontier reaching from Persia across the Indus Valley and the Himalayan foothills well into the Indo-Gangetic Plain (Khan 2004).

It is this engagement between *ways,* we will argue, which is constitutive of a specifically *theological* discourse, and which gives birth to the great synthetic ways which were the highest achievement of the Silk Road Era: the Catholic synthesis and its progenitors in Judaism and Islam, the higher Mahayana and Varjayana Schools, the "Neo-Confucian" (but actually also profoundly Buddhist and Taoist) *dao xue* and the diverse complex of *ways* including a range of later developments of the Ismaili tradition, Sufi currents, the Sikh tradition, and at least some of what was eventually classified by colonial authorities (and came to understand itself) as Hinduism along the western frontiers of the Indian subcontinent (Khan 2004).

These synthetic ways represent an enormous achievement, mapping out for humanity a process by which, if it cannot transcend finitude and contingency substantially, becoming God in *essence*, it can, nonetheless do so accidentally, taking on the form of God in increasing degrees by means of a protracted process of intellectual and moral self-cultivation, ethical conduct and active engagement in the struggle for justice, and the spiritual practice necessary to harvest the fruits of this engagement. It also created an infrastructure of institutions—academies and synagogues, temples and monasteries, the Papacy, and the Caliphate or Imamate, which supported humanity in its struggle for *thesosis*. We call this complex of institutions and the project they carried *Sanctuary*.

At the same time, the failure to address the patriarchal expropriation of female creative power left the sanctuaries which were created darkened and undercut the full realization of the axial project. The Great Silk Road Era was, ultimately, a period of stalemate in which *Sanctuary* and *Saeculum* held each other in balance. *Sanctuary* softened and humanized *Empire* and limited instrumentalization; *Empire* instrumentalized *Sanctuary* as a means of legitimation and ensured that the problematizing, rationalizing, and democratizing dynamics of the axial project were held in check.

This stalemate has now been broken and the *Saeculum* has become globally hegemonic. Breaking this stalemate was, historically, the work of one particular group of warrior tribes—the Germanic peoples, and especially the Normans—whose movement into Europe set in motion a process which, by way of the Norman conquests, the Crusades, the Reconquista, and their prolongation into the conquest of Africa, the Americas, and much of Asia, led to the scientific and industrial revolutions, and eventually to the hegemony of Global *Capital* under which we live today (Mansueto 2010a). At first this process was legitimated as a way of advancing the sovereignty of the Christian God, and of participating in His creative activity by means of ever more advanced technology and ever more efficient exploitation of human labor. This *way* found its expression in the diverse forms of Protestant Christianity, and its highest expression in the evangelical (but prefundamentlaist) and liberal variants of the Reformed Tradition (Heimart 1966, Howe 1966, Hatch 1977, Marsden 1980). We call this way *theistic secularism* (Weber 1920/1968). But soon humanity's conviction of its own potential and power grew to the point that many began to believe that they could actually *build* God, or at least transcend finitude by means of scientific and technological progress and the economic development they make possible. This is the *way* that we are living today, the *way* of *technocratic secularism* (Tipler 1994). We are chained to this way by industrial technology and proletarianization and we live it whether we embrace it or not.

Over the course of roughly the same period the democratic impulse which had always been part of the axial tradition, but which had been eclipsed during much of the Silk Road Era by the reality of stalemate with the *Saeculum*, began to reassert itself, especially in Europe. Peasants, emboldened by the rising value of labor power and the demographic collapse that followed the Black Death fought to liberate themselves from feudal obligations. Cities governed by guilds of artisans and merchants demanded and won self-government from the Holy Roman Empire and the Church

(Anderson 1974a). These movements almost always articulated their emerging understanding of what it means to be human in terms derived from the axial traditions. Joachism (de Lubac 1979, Leff 1999, Reeves 1969, 1976), which proposed to replace the rule of priests and kings with a sort of monastic communism led by the spiritually most developed[2], and Radical Aristotelianism[3], which began to give political content to the ancient ideal of the philosopher king (Dahm 1988, Crone 2004), are typical in this regard.

---

2. Drawing on the work of Gillian Rose (Rose 1984), John Milbank (Milbank 1990, 2014) has argued forcefully that the univocal metaphysics which defines the *Saeculum* is ultimately derivative from the Franciscan movement. This is based, of course, on the defense of the doctrine of the univocity of Being by John Duns Scotus. The argument has considerable merit, especially considering the implication of the Fransciscans in the Augustinian Reaction of the thirteenth century, which was in every sense a run-up to the Reformation. What this analysis misses is 1) the distinction between a univocity like that of the Spirituals which treats all Being as necessary, i.e. as immanently divine and one which, like that of much Protestantism, does not even recognize the difference between the necessary and the contingent, and thus fails to actually rise to the idea of Being as such. 2) the fact that Francis' original charism was interpreted in radically different ways within the order from the very beginning and that as a result of the influence of Joachism and the Spiritual controversy the movement was, effectively dismantled and rebuilt under the control not even of its own Right wing but of tendencies much further to the Right than even the Conventual tendency. This is apparent from the fact that when many Franciscans today defend the doctrine (Rohr 2015) they are clearly defending the participation of phenomenal reality in the life of God, in much the way that Dominicans would using a doctrine of the analogy of Being, with perhaps a bit less sensitivity to the distinction between "participation" and "identity," and a resulting tendency to constantly reproduce the radical immanentism of Joachim and the Spirituals. We will consider this question in great depth in a later chapter.

3. There is, similarly, a much longer standing tendency, based on the work of Etienne Gilson (Gilson 1952) that it was only Thomas who final developed a coherent doctrine of Being and that earlier Jewish and Islamic Aristotelianism, especially the thought of ibn Sina, was dominated by a marked tendency towards essentialism. While there can be little doubt that Thomas' doctrine of Being is more developed than that of his predecessors, a careful reading of the ibn Sina's only major philosophical work in Persian the *Danish* (ibn Sina c 1025/2001) shows a clear distinction between necessary and contingent Being and a clear identification of God with the former. What defines Radical Aristotelianism, and especially Latin Averroism, is above all a tendency to invest phenomenal being, at least in its totality, with the characteristics of Being as such, resulting, again, in a radical immanentism. While we will argue that this radical immanentism is mistaken, and that this mistake is responsible for many of the errors of later humanistic secularisms of both the left and the right, it is quite different from the univocity which conceives God simply as an infinitely powerful instance of the kind of being we are, stripping the universe entirely of the creative and generative power of Being as such and creating a metaphysical zero-sum game in which the only spiritual alternatives are submission or radical depravity. It is also quite different than the technocratic secularism which denies the existence of such an infinitely powerful being but aims to create one by means of scientific and technological progress, or at least to approach such technodeification as closely as possible.

Similar movements emerged in China, India, and Dar-al-Islam. While most Chinese peasant revolts were inspired by Taoism and Buddhism (Ter Haar 1992), there is some evidence of an esoteric Confucianism with revolutionary tendencies (Lai 1977). Tantric and related movements in the Indian subcontinent were quite explicit both in mobilizing subaltern spirituality and in popularizing and radicalizing the philosophical monism of the *advaita vedanta*. The most important of these movements was almost certainly the Mahavidya trend, which focused on the veneration of low-caste and even *dalit* female manifestations of the divine (Kinsley 1997). The devotion to Kali in particular has a long history of association with movements of popular resistance. The Nizari Ismailis, meanwhile, who taught a synthesis between the Islamic variant of the *way of justice and liberation* and Hellenic dialectics completed and enriched by contemplative practice, emerged as a revolutionary force with *Dar-al-Islam,* which resisted the Turkic invasions which eventually imposed an Asharite Sunni consensus (Darfatary 1992, 1994, 2005).

These revolutionary tendencies were soon crushed by a series of reactions across the planet. The most important of these was the Augustinian reaction which accompanied the formation of sovereign, absolutist states in Europe as a result of the Norman conquests, the Crusades, the Reconquista, and the Conquest of the Americas. But the Turkic and Mongol invasions had similar consequences, marginalizing not only the Ismaili Imamate but the more advanced schools within the Sunni tradition, and transforming the *dao xue* from an elite reformism into an ossified doctrine of imperial legitimation. The result, at least in Europe, was an intensification of their immanentist orientation and a tendency to assert the already "divine" character of the human and even of the material in general. It took 700 hundred years, but the popular messianisms of Joachim of Fiore and Sabbatzi Zvi (Scholem 1973) on the one hand and the and idealist and materialist mysticisms of Amalric of Bena and David of Dinant (Dahm 1987) on the other eventually became, by way of Gersonides, Spinoza, Kant, and Hegel, together with countless movements of resistance and revolution by peasants, artisans, and the emerging proletariat, the dialectical and historical materialism of Marx and Engels and Lukacs. This *way* we call *humanistic secularism* of which we will identify liberal, democratic, socialist, and populist variants.

Understood properly, modernity *is* secularism, but not in the sense of a rejection of the spiritual aim of humanity, which remains constant and which cannot be anything other than deification. Rather, modernity is defined by the conviction that deification can be achieved, if at all, through innerworldly civilizational progress: either scientific, technological, and economic (what we call technocratic secularism) or through the construction of a political subject (the rationally autonomous individual, the *demos*, the proletariat, the *ethnos*) capable of making humanity the master of its own destiny, transforming contingent into necessary Being.

Theistic, technocratic, and humanistic secularisms were doomed from the beginning, but for very different reasons. Theistic secularism was unable to reconcile the Jewish and Christian (and in some later variants Muslim) story on which it was based with the imperative to exploit and accumulate. The First and Second Great Awakenings in the United States can be understood in large part as movements of resistance to liberal tendencies to assess election on the base of "usefulness to society." The resulting Evangelical movement focused as much on social reform as on individual conversion. It was only when the Civil War ushered in not the millennium but rather industrial capitalism that evangelicals abandoned their historic commitment to social justice and focused their efforts on preparing for an divinely initiated (but still very worldly) return of Jesus as messianic king (Marsden 1980). Liberals, meanwhile, struggled to reconcile their profound attachment to secular concepts of "progress" with efforts to ameliorate the injustices of industrial capitalism in a way that rendered it compatible with the Christian story. Their failure in this regard (not for lack of creativity, but because the task is inherently impossible) is, more than anything else, the reason for their decline, an issue to which we will return later in this work.

Technocratic secularism was doomed because it radically misunderstands the nature of the sacred and thus seeks to build something (a being of infinite power) which is itself ultimately unsatisfactory. The Being we long for is not the Infinite but rather the creative and generative power of *Being as such* and no increase in our ability to accumulate contingent beings will quench that thirst. Unlimited accumulation, as we are discovering, degrades the creative expressions of being at the mineral, plant, animal, and rational/social levels.

Both theistic and technocratic secularism are, furthermore (whatever the role of technology in liberating women) ultimately the most radical possible expressions of the patriarchal expropriation of female generative power. Theistic secularism requires the radical submission of women to a God conceived in a way which cannot but resonate psychosexually as male and patriarchal. Even radical institutional reforms, such as the ordination of women to positions of leadership, cannot change the fact that the feminine dimension of the divine has been banished utterly from theistic secular movements.

Technocratic secularism, through the medium of industry, seeks to find another way of creating. Rather than tapping into the immanent creative and self-organizing potential of matter, which is a reflection of its participation in Being, and which we humans experience first and foremost in our generation from the womb, it breaks down existing forms of organization by means of combustion and uses the energy released to do work. Where the sacral monarchic and imperial projects rendered the feminine captive and subject; industrial Capital attempts, at least, to make it redundant.

Humanistic secularism, on the other hand, seeks Being authentically, and seeks it in an authentic locus of its self-disclosure, i.e. the human, but it fails to recognize that the boundary between contingent and necessary being is impermeable and that *no* political subject can render us the masters of our own destiny. Marx's critique of liberal and democratic humanism is quite correct. Capital makes both individual rational autonomy and authentic democracy impossible. But socialism has its own contradictions. Merely "organizing and directing the historical process," does not carry humanity across the boundary between contingency and necessity, especially in a universe which physics tells us may eventually become inhospitable to complex organization, life, and intelligence. It would be necessary, at the very least, to "organize and direct the entire cosmohistorical evolutionary process." Thus the necessity of technological god-building, of the sort advocated by Bogdanov and Gorky and Lunacharsky (Rowley 1987). But once we make this move we are back on the terrain of technocratic secularism which is the terrain of univocity and terror. It should thus come as no surprise that when, after liquidating its philosophical advocates, Stalin made technological godbuilding into his principal strategy for socialist construction, the result was a complete liquidation of socialism's humanistic aims and transformed socialism into an *alter-imperial* development strategy, and ultimately, as the constraints which socialism placed on development beyond a certain point became apparent, just a regional strategy for primitive *capitalist* accumulation.

But avoiding the technocratic turn does not solve the problem. The truth is that any collective political subject coherent and disciplined enough to act as the unique subject-object of the cosmohistorical evolutionary process would also, inevitably, be incompatible with meaningful individual rational autonomy (the liberal form of the humanistic ideal) or internal democracy (the democratic form) which were nonetheless integral to what humanists from Marx through Lukacs were trying to accomplish through socialism. Attempts to make socialism something other than a strategy for building industrial capitalism on the periphery of the world capitalist system, such as that undertaken by Maoism during the Cultural Revolution, by abolishing *selfishness* before the abolition of *scarcity*, thus inevitably result in totalitarian nightmare.

The attempt, finally, to substitute the *people* as *ethnos* for the proletariat as the locus for the self-disclosure of Being, already well developed in the nineteenth century and articulated most fully by Heidegger (Heidegger 1934/1989) has proven itself to be a catastrophic dead end. While it *does* matter whether the *ethnos* in question is engaged in empire building, like the NAZI Germany of which Heidegger aspired to be *the* philosopher, or a struggle for national liberation, like the anticolonial struggles which form the background for most poststructuralist and deconstructionist "left" Heideggerianism (Chiesa and Toscano 2009), the internal dynamics of postcolonial societies, especially those which claim to be revolutionary, have looked strikingly like soft fascism, with national, popular and religious traditions used to mobilize the people in a way which leaves little room for rational autonomy or democratic process. In both cases, as with socialism, the technocratic turn seems all but inevitable as the realities of state-building in a world dominated by *Capital* and *Empire* assert themselves. Prioritizing difference rather than the "event" of Being (Millerman 2013) does nothing to guarantee either a spirituality or a politics which is authentically liberating. Both are just substitutes for an assertion of ethnic identity in which the line between the *anti-imperal* and the *alter-imperial* is always a fine one at best. And as for socialism, competing with the dominant *Imperium* meant embracing the very practices of technopolitical control which the philosophers of this trend, such as Heidegger (Heidegger 1977) so decried.

The long epoch between 1848 and 1989 was dominated by two principal dynamics. On the one hand, in the metropoles, there was a struggle between technocratic and humanistic secularism and within the humanistic camp between liberal, democratic, socialist, and populist tendencies. Meanwhile, on the peripheries, peasant and sometimes artisan and clerical sanctuaries resisted vigorously the penetration of capitalist relations of production into their "countrysides" and the incorporation of their homelands into rival *Imperia* among which the American *Imperium* was ultimately victorious (Hobsbawm 1958, Wolf 1969).

This struggle was won decisively by technocratic secularism not because it was able to deliver on its promise to transcend finitude by means of scientific, technological, and economic progress, but rather because it delivered *enough* technologically and economically to defeat the other alternatives in a protracted war of position and because, as we have seen, humanistic secularism had to make massive concessions to technocracy in order to even compete, concessions which echo the earlier concessions of the axial movements to patriarchy and empire. The result is the decisive victory of the *Saeculum* and the reduction of *Sanctuary* to a dwindling number of marginal enclaves.

This is a defeat and in many ways it is a decisive one. Even more so than in the case of the great Iron Age manifestations of *Empire* the *Saeculum* has constituted itself as an autonomous power, acting through *Capital* and *Empire* but quite independent of anything which might be called a "ruling class." The bourgeoisie which created *Capital*, for which *Capital* was the vehicle of a great spiritual and civilizational project, and which still, in many ways benefits from *Capital*, now finds itself at the mercy of the power it has created, unable to bring it heel or make it serve their spiritual and civilizational aims. They—and we—are truly in the grip of an *asuric* power.

But this defeat is not final and it clarifies for us the conditions for any renewed struggle to liberate and extend the reach of our sanctuaries. Not just for the individual, as Lukacs himself recognized (Lukacs 1921/1971) but for humanity as a whole, understood as either substance or as subject, alienation is irreversible. It is only by understanding Being as neither substance nor subject, but rather pure generativity, ceasing to cling to inherent existence, that either the spiritual aims of the axial traditions or the political aims of humanistic secularism can be realized. And this means going back and resuming the axial and humanistic secular projects, engaging the patriarchal expropriation of female generative power and the resultant compromises with empire. It means extending and radicalizing the problematizing, rationalizing, and democratizing dynamics of the axial project, as humanistic secularism attempted to do, while avoiding the mistake of radical immanentism. And it means discovering a new sense of *techne* (or perhaps rediscovering an older one) as cultivation of the self-organizing potential latent in matter, which will best the technological achievements of the *Saeculum* while avoiding the instrumentalization and ecological destruction the latter has wrought.

The Terrain

This is the quest. We need now to analyze in greater detail the specific terrain on which we undertake it today.

An Era of Civilizational Crisis

The victory of the *Saeculum* is, we will argue, ultimately Pyrric in nature. This is because, even has as the *Saeculum* approaches total hegemony, it is entered a period of profound and unprecedented crisis, a crisis which threatens civilizational retrenchment perhaps on the scale of the late Bronze Age collapse (Cline 2014) and at least on the scale of the partial collapse which affected some of the great Iron Age empires (such as Rome) during the more recent Dark Ages (Anderson 1974, de Ste. Croix 1982, Frank 1998).

There are several dimensions to this crisis. We are, first of all, in the early stages of a profound ecological crisis which will, at the very least, result in major traumas to essentially all major civilizational centers and which, at worst, could lead to complete civilizational collapse. *Industry*, which is the technological expression of the *Saeculum*, relies on combustion which breaks down existing forms of organization to release energy and do work. Unless significant progress is made very soon in developing renewable and thus fundamentally nonindustrial energy sources, we will eventually deplete the fossil fuel sources on which the industrial regime depends, undermining its material basis (Hubbert 1956, Campbell 2007). The same principle applies to all of the other mineral inputs required by an industrial civilization.

Meanwhile, the by-products of industrial production are significantly altering our ecosystem. The most important such effect is the climate change induced by increasing carbon dioxide levels, the most important direct effect of combustion. According to the Intergovernmental Panel on Climate Change "warming of the climate system is unequivocal, as is now evident from observations of increases in global average air and ocean temperatures, widespread melting of snow and ice, and rising global average sea level (Intergovernmental Panel on Climate Change 2007: 5)." Furthermore, "for the next two decades a warming of about 0.2°C per decade is projected for a range of SRES emission scenarios. Even if the concentrations of all greenhouse gases and aerosols had been kept constant at year 2000 levels, a further warming of about 0.1°C per decade would be expected (Intergovernmental Panel on Climate Change 2007: 12)." And these averages are deceptive. Climates are complex, nonlinear systems and even small fluctuations can have large effects. Some analysts, for example, have claimed that melting of the polar ice caps for example, could desalinate the Atlantic Ocean, undermining the Gulf Stream and depriving Europe of its mild climate (McGuire 2003).

Resource depletion and climate change are, furthermore, only two dimensions of the emerging ecological crisis. There is broad evidence that the pollution of the environment and food supply with the byproducts of industrial production is contributing significantly to rising cancer rates and other health problems. Far from allowing us to transcend the limits of material finitude, industrial civilization may well bring us crashing up against those limits in an unprecedented way.

Capital, meanwhile, which is the economic modality of the *Saeculum*, is holding back both the development of new technologies which might resolve the crisis of industrialism, largely because they are not easily monetized. It was precisely the relative scarcity of fossil fuels which made investment in them attractive, as a source of mineral rents. The sun, wind, and even hydrogen, which are abundant, might yield profits of enterprise, but they will yield no monopoly rents. And the technologies which capitalism *has* developed (the information technology revolution) are coming close to rendering all routine human labor (including all but the most innovative intellectual labor and a cluster of boutique "artisan" practices) redundant. And even in advance of this development, the emergence of a global market in capital is leading to a convergence in wages which is rapidly undercutting the privileged status of workers in the old "First World." As even more regions of the planet are incorporated into this global market, the supply of labor, including of skilled labor, will so far exceed the demand that both the value and the price of labor power will decline (towards zero), creating a permanent condition of structural underconsumption which is increasingly difficult to ameliorate by means of corrective regimes of accumulation such as the welfare state, military spending, obscene luxury consumption combined with easy credit, etc.

Capital has also, effectively, undermined the state as an authentic institution of governance. The nation state, for all its failures, provided the people with the leverage they needed to wrest concessions from their ruling classes which were, ultimately, stabilizing for the system as a whole. But when *Capital* can simply redeploy to evade measures designed to protect the ecosystem, workers, or the social fabric, the nation state becomes impotent not only as an instrument for structural reform or social revolution but even for stabilization. The only effective global political authorities exist to create an hospitable global framework for *Capital* whether through economic regulation or deregulation or through military intervention to protect the interests of *Capital*. This global political authority which, while exercised through nation states and their governments is actually independent of and superior to them, we call *Empire*. And *Empire* has local expressions in the form of the repressive state apparatus. As recent events in the United States show, even where elected leaders are benign or better, *Empire* ensures that the growing surplus population is kept in a state of subjection and terror.

The most profound sign of crisis of the *Saeculum*, however, is the fact that people have ceased almost entirely to *believe* in the ideal to which it is ordered. There are, to be sure, pockets of transhumanism, the most radical of which center around Frank Tipler's Omega Point Theory, which revives Bolshevik godbuilding but strips it of its humanistic ideals (Rowley 1987, Tipler 1994), reducing intelligence, life, and complex organization to simply degrees of informatic complexity. But the scientific evidence has not been kind to the *Omega* tendency, especially since the Higgs Boson weighed in well below the levels Tipler's theory requires (CERN 2012). More modest transhumanisms, which promise radical extension of human life and capacities and an end to human drudgery through advances in biotechnology and robotics are failing to speak to the majority of the planet's population, who see little prospect of access to life extending and enhancing technologies and who experience the redundancy of routine labor as the redundancy of their very existence. For the *Saeculum* everything that exists exists to be exploited. Universal "employment"—the goal of even most progressive economic policy—is essentially universal exploitation. This seems like a good alternative only because we know, in our heart of hearts, that redundancy could easily mean anihilation.

This is not to say that the apocalyptic nightmare visions of cyberpunk fiction are inevitable or even likely, but rather that the *Saeculum* is spent and that only a new *techne* grounded in a new science and new vision of what it means to be human can give birth to a new, truly human future. People are, quite simply, tired of being turned into batteries. They are tired of having every aspect of their lives regulated and controlled. And they are tired of being told that the *only* thing that is meaningful about their lives is their contribution to the accumulation of capital or to the scientific and technological progress which it makes possible.

The Current Conjuncture and the Configuration of Forces on the Terrain

Within this broader context of civilizational crisis, it might be useful, finally, to analyze the configuration of forces which define the current conjuncture. We are, broadly speaking, still within the third conjuncture since the collapse of the Soviet bloc. The first of these conjunctures was dominated by the aftermath of this collapse and the wave of growth and development made possible by the information technology revolution and given scope, in part, by the collapse itself and the subsequent formation of a global market in capital. This conjuncture lasted from roughly 1989-2001. The second conjuncture was defined by the collapse of the "dot.com" bubble, which marked the limits of the new "information economy" as a force for driving growth and development. The collapse of this bubble led to the resurgence of reactionary, resource based economies—and the conflicts between them, which took the form of the "clash of civilizations" and the "war on terror." This configuration of forces was already emerging in 1999-2000 and was dominant from 2001 until sometime between 2006 and 2008. The third and still dominant configuration of forces has been defined by the global

"Great Recession" which began in 2007 and from which we have not yet fully emerged. This recession was the catalyzed by the collapse of the speculative bubble created by easy credit, the principal means used by *Capital* to spark a recovery from the "dot.com" bust, but has been so recalcitrant largely because of the underlying technoeconomic changes noted above: the declining demand for human labor as a result of the advance of information technologies, which drives down the value of labor power, ultimately towards zero, and creates a situation of structural underconsumption. The resistance of the recession to ordinary modes of stimulus (at least those considered ordinary within the framework of a global neoliberal outlook which takes the market as the ultimately, long term allocator of resources) is gradually beginning to expose the underlying structural and civilizational contradictions which define our period and epoch.

In our last major work (Mansueto 2010a) we argued that the present conjuncture would be characterized by serious but modest efforts to address global challenges. And this was clearly the intent of the Obama government. These efforts have been hindered by the underlying resistance of the global economy to traditional means of stimulus (coupled with the refusal of most European regimes to even attempt such methods). At the same time, the Democratic Party, as the party of the advanced, progressive, information-technological sector of Capital, *cannot* put forward proposals which would seriously compromise the hegemony of *Capital* itself. Where it *has* undertaken initiatives, as in the case of health care reform, immigration reform, and climate change, they are largely within the scope of the program of the progressive sectors of *Capital* themselves, which favor rationalization and mobility and which are not especially dependent on mineral rents. This has left its own base dissatisfied and demoralized, while increasing the anger of those in the hinterlands who do not see themselves as benefiting from continued expansion of the information technology sector and who have gravitated to a Republican Right so radical that it has left even core sectors of finance capital frightened. Similar dynamics are apparent in Europe, where efforts to streamline the welfare state in response to demographic inversion and open up labor markets have led to a shift among working class voters from social democratic to neofascist and protofascist parties. India has just elected a Hindu nationalist government and the principal beneficiaries of the Arab Spring seem to have been moderate Islamists. Even China, which has long seemed to be the stronghold of technocratic secularism, is experiencing a bit of a populist and fundamentalist reaction, as Xi Jiping revives elements of the old Maoist cult of personality (*The Economist*, 2014.09.24)

This is not to suggest that a global turn to the right is inevitable. More likely we will see a continued swing between "progressive" secular governments backed by the more advanced sectors of *Capital* and "conservative" populist governments, sometimes with a fundamentalist veneer, based in the extractive sector, with the people becoming more and more disillusioned with each in turn, as neither tendency acts to address either global challenges or the aspirations of the increasingly redundant masses.

We have argued elsewhere (Mansueto 2010a) that the current civilizational and structural crisis can have four possible outcomes:

- civilizational collapse, probably due to the inability to address ecological challenges within the context of existing civilizational ideals and social structures
- a transition by decadence, during which new a new civilization or civilizations will gradually emerge as the old one decays,
- a transition by reform, in which an alliance between the carriers one or more of the dominant civilizational ideals (technocratic or humanistic secularism) collaborates with carriers of a new ideal to resolve the most critical global challenges and the carry out a transition to a new civilizational pattern which integrates significant elements of both old and new, or which allows diverse forms to exist side by side, or
- a transition by revolution, in which the carriers of a new civilizational ideal systematically reorder human civilization to a new ideal over the course of the relatively brief period of a few centuries.

Obviously these are ideal types; outcomes combining one or more are certainly possible, but our assessment has been and continues to be that the forces for transition by decadence are strongest. *Capital* and *Empire* are ultimately unable to solve the principal challenges facing humanity, but they are not utterly incapable of or unwilling to take action with respect to the gravest problems, such as climate change; forces carrying a new civilizational ideal are just barely beginning to emerge. The current global political stalemate between the technocratic consensus and the conservative populist opposition suggests that this assessment is, indeed, correct.

Here we add to this standing analysis the fact that on the civilizational battlefield we have analyzed we find arrayed, broadly speaking, three principal forces:

- The party of *technocratic consensus*. This includes the entire mainstream of *Capital* together with its supporters among the technocratic middle strata and those sectors of the working classes (mostly in the old "Third World") which still believe that they are profiting from globalization and the information and biotechnological revolutions. For the most part the outlook of this alliance is one of a much sobered technocratic secularism, though it includes *transhumanists* at one extreme and *liberal theistic secularists* (mostly liberal Protestants) at the other. It shares the consensus that "there is no alternative" to global capitalism but there are significant internal differences regarding the extent to which markets can and should be regulated and the extent to which states should invest in promoting scientific and technological progress and cultivating new comparative advantages. It understands the need to address "global challenges" such as climate change, the growing redundancy of labor, the need for effective global governance, etc., but drawing from the "best and the brightest" though it may, it has few solutions which are both technically and politically credible. As Daniel Bell's new book *The China Model: Political Meritocracy and the Limits of Democracy* (Bell 2015) suggests, despite its experimentation with Neo-Maoism as a strategy for social control, all dominant sectors of the Chinese leadership are ultimately in this camp. The same is almost certainly true of India, despite its experimentation with conservative populist strategies of control.

- *Conservative populism.* This camp is controlled largely by the extractive sector of *Capital* and secondarily by low wage, low technology industry and what remains of agrarian capital, with support from those sectors of the middle strata and working classes which feel "left behind" by globalization and technological change. While it includes elements which are authentically oriented by axial and theistic secular ideologies, its ideological dynamics are ultimately driven by populist secularisms for which religion defines identities which support resistance to globalization. This is true, as we will show, both for theistic secularisms such as Christian and Sunni Islamic (especially Wahabi) fundamentalisms and for conservative ideologies with roots in authentic axial traditions (such as the Catholic *Communio* trend and the Islamic Republicanism of Iran). The tendency is defined above all by its commitment to patriarchal pronatalist policies and by resistance to the liberation of women, which is seen as threatening the viability of low technology "r" strategies and the survival of threatened European identities. Russia, with some qualifications, may actually have located itself in this camp.

- *Multitude.* This is what currently exists in the way of a "left" opposition to the technocratic consensus. It draws its support from the humanistic intelligentsia and those sectors of the working classes which, while they may feel "left behind" also feel threatened by the authoritarian and patriarchal tendencies of the conservative populists: women and ethnic and sexual orientation and gender identity minorities, together with what remains of the old proletarian and peasant movements of the previous epoch. This camp is currently oriented by a range of radical humanistic secularisms, though some elements embrace axial (religious) left ideologies. I have taken the name for this trend from the recent work of Michael Hardt and Antonio Negri (Hardt and Negri 2001), but it also includes, in addition to "autonomist" communists like them a broad range of critical theorists and left Heideggerians, especially those engaged in what might be called "atheology," such as Zizek, Agamben, the late Derrida, Raschke, Massimo (Chiesa and Toscano 2013), etc. who serve as a kind of bridge to both the small religious left intelligentsia and to working class and peasant communities which articulate their resistance to *Capital* and *Empire* in religious terms. *Multitude* lacks a grand strategy, and looks a great deal like left wing communism without the party.

As we have noted, all three camps include elements which are located where they are largely by the absence of credible alternatives and by their own inability to create them. Liberal theistic secularists and liberal and democratic humanistic secularists based above all in the philanthropic and nonprofit/nongovernmental sector, including academia, tend to ally themselves with the technocratic consensus but find less and less support for their interests and initiatives there and occasionally defect to one of the other camps. Authentic religious conservatives based in religious institutions often align with conservative populists but have a very different economic base and core ideological orientation. The religious left tends to support the *Multitude* but to the extent that it has not accepted the reduction of its spirituality to "religion without religion" or "weak theology" it can never find a real home there. There are also elements of the conservative populist right which, even though based in extractive economies, have opted, largely for geopolitical reasons, to align themselves with *Multitude* and in fact represent the antistatist *Multitude's* few bases of state power. This is especially true of the Bolivarian tendency in Latin America.

Our Trajectory

This is a time of crisis, but it is also a time of opportunity. While the *Saeculum* has achieved an unprecedented hegemony, it is also in a state of unprecedented crisis. *Sanctuary* has the opportunity to recover the terrain it has lost over the course of the past three decades and position itself to develop and advance a new spiritual and civilizational ideal as the *Saeculum* decays or collapses. But to do this we need a *theory* and a *strategy*.

The Ways of Wisdom is first and foremost an effort to theorize *Sanctuary*. *Sanctuary* itself is nothing new. It is as old as humanity itself. It is the distinctively human *way*—or rather the distinctively human complex of *ways*—of *Being*. But it has not hitherto been adequately theorized. Primal traditions were pretheoretical and thought themselves through the medium of image and story. The great axial *ways* theorized particular forms of *Sanctuary*, but they were brought only partly into dialogue with each other during Silk Road era, so that a global deliberation regarding either what it means to be human or what was involved in resistance to the *Saeculum* was never really possible. Nor did the axial *ways* ever fully come to terms with the problem of patriarchy, which is the constitutive "original sin" behind the *Saeculum* and the reason why so many sanctuaries are themselves darkened. The axial *ways*, finally, never had either the challenge or the opportunity represented by the third and final form of the *Saeculum*, that represented by the contemporary fusion of *Capital* and *Empire,* nor did they ever fully and adequately locate themselves *collectively* in relationship with the various humanistic secularisms.

Any adequate theorization of *Sanctuary* must be *theological*. This is true for four reasons. First, as we have suggested above and as we will argue at length in the next chapter, theology is the discourse constituted by intercultural encounter between competing *ways* of being human, and any theorization of *Sanctuary* must, at this point in history, be a comprehensive, global encounter of all *ways* with each other. Second, as we have already suggested and as we will argue across all of the chapters which follow, humanity is *naturally* ordered to an end which transcends our natural capacities. We are finite and contingent and seek the infinite and necessary. We are human and want to be God. Any theorization of this attempt thus necessarily draws on transconceptual as well as conceptual and imaginative resources, and is thus theological in the classical sense of engaging "revealed" or mystical wisdoms as well as a rational dialectics. Third, any theorization of *Sanctuary* is a practical as well as a theoretical discipline. As Thomas points out (Aquinas, *Summa Theologiae* I:1:a4) , this is yet another way in which theology differs from philosophy (though it might be argued that materialist dialectics, as an attempt not just to interpret the world, but to change it (Marx 1846/1978) is in this sense, as much theological as philosophical). Fourth, in a pluralistic society in which competing *ways* contend openly in the public arena, even claims which transcend the limits of a rational dialectic must defend their reasonableness, and explain and interpret themselves, to those who do not share them, by means of a rational dialectics. And so a purely imaginative or mystical religious discourse would be inadequate.

The Ways of Wisdom is theological in all these senses. First and foremost, it defines a new way of doing theology, what we call a "world," "global," or *Convivencia* theology, which engages questions of meaning and value across as well as within traditions, primal, axial, and secular, and which addresses claims made on the basis of supra-rational forms of knowledge as well as those made on the basis of reason alone. This will entail developing a radically new way of looking at such key questions of theological method and fundamental theology as the possibility and nature of supra-rational or transconceptual knowledge and its relationship with both imagination and reason, the relationship between theology and science (including the social sciences), theology and philosophy, and theology and hermeneutics and the sacred texts and other artifacts of which theology is, in part, an interpretation, and the nature of specifically theological reflection itself. More specifically, we will treat these methodological questions, and ultimately theology itself, as encounters between spiritual and civilizational traditions, i.e. between competing *ways* of being human. This will involve us in extending the Silk Road dialogue between the axial traditions, so that Jewish, Christian and Islamic claims are brought fully in to dialogue with, for example the claims of various Hinduisms, the Higher Mahayana and Vajrayana schools and the *dao xue*. But we will also show that the question of religion and science is fundamentally about the encounter between the axial traditions and theistic and technocratic secularism, that between theology and social theory about the encounter between the axial and theistic and humanistic secular traditions, and the questions of hermeneutics which have so dominated Protestant theology in particular about the engagement between the axial traditions and theistic and populist secularism. Throughout we will be laying the groundwork not only for a more systematic elaboration of our *theoria* in later works, but also for a spiritual and political *practice*. Finally, we will show how our claims are credible, even where those which are based on transconceptual insights cannot be rigorously demonstrated, by means of a rational dialectics which builds on the application of hermeneutic and social scientific methods to the understanding of the sources of our discourse.

Substantively, *The Ways of Wisdom* argues that the issue between *Sanctuary* and *Saeculum*, is ultimately, ontological. Following Milbank (Milbank 1990, 2014) I will argue for an analogical metaphysics of participation as against the univocal metaphysics which dominates theistic and technocratic secularism. But I will dissent significantly from Milbank's analysis and argue that *all* of the axial *ways* ultimately embrace an analogical metaphysics, even if it is not the Thomistic metaphysics of *Esse*. Thus an analogical metaphysics may be stated in either positive, cataphatic, or negative apophatic terms. We can say with Thomas that not everything exists in the same way—that in particular for anything to exist in the way we do, as contingent beings dependent on others, *something* must have the power of Being in itself. In order to exist we must participate in this Being. But we cannot, no matter what we do, actually *become* Being, at least not in essence. The best that we can do is to become partly or wholly connatural with it by growing in wisdom and acting justly. But we can also say with the Higher Mahayana and Vajrayana that *nothing* has inherent existence. We live in each others' embrace. That which allows existence is the very negation of self-possession or substance of any kind. Becoming connatural with this nonself-existent embracing, or enlightened compassion is the very essence of Buddhahood. Or, better still, we can attempt a synthesis of the cataphatic and apophatic *ways*, following Zhou Dunyi (Zhou c1050), the *advaita vedanta* (Sankara c 750/1890), the cluster of Sufi and Ismaili ways which developed along the borderlands between India and *Dar-al-Islam* (Khan 2004), the kabbalists (Silberman 1998) or Meister Eckhardt (Kelly 2008), recognizing that such a synthesis is almost certainly beyond not only image and story but also concept and argument.

Saeculum, on the other hand, is predicated on what I will argue is the false claim that all things exist in the same way: that Being is univocal. But here as well I will dissent significantly from Milbank's analysis, arguing that there are two very different forms of univocal metaphysics. The dominant form sees only contingent being, and then asks whether or not there is already one of these beings which is infinitely powerful Being to which the only reasonable response is one of absolute submission. Those that answer yes comprise what we call the *Theistic Saeculum,* which includes most Protestantisms and at least some Asharite Islam. Those who answer no and then dedicate themselves to building God (or getting as close as the laws and constants of physics will allow us) comprise the *Technocratic Saeculum.*

But it is also possible to recognize the conceptual distinction between contingent and necessary Being but then confuse *participation* in the power of Being as such with *possession* of that power—to mistake contingent being for *Being as such*. This error is a particular danger for those who, intensely aware of how many sanctuaries have become darkened return to secular activity and seek—and find—the sacred there. This is the way of most Silk Road revolutionary millenarianisms (culminating, especially in Joachism and the Franciscan Spirituals), as the project of creating "heaven on earth" presupposes the claim that the boundary between contingent and necessary being can, in fact be broken. It is also the way of the *Humanistic Saeculum*, the way of the great liberal, democratic, socialist, and populist revolutions.

We will argue that radical immanentism of this sort is mistaken in all its forms. There is no solution to the riddle of history, no resolution of the conflict between existence and essence (Marx 1844/1978), and attempts to find one or force one lead to "final solutions" marked by terror and repression. At the same time, I will argue, radical immanentism must be engaged for two reasons. First, it is a protest against the axial compromise with *Patriarchy* and *Empire*, the metaphysical signature of which is a hierarchical metaphysics and an emmanationist cosmology. This may seem like metaphysical hairsplitting to some, but we will attempt to show that the criticisms raised by the radical immanentists from Joachim and David of Dinant through Marx and Engels *can* be addressed in the context of an analogical metaphysics if we begin by reversing the patriarchal expropriation of female generative power and what I will argue is the associated incorrect identification of Being with Substance and Subject. Once we have rectified this error, it will be possible to show how the great axial ways, authentically distinct though they are, can be reconciled with each other and the axial project completed in a way that fully answers the objections of humanistic secularism. Second, because humanistic secularisms seek *Being* in its authentic form as relational, transformative, generativity, except where humanistic secular projects have been hegemonized by *Capital* and its technocracy, they are objectively part of *Sanctuary* in the sense that they seek to defend and advance an authentic humanity in the face of advancing capitalist instrumentalization.

The resulting ontology will position *Sanctuary* decisively to the left of both perennialism and Radical Orthodoxy, with which it otherwise shares common ground. Specifically, it will avoid the danger both run of being hegemonized by conservative populisms—Radical Orthodoxy as a defense of European Christendom in a time of demographic and spiritual crisis, and perennialism as an *altercosmopolitanism* of the Right. But it will also differentiate our position clearly from that of *Multitude*, grounding an argument for authority and conscious spiritual and civilizational leadership[4], institutions, civilization and even tradition against the soft anarchism and leftwing communism of thinkers like Negri, Agamben, Vatimo, and Zizek. My posi-

---

4. These are, I know, extraordinarily controversial terms, given their political association with both the "authoritarian" right and the "totalitarian" left. And I will grant, up front, that they follow necessarily from my option for an analogical rather than a univocal metaphysics of participation. But I will show how, in the context of such a metaphysics, where the patriarchal expropriation of feminine generativity is transcended and the recognition of participation is authentic, the result is a "mixed polity" or *politea* (as opposed to either tyranny, oligarchy, or democracy, monarchy or aristocracy) at both the metaphysical and the political levels. It is possible to recognize conscious leadership and authorities independent of popular will *without* constituting ideological monopolies or monolithic hierarchies.

tion is closest to that of Merton (Merton 1968) and Cardenal (Cardenal 2000) and can be read as an attempt to carry their lineage, including their engagement with Buddhism and communism, to a new level under vastly different social and historical conditions.

This theological and ontological argument has, furthermore, definite practical implications. *Sanctuary* is a form of rule and a way of life. Ecologically and demographically it argues for a k strategy which invests in a small number of offspring and ripens their capacity to Be and against an r strategy which turns wombs into factories and generates as much raw labor power as possible. Technologically it nurtures matter's immanent drive towards complexity and organization (hortic and alchemical technologies) rather than breaking down existing forms of organization to release energy and do work (industrial technologies). Economically it invests in service of human development rather than in service of accumulation, capitalist or statist. Politically it cultivates the power to do and to Be, not command and control of the Other. Psychosexually it respects the generative power of women and regards sexuality as sacrament, wiping from our lips forever the claim of the *ba'alim* to own and use this power (Hosea 2).

This said, *Sanctuary* includes many different *ways*, many trends, and many tendencies. *The Ways of Wisdom* represents a specific position within the broader camp of *Sanctuary* for the simple reason that as a *way* it has a specific starting point and a specific trajectory. These are, in significant measure, autobiographical. I write as a North American man who is, on my father's side the gransdon of a Trapanese immigrant with deep roots in both the Franciscan Spiritual tradition and the Latin anticlericalism which was the popular form of Latin Averroism. My grandfather was profoundly devoted to the *Magna Mater* in the form of the Dark Virgin and profoundly committed to the international workers movement. I was raised as a Catholic and continue to regard the Catholic Church as my home. But I have continued my grandfather's tradition of socialist politics and my criticism of socialist humanism is in many ways a work of self-criticism. I am also an academic with roots in both the humanities and humanistic social sciences on the one hand and theological faculties on the other. I am, in other words, both a humanistic and a clerical intellectual. And on my mother's side I am descended from (very much decayed) English gentry and German-American yeomen. While I was raised within the Catholic Church, I was also raised with the *Protestant Ethic* which Weber analyzes so powerfully. Finally, while my journey has presented me with the opportunity to learn deeply from friends (and adversaries) from many different traditions, certain of these intercultural encounters came earlier and were more fundamental. I grew up with and around Jews and understanding the Jewish critique of Christianity and finding a way to affirm my Catholic identity while rejecting Christological claims which are inherently antisemitic was fundamental to my process of spiritual and theological maturation. And my first deep immersion in a radically "Other" cultural reality took place during extended periods spent during my childhood in Theravada Thailand. My most powerful *altermaternal* figures were young Thai and Khmer women who introduced me to the *dhamma* and planted the seeds of what has become a thriving contemplative practice.

What this means in terms of the way in which I have chosen to write this book is that I write as a Gentile, who approaches life with a "Greek" problem: I want to transcend my finitude and contingency. I write from a vantage point which is close enough to real privilege to understand the temptation of pursuing this aim by means of conquest and exploitation. I write, in other words, from the vantage point of the *way of the search for Being* and its prolongation in to secular and specifically socialist humanisms. But I also write as someone for whom the answer to this question, both in the sense of (at least one of) the broader historical stream(s) of which I am part (Catholicism) and in terms of my own personal journey has come from the people of Israel: we know (and become) God in and only in the just act. And both my "Greek" question and the Jewish answers I have found to this question have been transformed profoundly by the gradual awakening to the Dharma I began to learn nearly half a century ago from the young Thai and Khmer women who cared for me: that nothing has inherent existence, that we all live in each others' embrace. Being is neither Substance nor Subject, but relational, transformative, generativity.

And so our journey beings. First we will show that theology is, in fact, intercultural engagement. We will then look in some depth at both the original axial *ways* and their internal development and engagement with each other, making the argument that once we reject the idea of Being as Substance the difficulty in reconciling these *ways* (as well as feminist and deconstructionist objections to them) are largely overcome. The result will be a preliminary synthesis and an agenda with which to approach the challenges posed by theistic, technocratic, and humanistic secularism. We will then address these challenges both methodologically and substantively in the forms in which they have presented themselves theologically in the secular era: the challenge of science, social theory, and hermeneutics and show that by leaving behind the idea that Being is Subject we not only overcome secular objections to the axial ways but also the patriarchal residues which affect even most humanistic secularism. This will, finally, set the stage for a systematic explanation of *Sanctuary* as a way of being human centered on seeking wisdom, doing justice, and ripening Being understood neither as substance nor as subject, but as relationship, generativity, and creation.

2

Theology *Is* Intercultural Engagement

In the previous chapter we said that *Sanctuary* needs a theory and a strategy and that the theory and strategy it needs is a *theology* and indeed a theology of a very specific kind: a theology understood as an engagement between competing *ways* of being human. We now need to explain in greater detail what such a theology might consist in, and show that it is, in fact, possible.

We will proceed by answering first the principal and obvious objection to our approach. Theology has historically been understood as *fides querens intellectum*, and therefore as operating within the context of commitment to a particular religious tradition. This is a consequence of the fact that theology, as distinct from philosophy, consists in the attempt to understand, explain, and/or demonstrate the reasonableness of a wisdom which, by its very nature, transcends discursive reason or dialectics, so that engaging the wisdom in the first place presupposes a prior faith commitment. We will show, however, that engagement with suprarational wisdom does not by itself generate *theology*, and that the efforts to understand, explain, and justify such wisdom which constitute theology in fact emerge only when competing *ways* encounter each other. With this task complete we will proceed to analyze in some depth the various approaches to intercultural engagement which have defined humanity's great *ways*, both historically and in the present period. In the process we will discover that we have been reflecting on the question of theological method all along. We will then situate our approach in relation to these, arguing both for its continuity with the great synthetic and syncretic movements and for its superiority to the existing contemporary alternatives.

Primal and Sacral Monarchic Societies

We begin then by demonstrating that nothing which meets the description of theology is possible prior to intercultural encounter and that theology is, in fact, precisely what happens when competing *ways* of being come into contact with each other.

The most straightforward way to proceed in this regard is from a comparative historical sociological perspective, looking at each stage in the development of human civilization to see whether and in what sense something like a theological discourse is discernible. There have never been claims that anything like a strictly theological discourse is present in primal societies. At this stage human beings participate in Being largely through the modality of hunting and gathering, cultivating and husbanding plants and animals, through the construction of increasingly complex kinship and cross kin village structures, and by assigning meanings to these activities, meanings which are expressed through the medium of image and story as totemic symbols and rituals of collective effervescence, creation stories and legends about founders and culture heroes, and eventually in the widespread cult of the *Magna Mater* (Durkheim 1911/1964, Stone 1976). There is no reason apart from confessional presuppositions to deny that the wisdom achieved at this stage is, at least partly, transconceptual, though formal abstraction has not yet emerged as a differentiated activity, so very little distinction is made between insights which are empirical, those which are rational, and those which are mystical in character. What *is* absent is any attempt to *understand* supra-rational insights in terms of a rational dialectics for the simple reason the latter has simply not yet emerged. To the extent that intercultural engagement takes place, the approach to such engagement tends to be integrative. We know, for example, that among the Hopi, when new clans wished to join a village, they were asked what new ceremonies they might bring. The decision on whether or not to admit them depended on the perceived value of their rituals (Waters 1963). Integration between different *ways* was clearly possible, but by no means assured.

This orientation persists today in the form of the "fourth world" movement, where this term is used to describe native and indigenous peoples who historically rejected the development of urban civilization and even, in some cases, settled villages (Griggs 1992) and is represented by organizations such as the *Center for World Indigenous Studies* (www.cwis.org).

For primal societies the principal form of discourse generated by humanity's encounter with the sacred—or rather by its own inherently theotic project—is that combination of image and story we call myth. Carried into action as a way of producing and reproducing collective effervescence, myth becomes ritual. Both can be sources for theology but neither by itself is theological in character.

In sacral monarchic societies the vast majority of human beings continue to participate in Being as they did in primal societies, while the warlord class undertakes a project centered on conquest and sacrifice, attempting to divinize themselves by means of exploitation and accumulation, by building (rudimentary) empires, and by assigning meanings to these activities through, once again, the modality of image and story (Mansueto 2010b). Once again, there is no reason to deny the possibility of suprarational wisdom here. Indeed, if we do, we will have to do without key concepts such as sacrifice which, in more spiritualized form, are essential to axial and post-axial *ways*. Once again, though, since formal abstraction and rational dialectics have not yet emerged as differentiated activities, theological reflection on supra-rational wisdom is not really possible. Where intercultural engagement takes place it tends, as in the case of primal societies, to be integrative in character, albeit with the addition of a hierarchical element, so that the gods of conquered peoples were subordinated to those of the conqueror.

This trend is reflected in the present period in the integral traditionalist movement which emerged around Rene Guenon (Guenon 2007) and Julian Evola (Evola 1995). This movement, which is often associated with but different in certain fundamentals from the *perennialist* trend which we will discuss later, advocated a restoration of a sacral kingship which joined warrior and priestly functions. Below such sacred priest-kings ranged what he regarded as inferior castes: degenerate feminized priests, desacralized warriors, money-makers, and laborers concerned with nothing but sustaining organic vitality. The political valence of the doctrine gives reason for concern, in so far as many of its adherents inclined, at least for a time, to support fascism during its apogee in the 1930s. This was, at least, true of Evola.

The root of this error resides ultimately in their response to the crisis of industrial capitalism which first became apparent in the middle of the nineteenth century. Far from fulfilling the promise of the technocratic secular ideal (transcending finitude and contingency by means of scientific and technological progress) capitalism was in fact beginning to hold back these processes and could be sustained only by means of renewed militarism and empire building and by the exploitation of the peoples of the Latin, Celtic, Slavic, Asian, African, and American peripheries. One option, that taken by the communists (Marx 1844/1978), was to resist capitalism and imperialism in the hope that socialism would eventually end the instrumentalization of human creative power. Clearly this option eventually ran into its own contradictions. But the alternative—alliance with emerging imperialism in the hope that it would restore an "heroic" ethos—the option chosen by

Schelling, Nietzsche, Heidegger, and Jung (Lukacs 1953/1980), was much worse. It helped pave the way for fascism.

Integral traditionalism is one variant of this later option. It differs from the core tradition of Germanic romanticism and authoritarianism in being far more ecumenical in the range of cultures from which it drew its inspiration and far less inclined than Heidegger and his followers to imagine that it had invented something radically new. Eventually most of the integral traditionalists recognized the fascists for the techno-thugs that they were. But it was much, much, to late.

As with primal societies the principal form of discourse generated by the sacral monarchic project is that combination of image and story we call myth. Carried into action as a way of producing and reproducing collective effervescence, myth becomes ritual. Both can be sources for theology but neither by itself is theological in character.

The Axial Age and the Silk Road

The Axial Age brought significant changes in the forms of religious discourse, but still nothing which could properly be called a theology. As old stories cease to make sense under new circumstances and are retold they become *literature*. Hellenic drama and the revised and retold epics of Greece and India and the prophetic discourse of the sort found in ancient Israel might all be regarded as a special cases of this broader form of discourse. Struggles for justice lead become crystalized in legal traditions and eventually legal codes, as well as in histories. The emergence of formal abstraction, itself a reflex of petty commodity production, leads to the supplementation of image and story by concept and argument as ways of engaging questions of meaning and value, and eventually to the emergence of philosophy. Somewhere in between the prophetic oracle and the philosophical treatise lies the "saying" of the Sage, of which the works of Lao Tzu and Kung Fu Tze are the best examples, though many of the pre-Socratics look similar in form (Mansueto 2010a).

Intercultural engagement increases during this period, but it is not of the sort that yields a specifically theological discourse. On the one hand, as the emergence of specialized agriculture and crafts production and, along with them, petty commodity production and the creation of regional trade networks brought peoples into ever closer communication with each other in the context of a broader dynamic of religious rationalization, there was a tendency towards not just integration of cults but actually towards synthesis and syncretism, a dynamic we see, perhaps for the first time, in Hesiod's

Theogony (Hesiod c750 BCE/1988). On the other hand, the emergence of a rational dialectics led to conceptual refinement and to differentiation and to what eventually became sharp polemics between otherwise quite close philosophical schools (Collins 1998).

The great Iron Age empires which emerged at the close of the Axial Age alternated between exclusivist cultural programs of the sort implemented by the Seleucids, the Qin and the Late Roman and Byzantine Empires and what eventually became a more hierarchically integrative norm in which many *ways* were patronized, with tendencies which served imperial interests favored and those which presented a real or perceived threat subject to persecution.

It is only with the Silk Road Era that theology as a well defined mode of discourse first emerges. This is true for the simple reason that it is in this period that we find the large scale encounters between competing *ways* of being human which makes such a discourse necessary. It is worth looking at each of these principal encounters in greater depth.

The first of these encounters, and the one which defines the actual trajectory of development of Judaism, Christianity, and Islam, is that between *Athens* and *Jerusalem*. This encounter is, in turn, set up by the unique character of the religion of earliest Israel, which, as Norman Gottwald has demonstrated (Gottwald 1979), emerged from a Late Bronze Age peasant revolt, so that *seeking wisdom* and *doing justice* become fully convertible with each other as Israel meets here God on the battlefield of the revolution. The *ba'a'lim* which Israel rejected were the heavenly reflex of the earthly warlords and rejection of the *ba'alim* was the condition of any possible liberation.

As *Empire* reasserted itself during the Iron Age, this revolutionary posture became more and more difficult to sustain. Broadly speaking three options were available. The first, gradually developed by the Pharisees and eventually consolidated in the dominant rabbinic form of Judaism (Neusner 1975/1998), accepted that the Jews were and would remain an ethnoreligious minority incapable of re-establishing an independent polity, much less of systemically remaking the world, at least for the foreseeable future. There was also a growing sense that the legal and prophetic traditions needed to be reinterpreted for the new conditions represented by the Silk Road, in which Jews were as often craftsmen and merchants as they were peasants and the place of both the land and that of the Temple were radically relativized, a trend which became even more marked after the destruction of the Second Temple at the end of the Jewish War. Finally, especially after the Jewish War, there was no longer any central teaching or governing authority and the priesthood no longer had a well defined function, so that there was no authority left except that of a good argument. The result was a focus on serving as a "light to the nations," a catalyst for justice in an unjust world, in a context where all decisions were regarded as having spiritual significance and in which deliberation around just what constituted justice became near as important as the just act itself. Much of this deliberation took place in the context of Talmudic legal scholarship, but as Jacob Neusner points out, the dominant legal hermeneutic within Judaism was always rationalistic, focusing on extracting the principle behind the law and applying it critically and creatively in the present period, something which puts all Jewish jurisprudence well to the "left" of even the most liberal Muslim *fiqh*, such as that of the Jafari tradition, which stresses *ijtihad* and *aql*, analogical reasoning and intelligence. And the absence of any centralized religious authority, creating an environment in which there was no authority but a good argument, introduced into later "western" appropriations of Hellenism a critical element much stronger than that present within the Hellenic tradition itself, paving the way for Marx's *Ruthless Criticism of Everything Existing* (Marx 1843a/1978).

The second alternative was messianism and armed struggle. There were many such attempts, culminating in the Jewish War of 66-70 CE and the Bar Kokhba revolt in the second century of the common era. Christianity probably emerged from such a movement, though just how far along the path to armed struggle that movement traveled remains contested (Eissenman 1997, Tabor 2006). But when messianism failed, at least in the context of Christianity, it gave birth to an entirely new spiritual *way*. The struggle for justice, specifically in its *failure* as represented by the cross, became as a spiritual discipline which stretches us, helping us grow towards God. This new *way* was articulated almost from the beginning in the language of the Hellenistic mystery cults as Jewish solution to a Greek problem, and it is thus all but impossible to isolate in "pure form." Rather, it exists *between* the two broader *ways of justice and liberation* and the *search for Being*. This allowed, ironically, for a rapid accommodation with *Empire* as the new Christian ideal displaced Hellenism and the principal form of legitimation for the Late Roman and Byzantine states as well as the Germanic and Slavic states which surrounded and partly succeeded them and eventually emerged as the Holy Roman and Russian Empires (Theissen 1982, Kyrtatits 1987). But it also made *internal* to Christianity the question of the relationship between Athens and Jerusalem, so that this question *constitutes* Christian theology. On the one hand, core Christian doctrines such as the Trinity and the Incarnation could never even have been formulated apart from the categories such as *being, essence*, and *hypostasis* drawn from Hellenic philosophy. On the other hand Christianity has always been marked by a profound tension between the Greek problem it tries to solve (finitude and contingency), the

Jewish answer that it offers to this problem (*da'ath 'elohim* in the supernaturally just act). What might justice mean for a *failed* messianism? How is the failure of this messianism *divinizing*? It from this half-hidden complex of questions that the surface Christian debates around the Trinity and the Incarnation, nature and grace, sin, atonement, justification, and sanctification all emerge and for which they are all ultimately just a code.

The result has been the development within Christianity of a theological spectrum which reaches from Tertullian (Tertullian c 197/1956) on the "right," through Augustine (Augustine 426/1972), up to the central Orthodox and Catholic tradition represented by the majority of the Greek Fathers and, in its fullest form, by Thomas Aquinas (Aquinas 1927/1952). Thus we have from Tertullilan the oldest rejection of any engagement between Athens and Jerusalem.

> Whence spring those "fables and endless genealogies," and "unprofitable questions," and "words which spread like a cancer?" From all these, when the apostle would restrain us, he expressly names *philosophy* as that which he would have us be on our guard against. Writing to the Colossians, he says, "See that no one beguile you through philosophy and vain deceit, after the tradition of men, and contrary to the wisdom of the Holy Ghost." He had been at Athens, and had in his interviews (with its philosophers) become acquainted with that human wisdom which pretends to know the truth, whilst it only corrupts it, and is itself divided into its own manifold heresies, by the variety of its mutually repugnant sects. What indeed has Athens to do with Jerusalem? What concord is there between the Academy and the Church? what between heretics and Christians? Our instruction comes from "the porch of Solomon," who had himself taught that "the Lord should be sought in simplicity of heart." Away with all attempts to produce a mottled Christianity of Stoic, Platonic, and dialectic composition! We want no curious disputation after possessing Christ Jesus, no inquisition after enjoying the gospel! With our faith, we desire no further belief (Tertullian *De praescriptione haereticorum 7*).

This methodological rejection of engagement between Athens and Jerusalem is associated, from Tertullian on, with an option for a univocal metaphysics, a strong doctrine of original sin, a tendency to emphasize God's role (as opposed to human cooperation and self-cultivation) in the work of redemption, and a premillenialist eschatology marked by a literal return of Jesus to establish his kingdom on the Earth, doctrines which we see today on the Christian Right. But Tertullian, we should remember, was marginal to the broader Patristic tradition and the sort of theology he advocated became normative—and then only for a trend within Christendom—after the Norman Conquests and the beginning of the Augustinian Reaction. And it is only with the Reformation, and the advent of the *Saeculum* that it really becomes dominant.

In the middle of this spectrum we find Augustine and the Augustinian tradition up to the time of the Norman Conquests. Augustine *clearly* understood Christianity as the answer to what had been a distinctly Hellenistic personal quest for wisdom and had no hesitation either in using Hellenistic philosophy to interpret Christianity or in regarding it as an authentic path towards Christianity. What distinguishes Augustine from the Greek Fathers and from Thomas is a more radical internal critique of the Hellenic *way of the search for being*, and especially of humanity's *theotic* project, which he is inclined to regard as ultimately vain and rebellious and which he associates, at least implicitly, with the *City of Man*, which is founded on the love of honor (Augustine 426/1972). This in turn leads to a tendency to give priority to the will over the intellect and to love over knowledge. For Augustine sin is the result of an act of the will rather than a failure of the intellect and it is through the right ordering of our loves rather than by taking on the *form* of God that we become Godlike. And since once we have chosen self over God we cannot choose God for any reason other than self, only God can redeem us.

There has been considerable debate in recent years regarding the extent to which this excludes a doctrine of *theosis*. Certainly the doctrine is less prominent here than it is in the Greek fathers and it has not historically been emphasized in most Protestant or indeed in most Catholic readings of Augustine. But recent scholars have argued that a more modest concept of *theosis* is indeed present in Augustine (Hallosten 2007, Persons 2010). A similar case might be made for Luther, in spite of his harsher judgment on reason and philosophy, which he regarded as the devil's whore. Recent Finnish scholarship has affirmed the presence of a genuine doctrine of *theosis* in Luther and the Lutheran tradition (Mannermaa 2000).

It is, rather, when we look especially at the English tradition from Anselm on (Anselm who became Archbishop of Canterbury after the Norman Conquest) that we begin to see the re-articulation of Augustine's theology in terms of a strict univocal metaphysics, a zero sum game struggle between humanity and God, leading to a divine command ethics, a strong doctrine of original sin and of the substitutionary atonement, and spirituality of submission. These themes are then taken up by the English Franciscans, especially Scotus and Occam (Boler 1993, Ingham 1993, MacAleer 1996, Mansueto 2011) and ultimately by the Reformed tradition which, of course, reaches its most advanced expression in the Anglo-American domain. In this context the emerging doctrine of divine sovereignty—reflex of the emerging absolutist state and, in its more advanced form of the abstract, invisible, and utter inscrutable Sovereign which is *Capital*—excludes any meaningful concept of *theosis*.

On the "left," finally, Christianity is understood as the solution to the Hellenic problem of humanity's *theotic* ordering in and through the fundamentally Jewish practice of justice. This is Thomas' solution (Thomas, *Summa Theologiae* II Q 45 a2) and even more so that of Eckhart (Kelly 2010). Here the struggle for justice remains not merely integral to the Gospel but constitutive of it, while carrying us beyond the political towards a real if nonentitative connaturality with God. This has the effect, as Milbank puts it (Milbank 2014), of democratizing virtue by rooting the highest wisdom not in metaphysical inquiry but in *caritas* or the supernaturally just act.

Islam, finally, is fundamentally about a refusal to accept the marginalization of the struggle for justice as a minority ethnoreligious current and a refusal to accept the defeat of the messianic project. Islam means "commanding right and forbidding wrong (Crone 2004)," establishing God's rule, which is the rule of justice. But this does not exempt Islam from either the internal problems of the messianic project, which do not disappear when this project is (at least partly) successful. Nor does it exempt Islam from the problem of the relationship between Athens and Jerusalem. Islam was *so* successful that it paid no attention to the problem of succession and leadership before the prophet died, leaving two parties to contend with each other. The first party, that of Ali (the *Shia*), stressed the primacy of the Prophet's lineage, traced most especially through his daughter Fatima, and the imperative that the successor of the Prophet by wise and just. The result was a doctrine of the Imamate which represented at least a partial movement towards the Christian doctrine of the Incarnation. The second party, that of community and tradition (the *Sunni*), stressed the need for the unity of the *ummah* and for effective political military leadership if *Dar-al-Islam* was not to be reduced to the status of a pious but impotent sect. This fundamental contradiction was layered over by the partly—but only partly—overlapping difference regarding the extent to which Islam should draw on other traditions, particularly those of Hellenic philosophy. The Shia went furthest in their engagement with Athens with some communities, such as the Ismailis, eventually coming to regard Hellenic philosophy as the esoteric or *batin* content of the *Quran* passed on through the lineage of the Imams, while the Sunni differed widely, with some (the Mutazilites and most later Sufis) embracing Hellenism in various forms while others (the Asharites and especially later movements such as the Wahabis) rejecting such intercultural engagement as a betrayal of Islam and *de facto takfir*.

In India the dynamic which led to the emergence of a theological discourse was driven by the encounter between Indo-Aryan and indigenous Dravidian traditions on the one hand and, encounters of both of these root traditions with Chinese *ways* which reached India along mountain trade routes through Tibet (Capriles 2003) and maritime trade routes through the Tamil and Mayalalam South on the other (Samuel 2008). The Indo-Aryan tradition contributed an understanding of sacrifice as the generative power of the universe. This understanding was rooted in the Vedic myths which recounted the creation of the universe from the sacrifice of primordial human, *Purusha* and in the rites of deification, such as the *rajasuya*, practiced by the Indo-Aryan warlords and their *brahmana* ritualists. This sacrifical complex was increasingly rationalized during the early part of the Axial Age with the creative principle of the universe understood as either *Brahman*, after the manner of the *Upanishads* or *pattica samupada*, or dependent origination in the Buddhist tradition. Physical austerity (*tapas*) and contemplative practice at least partially displaced animal sacrifice. What the borderlands contributed was above all a complex of yogic and tantric disciplines which mobilized the human body and the human mind as instruments for achieving union with—or more often realization of our identity (and that of the entire phenomenal universe) with—the divine. This was generally accompanied by both a higher degree of comfort with worldly aims and a sense of the world as itself sacred, a feature of both the indigenous, primal traditions of India and of Chinese *ways* generally.

On what eventually emerged as the "Hindu" side this encounter led to a hierarchization of spiritual aims and a pluralism of spiritual methods. *Kama, artha, dharma,* and *moksa* (pleasure, power, duty, and liberation) are recognized as legitimate aims, even if the highest remains *moksa*. There is, meanwhile, sharp debate regarding what *moksa* entails (freedom from matter, devoted union with or recognition of our prior identity with Brahman) and the best ways to attain it (*bhakti, karma, jnana,* or *raja yoga*: devotion, good works, study, and contemplative practice).

On the Buddhist side, on the other hand, the primacy of *bodhi* (enlightenment) was more resolutely upheld, but the debate around what this entailed and how to achieve it was, similarly, informed by a similar engagement with more world-affirming Dravidian and Chinese doctrines and practices. This resulted in a wide range of opinion from the austere doctrine of the *Pali* canon (especially as interpreted in the later *Theravada*), which eschewed theism and metaphysical speculation and understood *bodhi* as release from suffering, with the more expansive claims of the emerging

Mahayana and *Vajryana*, which envision and enlightenment which is tantamount to full deification in all but name, and which, especially for the *Vajrayana,* regards the entire universe as manifestation of enlightened mind and energy. (Capriles 2003).

In China, the encounter between Indian traditions in the form of Buddhism and indigenous Chinese traditions generates a discourse which is clearly theological. On the side of the indigenous traditions there was significant resistance, especially from the *ru xue* or Confucian tradition, and periods of imperial patronage under the Sui and Tang culminated in sharp repression towards the end of Tang Dynasty. Ultimately, however, Buddhism proved itself too compelling to definitively defeat, but not strong enough to best indigenous Chinese traditions. The result was a kind of functional integration, in which Taoism provided guidance for health and worldly happiness, Confucianism guidance for intellectual and moral self-cultivation and social order, and Buddhism guidance for achieving enlightenment, at least for those who chose to pursue it. It is important to remember, in this context, that even the most rationalistic of the Song Dynasty advocates of the *dao xue* (Neoconfucian) synthesis such as Zhu Xi were regular practitioners of sitting meditation in the Cha'an (Zen) tradition. This approach was mirrored in Chinese Buddhism in the *p'an chiao* (Williams 1989) system, in which the teachings of various Buddhist schools are ranked in terms of their relative completeness, with the lower ranked schools treated as skillful means (*upayakausaya*), teachings directed at the less developed, and the non-Buddhist schools ranked below that, generally with a generic Hinduism ranked below Buddhism and a generic Confucian-Taoist synthesis ranked at the bottom, but still recognized as promoting basic ethical conduct. This approach was then taken up by the various Vajrayana schools, especially on the Tibetan plateau, each of which regards the others as a "preparation" for its own higher wisdom.

There is, finally, one attempt at a self-consciously intercultural (and global) theological discourse which remains wholly within the framework of the axial project: *perennialism*. Perennialism (Nasr 1989) is a philosophical and religious school which teaches that, behind their diverse exoteric forms, the world's great wisdom traditions, philosophical and religious, share a common esoteric and mystical core. It advances this claim in conscious continuity with Neoplatonic attempts to unify Hellenistic and Semitic spiritual culture, the Hindu concept of *Sanatana Dharma* or universal wisdom and the Chinese Buddhist *p'an chiao*. But the term itself derives from the Catholic Humanist Agostino Steuco (Delph 2006a, 2006b), for whom it represented the great tradition of human wisdom which had culminated in Catholic Scholasticism, and which was then under assault by the

Reformers. For Leibniz the idea of a perennial "philosophy of harmony" was at the center of a strategy to heal the religious divisions of Europe (Schmitt 1966). And the idea gained popularity as Europeans became aware of the significant common ground between their own mystical traditions and those of the peoples they had colonized. Advocates of the position include Huston Smith, whose introduction to world religions (Smith 1995) has promoted a moderate version of the doctrine among an enormous number of undergraduate students studying comparative religion, the Persian Islamic scholar Seyyed Hossein Nasr (Nasr 1989), Ananda Coomaraswamy (Coomaraswamy 1987), and Fritjjof Schuon (Schuon 1992). The neotraditionalist leaders Rene Guenon (Guenon 2007) and Julian Evola (Evola 1995) also identify with this trend and are often included within it, but they differ in looking back behind the Axial Age to the sacral monarchic project as their principal source of inspiration.

Substantively, the esoteric core of human wisdom is taken to center around the claim that behind phenomenal reality there lies a rationally and mystically knowable first principle: Being, the Good, the One, Brahman or Tian. Humanity's end consists in understanding our unity and/or identity with this principle. This is achieved through any of a variety of means, usually centered on some combination of intellectual self-cultivation and spiritual discipline, though many perennialists have shown significant interest in mystery cults and have written extensively on what they regard as the degradation of the mystery tradition by Theosophy, modern day Rosicrucians, and Masonry.

This trend is, fundamentally, a reflection of the position of axial intellectuals who, in an era of globalization, now believe themselves to be in a position to complete the global intellectual synthesis which was emerging during the Silk Road Era while offering that synthesis as a remedy to the ills of secularism. Politically the movement leans to the moderate right, in that its metaphysics and cosmology, and thus its social doctrine are organically hierarhical and emmanationist. Integral to this conservatism is a failure to address the patriarchal expropriation of female generative power, though some members of the trend have been devotees of various goddess cults, especially those associated with the Hindu *mahavidya*. It also reflects a failure to engage full the humanistic secular project, especially in its democratic and socialist forms, which advocate a more emergentist and less hierarchical cosmology and metaphysics.

Perennialism is by no means globally in error. There *is* significant common ground between *many* of humanity's wisdom traditions, and especially between their mystical doctrines. This is because they represent responses, on the basis of a common humanity, to a common ultimate reality. And, as we have argued elsewhere, humanity's *telos* is nothing other than deification, even if full deification remains always and only a horizon, drawing us forward to the connaturality with God which we have in caritative wisdom and the supernaturally just act. There is even an element of truth in the school's political doctrine. The modern world, by glorifying a "science" which unlocks the secrets of nature, telling us *how* the world works, has radically devalued wisdom, which asks *why*, unlocking, if only partially, the secrets of the divine. And the modern world hates nothing more than the authentically wise and the authentically just, regarding them as a threat to freedom and democracy. *Knowing God: The Journey of the Dialectic* (Mansueto 2010a) and *The Death of Secular Messianism* (Mansueto 2010b) explain this broad common ground between humanity's spiritual traditions—and the difficulties with the modern era—in a sociologically and philosophically rigorous way.

This said, there are also serious problems with perennialism. First, its claims regarding the underlying unity of humanity's wisdom traditions go much too far. Even among the many traditions which share a common analogical metaphysics of Being/the Good/the One/Brahman/Tian, there are significant differences in how this first principle is understood and even greater differences regarding its relationship to the universe and to humanity. While I have generally emphasized the common ground between the Platonic metaphysics of the Good, the Aristotelian metaphysics of the Unmoved Mover, and the Avicennan/Thomistic metaphysics of Necessary Being or Esse, there are real differences even between these. The latter in particular privileges creativity and thus has rather different spiritual and political implications than its predecessors. Platonic and Aristotelian metaphysics leaves humanity little to add to the universe, and the values the contemplative life the most; Avicennan and Thomistic metaphysics make human beings co-creators with God and place more value on the active life—and on creative work of any kind, as well as on those who do such work. The differences between this Western metaphysical tradition and the doctrine of Brahman or of Tian are even greater. While the *word* Brahman probably has its origins in the Sanskrit term for a certain creative swelling, most Vedanta defines Brahman by contrast with the creative play of Maya or illusion. And the Chinese Tian (heaven) serves more as a metaphysical anchor, grounding moral claims and known as much through practice as through dialectics, than as carrier of rich metaphysical content. Indeed, there is a good case to be made that China developed a fully elaborated positive ontology centered on Tian only in response to the challenge posed by Buddhism, something which suggests that the common ground identified by the perennialists is *in part* at least an Indo-European phenomenon.

Even within the very restricted realm of Indo-European spiritual traditions, the perennialists fail to come to terms adequately with the Buddhist denial that *anything* has intrinsic existence, which seems the exact negation of their preferred Neo-Platonic/Advaita Vedanta ontology. While I have argued that Buddhism historically evolved *towards* a more positive ontology, centered on the ideas of the *tathagatagarbha* in the Mahayana tradition and the *bhavanga* in the Theravada tradition (Mansueto 2010a), the tendency is to understand the first principle in terms of Mind rather than Being or one of the other transcendentals. This, not surprisingly, privileges contemplation even more than the Platonic, Aristotelian, or even Vedanta schools.

Finally, while I have argued extensively that the univocal metaphysics which characterizes Augustinian Christianity and Asharite Islam is *wrong* (Mansueto 2010b), we cannot simply exclude them from the list humanity's wisdom traditions because failing to do so would call into question a cherished and attractive claim regarding the unity of the world's religions. And here, of course, the spiritual and political implications are *very* different: faith, devotion, surrender, submission . . .

These differences become even more apparent when we move to the question of the relationship between the first principle and the universe. Did the universe emanate from the first principle (the most common view among perennialists and the philosophers they favor), a cosmology which suggests a hierarchical and degenerating universe, or does it evolve towards it, the view of many Radical Aristotelians and modern dialecticians? This latter view, while certainly not excluding an emphasis on excellence and conscious leadership, has more democratic possibilities. Vedanta, meanwhile, to which perennialists tend to reduce *Sanatana Dharma*, is *constituted* by the debate between the *advaita*, the *dvaita*, and those in between, over whether the human soul (atman) is identical with Brahman, has Brahman immanent in it, or radically separate, a view which tends towards quasi-Protestant devotionalism.

Finally, while the main body of perennialism avoids the serious political errors of the integral traditionalists, clearly upholding the primacy of the teaching and sanctifying over the governing and warrior offices, it also argues, at least implicitly, against any possible political solution to the evils of this *kali yuga*. This is, in a sense, consistent with an axial rejection of the secular project generally, in both its technocratic and humanistic forms. But it also marks the failure of the perennialists to fully integrate into their understanding of the *sophia perennis* the *way of justice and liberation*, for which the struggle for justice, even when it fails, is constitutive of *da'ath 'elohim* and both an occasion and an effective of authentic spiritual progress.

In the context of the "long twentieth century" which lasted from 1848–1989 this cannot but be seen as an antisemitism by omission.

Saecular Theologies

The dynamics of theological discourse changes radically in the period beginning with the Norman Conquests, the Crusades, the *Reconquista*, and the European conquest of Asia, Africa, and the Americas, conquests which constituted the third and final iteration of the *Saeculum*. We have already noted that the Norman conquests coincided with a sharp turn towards Christian exclusivism and with the emergence of a well defined univocal metaphysics within Christendom, as reflected in the theologies of Anselm and later of Scotus and Occam (though it is worth noting that the Normans in Sicily and in the Slavic lands were far more integrationist in their approach to local cultures than they were in their French and British headquarters). While the Catholic powers followed the more traditional pattern of hierarchical integration, subsuming local cults within the context of the broader Catholic synthesis, and more specifically in the context of the cult of Mary and of the saints, Protestant England became the point of origin of an exlusivism previously unforseen on the planet. The internal logic of Reformed theology, adopted in one or another degree by essentially all parties in the Church of England, left no room for the recognition of truth outside the Gospel of the crucified and resurrected Christ, even where, as in the case of a some late Puritans and Early Evangelicals such as Jonathan Edwards and his followers, there was an authentic commitment to justice of Native Americans and other oppressed peoples (Heimart 1967).

This approach persists in what have come to be called *exlusivist* or *restritivist* theologies of religion, which are most common among Evangelical Protestants but which sometimes appear in Catholic and Orthodox circles as well. Exclusivist theologies (Newbigin 1969) theologies can be defined as those which reject the existence of religious truth sufficient for salvation outside of Christianity and in many cases rule out salvation for non-Christians. The argument behind such theologies generally draws on an Augustinian and or Evangelical Protestant reading of the New Testament, especially Paul, which stresses the depth and seriousness of original sin, the need for a redemption which can be effected only through the death and resurrection of Jesus understood as both Christ and divine Son of God and, finally, the necessity of appropriating this redemption through faith in Jesus (again understood as Christ and divine Son of God). The exclusivist position is dictated and follows necessarily from such the underlying univocal metaphysics of the Augustinian/Evangelical tradition, and from the anthropology and a soteriology which follow from that metaphysics, which really do not allow *redemptive* value to be recognized in spiritual traditions which understand the human condition or the conditions for redemption in a different way (though this does not rule out recognizing that non-Christian traditions might have ethical or spiritual insights of a lesser order).

From a methodological vantage point the defining characteristic of this kind of exclusivism is the reduction of theology to hermeneutics, a position we will analyze and subject to criticism, bringing it into dialogue with the much richer hermeneutic perspectives of other spiritual traditions, in a later chapter.

While modern *Science* has historically understood itself as a force for free thought and open-mindedness, we have shown, following Duhem (Duhem 1909) that the scientific revolution of the seventeenth century actually had its roots in the Augustinian reaction of the thirteenth century (Mansueto 2012) and in the repression of Radical Aristotelianism. What we are calling the technocratic *Saeculum* is simply a logical development of the theistic *Saeculum*. On the theoretical side this is a result of the gradual realization of the fact that, as Laplace put it (Laplace 1799–1825), in the context of a univocal metaphysics, "God is an hypothesis of which we have no need." Where all Being exists in the way in which a univocal metaphysics understands it, the problem of Being, of why there is something rather than nothing, simply disappears. Science tells *how* Being is, i.e. according to what laws it operates, and theology is, as Frank Tipler (Tipler 1994) puts it, effectively reduced to physics. Within this basic problematic there are, to be sure, a wide range of positions available, from one of sharp conflict with religion, such as that advocated by the new atheism (Harris 2004, Dawkins 2007, Dennett 2007, Kraus 2012), through an integrationist position advocated by God builders such as Tipler (Tipler 1994). We will address these positions in a later chapter. On the practical side the development from theistic to technocratic secularism takes the form, on the one hand, of technological progress which increases the weight of humanity in the universe and which ultimately begins to make god-building seem possible and, on the other hand, of the "disenchantment" of the Protestant Ethic which Weber describes (Weber 1920/1968), resulting in the "iron cage" of the technocratic *Saeculum*. It is a very short distance from superexploiting oneself and everyone else for an entirely inscrutable divine purpose to superexploiting oneself and everyone else for the sake of unlimited accumulation—or, perhaps even more straightforwardly—for no purpose at all.

Humanistic secularism, in its liberal, democratic, socialist, and populist forms presents a rather different cluster of problems. Humanistic secularism, we have suggested in the previous chapter, argues that Being is univocal not in its contingency, with God differing form other beings only in His infinite power, but rather in its necessity, so that everything is, at least potentially divine not merely by participation or accidental connaturality, but by nature and in essence. And the humanistic secular tradition as a whole is, in this sense globally *theological* in the sense that it takes the form of a critique of axial and specifically Christian theology with the aim of demonstrating the possibility and explicating the conditions of such immanent deification. In this sense Marx spoke not just for the emerging communist movement but for all humanistic secularisms, liberal, democratic, socialist, and populist when he said that "the criticism of religion is the beginning of all criticism (Marx 1843b/1978)."

This religion-critical discourse takes two variant forms, though ultimately it is difficult to define rigorously the boundary between them. We have, on the one hand, discourse which understands itself as philosophical, which articulates the humanistic secular project of deification by means of the construction of a political subject which can make humanity the master of is own destiny. Hence Hegel:

> The divine spirit must interpenetrate the entire secular life: whereby wisdom is concrete within it, and carries the terms of its own justification. But that concrete indwelling is only . . . ethical organization (Hegel, G.W.F. *Encyclopaedia of Philosophy: Part Three: Philosophy of Spirit:* Paragraph552).

And Marx, for whom communism is the

> . . . the definitive solution of the contradiction between man and nature and between man and man, the true solution of the contradiction between existence and essence, between objectification and self-realization, between freedom and necessity, between the individual and the species. Communism is the solution to the riddle of history and knows itself to be that solution (Marx 1844/1978: 84).

Second, we have the sociology of religion, always intimately bound up with and the real font of modern social theory, which engages in empirical analysis of historical and living religious traditions from the vantage point of categories derived from one or another variant of the humanistic secular project. Weber represents an engagement first with the Reformed (theistic secular) tradition and later with other religions from the vantage point of a peculiar combination of liberal and emerging populist secularism. Durkheim represents an engagement with primal religions (and provides a framework for engaging other religions) from a vantage point on the far left of democratic secularism. An historical materialist sociology of religion was slower to develop, given the force of the communist critique of transcendence in any form, but is now well represented in the work of Otto Maduro (Maduro 1982) Francois Houtart (Houtart 2000), and Roger Lancaster (Lancaster 1988), as well as in my own work (Mansueto 1988, 1995, 2002a).

It is worth pointing out that there seems to be a new phase in the development of this tradition with the re-emergence of a dialectical critique of religion explicitly sympathetic to the values of the religious traditions in question, a critique which often approaches what might be called an "atheology." Of particular import here is the work of late Derrida (Derrida 2001) who clearly recovered his Jewish roots, but persisted in an essentially anti-Catholic polemic against "globolatinity," as well as the work of Zizek (Zizek 2009, 2012) Agamben (Agamben 2011, 2013a, 2013b), Baudou (Baidou 2003), and Vattimo (Vattimo 2013). Radical Orthodoxy, which began with an argument that, Christianity and secular social theory represent fundamentally different and contradictory spiritual projects (Milbank 1990) might be regarded as a Christian response to the critique of religion which is now engaging this newest phase of the critique very creatively (Milbank 2014).

The populist variant of humanistic secularism has also generated a "theological" discourse which skirts the boundaries between philosophy and the sociology of religion. Here, we will remember, it is the people or nation which is to be the political subject which makes humanity the master of its own destiny. There is thus a sharp rejection of the cosmopolitanism of both the axial project and the liberal, democratic, and socialist variants of the humanistic secular project. The key thinker here is Heidegger, who presents himself as a critic of the entire axial and humanistic secular project, but who is in fact located squarely within the latter. It is just that for Heidegger Being manifests itself not in the rationally autonomous individual, the people as *demos* acting through the secular state, or the working class acting through the Communist Party, but rather the people as *ethnos* or *Volk*, which finds its voice through the discovery of its unique "god" (Heidegger 1934/1989:319, 398–99).

There has been considerable debate among scholars regarding the extent to which Heidegger's own option for fascism is in fact integral to his philosophy. Millerman (Millerman 2013) argues that the key question here is whether one gives priority, as Heidegger himself did, to the "event" as defining a people or to "difference." This is the distinction, Millerman argues, between the Heideggerian Right, with which he, interestingly enough, openly identifies, and where we would also locate the work of Pierre Krebs (Krebs 2012) and the Heideggerian left, which includes Derrida (whose lineages include one which reaches back to Heidegger) and the other religious deconstructionists. I am skeptical of this approach, given that leftwing populisms have historically been defined as much by events (e.g. national liberation struggles and populist revolutions) as by difference. The critical difference I would argue is simply whether the people whose voice and god are being defending is in the process of building or defending an empire or liberating itself from an empire—or is, perhaps, up to something else. We will argue that there are good reasons to prefer liberation from *Empire* to its creation, but the danger of authoritarianism, as well as the co-optation by technocracy, essential to prosecute effective political struggles in the *Saeculum*, remains.

Millerman's typology also fails to define accurately the distinctive character of what might be called the populist "center," represented by Weber (Weber 1920/1968) and Gadamer (Gadamer 1960/2004), both of whom have been central to theological discourse and intercultural engagement in the past century. Here the sense that history is about "peoples" or "civilizations" defined by distinctive ideals remains, but the focus is less on constituting peoples as subjects than on understanding the ideals which motivate them and (in the case of Weber) explaining why some are more successful than others. This project can be mobilized both in the service of liberal tolerance and pluralism and in helping alterimperial or colonized powers define the conditions of their own "success." These alternatives as well must be engaged when we consider in a later chapter, the relationship between the axial projects and humanistic secularism in both its philosophical and social theoretical forms.

Theology in the *Saeculum*

We have shown that the constitutive *theoria* of the *Saeculum* in both its technocratic and humanistic forms is organically theological. In the case of technocratic secularism this takes the form of a logical working out of the implications for the univocal metaphysics which is the foundation of the theistic and the technocratic *Saeculum* alike. If all Being exists in the same way then it might, at least in principal, be possible to *build* God technologically rather than simply submitting to a pre-existent God or resigning ourselves to the ultimate meaninglessness of the universe. Humanistic secularisms, on the other hand, are directly *constituted* by the criticism of religion and specifically of Christianity, a criticism which purports to show that the rationally autonomous individual, the *demos*, the proletariat, or the *ethnos* themselves are, at least implicitly, divine. This leaves, however, the question of what form theological discourse within the axial traditions and theistic secularism, which have by no means disappeared, take in the technocratic and humanistic *Saeculum*.

It should be apparent from what we have already said that in the *Saeculum*, theology has been almost exclusively *about* the relationship between the axial traditions theistic secularism on the one hand and the *Saeculum* on the other. Thus all of the great disputes regarding theological method over the course of the past 500 years (and even more so the past 100 years) can be reduced to differences regarding how to respond to modern secular science, social theory, and exegetical and hermeneutic techniques. There is no better argument for this claim than David Tracy's *Blessed Rage for Order* (Tracy 1975), which retains its relevance in this regard even four decades after its original publication. Tracy identifies five approaches to doing Christian theology in the present period:

- orthodoxy, which rejects any real dialogue with secularism,
- liberal theology, which looks to theology to provide a Christian justification and/or interpretation and of the secular project,
- radical theology, which, rather like the "atheology" of the religious deconstructionists affirms reads Christianity, properly understood, as itself pointing to the death of God,
- neo-orthodoxy, which provides distinctively Christian answers to the problems raised by the secular project, and
- what he calls "revisionism," which seeks to bring Christianity into authentic dialog with the secular project, by engaging Christian sources using the tools of secular.hermeneutics while insisting on the existence of an authentically religious dimension to what he calls "common human experience."

The power of Tracy's analysis not withstanding, I would suggest some amendments. First, because technocratic secularism is derivative from theistic secularism and because this derivation takes place largely within a Protestant Christian context the spectrum he describes is originally a *Protestant* spectrum. The original division, which emerged as early as the seventeenth century, and in a specifically Puritan context, was between those who focused more on the objective value of the individual's contribution to God's work of redemption (the liberals) and those who focused a person's subjective spiritual state (the evangelicals) (Heimart 1966, Hatch 1974). A *political* "united front" in support of the Anglo-American industrial capitalist project as *the* way to build the Kingdom of God on earth, remained between these two parties, which differed more in emphasis than in essentials, up through the Civil War (Howe 1979). But when the Civil War failed to usher in the millennium those left behind by the industrial revolution largely abandoned their support for the technocratic secular project in favor of dispensational premillenialism (Marsden 1980). This too is a secular ideology, in the sense that redemption unfolds entirely within the realm of ordinary sensible reality, which is why the literalist reading of the scriptures as a body of facts reported by reliable witnesses, and the literal return of Jesus to establish his kingdom are so important. But it is a reactively theistic secularism which rejects the technocratic (and humanistic) projects as a rebellion against God.

Liberal Protestantism, on the other hand is that Protestantism which still seeks to find Christian meaning in the *Saecular* project. Even for liberals, however, the realities of industrial capitalism have been hard to swallow. Thus, while a small section of the old Anglo-American ruling classes still believes, at least silently, that their superior "usefulness to society," as demonstrated by their economic contributions, marks them as *elect*, spiritually as well as civilizationally, there has been a tendency for liberal Protestants to become more critical of the technocratic secular project. In some cases this amounts to little more than socializing *noblesse oblige* in government welfare programs; but in other cases it has led to an embrace of liberal, democratic, and even socialist currents of secularism as better expressions of Protestant principle than technocratic capitalism.

Neo-Orthodox theologies, however much they may have understood themselves as rooted in a new and more faithful reading of the Christian *kerygma*, are fundamentally a reflection of the fact that it has become more and more difficult to find and affirm a Christian meaning for either the technocratic or humanistic secular project. Neo-Orthodoxy responds by offering an incisive Christian critique of the *Saecular* projects without actually challenging *Saecular* hegemony. Reinhold Niebuhr's image of the *Moral Man in an Immoral Society* (Niebuhr 1932) captures this orientation quite precisely. Rather than baptizing the technocratic *Saecular* project as implicitly the Christian project, the neo-orthodox Protestant insists that the rejection of divine sovereignty generally and the attempt to build god technologically and politically represent a fundamental mistake. And yet precisely because of their rejection of the *Saecular* project they also reject any global attempt to challenge the *Saeculum*. In this sense neo-orthodox Protestants are still Liberal Protestants in the broader sense in that they find religious meaning first and foremost in an attempt to do the will of God on the basis of their justification by faith in the *Saeculum* as it actually exists. They are just rather more critical with regard to the extent to which the

Saeculum itself, in either its technocratic or humanistic forms, can ever fully embody that will.

Second, Tracy's category of "radical theology" seems to me to cover some fundamentally different options. In the case of Altizer and Hamilton (Altizer and Hamilton 1966) there seems to be an affirmation of the secular project, especially in its humanistic form, as a *full* expression of the Christian, which stands somewhere between Hegel, in that it persists in using Christian language and affirming the enduring relevance of the Christian story, and Marx or even Nietzsche, in using the language of the "death of God" and affirming what appears to be a metaphysical atheism. Altizer, in other words approaches a position similar to that of the new critics of religion or "atheologists" such as Agamben, Zizek, and the late Derrida, but from a Christian rather than humanistic secular vantage point. For Vahanian (Vahanian 1961) the death of God, on the other hand refers to a loss of the sense of the sacred in society, a perspective which might be read as within the neo-orthodox camp. For Rubenstein (Rubenstein 1966), finally, the term "death of God," is a response to the Shoah and to the sense that it is obscene to talk about God in the wake of the attempted and nearly successful extermination of His people. This is, of course, a Jewish insight, though by no means irrelevant for other traditions, and quite different from a Neo-Hegelian embrace of the secular.

Tracy wrote at a time when the original wave of Death of God theology was ebbing. The emergence of atheology, weak theology, and the like require greater attention to this current.

Third, the application of Tracy's typology outside the Protestant arena is, as we have suggested, possible, but requires some care. Even in the Catholic context there are ambiguities. Thus it is not clear that there was ever a "liberal Catholicism" in the sense of a Catholicism which affirmed the technocratic, capitalistic *Saeculum* as *the* definitive realization of the Catholic ideal. It is more useful to follow the historic divisions which developed within the Catholic Church. There have been many of these but several seem especially important. There is, first, the division between the Radical Aristotelians (Dahm 1987), the Dominican Thomistic center, and the Neo-Augustinian Right (Mansueto 2010b), which emerged in the thirteenth century and which was then followed almost immediately by the schism within the Augustinian camp first between the Franciscan Spirituals and Conventuals and eventually between the Franciscan order as a whole and the rest of the Church. The issue here was above all the reaction to the completion, or at least further radicalization of the axial project of religious problematization, rationalization, and democratization by the emergence of the urban communes and peasant movements in the high and late Middle Ages, and to the emergence of sovereign states as a result of the Norman Conquests, the Crusades, the *Reconquista*, and eventually the conquest of the Asia, Africa, and the Americas. The political theological fissures and alliances of this period are extraordinarily difficult to trace, since advocates of radical immanence emerge in both the Radical Aristotelian and Franciscan camps and both, separately sometimes ally themselves with *one* of the emerging absolutist states (interestingly enough the least effective one, the Holy Roman Empire). Advocates of the emerging doctrine of divine sovereignty, similarly, emerge among ideological operatives of the French crown (Stephen Tempier), the Normans (Anonymous of York), and undoubtedly elsewhere, while the papacy, resisting the movement towards absolutism gradually embraces but also co-opts the Thomistic center. This latter phenomenon is, in turn, further extended and complicated in the Counter-Reformation as the Catholic powers reach some measure of detente with the papacy as they struggle to resist their emerging Protestant rivals, and the papacy gradually moves toward absolutism, a movement completed with the embrace of papal infallibility at the first Vatican Council. Cutting across all of these currents are the projects of competing religious orders, each of which takes its own distinctive approach to the emerging *Saeculum*. The Dominicans look to find a place for the secular within a renewed Christendom, while the Jesuits seek to find a place for a renewed Church in a *Saeculum* they know will be victorious, at least in the middle run of the next few centuries or millennia. The Franciscans, finally, attempt to build the Third Age of the Holy Spirit among the poor in the Americas and elsewhere, but end up largely agents of Spanish absolutist state. A bit later the principal Catholic powers, especially France, pull away from Rome and embrace a new Augustinianism rooted in the philosophy of Descartes and Malebranche (Thibault 1971) and Thomism reasserts itself in the nineteenth century as part of a movement to restore Catholic fortunes based on a new alliance with the peasantry and working classes.

None of this means that the category of "Liberal Catholicism" is meaningless. On the contrary, especially in North America, the category is an important term of self-identification. But it is a much less precise term than Liberal Protestantism and refers simply to a Catholicism which is more open than other trends within the Church to dialogue with and learning from dissident currents within the Church (though it is rarely comfortable with the radicalism of groups like the Beguines or the Spirituals) as well as from Protestantism, technocratic and humanistic secularism, and other axial spiritual traditions. It is also, perhaps, less committed to and often uncomprehending of the complex geopolitical *realpolitik* of the Papacy and the *curia* which has driven most of the actual doctrinal and pastoral decisions of the Catholic Church throughout its history than are other currents in the

Church, something which is further complicated by the fact that this *realpolitik* belongs *both* to a global power carrying a powerful spiritual and civilizational ideal *and* a rather peculiar patriarchal celibate clerical corporation.

This means that Liberal Protestantism and Liberal Catholicism have two entirely different political trajectories and destinies. Liberal Protestantism was once integral to the ideological strategy of the *Saeculum* and is slowly dying as the *Saecular* project loses its credibility and becomes more and more difficult to either defend or reform in ways that are recognizably consistent with Christianity. We will see shortly what replaces it. Liberal Catholicism is not itself a single coherent political-theological project but rather an umbrella term which includes *all* those who are especially faithful to the *catholicity* of the Catholic Church, in the sense of its historical openness to dialogue with and learning from Athens or any other political-theological metropole (or micropole) but who do not fully understand that the Catholic Church, unlike nearly any other religious community on the planet operates politically as at least a "great power" and quite possibly as a "superpower," even in the *Saeculum*, and must be understood—and led—as such.

With the same qualifications Tracy's application of categories such as neo-orthodox, radical, or revisionist might be applied in a Catholic context, but the qualifications are important. Internal Catholic lines of demarcation are as important or more important than attitudes towards the *Saeculum* and the most important relationship between the Catholic Church and the *Saeculum* is the geopolitical one.

What has been said about Catholicism applies with even more force to discussions of Jewish, Muslim, Hindu, Buddhist, Confucian, and Taoist liberalisms or modernisms, neo-orthodoxy or radicalisms or revisionisms. The divisions between Assimilationist, Bundist, Territorialist, or Zionist, Liberal, Religious, Labor, or Spiritual Zionists (Avinieri 1981) are as important as the divisions between Orthodox, Reformed, Conservative, or Reconstructionist (which otherwise corresponds eerily to Tracy's typology). The same is true of the divisions between and within the Sunni and Shia camps (Crone 2004), the incredible diversity of "Hinduisms (Khan 2004)," and the complex engagement and contest between Indian and Chinese civilization which *is* actually existing Buddhism. It *is* true that the global hegemony first of theistic and later of technocratic (and in the Soviet sphere humanistic) secularism has *forced* all other traditions to define their global political-theological position with respect to the hegemonic ideals. But we cannot assume that the positions taken are taken for the same reasons, or have the same meanings as "analogous" positions within Protestantism. Anyone who has doubts about this should spend some time working with Muslims who understand themselves as friendly to modern science and democracy, but who are anxious to demonstrate that its all in the Quran after all or to Burmese Buddhist democracy advocates who care very little about the human or democratic rights of the Rohinga. The issue here is not backwardness or insensitivity. It is the theological imperatives of global civilizational politics.

Finally, we need to consider two "types" which Tracy does not address, one because it is not generally considered to be in the mainstream of Christian theology and the second because it emerged since he wrote. I am referring to the New Thought/New Age movement and Radical Orthodoxy.

The New Age movement is best understood as the heir of the New Thought (Albanese 2007) movements of the nineteenth century. The term New Thought refers to a cluster of religious sects, including Religious Science, Unity, Divine Science. Christian Science represents a closely allied tendency, but differs from New Thought in emphasizing the unique manifestation of divine truth in Jesus. Like perennialism, this tendency promotes the idea that most, if not all of humanity's great religious traditions contain a common spiritual core. But where the perennialists find this core in Neo-Platonism and authentically similar, cognate ideas in other traditions (Advaita Vedanta, Sufi mysticism), New Thought tends to reduce all religion to a kind of subjective idealism which regards reality itself as a projection of the mind. In this sense it betrays its modern, Anglo-American Protestant roots, which ultimately go back to Bishop Berkeley.

While New Thought organizations, such as those named above persist and form part of the larger New Age movement, the tendency has also had a broader influence on the Western reception of Hinduism and Buddhism. In particular, it has tended to promote a (mis)reading of Advaita Vedanta and several Buddhist Schools, including most Vajrayana, and especially the Karma Kagyu and Nyingmpa Schools, as subjective idealisms.

If perennialism is an oversimplification of the relationships between humanity's mystical traditions the New Age movement is an outright falsification. This is easiest to see in the case of Buddhism. The first of the great noble truths—that life is suffering—is lost on the New Thought/New Age movements. For an authentic Buddhist the root of suffering is metaphysical and not merely mental. It lies in the reality of life as a finite, dependent being. The change in outlook by means of which we overcome suffering does not change our circumstances but rather involves a radical coming to terms with the unreality of the self and the impermanence of everything we hold dear. Even the more advanced Mahayana and Vajrayana Schools, which promise the bliss of full enlightenment, do so in the form of a purely generative, egoless life of ripening Being. For the New Age, on the other hand, overcoming illusion allows us to make the world what we will it to be, an attitude possible only for those who live on accumulated wealth.

In the case of Hinduism the line between an authentic Western adherent of Advaita Vedanta and a New Age dilettante may, at first, seem a bit more difficult to catch. Hinduism, after all, is comfortable with the pursuit of religious aims other than enlightenment. But philosophically the difference is clear. Advaita Vedanta is an objective idealism for which the ego is as much an illusion as it is for Buddhism, to which it was the Hindu answer and from which the advanced Mahayana and Vajrayana schools derived much of their inspiration. Brahman is first and foremost an infinite and necessary generativity, not simply a universal mind. New Age movements, on the other hand, are subjective idealisms for which mind is always and only the primary reality.

Radical Orthodoxy, on the other hand, represents a fundamental rejection of the *Saeculum*, understood as defined by the embrace of a univocal metaphysics from the late Middle Ages on. This analysis has obviously influenced my own profoundly. But John Milbank (Milbank 1990, 1999, 2006a) argues that only Christianity provides the theological context for a metaphysics of participation, and includes what we have called humanistic secularism (and, in his earlier work at least, Hellenic philosophy) in his condemnation of the *Saeculum*. Where Milbank seems to me to err is in the claim that only Christianity can sustain a metaphysics of participation. As we will see there is ample evidence for such a metaphysics in Judaism and Islam and Hinduism, Buddhism, Confucianism, and Taoism all operate (with the exception of a few sects) with metaphysical foundations that are clearly not univocal even if they are not identical to, say, a Thomistic metaphysics of *Esse*. We will also argue for a distinction between two types of univocity: that of univocal contingency, with or with out an infinitely powerful being (God), which is the univocal metaphysics of the theistic and technocratic *Saeculum,* and that of univocal necessity, which endows all beings with the power of *Esse* as such, which is the univocal metaphysics of humanistic secularism. This latter metaphysics, we will argue, is also incorrect, but it is far less damaging that the metaphysics of univocal contingency, in that it does not drive the authentically divine from the world, but simply overestimates what ordinary beings can do. This will lead us to a political-theological alignment which is both more cosmopolitan than Milbank's and more sympathetic to the humanistic secular project, if also concerned to define clearly the metaphysical as well as the political reasons for its failure.

It is necessary, finally, to mention an entirely new way of engaging questions of meaning and value across traditions which avoids many of the problems of both cosmopolitanism and particularism. I am referring to the emerging discipline of comparative theology (Clooney 2010). Specifically, where *theologies of religion* are concerned primarily with evaluating the status of other religions, with respect to their truth claims and capacity to promote the spiritual development of their adherents, *comparative theology* is focused on what one can learn from inter-religious engagements. Thus, where a theologian of religions might ask how a Christian should evaluate the spiritual impact of the Buddhist doctrine of *sunyata* or emptiness, a comparative theologian would ask what we can learn from it without, however, calling into question core Christian metaphysical and theological commitments, e.g. for the Thomistic Catholic tradition, a theism grounded in an analogical metaphysics of *Esse*. Thus in *Zen and the Birds of Appetite* (Merton 1968), Thomas Merton (long before comparative theology had emerged as a distinct discipline), shows how Zen Buddhism can inform the apophatic moment in Catholic theology and deepen a Christian's passage through the *via negativa*, and the "dark nights," preparing us for the breakthrough beyond mystical union which only Eckhart, among Catholic mystics, has adequately described.

This trend is also important to our work and we differ from it primarily in arguing that while we begin and may well end our engagement with questions of meaning and value within a particular spiritual tradition, the present period requires an engagement which is radically open and looks forward to both new syncretisms and radically ways of understanding the sacred and humanity's *theotic* project.

From Intercultural Engagement to Theological Method

We are now in a position to define our own method, which is at once a theological method and a approach to the engagement between civilizations which we have shown to be constitutive of theology. As we will see, it looks a great deal like Tracy's revisionism, but differs in taking a much longer and much broader view, so that the engagement between the theistic, technocratic, and humanistic *Saecula* are only a few among many such engagements with theological relevance.

We begin with an insistence on the existence of a common human nature and a common human project which is ultimately *spiritual* and *religious* in nature. Up until now we have used the terms spirituality and religion more or less interchangeably, and have been gradually defining theology as a specific discourse within and about the spiritual and the religious. As we move to define our method we need to be more precise. Henceforth, by *spirituality* we will mean humanity's fundamental ordering to the sacred, understood as *Being as such*. By *religion*, on the other hand, we intend the structures by which humanity seeks *Being*. There is, in this sense, no contradiction between the claim that human beings are, by nature, both spiritual and religious animals (and would be even if the spiritual impulse turned out to be in vain) and the claim that religion is a social product and spirituality itself a social phenomenon.

Within this context the *secular* takes on a very distinctive meaning and one by no means essentially opposed to either the spiritual or the religious. The secular is simply the worldly. All religions bear on the worldly. In the process of seeking Being we define distinctive civilizational ideals or normative orders which in turn affect everything that we do. Some religions are, however, focused *exclusively* on the secular, constituting the civilization we will call the *Saeculum* (what most call *modernity*) and the doctrine we will call *secularism*. Secularisms attempt, that is, to find the infinite and the necessary, to the extent that they believe that it is possible, entirely within the realm of this world, through human development and civilizational progress. Humanistic secularism seeks divinization through the creation of a political subject (the rationally autonomous individual, the democratic state, the Communist Party, or the people or nation) which makes humanity the master of its own destiny. Positivistic or scientific-technological secularism seeks divinization through scientific and technological progress which pushes back the limits of finitude until they have, for all intents and purposes, disappeared. But neither is any less spiritual, in the sense of seeking Being, or religious, in the sense of being social determined and institutionalized ways of seeking Being, because of their radical secularity. Nor do ideologies which regard the secular project as ultimately vain and hopeless, such as existentialism or deconstructionism, cease to be spiritual or religious simply because they believe that humanity's spiritual longings are ultimately in vain.

Being spiritual and being religious are, in other words, *constitutive* of humanity and are so in and through our other human distinctives such as language and reason, labor and sociality, which are simply our ways of representing and pursuing our longing for Being. And this is true however much religious dogmatists may want to exclude experiences of the sacred different from their own or however much secularists may want to represent the sacred itself as a delusion. Both attitudes represent a fundamental misunderstanding of human experience. Hunting and gathering, plowing, sowing and harvesting and herding, eating and drinking, urinating and defecating, making love and making war, building cities, ruling them and governing them and razing them, art, science, and philosophy—each of these is a spiritual and a religious act. And they are and would remain so even if God were to turn out "not to exist" (whatever that means) and Enlightenment to turn out to be impossible.

Second, we will insist on the existence of real differences between *ways* of being human. This includes openness to the possibility at least of real differences between human *ends*. While our underlying commitment to the primacy of seeking *Being* would seem to imply a single shared final goal, even if the paths really differ, it is quite possible that we are seeking something that does not exist or that we play a significant role in creating. If this is so, then just as seeking *Being* leads to the evolution of diverse species of plants and animals, it may well lead to an increasing diversity of spiritual goals, even if there is an implied *telos* operating in an through all of them.

Third, these first two points imply that there is a basis for real dialogue, debate, and deliberation between ways, with the possibility, but not the inevitability, of persuasion. This deliberation, furthermore, while it certainly takes the form of theory, also takes the form of practice and the analysis and critique of practice. It is, in other words, a geopolitical-theological engagement (collaboration and contest) as much as it is a scholarly debate, and the scholarly debate becomes useful only to the extent that it takes into account geopolitical-theological realities.

Fourth, there is no implication in what we have said either that there is a final truth accessible to finite and contingent beings, or that all perspectives are equally valid or in any case not susceptible to rational validation or critique or both. Our work is more likely to lead to a tentative and uncertain hierarchization of perspectives, a kind of modest *p'an chiao* than it is either to final solutions or radical relativism. This is true partly because, as we will show, the truth transcends any particular expression or formulation, whether imaginative or dialectical, verbal, visual, or musical and partly because its possible two different *ways* will show themselves—even at the supra-rational level—to be equally but not completely adequate attempts at the Truth.

All of this, finally, will affect profoundly our substantive claims. While our starting point is a critique of the currently dominant spiritual project, that of the technocratic *Saeculum*, and while we will mount this critique quite vigorously, our fundamental orientation prevents us from denying that even our adversaries see at least a part of the truth. Our aim will be to save their contributions and to integrate them into a higher synthesis, recognizing that this synthesis itself will remain partial and incomplete.

With these methodological notes in mind, we now turn to the substance of our work beginning with an attempt to address the contests within and between the principal axial *ways*.

3

Being and Dependent Origination

Our next step is to bring the principal axial traditions into dialog with each other, completing the axial project and the emerging global dialogue which began during the Silk Road Era and which was interrupted by the advent of the third iteration of *Saeculum*. This will entail, first of all, engaging the debates *within* the principal axial *ways*, and then asking how, if at all, these ways can be brought together in a higher synthesis. In undertaking this project we will need to begin with the *way of seeking Being*, understood to include Hellenism, Hinduism, and Buddhism. This is because the internal struggles within the *ways* of harmony and of justice and liberation are affected from the very beginning by their interactions with the *way of seeking Being* and cannot be understood apart from this way.

We will begin by defining the basic, shared characteristics of this way. We will then analyze each of the particular spiritual and civilizational traditions within it, situating each within its particular historical context. This will, in turn, allow us to frame the fundamental question at issue within this *way* in both theoretical and practical, ontological/theological and political/civilizational terms. Finally, we will propose a resolution to the question which not only advances the *way* to a higher synthesis, but which substantially answers deconstructionist critiques of ontotheology.

What unifies the *way of seeking being* is a shared perspective with respect to the sacral monarchic way. As we argued in the first chapter, neither hunting and gathering with its totemic ideologies, horticulture with its attendant cult of the *Magna Mater*, nor the sacrificial cults of pastoral-nomadic peoples could ever satisfy humanity's desire to be god. Each, in fact, while celebrating our participation in the divine, is also, at the same time, an acknowledgement of our finitude and contingency, our limitation and our insertion in a complex web of interdependence.

Humanity's first attempt to liberate itself from these limitations and this dependence comes with the development of metal (specifically bronze) technology around 3000 BCE, which opens up for humanity an entirely new strategy for development: that of conquest and exploitation. It is, of course, the pastoral/raiding peoples who first pioneer this way, not because of any innate predisposition towards violence but simply because it represents, for them, the only way forwards towards the enjoyment of the fruits of urban life. The spiritual question which emerges as a result of this process is starkly simple and was perhaps first represented clearly in Hegel's analysis of the master/slave dialectic in his *Phenomenology of Spirit* (Hegel 1807/1977). *Do we more nearly realize Being through conquest and mastery or through defeat, enslavement, and abstract, uncompensated labor for the Other?*

Sacral monarchy answers this question in what seems, at first, like the obvious way. Human life—indeed the universe as a whole—is a participation in Being. Conquer it and one becomes the lord of Being, a kind of god. There is, to be sure, as yet no clear concept of *Being as such*, and thus the king is *a* god, not God. But the strategy makes sense. If it a good thing to plow and sow and reap and herd and build cities, is it not better still to have at one's disposal entire villages and cities full of people who can do this in your name? If it is a good thing to bear and rear children, is it not better still to have at one's disposal an entire harem of women who can do this for us at our will?

What defines the common ground on which the various forms of the *way of the search for Being* develop is a simultaneous recognition that the sacral monarchic project is a failure, and in fact deeply destructive, and a re-affirmation of the *desire to be god* as the fundamental aim of human life. Some strains of the tradition will look for ways to approach realization of this end; others will argue that it is an impossible desire, not because a sovereign God stands in our way but because *nothing* has the power of *Being in itself*. Still other strains stand somewhere in between. The result is a profound dialogue regarding just what *Being* is and just how, given what we believe it to be, we might best approach it.

Hellenism

Of the variants of the *way of seeking Being*, what we will call Hellenism and two Indian *ways*, Hinduism and Buddhism, were clearly the most important. Hellenism emerged out of the crisis of a peripheral variant of the sacral monarchic project—the Mycenean Civilization—which collapsed at the end of Bronze Age and ushered in a period of as many as four centuries during which urban civilization and written language all but dissapeared from the Hellenic domain. We call this civilization "peripheral" in the sense that rather than great urban centers like those of the Nile, Mesopotamian, Indus, and Huang He valleys, we find what were little more than palaces and rather than building empires, the Mycenean warlords were little more that raiders and cattle rustlers.

Hellenism begins with the memory of the collapse of the sacral monarchic project, and remembers it as a great war. I refer, of course, to the Trojan war, preserved in what is left of the great epic cycle we associate with Homer. We should note, to begin with, that unlike the events of *Kurukshetra*, which were the result of a lawful attempt at deification through conquest, ratified by the Vedic ritual of the *rajasuya*, which nonetheless led to disaster and the advent of a new Dark Age, the *Kali Yuga*, the Trojan war was more of a human participation in a conflict among the gods, into which they were invited by the Gods as a kind of challenge and test. At no point, at least as the events are remembered in the Homeric text, which is from around 750 BCE, is full divinization ever on the horizon. Rather, the Gods, and above all Athena, who serves as "mentor" to Achilles, Oddyseus, and Telemachus (indeed, in the form in which she appears to the last of these, she is the eponymous Mentor), challenge humans to stretch themselves *towards* the divine, leading them into situations which will reveal to them their limits. It is in this realization of limit that the idea of the unlimited emerges and that Greece is challenged to develop a deeper and richer understanding of the *theotic* project.

By comparison with the *Mahabharata*, in other words, both the drive to deificaiton through conquest (as we might expect in a peripheral sacral monarchic formation) and the critique of this drive are relatively muted. Still, the events at Troy are remembered as catastrophic for the Greeks, *in spite of the fact that they are the victors* and what emerges out of this memory are quite different ways of *seeking Being*.

As civilization revived in the eastern Mediterranean from around 800 BCE on, it did so on the basis of specialized agriculture and petty commodity production, developments which in turn catalyzed the Axial Age breakthroughs. We have already analyzed these breakthroughs—the process of religious problematization, democratization, and rationalization—in some detail elsewhere (Mansueto 2010b). Here we focus on the new *ways of seeking Being* which emerged during this period. Two in particular stand out: *democracy* and *philosophy*.

Petty commodity production, while it opened up the possibility of the accumulation of wealth without exploitation, tended in fact to lead to economic differentiation and eventually to indebtedness, loss of land, and servitude for those peasants who had poorer quality land, were further from markets, or had opted to grow barley and wheat rather than grapes or olives.

The result was a series of peasant revolts in the late seventh and early sixth century. These struggles were resolved in different ways throughout Greece. In Sparta, for example, the landed elites co-opted the masses by enserfing the surrounding Messenians and transforming the whole population of the *polis* into a "mass" warrior aristocracy which played no role in production or commerce whatsoever. In other places the uprisings were suppressed with only a few concessions and an oligarchic constitution predominated. In Athens, however, there were fundamental structural reforms which improved the situation of both the peasantry and the emerging bourgeoisie[1] at the expense of the *eupatridae*. The first of these reforms was carried out by Solon in 594–593 BCE. All debts secured by land or personal liberty were cancelled in what was known as the *Seisachtheia* or "shaking off of burdens." This was accompanied by limited land reform and by the establishment of a mixed constitution which replaced birth with wealth as the criterion of eligibility for higher office and gave even the poorest citizens some voice in shaping public policies. Later reforms further extended the sphere of democratic participation, so that at times essentially all laws were made by a democratic assembly in which all male citizens had voice and vote and many key offices were chosen by lot, though there were also periods of oligarchic reaction.

The development of Hellenic democracy was closely associated with the emergence of new military technologies. The advent of iron technology made it possible for a far larger percentage of the population to arm itself, leading to the emergence of a light armored infantry—the hoplites—who formed the backbone of the Greek military during this period. An armed population, of course, is difficult to subdue, making some element of democratization nearly inevitable.

As we will see, these reforms did not actually bring the Athenian peasantry and artisanate to power. The *nouveau riche* elements which were gradually displacing the *eupatrid* families had the time and resources to participate in public life in ways than the peasants and artisans could not, and found ways to manipulate the passions of those who could participate. The effects of the revolutions should not, however, be underestimated. On the one hand, the economic reforms of Solon and his successors guaranteed the continued existence at Athens of a small peasantry, something which cannot be said of Rome and most other cities in the ancient Mediterranean.

---

1. The term bourgeoisie is taken here to apply to any social class which drives its revenue from the exploitation of the labor of others and the sale of the resulting goods and services in the marketplace, even if the exploitation in question is not strictly capitalist in character (i.e. based on wage labor), but depends rather on coercion of some kind, in this case on chattel slavery.

Second, and more importantly, the revolutions brought into being a democratic public arena in which matters which had formerly been divined or simply decreed by the *basileus* were now matters of public deliberation. Indeed, what the revolutions did, ultimately was to make the position of *basileus*, who, while not regarded as divine, was a sacred king, into an elected office. This in turn opened up the sacred court of the Areopagus, now expanded to include those who had held senior offices, such as that of *basileus* archon to the entire population.

The reforms also added a second official, the *eponymous archon*, who was responsible for organizing a new religious festival—that of Dionysus. This festival which included contests in the various dramatic disciplines: tragedy, comedy, and satyr plays. The development of Greek drama was itself an integral part of the process of religious democratization. The old myths and legends which formed the imaginative content of Greek religion concerned, for the most part, a vision of human excellence which would have made sense only to the old *eupatrid* families, and then only during the period in which warfare was still their principal occupation. They had little to say to a commercial wine or oil producer, much less to a peasant or artisan. The various forms of drama, but especially the tragedies, took these stories and retold them in a way which made them relevant to contemporary concerns. Thus rather than focusing on the divine challenge to excellence—most especially on the field of battle—and on the inevitable limits imposed on human achievement, Greek drama addresses themes such as the contradiction between kinship and political relationships (*Antigone*), between mother-right (still very important among the peasantry) and the patriarchal order of the *polis* (the *Orestaia*), and eventually the conflict between myth and philosophy (*The Clouds*). And each dramatist offered differing answers to these questions, so that drama itself became the locus of an authentic public debate regarding fundamental questions of meaning and value.

The other great locus of religious democratization was, of course, the mystery cult. Traditional Greek religion seems to have afforded hope of immortality only to the semidivine members of the *eupatrid* lineages who were descended from the gods. The new mystery cults extended this promise to literally anyone who underwent an initiation into the cults. The basic structure was always the same: catechesis or instruction regarding the mysteries, initiation, usually through a symbolic experience of death and rebirth by passage through water or a cave, participation in a communion meal and, later, the possibility of still higher degrees of initiation. The most important of the mysteries in the early period were the cult of Demeter at Eleusis and the Orphic mysteries. By participating in a secret initiation process members of the mystery cults gained access to knowledge which afforded them the prospect of immortality or at least of a more favorable reincarnation. Eventually, these cults emerged as the principal forms of religious life throughout the ancient Mediterranean. The form of the mystery cult, which originated in Greece, was joined to content from Egypt (the cult of Isis and Osiris), Persia (the cult of Mithra) and eventually Israel (Christianity).

As a *way of seeking Being*, then, Hellenic democracy was, fundamentally, a democratization (and to *some* extent a pacification) of the sacral monarchic way. Rather than being the privilege of the sacral monarch alone, or perhaps of his family and a few other aristocratic lineages, *theosis* is opened up, at least in principle, to the people as a whole. But the *means* remain remarkably similar: warfare as a hoplite or the more civil *agon* of the athletic field or the democratic arena, and participation in and even leadership of the cult, though more likely in the form of the new Dyonisian drama festivals or the mystery cults than the old civic cults which tended to remain strongholds of the old ruling class.

The second *way of seeking being*, philosophy, emerged alongside of, but also in tension with, Hellenic democracy. Initially, philosophy was simply a reflex of the spontaneous process of religious rationalization which accompanied the emergence of petty commodity production. Thus the gradual evolution in understanding of the first principle which we have traced elsewhere (Mansueto 2010b). At the beginning of the Axial Age (e.g. for Homer) the gods are characters in a story, with fully developed personalities. A bit later, for Hesiod, they are personified natural forces. Still later, they appear as natural forces without personification (e.g. in the natural philosophers), and are eventually described by mathematical terms such as the One (Anaximenes) or the Infinite (Xenophanes). To the extent that philosophy at this stage becomes a real *way of seeking Being*, it operates as a kind of intellectualized mystery cult. This was certainly the case with the Pythagoreans and some other schools as Kingsley (Kingsley 1995) has shown, and it remains a dimension of philosophy until its absorption by Judaism, Christianity, in the middle of the first millennium of the Common Era.

The emergence of the dialectical tradition with Socrates, Plato, and Aristotle, however, marks a sharp break with the democratic current of Hellenism. As we have argued elsewhere (Mansueto 2010b) the Socratic tradition was first and foremost a critique of democracy as an instrument by which the *nouveux riches* elite of large landowners and merchants (from which some philosophers, such as Plato himself were in fact drawn) exercised hegemony over the *polis* and turned it into a means of private profit.

Plato describes his *way* in dramatic terms in the *Republic*. The dialogue opens with Socrates returning from a festival, probably of the goddess Bendis, in the Pireaus (Plato, *Republic* 327a), situating the action firmly in the context of the Hellenic practice of *theoria*. This was the practice undertaken by Hellenic *poleis* (and no doubt by individual citizens and groups of citizens) of observing the festivals of other *poleis* and other political actors in order to understand their political-theological orientation (Bellah 2011). Socrates is all but kidnapped by a group of rich young men, who drag him to the house of Cephalus, a leading citizen, as sort of court-jester. A debate ensues concerning the nature of justice in which Socrates demonstrates the internal contradictions of the concepts of justice typical of the older *eupatrids*, represented by Cephalus (for whom justice is paying your debts), and the emerging bourgeoisie, represented by Thrasymachus (who argues that justice is just a nice term for the will of the stronger) and the *demos* (who argue that justice is just a social convention). The bulk of the dialogue is a critique of this last position, which Socrates carries out by analyzing what would be involved in actually creating an ideal city.

The core of this argument is a demonstration that a city must be protected not only from outsiders (making a military necessary) but from its own protectors. Thus far, of course, this is just the broader axial critique of sacral monarchy. But Plato then shows that they only reliable way to protect the city from its protectors is to ensure that the protectors themselves are virtuous. This is to be achieved by means of a decades long process of preparation. Plato's Guardians begin their preparation with military training as well as training in music and mathematics generally. This is followed, for the most capable, by the study of dialectics. But before they become "philosopher-kings" (actually members of a council of the wise governing the *polis*) the Guardians spend something on the order of two decades in increasingly responsible political posts. Plato's model for cultivating his Guardians is, in other words, very much that of the emerging *cursus honorum*, infused, to be sure, with philosophical training, but still very much embedded in the political process (Plato, *Republic* 471c–541b). Participation in the public arena is an integral, indeed constitutive element of the dialectical ascent which terminates, for Plato in what he calls *noesis*.

> And when I speak of the other division of the intelligible, you will understand me to speak of that other sort of knowledge which reason herself attains by the power of dialectic, using the hypotheses not as first principles, but only as hypotheses—that is to say, as steps and points of departure into a world which is above hypotheses, in order that she may soar beyond them to the first principle of the whole; and clinging to this and then to that which depends on this, by successive steps she descends again without the aid of any sensible object, from ideas, through ideas, and in ideas she ends (Plato. *Republic* 511e)

Those who do not complete this sort of philosphically enriched *curus honorum*, Plato compares to people chained in a cave watching the play of shadows on a wall. On the rare occasion that someone escapes they must not stop at discovering the mechanism by which this shadow play is generated (perhaps a reference to the art of *rhetoric*) but must exit the cave, discover the real things of which the shadow puppets are but a reflection, and ultimately the sun itself, which is the source of all things. Should one thus liberated return and try to enlighten his fellow citizens, s/he will be regarded as insane. Those who remain in the cave, or only get part way out are slaves. The *way* is steep and narrow and because of this *the ordinary condition of humanity is a slavery which it is all but impossible to escape* (Plato, Republic, 514a–520a).

Dialectics, as an axial *way* and a variant of the *way of the search for Being*, then, does not abandon the political or the cultic, but enriches them with the practice of philosophy. It is at once a critique of the democratic way and an argument regarding the conditions of its realization. In order to fulfill its promise, democracy would require that everyone become a philosopher. And by this we mean not just a student of philosophy with a few years of liberal education or a scholar of philosophy who has mastered the existing state of the tradition, but a virtuoso practitioner of a crushingly difficult spiritual discipline.

And for Plato, even if this were to be accomplished, the result would be a gradual degeneration. Aristocracies, societies governed by the intellectually and morally most advanced elements degenerate into timocracies, societies governed by the courageous and proud (i.e. warriors). Timocracies degenerate into oligarchies, governed by the rich, oligarchies into democracies, governed by the people as a whole, who do not know the Good, and democracies into tyrannies, which transform the state into an instrument for satisfying the rapacious desires of a single individual. Errors in the training and selection of the Guardians would bring to power leaders more interested in wealth and honor than in truth and justice. Eventually these decadent elements would force a restoration of private property not unlike the *nomenklatura* privatization we have witnessed in the former Soviet bloc. Even if at first the property holders were persons formed under the old system and concerned at least for their own honor, if not for the highest values of truth and justice, gradually, from one generation to the next, the growing opportunities for making money would encourage its pursuit and the "timocracy," rule by lovers of honor, would degenerate into an oligarchy or a plutocracy—rule by the wealthy. But the degeneration does not stop there. The people see that the rich are able to indulge in the most various pleasures without negative consequences, and they too become infected with greed, rising up at the first possible moment to seize the wealth of the few and share it out among themselves. The rich respond with force, and the result is inevitably tyranny, as the most unscrupulous, playing one class off against the other, make the state their private plaything (*Republic* 543a-576b). Plato takes up this same theme in the *Timaeus*, but goes further, arguing that social disintegration is part of a larger and inevitable cosmic dynamic.

Then why bother? Plato answers this question at the end of the *Republic* recounting the story of the *Myth of Er*. After death, Plato suggests the wisdom accumulated in previous lives informs our choice of our next life. Whether this is taken as a literal embrace of *metempsychosis* or as a metaphor for the choices we make in this life, the point is the same. There is no deification, no remedy for our finitude and contingency, not even any final enlightenment. It is just that it is better to be wise than not. It brings us closer to the Good without ever actually carrying us to our destination.

> And here, my dear Glaucon, is the supreme peril of our human state; and therefore the utmost care should be taken. Let each one of us leave every other kind of knowledge and seek and follow one thing only, if peradventure he may be able to learn and may find some one who will make him able to learn and discern between good and evil, and so to choose always and everywhere the better life as he has opportunity. He should consider the bearing of all these things which have been mentioned severally and collectively upon virtue; he should know what the effect of beauty is when combined with poverty or wealth in a particular soul, and what are the good and evil consequences of noble and humble birth, of private and public station, of strength and weakness, of cleverness and dullness, and of all the soul, and the operation of them when conjoined; he will then look at the nature of the soul, and from the consideration of all these qualities he will be able to determine which is the better and which is the worse; and so he will choose, giving the name of evil to the life which will make his soul more unjust, and good to the life which will make his soul more just; all else he will disregard. For we have seen and know that this is the best choice both in life and after death. A man must take with him into the world below an adamantine faith in truth and right, that there too he may be undazzled by the desire of wealth or the other allurements of evil, lest, coming upon tyrannies and similar villainies, he do irremediable wrongs to others and suffer yet worse himself; but let him know how to choose the mean and avoid the extremes on either side, as far as possible, not only in this life

but in all that which is to come. For this is the way of happiness (Plato, *Republic* 621c).

Aristotle enriches and modifies Plato's argument in many ways. Specifically, he develops a more complex cosmology which has significant room for growth and development and he examines more formally and rigorously the extent to which human beings might realize their end. His cosmology is dynamic and vital, with all things drawn into Being by their desire for the Unmoved Mover, the existence of which, unlike Plato, he rigorously demonstrates (Aristotle, *Metaphysics* 1072a).

The result is a much more complex and nuanced Ethics than Plato's. Aristotle begins with a scientific analysis of human nature, noting that we possess distinctive capacities which transcend those of the other animals. We have an intellect and a will. The Good draws us into motion, growth and development just as it does everything else in the universe, but it does so in a different way, by acting on the intellect and thus informing the will. The good for human beings consists in virtue—in habitual excellence in the exercise of our distinctively human capacities. This means, on the one hand, the cultivation of the intellect, through *techne* or excellence in making, *phronesis* or excellence understanding the means to the ends of human life, *nous* or excellence in understanding first principles, *episteme* or excellence in explaining things, and *sophia* or excellence in rising to first principles, and, on the other hand in the moral virtues of temperance, courage, and justice. The intellectual virtues we develop through study, the moral virtues through habituation, something which requires, in turn, a just social order. While his preference, like Plato's, is for a monarchy in which the king is authentically wise and just, or an authentic aristocracy, Aristotle already begins to recognize the merits of a mixed constitution which includes democratic elements (Aristotle *Ethics, Politics*).

This said, distinct limitations remain. On the one hand, the dialectical tradition offers a sharp challenge to the hegemonization of Athenian democracy by moneymakers. Resolution of the contradictions of the petty commodity system, unlike those of capitalism, does not require that the system itself be radically transcended. It is merely necessary that economic differentiation be contained, that a mechanism be developed for centralizing and allocating the resources necessary for human development, and that debt servitude, chattel slavery, and other degrading ways of organizing labor be abolished. It is just precisely this sort of regulation which Plato (more radically, but with less practical intent) and Aristotle (more modestly and with more practical intent) proposed to introduce. But the price of this economic regulation is a retreat from the democratic project of the Axial

Age. Neither Plato nor Aristotle can actually imagine a society in which *everyone* is sufficiently developed intellectually and morally to participate authentically, as free human beings, in a public arena which does not become hegemonized by moneymakers. Plato, in the *Republic* at least, is clear that there is no room whatsoever for slavery in a just social order. Slavery is seen to emerge only as a result of the disintegration of the ideal state (Plato. *Republic*. 546). Aristotle's discussion of slavery, on the other hand, while it implies a critical perspective on the institution as it actually existed in Athens, seems to suggest that, because of the limitations to their intellectual and moral development, slavery is, in fact, the ordinary condition of the vast majority of human beings.

> For he who can be, and therefore is, another's and he who participates in rational principle enough to apprehend, but not to have, such a principle, is a slave by nature. (Aristotle. *Politics*, 1254b).

Two points are in order here. First, we should note that Aristotle acknowledges the difficulty in ascertaining who is fit for freedom and who is fit for slavery, even if he does not draw the obvious conclusion: that slavery will inevitably result in injustice to those who are mistakenly enslaved. Second, however, given the broader framework of Aristotle's analysis of human nature and the conditions for the cultivation of virtue, it is by no means clear that anyone except the philosopher really has full use of his or her rational faculties and is, in this sense, a slave. It is not, of course, clear that this is the result of "natural" limitations as opposed to social conditions—i.e. a level of development of the productive forces which requires that the majority of people be employed from an early age in producing the basic means of subsistence—or that "slavery" in this sense is a justification for treating the individuals in question as chattels. But the implications are nonetheless quite stark for anyone who sees merit in the Hellenic ideal and indeed has enduring relevance as we come to terms with more recent developments such as the collapse of the socialist project—in part, perhaps, because we never found a way to create the "spiritual conditions for communism," which certainly include the requirement that everyone have full use of their rational faculties, use them to make rationally autonomous judgments regarding questions of meaning and value and act accordingly.

Similarly, Aristotle remains unclear regarding the possibility of a purely spiritual realization of humanity's quest for Being. Of particular relevance here is his discussion of the Agent Intellect (Aristotle. *De Anima* 3), the part of the intellect which illuminates the images which extract from our senses in order to reveal their intelligible content. Since the Agent Intellect is a rational principle and since individuation for Aristotle is by matter alone, it would seem that there can be only one Agent Intellect. In later Platonizing syncretisms, this was conceived as the intellect of the sublunar sphere. The implication would seem to be first of all that the limit on human development is identity with the Agent Intellect and that this was not in any sense an authentic individual immortality, but rather simply a statement that what endures in us is the part which is eternal and which is not individual or specific to us in any way.

Further developments in the dialectical tradition prior to its syncretism with the *way of justice and liberation* if anything exacerbated these limitations. By the fourth century BCE the Hellenic economic strategy of insertion into the emerging global market as exporters of wine and oil was being replicated throughout the entire Mediterranean Biome, resulting in an erosion of the comparative advantage originally enjoyed by the Greek homeland and a rapid decline in incomes. The only way to sustain the level of civilization which had emerged in Greece was by taxing trade over a much wider area. This meant *Empire*, first Macedonian and then Roman. And much as the *Imperium Romanum* presented and even understood itself as extending and defending the ideal of life as a free human being and citizen, the whole structure depended, at least in the West, on mass chattel slavery. And *Empire means* the development of a military apparatus which renders the democratic institutions it is intended to protect ultimately impotent and irrelevant. As a result the political dimension of the dialectical tradition, always problematic because of its uncomfortable relationship with Hellenic democracy, became largely irrelevant. Dialectics gradually retreated from its critique of sophism (the direction of the New Academy) or merged with the mystery cults, seeking ritual methods of *theurgy* to complement a discipline of dialectical ascent which always knew itself to be insufficient.

This brings us to the limitations—and contemporary situation—of dialectics as a *way*. In its original Hellenic form, dialectics remains a partial and ultimately tragic way which shows us a *telos* that we can never reach. It allows us to rise rationally to a first principle in terms of which the universe can be explained and human action ordered. It gives us a glimpse of the God we actually want to be, and demonstrates once and for all that this God is not a cosmic tyrant. But it also shows us no way to *become* this God. Similarly, it shows us what justice would actually look like while implying that it is quite impossible.

On its own dialectics at this stage of its development is the *way* of the philosopher-statesman. It values liberal education and treats both politics and philosophy as spiritual disciplines. It dedicates itself to the common good of a *laos* which it knows can never escape servitude. And while it offers the thinnest hope of a kind of impersonal immortality in identification with the Agent Intellect, it also seems to leave open the possibility that we are, in fact, trapped in the contingency hell that the Buddha would eventually name *samsara*, a hell from which there is no exit, or that our quest for Being notwithstanding, when we die we face sheer annihilation.

It is, therefore, not surprising that the place where dialectics survives on its own, in something like its original form, apart from syncretism with the *way of justice and liberation*—the secularized Academy—can be a rather sad place which makes the First Circle of Dante's *Inferno* seem pleasant by comparison. Its inhabitants follow a *way* which terminates in eternal frustration. Nor should it be surprising that the Academy has difficulty exercising its sapiential leadership function. We are, in effect, inviting our students along a *way* which, if we are honest, we do not believe very many of them can follow, much less complete, and on which our own claims to have advanced very far are tenuous indeed. We are saying that we are wiser and more just than they are and that they are poor slaves who are actually incapable of liberation. And we do not even have the prospect of full Enlightenment or Beatitude to offer them.

The alternative, of course, is to practice dialectics in syncretism with the *way of justice and liberation* which, as we will see, makes possible both a more democratic and more complete fulfillment of humanity's theotic project, or else to imagine a way in which it might become possible for everyone to become a philosopher, which is, we will argue, what the way of *communism* demands.

But before we can explore these alternatives, we still need to consider some of the the alternative forms of the *way of the search for being* which developed in India.

Indic Ways

The Indus Valley and Vedic Backgrounds

In India as in Greece the most enduring foundational text for the entire civilization, and perhaps *the* foundational text for what became its "Hindu" variant, is one that preserves the *memory* of a great war and a civilizational crisis. The *Mahabharata*, as we have already noted, recounts an attempt, fully lawful in the context of the Vedic tradition, on the part of the Pandava family to achieve deification by means of the *rajasuya*. The attempt sparks a great world war and, on the battlefield of *Kurukshetra*, the Pandavas recognize the fundamental futility of this *way*. The story of Gautama Siddhartha, which marks the foundation of the other variant of the Indian *way*, is similar in this regard. Born to a powerful *ksatryia* family, the sages tell his father he is destined to be either a great king or a great saint. Fearing the latter outcome, his father keeps him sheltered as long as he can from all of the sufferings which life (even for a *ksatriya*) entails. The implication here, rarely noticed, is that the Buddha's first great insight, that life is suffering, is not so profound or original after all. It was a simple truth which his father sought in vain to conceal from him. Eventually, however, he leaves his palace and discovers the truth, and sets out to liberate himself and all contingent beings from the suffering which, it seems, is their inescapable lot.

What is the sociohistorical reality behind these texts and what does that history tell us about the nature of the two principal Indian variants of humanity's *theotic* project? We have traced out the development of Indian civilization and the ways in which that development shaped the thought forms of the Indian *ways* in another context (Mansueto 2010b). Here we limit ourselves to what is essential in order to understand the form which the *theotic* project took in the Indian context. First, it is important to note that the principal Bronze Age civilization in this region was rather different from those in Egypt, Mesopotamia, or China (or for that matter in peripheral regions such as Greece). The so-called Indus Valley or Sarasvati Civilization does not fit into the general pattern of Bronze Age river basin civilizations, in that it appears to have developed neither the monumental religious architecture of the sort we ordinary associate with archaic structures nor the sort of palaces and fortifications we generally associate with tributary structures. The impression is of a civilization which was more mercantile than warlike. Such evidence of religious imagery as we can find seems focused water, especially the rivers which were the lifeblood of the region, and the goddesses associated with them.

This civilization seems, in any case, to have declined during the middle of the second millennium BCE. Scholars long assumed that this was the result of attacks by the invading Indo-Aryans, but current thinking suggests a combination of factors: changing climate, disease, and internal contradictions, with pressure from the Aryans constituting, at most, a secondary factor. The Indo-Aryans appear to have entered the region gradually, searching for pastures and farmland. Most of their interactions with indigenous peoples, at least as described in their own sources, appear to have been with forest dwellers and villagers, not with a major urban civilization.

Second, the Indo-Aryan successor civilization *did* develop a highly sophisticated doctrine of deification by means of conquest and sacrifice. The Aryans brought what was, essentially, a pastoral and raiding economy and a tribal structure centered on patriarchal clans. Clans or groups of clans gradually came to control particular territories governed by a *raja* or chief, assisted by the *purohita* or chief priest and the *senani* or military commander. These rajas were far from exercising absolute authority. They were, rather, constrained by various assemblies and councils: the *sabha*, a council of elders, the *vidatha*, an assembly, probably of warriors, which distributed the booty taken in raids, and the *samiti*, the assembly of the whole clan. Initially the *vish* or clan chose the *raja*, who was essentially a war leader, whose economic privileges were based on voluntary gifts—*bali*—and a special share of the booty, the *bhaga*.

Gradually, however, the role of agriculture increased and larger settlements were established. This led to a number of changes. The warrior elite seems gradually to have evolved from a stratum privileged but still essentially acting on behalf of the *vish* into a group of exploiters. A popular saying developed that the *raja* eats the *vish* like a deer eats grain. Most likely, at this point, this reflected a tendency for the "gifts" required of the *vish* to become mandatory and onerous. A fourth group of dependent producers, the *sudra* appeared, probably from among indigenous peoples on whom forced labor obligations were increasingly imposed. (Thapar 2002: 117ff).

These political-economic changes were reinforced by a perverse synergism between the *Brahmins* and the *rajas*. Increased levels of exploitation required a more sophisticated strategy of legitimation. The *Brahmins* obliged by developing increasingly elaborate rituals which, over a period of many years and at the cost of vast quantities of wealth, promised the *raja* divinization. Thus, after assuming office, the *raja* would perform the year long *rajasuya*, which involved rituals of purification and rebirth. At the end of this, he was expected to make offerings to the "twelve jewels," various members of his family as well as craft and other specialists. The *raja's* rule could be further extended ritually by the *asvamedha*, or horse sacrifice. A horse would be set free to wander for a year, the territory it covered becoming part of the *raja's* domain. At the end of the year it would be sacrificed as part of a fertility ritual which also involved the *raja's* chief wife.

The effect of this dynamic was to set in motion a kind of synergism between the *raja* and the *brahmana*. The largely functional differences between *raja*, *brahmana*, *ksatrya*, and *vaisya* were given ritual significance. The *raja* stood out from the other warriors because, unlike them, he had been divinized—something which one would think would have given him an edge over the *brahmanas* even on ritual grounds. But the *brahmanas* argued that as the *makers* of divinity it was they, in fact, who represented the highest status group. Thus we see the emergence of what was to become a millennia-long status struggle between priest and warrior which, though certainly not unknown in other cultures, came to play a dominating role in India.

Third, the *archeological* evidence for the end of the Vedic period is not of civilizational collapse but of a gradual process of urbanization, with the development of specialized agriculture and petty commodity production (Thapar 2002). Broadly speaking Axial Age Indian civilization seems to have developed along two distinct lines. In some regions—especially the Kuru region and cities of the Indo-Gangetic plain—the *raja-brahmana* alliance seems to have effectively gained hegemony. In these regions we see the development of what amount to sacral monarchic city-states, some of which controlled significant territories. In other regions—especially in the foothills of the Himalayas—the *ksatrya* effectively resisted the *raja-brahmana* alliance and instead formed *gana-sanghas*, assemblies of "equals" in which the chiefs of warrior clans sat together to frame laws, presiding over not only the members of their own clans, but also dependent *dasa-karmakara* laborers. In both cases, however, there seems to have been a very significant development of specialized agriculture and especially crafts production, including woolen cloth for export, terracotta figurines, etc. Eventually this blossomed into an export trade in ebony, spices, and cotton cloth, and even iron work (Thapar 2002: 141, 160-64, 178).

It was in the context of these city states—just beginning to enter into petty commodity production and still emerging from essential tribal social relations—that the Axial Age breakthroughs took place in India. Broadly speaking, it is possible to identify five broad trends: a skeptical trend which eventually gave birth to the Caravaka School, the Ajivikas, who taught a radical determinism but nonetheless allowed the possibility of release through asceticism, the Jainas, who developed a dualistic metaphysics and also taught release through radical asceticism, the Buddhists, who rejected the idea of the inherent existence of anything whatsoever and sought release through detachment, and the rationalized Brahminism of the *Upanishads*, which taught that the material world was, in some sense, simply an illusion and that everything was ultimately identical with the first principle or Brahman. Of these we will focus on the last two, which are the most important both from the vantage point of their enduring global presence and from the that of their implications for our unfolding argument.

Buddhism

It may strike some readers as odd that we identify Hellenism, which in its philosophical form proposes a rational ascent to knowledge of *Being as Such*, and Buddhism, which rejects more radically than any other tradition on the planet the idea of *Being as Such*, as variants of a common *way*. But this is to treat *ways* of being human as metaphysical doctrines when in fact (as important as metaphysics is) they are much more than that. As a *way*, Buddhism is founded on the insight that life is suffering. While the initial statement of the Four Noble Truths in the *Dharmchakrapravartansutra* 2 attributes this suffering to attachment and craving, ultimately this suffering is the result of a deeper metaphysical reality which is first spelled out in the third section of the text.

> All things are produced with a condition and a cause, Having put aside all extreme views, (it is) as clear as the sky: There is no doer, nor is there one who experiences, He sees no deed done, whether it be bad or good.
>
> The constituent parts arise through conditions, and so there is suffering, It is produced just as thirst is through the cutting off of water. Seeing equanimity towards (conditioned) things through the Path, It is completely destroyed, with the cessation of those things subject to decay...
>
> Thus conditionality has been understood by the Realised One, Because of that the Self-made One declares himself (Awake). I do not say that the constituent parts, the sense-spheres, or the elements are the Buddha, Without an understanding of conditions no-one can become a Buddha. (*Dharmchakrapravartansutra* 3, *Samytta Nikaya* LVI: 11).

The implications here are clear. *Everything*, up to and including the imaginative and discursively rational consciousness that makes human suffering so acute, comes about through the complex interactions which *are* contingent being. There is no necessary Being which is behind this process.

> Inasmuch as it is dependently on each other and in unison and simultaneously that the factors which constitute dependence originate the elements of being, therefore did the Sage call these factors dependent origination (*Visuddhi-magga*).

Buddhism, in other words, addresses precisely the same *problem* as Hellenism: our craving for Necessary Being. But unlike Hellenism, it begins with the recognition that not only is it quite impossible for us to become Necessary Being; there is, in fact, no such thing. But understanding this, not just conceptually, but experientially and transconceptually, we can overcome our craving, thus the suffering inherent in the human condition.

The principal *means* of this way is, furthermore (like all variants of the *way of seeking Being*) the cultivation of wisdom, first discursive and then contemplative. The result of this process is the achievement of *nirvana*.

> There is that dimension where there is neither earth, nor water, nor fire, nor wind; neither dimension of the infinitude of space, nor dimension of the infinitude of consciousness, nor dimension of nothingness, nor dimension of neither perception nor non-perception; neither this world, nor the next world, nor sun, nor moon. And there, I say, there is neither coming, nor going, nor stasis; neither passing away nor arising: without stance, without foundation, without support [mental object]. This, just this, is the end of stress (*dukkha*; suffering), (*Nibbana Sutta* 1).

The question, of course, is just what these original insights meant, both spiritually and politically. It has become fashionable in recent years to stress the anti-metaphysical character of the Buddha's original teachings and to read not only Theravada but much early Mahayana philosophy in this light. David Kalupahana (Kalupahana 1992) is typical of this trend, arguing that Buddhism is based on rejection of metaphysics understood as a rational search for meaning, or rather on a rational recognition that there is no such meaning and thus on a radical anti-substantialism. This approach is a more specific variant of a broader tendency to accept at face value the claim of the *Theravada* (and more specifically the *Theravada* as it was reformed in the nineteenth century in response to colonial pressures) to represent the closest living a approximation to the original teachings of the Buddha, a claim which reflects the Protestant originalist bias of most western scholars and which is rather akin to accepting the claim of the nineteenth century Campbellite Restorationists to have precisely reproduced the Christianity of Jesus and his first disciples.

A more accurate picture of the development of the Buddhist *way* suggests a complex struggle to work out what Enlightenment and nirvana might actually mean, spiritually and politically, in a world dominated by a vibrant Silk Road economy and resurgent *Empire*. The underlying dynamic of Buddhism, we will argue, is towards the development of a spirituality which aims at full Enlightenment, like that taught by the higher *Mahayana* (*Tian Tai* and *Hua Yen*) and *Vajrayana* schools (though also, probably, by the Tantric Theravada which was probably the dominant tradition in most of Southeast Asia before the European Conquests), and towards a polity dominated by monastic institutions which gradually evolve away from such traditional monastic practices as celibacy and begin to take on dynastic characteristics. But this development has profound internal contradictions, because of its tendency to transform monastic institutions into large feudal landlords. It also brought Buddhism sharply into contradiction with the Chinese Empire and with peripheral state-building projects in Southeast Asia. Both the Cha'an-Pure Land synthesis which defines most contemporary Chinese Buddhism and the Theravada should be understood as attempts, only partially successful, to address these contradictions within a still fully Buddhist context.

The Ashokan System

Critical to the emergence and consolidation of Buddhism as a major spiritual and civilizational was the patronage it received from one of the first great Iron Age Empires, that of the Mauryans. As everywhere, the construction of empire was a brutal and bloody affair. Consider this account of Ashoka's campaign against Kalinga:

> When he had been consecrated eight years the Beloved of the Gods, the King Pyadassi conquered Kalinga. A hundred fifty thousand people were deported, a hundred thousand killed, and many times that number perished (Major Rock Edict XIII, tr. R. Thapar, in Thapar 2002: 181).

Here, however, the similarity ended.

> On conquering Kalinga the Beloved of the Gods felt remorse, for when an independent country is conquered the slaughter, death and deportation of the people is extremely grievous to the Beloved of the Gods and weighs heavily on his mind . . . This participation of all men in suffering weighs heavily on the mind of the Beloved of the Gods. *Major Rock Edict* XIII, tr. R. Thapar, in Thapar 2002: 181).

Because of this, Ashoka, "the Beloved of the Gods very earnestly practiced *Dhamma*, desired *Dhamma* and taught *Dhamma* (Major Rock Edict XIII, tr. R. Thapar, in Thapar 2002: 181)." Whether as a result of a sincere personal conversion or part of an unusually mature and sophisticated legitimation strategy—or both—Ashoka undertook the first effort to organize and administer a Silk Road empire in accord with the principles of one the major axial *ways*.

In many ways, the Ashokan system looks very much like an enlarged tributary state. By this time, the Indo-Gangetic plain had become a major agricultural center, though villages continued to engage in stockbreeding. While the state attempted to assert control over the land, private property rights were gradually established. Two crops annually were common. State and private lands were cultivated by tenants of various kinds, as well as *dasa-karmakara* laborers, who appear to have been wage laborers and slaves of various types. Taxes were assessed on the area of land cultivated (*bali*) and on the produce (*bhaga*), with the surplus extracted someplace between one sixth and one fourth of the total agrarian product. Nonagrarian activities were subject to a tax known as the *kara*, while craftsmen in particular were obliged to perform free labor for the state (*vishti*). Water was also taxed. Craftsmen were organized into associations known as *shreni* and *puga*, which gradually became large and complex, which at once organized large scale production, protected their rights—and facilitated the collection of taxes. Trade was strictly regulated, with superintendents of commerce inquiring into supply, demand, and costs of production, before approving pricing. A toll of 20% and a trade tax of 4% were levied on all transactions. Interest rates were fixed at 15% (Thapar 2002: 184–90).

Within the context of this basically tributary structure, however, Ashoka pursued policies which gave him a well-deserved reputation for justice. First, much of the revenue he collected was directed towards uses which served the common good. Thus, the imperial capital at Pataliputra is the only city at which we find monumental palace architecture (Thapar 2002: 189). Instead, the surplus he centralized was used for a large system of public works—including large scale irrigation systems, public granaries which provided for the poor in times of famine, and endowments for Buddhist and Jaina monasteries. The property of the rich (the local dynasties and coteries of nobles he had conquered) was seized, but to the poor Ashoka would lend without interest, and after three years forgive all debts (Sarkisyanz 1965: 28-30, 54-56).

What did Ashoka gain by this generosity? First, the Buddhist doctrine of dependent origination taught Ashoka that ultimately his power rested on the consent and even the support of the people. A king who improved the lot of his people would enjoy their firm support and his kingdom would be secure. In short, Ashoka used a program of public works and public piety to build an alliance with the masses against the local aristocracies who presented the greatest threat to his empire. Second, Buddhism solved one of the principal difficulties facing a prospective emperor in India: the system of *varnas* which made Brahmin superior to warrior or ruler, and which make all rulers members of a relatively egalitarian caste community in which, up until 500 B.C. a kind of rough internal democracy had prevailed. This system had made kings dependent on the *brahmanas* who performed the sacrifices which made them divine. Buddhism and Jainism made spiritual authority dependent on the individual characteristics of the person claiming it, not on their birth or ritual knowledge. A just king could thus claim to be superior to a priest. This did, to be sure, present a new problem. What about the *bikkhus* and other ascetics Ashoka patronized? Where they not superior to him in terms of their personal sanctity, especially from the standpoint of world-renouncing traditions such as Buddhism or Jainism? This question was probably not resolved within Askoka's lifetime, but he became the central figure in later Buddhist solutions to this problem. Ashoka was regarded as *chakavatti*, a monarch whose rule is *constituted* by the turning of the wheel of the *dharma*, and ultimately as a Bodhisattva, a being who has achieved or who is close to enlightenment, but who continues to be reborn in order to help ripen other beings. This made him, of course, superior to the ordinary *bikkhus*, who had only just started out on the road to enlightenment, and who, in the Theravada tradition at least, were only aiming at personal liberation rather than at the liberation of all sentient beings.

The Mauryan empire eventually fell, but Ashokan state Buddhism became the model for smaller kingdoms in Sri Lanka, Burma, Thailand, and Kampuchea. An entire tradition of lay Buddhism grew up, centered in the *Ashoka-sutras*, which spoke of just kings who had fed the poor, pardoned criminals, and invested the surplus they centralized in public works and the support of the Buddhist *Sangha* (Sarkisyanz 1965: 33). This lay Buddhism, like the monastic tradition of the Buddha himself, pursued liberation from the illusion of selfhood. Its principal means however, was not mediation assisted by monastic withdrawal from worldly attachments, but rather works of *Metta* or charity, through which one gained *karuna*, or a sense of identification with others. Ashokan Buddhism provided fertile soil not only for the emergence of reforming monarchies, but also, when these monarchies ceased to serve the common good, for the emergence of peasant revolts directed at restoring *dharmaraj* or the rule of cosmic law and setting humanity once again on the path to liberation.

The Mahayana

Whatever Asoka's personal degree of spiritual development, his historical impact was to effectively *best* Gautama Siddhartha, showing that someone who chose the road which the historical Buddha had rejected (that of the conquering king) was, in fact, able to both "turn the wheel of dharma" and advance the cause of enlightenment. Ashoka established that there was a higher calling than pursuing release from suffering, and that the truly enlightened lived lives of profound compassion and enlightening world-building. This in turn stretched emerging Buddhism and forced it draw out the internal logic of both its metaphysical and soteriological claims.

Whether we accept the traditional Mahayana claim that their sutras represent later, esoteric, and more advanced teachings of the Siddhartha Gautama himself (which is doubtful) or not, there is a strong case to be made that they more successfully draw out the metaphysical implications of the central Buddhist idea of dependent origination than do the texts of the Pali Canon. This is apparent from the very earliest Mahayana literature, the *Prajnaparamita* (Transcendent Wisdom) sutras, a group of sutras which first began to emerge in the period between 100 BCE-100 CE, and which were then elaborated between the years 100-300 CE, reaching completion sometime between 300-500 CE, though the texts later began to absorb some Tantric influence in the period between 600-1200 CE (Conze 1960: 9ff, 1968: 11ff). As Paul Williams points out:

> The principal ontological message of the *Prajnaparamita* is an extension of the Buddhist teaching of so-Self to equal no essence, and therefore no inherent existence, as applied to all things without exception. This is not some form of Monistic Absolutism, negating in order to uncover a True Ultimate Reality. The ultimate truth is that there is no such thing (Williams 1989: 46).

Similarly, Beyer argues that

> the metaphysics of the Prajnaparamita is in fact the metaphysics of the vision and the dream: a universe of glittering and quicksilver change is precisely one that can only be described as empty. The vision and the dream become the tools to dismantle the hard categories we impose on reality, to reveal the eternal flowing possibility in which the Bodhisattva lives (Beyer 1977: 340)

Practically, this is associated with an emerging emphasis on the Bodhisattva ideal, which, contrary to what world religions textbooks often teach, is a not simply a commitment to persist in rebirth until all beings have been liberated, but rather a commitment to cultivate one's capacity to enlighten others until it includes the capacity to build entire worlds devoted to enlightenment. Closely associated with this is the idea of skillful means—the notion that the Buddha and his followers must use a variety of different teachings in order to meet the needs of beings at different levels of development (Williams 1989: 46, 50–52).

There were, broadly speaking, two different ways in which this basic insight could be elaborated. Nagarjuna (who lived in the second century CE) and the Madhyamika tradition which followed him focused in the concept of *sunyata* or emptiness, which replaces for them the concept of *svabhava* (self existence or essence) as the basic metaphysical category. For the Abhidharma, *svabhava* was the defining characteristic of a *dharma* (in the sense of a basic constituent of reality) in general, as hardness is of the earth dharma. Only dharmas have essences. Conventional things do not. For the *Prajnaparamita*, all entities, including dharmas, are conceptual constructs. There are, therefore, no essences at all. In Madhyamika, *svabhava* means inherent existence. And as Nagarjuna argues,

> The origination of inherent existence from causes and conditions is illogical, since inherent existence originated from causes and conditions would thereby become contingent. How could there be contingent inherent existence, for inherent existence is not contingent. Nor is it dependent on another being (*Madhyamikakarika* 15, 1977 vv. 1–2 in Williams 1989: 60)

What Nagarjuna is doing here is, in effect, to reject the key assumption which governed the Western metaphysics of *Esse*—namely the idea that there can be no infinite regress. For Nagarjuna, the concept of dependent origination is, in effect, a claim that there is no first cause, no cause which is its own cause and thus grounds contingent existence. Everything is contingent.

Practically speaking, the *Madhyamika* pointed to the importance of a rather austere sort of meditative practice—one designed to clarify and simplify, and in this sense it remained in continuity with the earliest sutras, the analytic emphasis of which it simply carried to its logical conclusion.

The *Yogacara* or *Cittamara* (Mind Only) School traces its origins to the monk Asanga and his half-brother Vasubhandu, who lived between roughly 310 and 390 CE. Central to their teaching was the doctrine of the three aspects (*trisvabhava*) of things: the conceptualized or constructed aspect (*parikalpitasvabhava*) in which we perceive the objects of ordinary everyday life, the dependent aspect (*parantrasvabhava*) in which we recognize that these objects don't really exist in any absolute sense, and the perfected aspect, (*parinispannasvabhava*) (Williams 1989: 82–86).

> According to the *Samdhinirmocana Sutra* it is the "Suchness" or "Thusness" (*tathata*), the true nature of things, which is discovered in meditation (6:6). It is said to be the complete absence, in the dependent aspect, of objects—that is, the objects of the conceptualized aspect (*Mahayanasamgraha* 2:4). This is not as difficult as it seems. What it amounts to is that through meditation we come to know that our flow of perceptions, of experiences, really lacks the fixed enduring subjects and objects which we have constructed out of it. There is only the flow of experiences. The perfect aspect is, therefore, the fact of non-duality, there is neither subject nor object but only a single flow. It is also emptiness, explained for this tradition as meaning that one

thing is empty of another. That is, the flow of perceptions—the dependent aspect—is empty of enduring entities—the conceptualized aspect. What remains, the substratum which is empty of those enduring entities, is the flow of perceptions themselves. (Williams 1989: 84–85).

This is not, therefore, a subjective idealism of the Berkeleyan variety in which mind is real and "things" are merely ideas in our minds and that of God, but rather a rejection of the duality of subject and object itself.

This has definite practical implications, as Collins points out. "Whereas Madhyamika emphasized salvation through a simplifying skeptical wisdom, Yogacara made salvation dependent on a very complex training process of mastering many refinements of meditation simultaneously with their philosophical basis (Collins 1998: 223). "The result was the elaboration of complex hierarchies: numerous degrees of ultimate nothingness, ranks of bodhisattvas and monks, etc. Where the Madhyamika represented a turning of Buddhism to its lay base, Yogacara reflected the reassertion of the monastic impulse within the Mahayana context.

From here it was inevitable that the Mahayana would develop back in a quasi-theistic direction. The first step in this process was the emergence of the idea of the *tathagatagarbha* or Buddha-nature, which resides within all beings. All the living beings "are possessed of the Matrix of the Tathagata [*tathagatagarbha*], endowed with virtues, always pure, and hence not different from me . . . (*Tathagatabargha Sutra*, trans. in Takasaki 1958: 51, Williams 1989: 97)." One sutra, the *Mahaparanirvana Sutra* even goes so far as to call this latent capacity for Buddhahood "*atman*" Williams 1989: 98-99. Fully realized, as the *dharma-kaya*, reality is " . . . beginningless, increate, unborn, undying, free from death; permanent, steadfast, calm, eternal; intrinsically pure, free from all defilement store' and accompanied by Buddha natures more numerous than the sands of the Ganges . . . (Williams 1989: 101)."

What does such a fully realized Buddha look like? What does one do? This is the question is answered by the *Avatamska* sutra, which attempts to show how the world looks from the standpoint of a Buddha or advanced Bodhisattva. This sutra mixes Madhyamika and Yogacara themes, acknowledging that all things lack inherent existence but at the same time arguing for a pure non-dual consciousness as the source of all things. Paul Williams (1989: 121-123) argues that the purpose of this move is to endow the Buddhas and advanced Bodhisattvas with enormous creative power. If nothing exists besides mental constructs, then the images created by the Buddhas and advanced Bodhisattvas in their meditations will be as real as anything else. And their motive in creating these images will be nothing other than their compassion for all beings, who they seek to liberate.

The result is, in effect, to reinstate an analogical metaphysics of creativity in which the ultimate ground of the universe is Mahavairocana, the Great Illumination Buddha, who looks rather more like the God of Western monotheism than most traditional Indian deities.

> The realm of the Buddhas is inconceivable; no sentient being can fathom it . . . The Buddha constantly emits great beams of light; the Buddha body is pure and always tranquil. The radiance of its light extends throughout the world . . . In all atoms of all lands, Buddha enters, each and every one, producing miracle displays for sentient beings: such is the Way of Vairocana (*Avatamska Sutra* I.1 and I.4, in Williams 1989: 122 and in Cleary trans. 1984/6).

This universe which the sutra calls the *dharmadhatu* or realm of *dharma is* Vairocana Buddha, or in another image, the jewel net of Indra, a system of interdependent causality represented as a unified whole (Cook 1977).

This spirituality had definite political implications. First, while it is not strictly *theosis*, the higher Mahayana and Vajrayana schools both promise and provide a method for achieving an Enlightenment which approaches full *theosis* more closely than any other spiritual *way* on the planet. This makes its pursuit compelling in a way other spiritual paths are not. This helps explain why, at one point, fully 40% of the male population of Mongolia had embraced monasticism. At the same time, this *way*, even with the shortcuts promised by the *Tantras*, requires an enormous investment of time and discipline in activities which do not contribute directly to material production. This, in turn, requires the centralization of quite a large surplus. To the extent that this surplus *is* invested in material production, on the other hand, since there will be less draining of resources for luxury consumption, monastic estates can become powerful engines of economic development. Finally, the *mana* of anyone who is even on this path, much less that of an advanced practitioner who can successfully mount a claim to be a reincarnated *tulku* or advanced *bodhisattva*, far exceeds that of any warlord or sacral monarch.

The result was the development of a system of large monastic quasistates throughout China and the Himalayan Plateau. In Sui and Tang China, for example, both the Emperor (and Empress) and the landed elites made substantial donations of land to the monasteries, so that by the time Buddhism was finally repressed in 842-845 the monasteries may well have controlled up to 25% of the land in China (Gernet 1985: 263, Collins 1998:

277-279). In some parts of the country, the local population was even enslaved and bound to provide grain for the monasteries, which were used, as in Europe, to clear frontier lands and place them under cultivation. Monasteries were exempt from taxation. However they obtained it, many monasteries had far more grain than they needed and began to loan it at interest, establishing what they called "Inexhaustible Treasuries"—i.e. banks. They also invested heavily in crafts production and trade, becoming among the most important economic players in the Silk Road system. Ching-tu monastery in Tun-huang got half of its income from loans, another third from temple lands and rents on oil presses, investment in water mills, caravans, etc. The monasteries thus played a central role in promoting the development of petty commodity relations in the countryside and tended to draw the marketized peasants under their sway through the medium of pure land cults which promised rebirth in a "pure land" where enlightenment would be easier to achieve, simply through faith in Amitabha Buddha.

The *Vajrayana* and the Tantric *Theravada*

We have already noted that the development of the Indic variants of the *way of the search for Being* was driven by intercultural encounters between the Indo-Aryan traditions which entered India after 1500 BC and both indigenous Dravidian traditions and Chinese (and more broadly Sino-Tibetan traditions) entering from the North, by way of the Himalayan Plateau and from the south, by way of Maritime trade routes from China. The indigenous Dravidian traditions especially, but also the Taoist strain in the Chinese tradition (which seems to have been the strain which exercised influence in India) conserved a very strong sense of the universe as a participation in sacred which challenged the radical otherworldliness of the earlier Buddhist teachings, and which suggested powerful synergies with the later *Mahyana* tradition. Sino-Tibetan shamanism, in the form of Bon, and Taoism, also brought a rich portfolio of psychophysical disciplines which mobilized the whole body in service to the goal of Enlightenment, which was no longer focused so much on the recognition of the temporary or even the empty character of phenomena, but rather on a nondual realization of the universe itself as a manifestation of divine energy. The result is the emergence of what has come to be called Tantric Buddhism, or the *Vajrayana* or Diamond Way.

> Tantra is that Asian body of beliefs and practices which, working from the principle that the universe we experience is nothing other than the concrete manifestation of the divine energy of the godhead that creates and maintains that universe, seeks to

ritually appropriate and channel that energy, within the human microcosm, in creative and emancipatory ways (White 2000: 9)

There is a vigorous debate between scholars over whether the tantric tradition was primarily a product of royal courts, which drew on tantric rituals to deify, or at least "enlighten" their monarchs, building the mana necessary for state-building, with tantric symbols such as mandalas read by this school as symbolic representations of the quasi-feudal relations between central and peripheral monarchies (Samuel 2006) and those who see in *tantra* a popular movement, or at least one which opened up access to full enlightenment beyond the sphere of the monastic aristocracy (Kinsley 1995).

This debate reflects a fundamental misunderstanding of the the relationship between sacral monarchic and popular traditions. It is clear that many tantric rituals, especially empowerments, are in fact based on royal coronation rituals. Indeed may involve actual coronations. It would be ridiculous to deny the origin of these form in the Sanskritizing, statebuilding enterprises of South India, the Tibetan Plateau, and Southeast Asia when the formal and substantive similarities are so strong. At the same time, there is a well documented history of the appropriation of royal forms for popular and even revolutionary purposes. Witness the powerful revolutionary content of the oracles in Isaiah 9 and 11, which are clear based on royal coronation rituals, or the phenomenon of the mystery cults in the Mediterranean Basin, which opened up access to royal theurgic rituals to the *laos,* a pattern conserved in Christianity with the concept of the Church as a "royal and priestly" people.

What *tantra* does is to draw on both primal and sacral monarchic patterns to both retheorize enlightenment as a recognition that far from being *merely* empty, phenomenal reality is in fact always and already pure and divine, and that overcoming delusion means recognizing this, through the achievement of a nondual consciousness in which we recognize our own divinity as well, becoming full participants, alongside of or instead of the great kings, in the cosmohistorical process of relational transformative generativity.

Tantric practices include complex visualizations, including interactions with *yidams* or meditational deities and the imaginative construction of complex ritual complexes in which these interactions take place, the consumption of forbidden food and drink (meat and alcohol in particular) and both imaginative and, in some variants, actual sexual intercourse, with the aim of inducing in the not-yet enlightened an experience of the bliss that would come when enlightenment was complete. Like traditional shamanic practices, *tantra* also promised, to those who were not yet ready to pursue enlightenment, more immediate, worldly benefits as well.

It should also be noted that these development were not confined to the Himalayan or other East Asian movements (such as Shingon) traditionally associated with *Vajrayana*. There is growing evidence that similar tendency not only developed in Southeast Asia, but may in fact have been normative in Bagan, Angkor, and possible the Sukothai kingdoms (Cousins 1997, Crosby 2000).

Reform Movements

The Buddhism which we know today is largely a result of the collapse of this monastic model of civilizational development. The early part of the Tang period would be the last time Buddhism was hegemonic in China. Gradually the deeper dynamic of Chinese civilization, which was centered on the reforming activity of a centralizing state informed by a largely Confucian scholar-gentry reasserted itself. This Confucian resurgence was, no doubt, ultimately related to deeper contradictions in the Tang system. The growth of rice cultivation and the concentration of wealth in great estates lead to a shift from taxation of persons to a taxation of land, further increasing the burden on the poorest classes (Gernet 1985: 262–66). The economy was further undermined by the closure of the roads of Central Asia as a result of Islamic expansion, especially after the defeat by the Arabs at Talas in 751 Gernet 1985: 261-262). The emergence of a regional command structure undermined the control of the central government over an already decentralized and aristocratic military (Gernet 1985: 262-272).

The result of these setbacks was a radical rejection of all things foreign. In 842-845 of 260,000 monks and nuns were forcibly returned to lay life and 150,000 of their former dependents added to the census lists (and thus to the tax rolls). Fully 460 monasteries and 40,000 small places of worship were destroyed or converted to other uses. Nearly all of the vast lands of the monasteries were seized. And Buddhism fared better than other "foreign" religions. Mazdism, Manicheanism, and Nestorianism were completely proscribed (Gernet 1985: 295).

This does not, to be sure, mean that Buddhism disappeared completely from China. Rather, it changed, essentially abandoning sophisticated metaphysical speculation or at least displacing such speculation from the center of the path towards liberation. What was left was, at the elite level, the Ch'an tradition which had emerged out of the Hua-yen and uphold much of its metaphysics, but focused on the pursuit of sudden enlightenment (or rather on uncovering the latent enlightenment which is already present in all beings, through meditation on subtle paradoxes) and, at the popular level, various Pure Land sects which promised salvation largely on the basis of faith and which appealed primarily to the merchant population and to some marketized peasants. The intellectual center of gravity had shifted back to the Confucian camp (Collins 1998: 290).

The pattern in the Himalayan Plateau and Southeast Asia was somewhat different. In the Himalayan Plateau Buddhist monasticism was the cutting edge of Sanskritization in a marginally habitable frontier region. As in China it came with royal patronage, and was resisted by the local aristocracy which favored the indigengous Bon practice. Perhaps because of the strength of local traditions, perhaps because of the centrality of tantric practice, there were periods during which Tibetan monastics were not exclusively celibate and there remain lineages, such as the Nyingma, which acknowledge noncelibate, nonmonastic lamas known as *ngapas*. Celibacy was, however, eventually imposed by local rulers anxious to prevent the formation of hereditary monastic dynasties. And the establishment of the office of the Dalai Lama, understood as a reincarnate *tulku* entrusted with the temporal leadership of large parts of Tibet, required celibacy so that the choice (and education, and thus possible control) of the next Dalai Lama could be vested in the monastic aristocracy rather than becoming the property of a single family lineage (Samuel 1993, von Shaik 2011).

While the *vajrayana* monastic establishments of the Himalayan plateau remained, to be sure, quite large (and expensive, and therefore frequently oppressive), they were, nonetheless, forced to develop more accessible means of enlightenment than the "endless aeons" which might be necessary to progress through the various stages of Bodhisattvahood in the earlier *Tian Tai* or *Hua-yen* systems. Here *tantra* played a critical role. Drawing partly on indigenous Tibeto-Burman shamanic traditions, such as Bon and partly on Taoist influences from China (as well, now doubt, on influences which flowed north from the southern part of the Indian subcontinent, the other "homeland" of *tantra*, *tantra* mobilized the senses and passions to as "skillful means" to expedite the process of enlightenment. The effect was to bring monastic and popular practice much closer together, legitimating a monastic complex the expense of which would likely otherwise have been unsupportable.

Buddhist states in Southeast Asia were, for the most part, primarily royal establishments. There is very strong evidence that the Angkor complex drew on a variety of religious traditions, both Hindu and Buddhist, to build the *mana* of the Khmer ruler, though Mahayana tendencies seem to have been dominant (Snellgrove 2004, Chandler 2007, Higham 2001).

Eventually, however, the burden of the surplus extraction required to at once deify the king, along Vedic lines, and present him as an advanced *bodhisattva* was too much, and Angkor collapsed. The embrace of Theravada seems to have been a response to the collapse of Angkor. Burma, similarly, seems to have practiced what is sometimes known as Ari Buddhism, a synthesis of Tantric Buddhism, Hindu practices, and indigenous *nat* worship, until King Anawrahta unified the Irrawaddy valley in the eleventh century of the Common Era and converted the region to the Theravada (Coedes 1966). The Theravada, with its much more modest monastic establishment, was both less of a burden on a biome which could generate only so much surplus and less of a threat to the emerging monarchic states.

The *Theravada*, in other words represents the furthest development of a reform movement, and simultaneously rectified many of the worst abuses of the monastic system (rather like the mendicant movements in Christendom) but also crippled the *sangha* as an effective challenge to regional *imperia* and (because in a Buddhist culture an incarnate, fully enlightened *tulku* cannot help but be a threat to a mere sacral monarch or world emperor) also forced a significant retreat from the claims of the more advanced Mahayana and Vajrayana claims regarding the meaning of full Enlightenment.

The claim of the *Sthaviras* or *Theravadins*, however, to adhere most closely to the teachings of the Buddha as preserved by his earliest followers, is no more credible that the claim of the *Mahayana* and *Vajrayana* that their texts are authentic, if later and more esoteric, teachings of Gautama Siddhartha.

Theravada thought concentrated on defending what they regarded as core Buddhist dogmas and on harmonizing what remained. Thus Moggaliputa-tissa's *Kathavatthu* (Kalupahana 1992: 132–43) is first and foremost a refutation of the doctrine of a transcendental, eternal Buddha, which was emerging among the Mahayana. Buddhaghosa's *Visuddhimagga* (c. 410–31, see Kalupahana 1992: 206–16) on the other hand, focuses on harmonizing and systematizing the texts and teachings current in arrived in monasteries in Sri Lanka during reign of King Mahnama. In the process, however, he process ends up laying groundwork for what eventually emerges as the distinctive Theravadin metaphysics. "Buddhaghosa's philosophical language eliminated not only metaphysical conceptions, such as permanent and eternal subjects and objects, but also empirical distinctions such as woman (*itthi*) and man (*purisa*), retaining only the aggregates (*khanda*) . . . We have here recognition of an "unconscious" consciousness, referred to as the life continuum (*bhavanga*) to account for the continuity in the otherwise dissected and momentary mental events. Philosophically, this is not that different from the metaphysical conception of the *alya*-consciousness presented in the *Lanka*, except that it is not originally pure (Kalupahana 1992: 21–213).

The resulting *way* focuses the monastic part of the *sangha* on a pursuit of liberation from the cycle of rebirth which includes a full experience of *nirvana* but which rejects the broader claims of the Mahayana and Vajrayana schools regarding full enlightenment. An *araht*, unlike a Buddha or advanced *boddhisatva* is not omniscient and does not manifest *buddha-kshetra* and looks nothing like a god. The *Theravada* is very much an attempt to come to terms with the impossibility of *theosis* rather than a metaphysical work around which approachs *theosis* while remaining technically nontheistic.

The Theravada kingdoms which embraced this *way*, while far from perfect, enjoyed both a relatively modest *sangha*, mendicant in its economy, and a reformed sacral monarchic state which took Ashoka as its inspiration (Sarkisyanz 1965). The more modest claims of the *sangha* meant that it could not become a threat to sacral monarchic states forced to reduce their own levels of investment in divinizing *tantric* rituals.

Hinduisms

While it was dominant in India for some time, the Buddhist *way* ultimately found its principal centers elsewhere and was all but driven from the Indian Subcontinent, displaced by new developments within the Vedic tradition it challenged, developments which eventually led to the emergence of a distinct but internally diverse Hindu *way*. We need now to examine the development of this way and explain why and how it became dominant.

The *Upanishads*

Our starting point in this discussion must be the *Upanishads*, which represent an alternative path of religious problematization, rationalization, and democratization from that advanced by the Buddha and his followers. These texts, which date from the very beginning of the Axial Age—the seventh and eighth centuries—understand themselves as a commentary on or an attempt to get at the inner meaning of the Vedas. They focus above all on the emerging concept of Brahman—the creative first principle which they understand as the ground of the phenomenal world. Some of the texts refer to *Brahman* in personal terms, as a kind of High God (*Upanishads*, Svet. 6.17). Others speak of *Brahman* as an impersonal force. "Verily this whole world is *Brahman*.

Tranquil let one worship It as that from which he came forth, as that in which he will be dissolved, as that in which he breaths (Chand. 3.14.1)."

Coupled with this movement towards a more abstract concept of God was a concern for the relationship between *Brahman* and the self or *atman*. Thus the text which eventually became the *locus classicus* for debate within the Vedanta tradition between nondualistic, modified nondualist, and dualist positions.

> He who is awake in those that sleep,
> The Person who fashions desire after desire—-
> That indeed is the Pure. That is Brahman.
> That indeed is called the Immortal.
> On it all the worlds do rest.
> And no one so ever goes beyond it.
> This, verily, is That (*Katha Upanishad* 8).

The Upanishads were not, for the most part, as overtly hostile to Vedic orthodoxy as Buddhism. They did, however, depart from the teachings of the Vedas both regarding the *aims* and the *means* of religious practice. On the one hand, the inner worldly aims characteristic of Vedic religion give way to a search for *moksa* or liberation. "The wise one is not born, does not die; it does not come from anywhere, does not become anything. It is unborn, enduring, permanent; this one is not destroyed when the body is destroyed . . . . (*Katha Upanishad* 2.1.15–18)." The Upanishads, similarly, make a strong case for the inadequacy of sacrifice as a means achieving religious aims. "The sacrificial rituals, eighteen in number, are, however, unsteady boats, in which only the lesser work is expressed. The fools who delight in this as supreme go again and again to old age and death (*Mundaka Upanishad* 1.2.7)."

Finally, while the Upanishads did not represent as radical assault on Brahmin hegemony as did the other trends, it did tend to open up new possibilities for religious leadership. Thus, for example, by reducing the Vedas to the syllable "*om*," the *Katha Upanishad* reduces substantially the quantity of text which must be memorized and recited in order to achieve wisdom . . .

The Development of the "Hindu" System

Initially, in large part due to the patronage of the Mauryan Empire under King Ashoka, Buddhism fared much better than the spiritual impulses informed by the *Upanishads*. And the period following the collapse of the

Mauryan Empire was accompanied by a complex of diverse and often conflicting dynamics, so that it took a long time before a new coherent pattern emerged. Broadly speaking, however, as we have argued in another context (Mansueto 2010b), it is likely that the Ashokan model, which focused primarily on taxing the existing economy and especially on taxing trade with the Roman Empire, and which tended to favor Buddhist monasteries which were dependent on royal patronage, worked as long as trade with Rome remained vigorous. As this declined an alternative model developed which focused instead on expanding the area under cultivation and, of course, subjecting it to taxation and other forms of surplus extraction. Development was fostered largely by offering large grants of land to both Buddhist and Jaina monasteries and to Brahmins, who then undertook responsibility for development. Land granted to monasteries and to Brahmins was held tax free, in return for teaching and ritual services provided. Grants to collectivities of Brahmins were called *agrahara* grants, those to individual Brahmins *brahmadeya* grants (Thapar 2002: 291–92).

Ultimately, the Brahmin pattern won out for three reasons. First, Brahmins proved themselves better pioneers than Buddhist monks, who were not supposed to be so involved in worldly affairs. Monasteries seemed to flourish best in established agricultural zones with thriving trade centers (Thapar 2002: 487). Second, the opening up of new areas to cultivation, even when set in motion by royal sponsorship, ultimately led to decentralization, which ultimately left state structures in the Indian peninsula weakened. Provincial, district, and village officials came to hold their posts on an hereditary basis and when the central authority weakened often tried to establish individual kingdoms. This, in turn, meant claiming *ksatriya* status, something which required Brahmin sanction and thus opened up new possibilities for patronage for Brahmin intellectuals (Thapar 2002: 290, 487) At the religious level it meant both the emergence of great Buddhist monastery-universities, such as that at Nalanda, which were the recipients of *agrahara* grants, but also the gradual eclipse of these centers as more and more land was granted to individual Brahmins in the context of Gupta and post-Gupta development policies. Finally, the gradual re-assertion of Brahmin hegemony was further facilitated by the development of Puranic Hinduism.

The result of this process was, in effect, an entirely new religion, with new gods, probably derived from those of the indigenous peoples being absorbed as Sanskrit culture extended into the South, with new rituals and an entirely new kind of spirituality. Where Vedic religion had been focused on the act of sacrifice itself, with the gods understood as being bound by rituals properly performed, and eventually disappearing almost completely, Puranic Hinduism was centered on the worship of gods, especially Vishnu (the creator) and Shiva (the destroyer). These gods were understood as conferring a variety of benefits, including *kama* (pleasure) and *artha* (wealth and power), as well as encouraging right conduct and social justice (*dharma*) and providing various modalities of *moksa* or liberation, understood in many different ways. Offerings to the gods continued to be an important part of the ritual, and still required ritual specialists, though Brahmins who undertook these roles were generally regarded as of lower status than those who performed the old Vedic rituals. Animal sacrifice was no longer obligatory.

Buddhism had won support away from the old Vedic tradition in part because its practitioners could be regarded as authentically holy and because Buddhist monks were willing to make some accommodation to popular tradition. The *stupa*, for example, probably derives from traditional megalithic burial sites. Puranic Hinduism, however, had *both* authentic holy men (and women) of its own, *and* a more generous outlook on those for whom the idea of *enlightenment* seemed unattractive or unattainable. Gradually, indeed, the idea developed that one could achieve *moksa* simply by devotion to the god (usually one of the avatars of Vishnu) or by means of tantric practices like those discussed in the context of Buddhism And Puranic Hinduism was able integrate Buddhism into itself (as the cult of one of the avatars of Vishnu) in a way that Buddhism itself could not reciprocate. By 900 CE Buddhism had all but vanished from India, except in the East, where it continued to enjoy royal patronage (Thapar 2002: 488).

The question of just what defines the Hindu *way* is a difficult one indeed. Some authors, such as Dominque Sila Khan (Khan 2004) have argued, with considerable reason, that the category itself is an external imposition, an artifact of British colonialism, and to some extent of anticolonial intellectuals in the nineteenth century anxious to develop a national identity based on a distinctive national ideology. There is a great deal of merit to this view and the idea of a timeless *santana dharma* is clearly a product of this process. At the same time, we will argue, it is possible to distinguish Hinduism from Buddhism (and other *ways*) on a number of fronts, so that the term is not entirely meaningless, however important it is to keep in mind the political context in which it was defined.

One way of making this distinction is on the basis of the traditional organization of Hindu philosophy into the "six acceptable *darshanas.*" But this is not especially useful. This classification was originally developed by Jaina scholars during the eighth century as a way of classifying the Hindu intellectual field from the outside. The scheme was not used within Hinduism until the fourteenth century, by which time it was already long obsolete, since some of the *darshanas*—Yoga—for example had never really been philosophical schools in the first place, while others, such as Vaisheshika were no longer really complete and autonomous systems. By this point, Hindu philosophy *meant* Vedanta, with borrowings from the other traditions. Indeed, while later Hindu philosophers read the *darshanas* back into the Upanishadic period and beyond, there was almost certainly never really a period during which we could find these six *darshanas*, understood as living philosophical schools, competing against each other (Collins 1998: 227, 269). They are, rather, more like modes of speculation, somewhere in between specialized fields (*Nyaya*, for example, focuses on logic and epistemology, *Vaisheshika* and *Samkya* on cosmology, *Vedanta* on metaphysics) and competing perspectives. What makes them "acceptable" is there deference to the authority of the Vedas, though their actual engagement with the Vedas varies considerably.

At a deeper level, the emergence of Hinduism represents a re-assertion of the ideal of the self and of creation against the Buddhist emphasis on the in emptiness of phenomenal reality. This is reflected in different ways in different philosophical and spiritual traditions, from the atomism of the Nyaya-Vaisheshika, through the nontheistic dualism of the Samkya-Yoga, to the focus on the concept of Brahman and its relationship with atman which dominates Vedanta. This reaffirmation of the idea of the self and of the world is, in turn, is reflected in the affirmation of the legitimacy not must of multiple legitimate spiritual paths, but also of multiple legitimate spiritual aims. Hinduism retreats from the Buddhist claim that all life is suffering and suggests instead that as we develop spiritually we gradually find more worldly aims unsatisfying and seek *moksa* or liberation from the cycle of rebirth. But *kama* or pleasure, *artha* or wealth and power, and *dharma* or the struggle for justice are all aims as legitimate as *moksha* itself at various levels of spiritual development. That this coincides, to some extent, with the callings historically associated with the *varna* system is no accident. Becoming more accepting of the world meant being more accepting it its injustices and inequalities.

Hinduism also allowed a wider range of spiritual paths or *margas*. Those who sought liberation could do so by means *raja yoga*, or the contemplative practice and psychophysical discipline cultivated by both Upanishadic Hinduism and Buddhism, by *jnana yoga*, or rational dialectics, *karma yoga*, or right action, and even *bhakti yoga* or devotion to a particular deity. As on the Himalayan Plateau, the Indian subcontinent, especially on its southern, eastern, and northern coasts and frontiers, became the site of a flourishing of tantric ways, the product of engagement with indigenous traditions and, most likely, contact with Taoist disciplines from China. In the Hindu context the most important of these was the *Mahavidya* tradition, which is focused on devotion to tend female deities, generally regarded as forms of Durga. Traditional *bhakti* practices are integrated with the *yantra* (visualizations), *mantra* (repetition of certain sounds), *mudra* and *nyasa* (adopting certain bodily positions) and *kundalini* yoga designed to awake the power of the goddess within us. Tantric Hinduism explicitly crossed gender and varna lines, with women fully empowered to act as *gurus* and the *Mahavidya* themselves represented as dark-skinned women from *dalit* backgrounds. The tantric *Saraswati*, for example, is *Matangi*, who, in one version of her story, is a *Chandala* (dalit) woman who aspires to and achieves *Brahmin* status by study and spiritual discipline (Brooks 1990, 1992; Kinsley 1988, 1997; Samuel 2008).

As with late developments in Buddhism, Hinduism represented at once a reform of an earlier high tradition in directions which reflected both an effective defeat of efforts at monastic hegemony (a defeat far more complete in Hinduism than in Buddhism) and engagement with popular traditions in a way which made significant spiritual development accessible to the *laos*. This reduced the economic burden associated with monastic establishments and opened the way to development of lay spiritualities, but it also represented a loss of tension with the *Saeculum*, both in the sense of a loss of the rigor which was associated with earlier, monastic and "virtuoso" treatments of spiritual progress and in the sense of disempowering both monastics and enlightening world-builders in their struggle with resurgent Empire. We will see that this represents an enduring dilemma for essentially all of the *ways of wisdom*.

Wisdom and Enlightenment

We are now in a position to address the central question which is at issue within the *way of the search for Being*. From the vantage point of metaphysics this is the question of whether there is something which has the power of *Being* in itself, and if so what we can say about it. From the vantage point of spirituality, the question is whether our aim is primarily to know and become, or become as much like, this *Being* as possible, or rather to come to terms with the fact that nothing has inherent existence. Practically, the difference is between a politics of doing justice, creating the conditions for as many as possible to become as much like *Being* as such as they can, or a politics of compassion, creating the social conditions for ferrying sentient beings across the ocean of *samsara* to the far shore of Enlightenment. Hellenism, and especially the *via dialectica*, stands on one side of these questions and Buddhism on the other. The various forms of Hinduism are, on the whole, closer to Hellenism in affirming the creative power which is Brahman and the value of what it would call householder life as part of the prolonged evolutionary path which leads to enlightenment. But it is marked by its engagement with Buddhism and especially in the form of *advaita* Vedanta suggests the possibility of further progress towards identity with Being as such (or rather suggests that we are Being as such all along and simply fail to realize it because of the play of *maya* which creates the illusion of separate existence).

Stated in this way the difference between the Hellenic and Buddhist variants of the *way of the search for Being* would seem to be irreconcilable. And yet, when we analyze both the internal logic of the two *ways* and the trajectory along which they develop we discover something very different. First, as we have already noted, the *via dialectica* practiced by itself is a tragic *way*, in that it presents us with an aim—Being as such—and no way to attain it. This leads, inevitably, either to an abandonment of authentic dialectics for the skepticism of the New Academy (or the new New Academy represented by the modern and postmodern university), or else to a merger with the mystery cults in search of some means beyond dialectics which can bring us closer at least to full deification, a process which culminates in the syncretism with Christianity. It is only with the emergence of humanistic secularism and specifically only in Marx (Marx 1844/1978) and the godbuilders (Rowley 1987) that we see a claim from within the dialectical tradition that full deification is possible. And even then, as Lukacs points out, this deification is only collective. For the individual alienation remains (Lukacs 1921/1971). The wisdom of dialectics, in other words, terminates in the knowledge that we live in a contingency hell: that life is, indeed, suffering.

If, furthermore, we trace out the line along which dialectics develops in syncretism with the *way of justice and liberation*, while there certainly is an affirmation, especially in Christianity, of a positive theology superior to pure dialectics, this in turn gives way to a *via negativa* which in turn leads to a transimagimative, transconceptual contemplative practice not unlike that advocated by Buddhism (Merton 1968). Indeed, there are already traces of these developments in Plato and the later Neo-Platonists. Plato names the first principle not Being but the Good and understands it as beyond Being and the Neo-Platonists focus not on Being but on the One. And as we will see, in the highest development of the Kaballistic, Sufi, Ismaili, and Christian mystical syncretisms between the *way of the search for being* and the *way of justice and liberation*, and especially in Eckhardt, there is an extension of the quest for *theosis* which extends beyond mystical union and which seems to know something like the Buddhist "awakening to emptiness" only to transcend it in a "breakthrough" in which we know ourselves in and as Being (Merton 1968, Kelly 2008).

Buddhism, on the other hand, develops from a very austere understanding of enlightenment as a coming to terms with impermanence towards a vision of the universe as the manifestation of an underlying buddha-nature or *tathagatagarbha* in which countless beings have, over endless eons, already evolved to a full enlightenment in which they manifest countless worlds or *buddha-kshetras* for the purpose of leading other beings to a similar enlightenment. And it embraces life in the world, sacramentally or tantrically understood, as a way of achieving such an enlightenment.

What this suggests is that synthesis between dialectics and Buddhism is by no means impossible, and we have indeed already outlined, at the level of metaphysics, what such a synthesis might look like (Mansueto 2010b). Specifically, it involves a rejection of the idea that Being can ever be understood as *Substance* or impassive self-possession. Being must, rather, be understood as relationship and generativity. Full development of this argument depends, however, both on understanding the engagement between the *way of the search for Being* and the *way of justice and liberation* to which we turn in the next chapter, and with humanistic secularisms, and dialectical and historical materialism in particular, which will advance the idea that Being is *Subject,* an error which, we will argue, must also be overcome before than can be any real synthesis between the doctrines of being and dependent origination.

4

The Way of Justice and Liberation

We are now in a position to analyze the second of the principal axial ways, that of *justice and liberation*. Unlike the *way of the search for Being*, which we characterized as a chastened variant of the sacral monarchic *way of the master*, this *way* has its origins in a peasant revolt in Late Bronze Age Canaan, a revolt which set in motion the formation of a whole complex of spiritual and civilizational projects and which made *justice* one of the principal loci of humanity's encounter with the sacred. We need first to analyze this background event, and then turn to an exploration of the divergent variants of the *way of justice and liberation*, the history of which is, as we have suggested, intimately bound up with the that of the *way of the search for Being*, and specifically its Hellenistic variant.

The prevailing religious form of the Canaanite social formation was the cult of *ba'al*, which had, by the Late Bronze Age, hegemonized the older, gynocentric cult of the *ashtoreth*. This *ba'al* is generally referred to in the textbooks as a "fertility god," as indeed he was. But the root from which the term *ba'al* is derived means "to own" and the word was used in ways which signify "lord," "master," "owner of land," and . . . "husband." It was used for the local warlord, as well as for the deity. Identification of agrarian and human fertility with domination and lordship, and of both with the divine, provided the ruling classes with an especially effective system of legitimation. The Canaanite peasantry, to put the matter starkly, worshiped their landlords.

According to Norman Gottwald, the later Bronze Age witnessed a decline in great power hegemony in the Syro-Palestinian corridor, and correspondingly internal strife among the warlords who dominated the Canaanite lowlands. The resulting instability in turn led to an increase in rural unrest, which took the form of social banditry (Hobsbawm 1959). These social bandits—referred to as "'*apiru*" in contemporary sources—were essentially marginalized peasants who had been run off their land, or who had gotten into trouble with their lords, and had (quite literally) taken to the hills, from whence they preyed off caravans, or raided the city states, occasionally entering the service of one or another *ba'al*.

At roughly the same time the collapse of the Hittite Empire to the north broke the monopoly on iron technology, allowing the techniques for production of primitive bloomery iron to penetrate Canaan. Up until this time metal tools had been a ruling class monopoly, protected by royal control of the tin trade—tin being an essential component of bronze, the only metal thus far widely used in the area. This ruling class monopoly on metal tools had in turn held back the development of the hill country, which required metal tools for clearing and terracing. Bloomery iron, while inferior to the bronze used by the Canaanite aristocracy, was superior to the stone tools used by the Palestinian peasants, and could be produced with materials available in the region. The collapse of the Hittite iron monopoly thus put metal tools into the hands of the peasants, removing the obstacle to settlement in the hill country.

The hills were out of the reach of the chariots of the Canaanite warlords, and thus beyond the sphere of Canaanite military hegemony. The *'apiru* groups thus began to terrace and cultivate the hill sides, and their banditry gradually transformed itself into a kind of *guerilla*, or prolonged popular war—the record of which is preserved in the Book of Judges. They organized themselves into *mishpahoth*, or protective associations of extended families. These *mishpahoth* practiced a form of communal land tenure, holding land collectively and redistributing it periodically to individual families, according to need, for purposes of cultivation (Lev 25:8ff), and also constituted a kind of "popular militia" which helped to defend and extend the "liberated territories" without recourse to a standing army. Israel seems to have provided for a tax of roughly 10% of the agricultural produce to support the Levitical priests. At the same time, Israelite law insured that the priests could own no land of their own and thus could not degenerate into an exploitative landowning class. The people were led by *shophetim*, the term which is translated in the English Bible as "judges." The term seems to have included both charismatic military leaders and figures who, perhaps while also serving like Samuel as priests of local sanctuaries, resolved disputes that were beyond the reach of village elders.

Norman Gottwald has suggested, based in part on the frequency of Egyptian names among the Levites, and their subsequent role as a religious elite, that the Exodus story is in fact the story of the Levites, and perhaps other elements serving in Egypt as forced laborers, who became the carriers of the cult of *yhwh*, and whose flight from Egypt and penetration of Palestine played a critical role in catalyzing the formation of Yahwistic Israel out of the numerous *'apiru* bands. The Exodus is, according to this hypothesis, the story of the vanguard of the Yahwistic revolution.

The emergence of the cult of *yhwh* was at once a product of and a catalyst for this process. The name itself probably derives from an epithet attached to the name of the god El, who was *ba'al*'s father and the actual high god of the Canaanites but not, for the most part, the object of an actual cult. Revolutionary Israel appealed above the head of *ba'al*, as it were, to his father, who they worshiped as *'el yahwi sabaoth yisrael*: God who brings into being the armies of Israel. This was a mark of the fact that Israel first met her god on the battlefield of the revolution, and found in the struggle for social justice the basis of all her religious knowledge.

Gradually, partly as a result of the spontaneous processes of rationalization which accompanied the development of petty commodity production, and partly as a result of her own struggle with the continuous reassertion of "*ba'alist*" sacral monarchic tendencies, Israel recognized that the same power which had liberated them from their oppressors was in fact the creative power behind the universe as a whole. We thus see a movement from the still largely anthropomorphic *'el yahwi sabaoth yisrael*, to the God revealed in Exodus 3:13ff, who tells Moses that His name is *eyeh asher eyeh*. *Eyeh* is the imperfect indicative form of the verb "to be" indicating that this God is *Being as such*, acting still. In the same passage we also find the revelation of the name *yhwh*, which is the causative form of the verb "to be," and points even more clearly to the recognition of God as the power of *Being as such*.

Along with this we see the emergence of a sophisticated spirituality which identifies the struggle for justice with *da'ath 'elohim*. Generally translated "knowledge of God," the prophets continually placed *da'ath 'elohim* in poetic parallelism with phrases denoting justice and ethical conduct: "They shall not hurt or destroy in all my holy mountain. For as waters of the earth fill the sea. So shall the land be filled with knowledge *yhwh* (Isaiah 11:1-12)." We find similar passages in Hosea (Hosea 4: 1-2, 6:3).

This is a spirituality and a politics quite distinct from that which we saw in the *way of the search for Being*. Among other things there *theoria* precedes *praxis* in the encounter with the sacred; here *praxis* is itself already an encounter with the divine and the knowledge which it produces is transimaginative and transconceptual without ever engaging in either a dialectical critique of or abstraction from the image or a properly contemplative transcendence of concepts. Doing justice is, quite simply, knowing God.

The War About the War About Justice

But if the *way of liberation and justice* finds its origin in a war *for* justice, it endures as a *war about that war for justice*. The reasons for this are not difficult to find. Israel and its religion were *constituted* by a revolutionary political practice. But the later history of Israel made this revolutionary practice difficult, even impossible to sustain. The crisis of the great powers passed. Empires were reconstituted on the basis of new, iron age technologies and a new, petty commodity system centered on the emerging global trade network of the Silk Road. Simply in order to survive, Israel had to take on many of the features of the societies around it: a king with a standing army, supported by systematic taxation of the peasantry and engagement with emerging trade networks. The prophets condemned the resulting injustice as a violation of the covenant, of Israel's founding experience of the divine. But in the end it didn't matter. *Empire* struck back—and won. Israel was defeated.

This defeat of Israel is *also* the common heritage of the three great religions of the book. We are defined by it, and it is why we fight *about* divine justice rather than *for* it, why we fight a war about a war, rather than the war itself.

Wars are complex, messy affairs and the *war about the war for justice* is no exception. But it is, broadly speaking, possible to define three broad parties to this war, each of which responded to the defeat of Israel in a different way. The first response is that of Israel itself, at least during the long period between the destruction of Second Temple and the foundation of the State of Israel. It is a response which accepts political defeat as final and asks how one lives justly—and as a catalyst for justice—in a world in which *Empire* is triumphant. The second is that of Christendom, for which the struggle for justice, precisely in its defeat, stretches us beyond the merely human, and makes possible the *theosis* which Hellenism sought but could not find. Third, and finally, *Dar-al-Islam* refuses defeat, even at the cost of also negating Jewish peoplehood, and insists on actually "commanding right and forbidding wrong," actually creating a just society.

It is these three variants of the *way of justice and liberation* which we must now explore.

Judaism

Rabbinic Judaism

Judaism, as we have known it throughout the common era, began the moment the defeat of Israel seemed final and definitive and ended, or at least entered a period of profound crisis, when that defeat turned out not to be final and definitive after all.

For long centuries Israel struggled to liberate itself from imperial rule and to use a restored monarchy to rebuild the just social order which it remembered from the "days of its youth." While the prophets of the Assyrian and Babylonian periods sometimes counseled submission to the great powers in the short run, they nearly all looked forward to a future of liberation and restoration. The relatively benign rule of the Persians and the Ptolemies temporarily eased the revolutionary impulse, but when the Seleucids attempted to erect a statue of Zeus in the holy of holies as part of their project of Hellenization, Israel responded with a successful revolt, that of the Maccabees, which won them a brief period of independence. And while Rome's relative tolerance and sensitivity to Jewish religious sensibilities led many in Israel to counsel accommodation during the early years of the Principate, by 66 CE a broad spectrum of Jewish parties had been won over to the revolutionary project. Ultimately it was only the overwhelming force of the Roman legions which crushed the Jewish uprising of 66-70 CE and the Bar Kochba revolt of the next century and which convinced Israel that liberation and restoration were not on the agenda.

The result of this process was the emergence of the Pharisees, who had been merely one of many political-theological tendencies in Second Temple Judaism, as the branch out of which most later Judaism—what we now call rabbinic Judaism—emerged. The Pharisees, while not rejecting the temple and while certainly sharing a long-term hope in liberation and restoration, had focused the bulk of their attention on adapting the legal traditions of Israel to the new realities of imperial rule, petty commodity production, and insertion into the Silk Road trade. For example, rather, than waiting for a time when the Jubilee Law could once again be strictly observed to act justly, they focused on the central moral norm embodied in Leviticus 25—"When you buy or sell . . . amongst yourselves, you shall not drive a hard bargain . . . You must not victimize one another (Lev 25: 14:17a)"—and asked what it meant for merchants in the new global economy. As events turned against the people of Israel during the Jewish War a group of rabbis gathered a Jabneh (the Roman Jamnia) to begin to codify the oral traditions they had been developing. These they organized under six headings. The resulting collection is known as the *Mishnah*, which was completed by 220 CE at the latest. Further commentary on the *Mishnah* continued both in the land of Israel and in Babylon, where there was an important Jewish community. These further commentaries, which consist fundamentally in debates between rabbis regarding the proper interpretation and application of the Law, eventually became the Palestinian and Babylonian *Talmuds*, which were completed sometime in the sixth century, shortly before the Arab invasions.

In the absence of a Temple and with the prospects for political independence shattered, in other words, the Pharisees, and the Rabbinic Judaism which grew out of their movement, found a new way of living Israel's historic commitment to divine justice. But as Jacob Neusner (Neusner 1975) has pointed out, however, there is more to this way than simply adapting Jewish law, with its historic focus on social justice, to new social circumstances. The Talmud also suggests a new model of leadership. While the Jewish communities in Palestine and Babylon, and indeed in other cities as well, often had an official leadership recognized by the political authorities, and while in some cases, as in Babylon, there was even an Exilarch claiming descent from David, real authority belonged to the rabbis. But it did not belong to the rabbis as an officially sanctioned body, the judgments of which were taken as legitimate. Rather, authority belonged to which ever rabbi was able to make the most logically convincing argument regarding the particular point of law in question. While earlier opinions might, furthermore, serve as a point of reference or departure, there was, in principle, no point which was not subject to criticism and re-evaluation. The people of Israel became, in effect, a *logocracy*, where neither law nor persons but rather legal argument and scholarship alone ruled.

The result of this was to transform the Jewish people, deprived though they might be of land and king and temple, into one of the leading forces—indeed perhaps *the* leading force—in the development of Western society and the reason we call it Western rather than Christian or European. They became practitioners of "a ruthless criticism of everything existing, (Marx 1843a/1978)" a criticism grounded in a primordial experience of divine justice. It was, above all, the deliberative practice of the rabbis which shaped that of the Islamic *ulema* and through them that of the Christian scholastics (Makdisi 1989). And everything authentically critical in the modern Western tradition (as opposed to what is merely messianic) bears this same rabbinic seal.

The destruction of the temple, similarly, and the postponement of any attempt at reconstruction to an indefinitely distant messianic future, also meant that the *sacred*, previously encountered in a privileged if not exclusive manner by the High Priest, in the Holy of Holies, was now encountered equally in all aspects of life to which the Law might be applied. *Everything*, in effect, was regarded as sacred. This was already implicit, to be sure, in Israel's historic focus on the struggle for justice, which endows the world with a religious significance it lacks in other *ways*, but this might have been interpreted as simply the application of externally mandated divine mandates to a radically desacralized world. This is, indeed, how outside commentators like Milbank (Milbank 2014) understand Judaism. But this is not the Jewish *way*. Judaism, rather, means plowing and sowing and reaping, buying and selling, eating and drinking, making love and engaging in legal debate as if it were all a part of the old Temple liturgy. This will be important as we attempt to distinguish later between a *univocity of immanence*, which we will argue is associated with the Radical Aristotelian tradition, both as formed in Judaism and Islam and as appropriated by the Latin Averroists, and in later humanistic secularisms, and a *univocity of transcendence*, associated with Asharite Islam, Augustinian Christianity (especially most Protestantism) and (with the transcendent term absent or postponed until the future) technocratic secularisms.

Jewish Philosophy

The same point holds for Jewish philosophy and mysticism. The encounter between Athens and Jerusalem began early, with Philo of Alexandra. Drawing on a mixture of Jewish, Stoic, and Middle Platonic ideas, Philo argued that the ideas, or the forms of things, exist in the mind of God as a kind of intelligible world. In their latent form Philo called these ideas *sofia* or the divine wisdom. In their active, creative form, they became the *logos*, the word through which all things came into being. Unlike the Hellenic tradition, Philo rejects the eternity of matter, and teaches that matter itself was the product of divine creative activity. As such, it implicitly participates in the life of God in a sense neither Plato nor Aristotle could have adequately theorized.

According to Philo, the Law of Moses is nothing other than the law of the cosmos itself, fully accessible to reason and binding on all humanity. On this basis, Philo develops a harmonizing ethics which integrates Jewish and Greek elements, arguing that authentic freedom consists not in citizenship in Rome or some reconstituted Greek city state, but rather in service to the one true God who alone is authentically self-existent. It is the Jews, who know and follow this law, and not the Greeks and Romans, with their devotion to wealth and earthly political power who are the true cosmopolitans. Knowledge of the law flows out from the Jews to the other peoples of the earth who will eventually be united as in a single city, under the one law of the living God. History itself, driven by the people of God as a catalyst for justice, becomes a participation in the life of God.

Philo's innovations were in many ways foundational for Christianity and we will explore their impact there shortly. But specifically Jewish philosophy remained a powerful current throughout the Silk Road Era. There were both Neo-Platonist and Aristotelian wings. Of particular interest among the first tendency was ibn Gabriol, who argued that the emanations from God are themselves material in character, and that matter is in no sense negative or evil (Collins 1998: 436). It is difficult to see how such a doctrine could be regarded as a univocal metaphysics, since emmanationism, whatever else it does, defines a hierarchy of different degrees of participation in the life of God. But if there is a pull towards univocity here, it is clearly a univocity of immanence.

Jewish Mysticism

A third trend is represented by Kabbalism. While it was the rabbis who became the real leaders of the people of Israel in the period after the destruction of the Temple, the priestly tradition did not entirely die out. It was, rather elaborated into an esoteric wisdom tradition. This tradition reaches back at least to the *Sefer Yetzirah*, which is likely a product of the second century and which suggests a synthesis between a distinctly Jewish concern for justice and a Hellenistic Neo-Platonic theurgy. For emerging Kabbalism, the process of emanation is understood in a distinctly Jewish way as being embodied in language and especially in the divine name—the pronunciation of which, in the Temple cult, was thus a real participation in the creative life of God. The whole fabric of creation has somehow been ruptured, something which is reflected on earth in wrong action and social injustice. The process of return is also understood in a distinctively Jewish fashion as rooted in ethical conduct. By means of the just act we "raise sparks" towards God. Kabalistic ritual affects "things above," in the higher worlds, creating more favorable conditions for the redemption of Israel and the establishment of a just social order here below, but right conduct and the struggle for social justice also helps to mend the torn fabric of the universe in a process known as the *Tikkun Olam*.

Neil Asher Silberman (Silberman 1998) traces out this development of this tradition in some depth. Analyzing the Kabbalism of the prosperous and relatively protected Jewish communities of Provence during the time of the *Cathari* controversy, he writes

> ... the *Sefer Bahir*, the Book of Brilliance, provides a key to understanding the intimate and complex *connection* between an Unknowable God and His creation ... It combines many earlier, distinct systems of symbols to show that varieties of trees, the organs of the human body, the heavenly constellations, colors, sounds, and biblical heroes are all variations of a *single* pattern from which the world and everything in it is made. Like the sublime symmetry of the vortexes and whorls of modern fractal geometry, the creators of the Sefer Bahir saw a single master pattern endlessly reproduced (Silberman 1998: 60).
>
> ... through its unique biblical interpretations, mystical parables, and vivid juxtaposition of images, the Sefer Bahir offers a powerful Jewish alternative to the mystical speculations of the Cathari. Its image of the Tree of Life extending between earth and the heavens showed that the material and spiritual worlds—the realm of the here and the realm of the hereafter— were not opposites or opponents but were both part of the unity of God (Silberman 1998: 64).

This essentially positive outlook on the world is reflected in an embrace of the doctrine of reincarnation, not as something to which sentient beings are chained and must seek liberation, but as a kind of circulation of divine energy through an essentially good world, and as a school in which souls gradually grow towards God.

The *Reconquista* led Jewish mysticism to take a somewhat darker view of the world. Central to this tradition was the idea that something had gone deeply and profound wrong during the creation of the universe—something which had resulted in the emergence of the aggressive civilization of Christian Spain (Silberman 1998: 85–86).

These themes are extended in the *Zohar*. King Alphonso had made devotion to the Blessed Virgin central to the ideology of the emerging Spanish state. The *Zohar* countered this with a claim that the *Shekhinah* or divine presence, conceived of as feminine, had been captured by the forces of darkness, and would have to be rescued (Silberman 1998: 91).

We argued in an earlier work (Mansueto 2010b) that unlike the Jewish Aristotelians around Moses ben Maimon, the Kabbalism tended, at least, towards a univocal metaphysics. Our judgment in this regard was based on the idea, central to Kabbalism, that the universe could not bear the creative overflowing of divine power, and that the vessels into which the divine nature poured were somehow ruptured. This suggests that the divine power is somehow in contradiction with the existence of created things. It is further suggested by the representation of the highest of the *sephiroth*,

Keter, as Divine Will, which is characteristics of some, and especially later Kabalistic texts, such as the *Pardes Rimmonim* (The Grove of Pomegranates) attributed to Moses Cordovero (Silberman 1998: 154-55). It is even more apparent in the work of Isaac Luria, who argued that evil was present in the divine nature itself, which is conceived of as a simple infinity or unlimited (the *Ein Sof*), and that creation took the form of a withdrawal of God from the universe, something which alone made possible the existence of finite creatures, which were gradually purified as evil demonstrated its long-term unworkability (Silberman 1998: 172-74).

We would now qualify this earlier assertion with by saying that the univocity which characterizes kabalistic metaphysics is a *univocity of immanence*, similar to that found among the Averroists and on the Franciscan left. It is not that the world is devoid of the sacred, either because it is radically distinct from the sovereign God who created it *e nihilo* (the Reformed or theistic secular position) or because God has not yet been built (the technocratic secular position) but rather that the universe is itself an overflowing of the divine, so that divinization, in the sense of actual identification with necessary Being, becomes possible.

This led to two very different types or political and spiritual practice. On the one hand, if the divine power is immanent, it is in principle subject to (partial) human control. Thus the idea that the *sephiroth* (though not, of course, the *Ein Sof*) could, in fact, actually be manipulated by ritual means. Rabbi Joseph della Reina, for example, used special incantations to try to capture the demons of which they believed the Castilian monarchy to be the earthly reflection (Silberman 1998: 114). Ultimately this emphasis on taking charge of the portion of the divine power which had been transmitted to humanity, or at least to the people of Israel, lead to Judaism's last major flirtation with messianism, in the movement around Sabbatai Svi, which culminated in his conversion to Islam in 1666. (Silberman 1998: 198-216). We will see this tendency further developed by the great secular Jewish thinkers of modernity, who, of course, substitute rational technical or political for ritual action or messianism. Indeed Yiramayhu Yovel (Yovel 1991) attributes the origins of modernity itself to the transmission of certain tendencies from Judaism by way of the *converso* community.

For the most part, however, the idea of creation by *withdrawal* tended to serve as a counterpoint to the modern Christian obsession with sovereignty and is, perhaps, best seen as a precursor to certain strains of phenomenology and deconstruction, which identify spirituality with respect for the Other who, like God, remains always and only incomprehensible. One thinks especially of Levinas and Buber, but also of late Derrida. But this is a much later part of our story. For now we must turn to an examination of developments in Christian Europe.

Islam

The second possible response to the defeat of the Israelite project was to rebuild it on a social basis which had some prospect for success. In a world dominated by *Empire*, this meant creating an empire which could itself be liberating, and which would actually establish a just society on a planetary scale. It is this response which defines *Dar-al-Islam*. We now turn to analyze the Muslim *way* in some detail.

Islamic origins

Islam prides itself on the idea that, unlike the other great monotheisms, it emerged in the "clear light of history." A middling Meccan merchant of the Quraysh tribe began to have visions. He consulted his wife, for fear he was losing his mind, but she reassured him that the visions were authentic. These visions, which he was commanded to write down, were eventually compiled as the Quran. He then began public preaching, calling on the people of Mecca to reject their polytheistic religion and to return to what he claimed was their original monotheism. The Meccans rejected him, so he fled north to Yathrib, and established himself their as a prophet and *de facto* ruler. Within his lifetime the Arab tribes he converted united much of the Arabian peninsula; within a generation Islam had liberated most of the eastern Mediterranean and Western Asia and within another century it had built one of the largest empires known to humanity.

Unfortunately, like the stories which Jews and Christians tell about their origins, this story is simply untenable. The archeological record contains powerful evidence that the Arab expansion preceded the formation of anything like an established Islam: Arab coins issued in conquered lands, for example, show no evidence of the Islamic inscriptions which later became normative until the eighth century (Cook and Crone 1977). Nor does the text of the Qu'ran become anything like definitive before the ninth century (Wansbrogh 1977, 1978), which it surely would have if the document had already been completed in the Prophet's lifetime and—composition or revelation—functioned as the "little green book" of the Islamic revolution. Unfortunately, the historical-critical study of the Qu'ran and the historical sociological study of the origins of Islam are terribly underdeveloped by comparison with the historical critical and study of the Jewish and Christian scriptures and the historical sociological study of Jewish and Christian origins, and the best that we can offer is a rather schematic and probabilistic account.

We begin with an overview of the conditions in pre-Islamic Arabia. This is a challenging ecosystem, most of which could support human significant habitation—much less urban civilization—only on the basis of trade. The critical commodity in this regard, at least until the development of the coffee trade much later in the region's history, was frankincense, which was collected from trees which grow in the southern tip of the Arabian peninsula, what is now Yemen, and in the Horn of Africa. Beyond this, there were oases through at which merchants could stop on their way East from the Roman Empire, encountering only tribal sheep herders moving from oasis to oasis and subsisting on mutton and dates. By Roman times the Nabatean Arabs had established an important city at Petra, which was, in effect, the first truck stop heading east out of the Roman Empire. The Romans, however, grew tired of paying the tributes and tolls the Nabateans imposed, and re-routed trade through Alexandria and the Red Sea, effectively cutting the Arabs out of the Silk Road trade.

The decline of Roman power presented the Arabs with both an opportunity and a problem. On the one hand, they had a chance to break out of the peninsula and gain sufficient territory to secure a more favorable position in the global trade networks. On the other hand, they could not do this without finding a way to overcome tribal divisions and unite. It is in this context that the emergence of Islam must be understood.

Cook and Crone (Cook and Crone 1977) put a very specific interpretation on just how emerging Islam met the needs of the Arab tribes. Working largely from Greek sources, they argue that the initial preaching of Mohammed, whose historicity they do not question, was essentially a Jewish-influenced messianism aimed at united all of the Semitic peoples to throw off Roman (Byzantine) hegemony and to liberate Jerusalem. Because of the centrality of the idea of a common Abrahamic heritage, they call this early movement Hagarism, after Sarah's handmaid who was the mother of Ishmael, legendary father of the Arabs. Some historical sources suggest that Mohammed lived much longer than Islamic tradition acknowledges and actually participated in the liberation of Jerusalem. That done, however, the Arabs soon fell out with the Jews and began trying to carve out for themselves an independent religious identity, drawing on elements of Jacobite and Nestorian Christianity, Samaritanism, and Persian and Greek philosophical traditions as well as the Rabbinic Judaism which formed their point of departure. "Islam" emerged only gradually as various groups vied for leadership. These included varying types of religious scholars on the one hand (*'ulemma* or jurists, *mutakallim* or theologians, and practitioners of *falasafa* or philosophy) and generals on the other, as well as groups claiming descent from or designation by the Prophet or his kin and/or companions according to varying tribal traditions.

Whether or not we accept the details of this account, the broad outlines make sense. For one thing, had the movement not had a strong apocalyptic tone, it is difficult to imagine that the problem of succession, which drove later Islamic politics, would not have been better resolved, given the otherwise highly effective and pragmatic character of Islamic political strategy. More broadly, as one moves through the plethora of socioreligious movements and political-theological tendencies we meet during the first centuries of Islam, all of the various influences identified by Cook and Crone can indeed be identified, as Crone points out in her later book on Islamic politics, *God's Rule* (Crone 2004).

This said, it seems to me that Cook and Crone miss, or perhaps merely understate, the distinctive feature of Islam by comparison to the other Semitic monotheisms. Where Judaism grew up in an environment of political disenfranchisement, and thus had to find a way to realize the law without political power, and where most variants of Christianity the gave up early on the idea of actually building the Kingdom of God on earth, and redefined messianism in an otherworldly direction, thus laying the groundwork for an alliance with the Roman Empire and its successor states, Islam actually joined, from the very beginning, a religious orientation centered on realizing the law with the political power necessary to actually do so, or at least to attempt to do so. In this sense, the defining feature of Islam is no so much its radical monotheism but rather *al-amr bi'l-ma'ruf wa'nahy 'an al-munkar*: commanding right and forbidding wrong.

This said, Islam develops this orientation in the context of an emerging Silk Road empire which, like all other such empires aims first and foremost at profiting from insertion into the Silk Road trade, and is able secure the support of Arab and later Persian, Berber, and Turkic elites because it provided the ideological basis for the wars of liberation and conquest which were necessary in order to build the empire. And just what constitutes right and wrong, as well as how one discerns them and who has the authority to command and forbid them, remain open to diverse, competing, and ultimately incompatible interpretations throughout the early centuries of Islamic civilization.

Variants of the Muslim Way

It is not possible in this context to discuss all of the various tendencies which emerged in this struggle. Patricia Crone's *God's Rule* (Crone 2004) already does an excellent job of this. Instead, I will outline the principal social forces which shaped *Dar-al-Islam* and its diverse *ways of commanding right and forbidding wrong*. There was, first of all, the dynamic of empire building noted above. As we have argued, the price of effective action on behalf of justice and liberation turns out to be significant concessions to the *Saeculum* which is itself the source of injustice and oppression. It was this dynamic which led to the selection of Abu Bakr, who was known more for his political military skill than his learning or piety, as the first *kalifah* or successor to the Prophet and which, in general favored election of the *kalifah* rather than his designation by descent from a narrow line of relatives. It was also this dynamic which provided the social basis for the eventual formation of the *ahl al sunna wa'l-jama'a*, the Sunni "party of tradition and community," which rejected the persistent messianic tendencies in early Islam and compromised commitment to ideological purity and social justice in the name of the unity and peace necessary for civilizational progress. At times this dynamic could breed ruthlessness and oppression, and did so early on. Almost no one, even later Sunnis, regarded the Umayyads, who can nonetheless be credited as the real founders of *Dar-al-Islam*, as model Islamic rulers. And by the time of al-Ghazali (d. 1111), it was widely accepted that those who wielded political power (*dhu shawka*) were little more than rough soldiers with a fondness for luxury and a tendency towards cruelty. Often this oppression was rationalized as divine punishment. Thus the *hadith* which attributes to the Prophet the saying that when God is angry with a people, he sends to Turks to rule over them, and al-Ghazali's claim that however badly behaved the Turks may be, they are doing the will of God (al-Ghazali. *Fada'ih* 113 in Crone 2004: 237).

This dynamic of pragmatic empire building was, however, balanced by a recognition that unity and thus peace could be achieved only on the basis of a common religious identity and a higher degree of social justice than was common in the surrounding empires. It was this that served as the basis for divisions: how and by whom were religious unity and social justice to be defined. One very important force in this regard was the still essentially tribal tradition of the Arabs themselves, which pulled in two conflicting directions. On the one hand, the prestige of the Quraysh was already very strong, and the idea that authority descended within a closely defined lineage widespread. On the other hand, the tribes also had a tradition of selecting leaders by *shura* or election, though just who constituted the electorate varied and provided a basis for ongoing dispute.

Cutting across this division deriving from tribal practices was the conviction, characteristic of the early stages in the institutionalization of most charismatic religious movements, that the leader must be the most qualified person religiously. In emerging Islam, this requirement was often stated in maximalist terms: if the *kalifah* finds that he is no longer the most qualified he must step down. Early on the idea of religious pre-eminence as a qualification for the caliphate became associated with support for maintaining the succession within the Prophet's family, variously defined, but usually understood as involving descent from Ali, his son-in law, giving rise to the "Shi'ite" *shi'a al-Ali* or "party of Ali." There were, however, groups which upheld the requirement of religious pre-eminence, while allowing that it might appear or be verified by some means other than descent and designation.

The requirement of religious pre-eminence, in turn, raised the question of just what constituted the basis for religious unity. Here there were a number of competing and inter-penetrating tendencies. There was, first of all, a veneration of the text of the *Qu'ran* and the *Hadith* (sayings) and *Sunna* (practices) of the Prophet, and there developed very early on a tradition of scholarship devoted to preserving, validating, and interpreting these texts. As Cook and Crone suggest, emerging Islam probably drew on the model of the Jewish rabbinate as it developed this model of religious scholarship, which like the rabbinate was centered on textual and especially legal interpretation. But while there was significant room, at least according to some of the legal schools, for *ijtihad* (independent judgment) regarding the interpretation and application of the law, the Islamic *'ulemma* never developed the idea, which we have seen became central to rabbinic Judaism, that debate itself is a participation in the life of God.

Second, we see very early on the emergence of *kalam* or theology, which attempts to support revealed doctrine with rational arguments and ends up, as theology always does, entering as well into its interpretation. The relationship between this sort of theology and the tradition of Greek philosophy is not entirely clear. Perhaps *kalam* represents an appropriation of the tradition of Christian apologetics, which used rational arguments derived ultimately from the Greek tradition but which could, at the same time, often be quite hostile to philosophy as such. The first school of *kalam*, the Mutazilites, stressed the unity of God, the basic goodness and freedom of humanity, and the power of human reason to discern what is right. Very quickly, however, an opposing school appeared, the Asharites, which stressed the sovereignty of God to the point of arguing that God creates each instant of the universe separately, so that there are no real causal relations between things which might for the basis for a physics, metaphysics, or natural law ethics. Moral judgment is radically dependent on divine command.

Third, we see early on the development of *falasafa*, which consisted mostly of a fusion of Neo-Platonic and Aristotelian philosophy and which was patronized by rulers primarily because its practitioners were also skilled physicians, astrologers, and alchemists, and could thus contribute to the welfare of the court and community in practical ways. The philosophers, for their part, following Platonic and Aristotelian tradition, regarded themselves as most qualified to rule, and in many cases even identified the *kalifah* with the Platonic philosopher king. We will, of course, have more to say about *falasafa* later on.

Fourth, there was a very strong tradition of esotericism, which seems to have had multiple sources: the Gnosticism which was pandemic in the Eastern Mediterranean, emerging Kabbalism, and possibly some Persian traditions. This esoteric tradition was picked up especially by the partisans of Ali, who declared that their *imam* had, in addition to the highest possible mastery of the exoteric tradition, i.e. the *Qu'ran, Hadith, and Sunna*, a knowledge of the esoteric meaning of the tradition. This esoteric meaning was identified, in varying degrees, with *falasafa* by the party of Ali in general and especially by the Ismailis, who eventually established a dynasty in Egypt, the Fatimid caliphate (909-1171). But it also provided a framework for the emergence of Sufi mysticism, which initially eschewed politics, but eventually gave birth to powerful orders which founded dynasties throughout *Dar-al-Islam*. Philosophical and Sufi esotericism, meanwhile, later flowed together to give birth to the highly imaginative *ishraqi* tradition, which blended philosophical speculation with Gnostic illumination.

The tension between the dynamic of empire building and the dynamic of religious and philosophical reformism made the early history of *Dar-al-Islam* unstable to say the least. Many of the partisans of Ali were too extremist and purist to effectively exercise political power. The vast majority of Shia—the Twelver or Imami communities—believe that there was an unbroken line of twelve Imams, the last of whom became hidden rather than dying, and who will eventually return to usher in a reign of justice. While they remain far more insistent than most Sunnis that the only legitimate ruler is one who is just and who has a profound grasp of the law or *sharia*, they tended, until the development of the ideology of Islamic Republicanism by Grand Ayatollah Ruollah Khomeini in the 1970s, towards political quiescence.

The Ismailis, on the other hand, who trace their own leadership from the seventh Imam, Isma'il bin Jafar, eventually built a state—the Fatimid Caliphate—based in Egypt, where they were responsible for making Cairo a major civilizational center and for founding the Al-Azhar University. They believe that there is a continuing and unbroken line of living Imams represented (at least for the largest, Nizari lineage) in the present period by His Highness Prince Karim Aga Khan. The Ismailis also believe that behind the external forms of the law there is a deeper mystical content which is passed on from one Imam to the next. This led the Ismailis to play an extraordinarily important role in the intellectual history not only of Islam, but also, indirectly, of Europe. This is because the hidden or *batin* content of the religion became identified with Hellenic philosophy. Ismailis played a critical role in translating the Greek texts of Plato and Aristotle into Arabic. It was in this form alone that most survived to be passed on, via Jewish translators in *Al-Andalus* (Muslim Spain) to Christian Europe. Ibn Sina, whose text on medicine was used not only in the Islamic world but also in the West up until the seventeenth century, and whose philosophy profoundly influenced that of Thomas Aquinas and thus the whole Catholic tradition, came from an Ismaili family. Other important beneficiaries of Ismaili patronage include the mathematicians al-Haytham and Nasir al-Din Tusi and the poet and philosopher Nasir e-Khusraw.

On all sides, relatively few of those who actually exercised power had sufficient learning or virtue to qualify as fully legitimate caliphs even by the more relaxed standards of the emerging Sunni tradition. Almost none, for example, were really *mujtahids*, scholars sufficiently learned to exercise independent judgment in matters of law, a task which fell increasingly to the scholars. This created enough discomfort that even Sunni scholars asked whether or not it was permissible to use public works built by oppressive kings (Crone 2004: 306)—a question which seems never to have occurred to even the most sectarian Christians.

Pressure from the legal scholars, theologians, philosophers, and esotericists, however, tended to hold the caliphs accountable to a higher standard than that of other earlier empires in the West. Of critical importance here was the *zakat*, or wealth tax, which took between 2.5% and 5% of the net wealth of those living in *Dar-al-Islam* each year. This tax—unlike the Roman impositions which it replaced—fell most heavily on the wealthy while providing an ample source of revenue which could be used to support the poor, subsidize debtors and slaves seeking to buy their freedom, and support institutions such as mosques, *madrasas*, and hospitals. The latter institutions were also supported amply by *waqfs* or charitable trusts. There were additional taxes: the *jizyah* or poll tax imposed on *dhmmis* or protected religious minorities and the *kharaj* or land tax, imposed on lands seized during the conquest, but both were to be used for the benefit of the whole community. While many rulers attempted to impose other taxes, they faced constant opposition on this front from legal scholars who warned that such taxes were uncanonical (Crone 2004: 304-307).

It was, no doubt, due to these low levels of exploitation and the productive use to which the surplus extracted was put that the Arab armies were most often greeted as liberators rather than conquerors and that once established, Islamic rule proved civilizationally so progressive. Revenues were invested in the arts, sciences, and philosophy as well as religion. The Abbasid Caliph al-Mamoun, for example, established the *bayt-hikhmah* to translate scientific and philosophical manuscripts from every language, but especially Greek and the languages of India. This, in turn, set in motion extraordinary progress in mathematics, science, and philosophy. It was the Muslim al-Khwarizmi who developed algebra. And investment in the alchemy led to the flourishing of laboratory techniques, including distillation, which proved essential for later scientific and technical progress. The Arabs also invested heavily in bringing water to their cities, which were like vast gardens, and in horticulture, developing many of the most important vegetables in the modern Mediterranean kitchen, importing others from India and China, and refining the techniques which, applied later on by the Portuguese and Spanish to plants from Africa and the Americas, reshaped diet world-wide.

Jerusalem and Athens

It is in the context of this dynamic by internally contradictory civilizational pattern that we must understand the specifically Muslim form of the encounter between Jerusalem (or Mecca?) and Athens. On the one hand, there can be little doubt that rational metaphysics generally, and Aristotelian metaphysics in particular, reached one of its high-water marks under the Abbasid caliphate, and another just a little bit later in *al-Andalus*. More specifically, it was during this period that the identification of Plato's Good and Aristotle's Unmoved Mover with the God of Exodus 3:13 was finally completed and that we see the emergence of a fully developed analogical metaphysics of Being as Such. At the same time, the situation of those who practiced *falasafa* was always tenuous. One caliph would patronize *falasafa* and the next would repress or at least ignore it, and the turn against philosophy came much earlier in *Dar-al-Islam* and was of broader effect than that in Christendom.

It, would, perhaps, be most accurate to say that *falasafa*, like so much else in *Dar-al-Islam* was caught in the crossfire between the two motors of Islamic civilization: the drive to build a military empire which would allow marginal, nomadic peoples—first the Arabs and then the Turks—to control a large section of the Silk Road trade and the insistence, originating the earliest preaching of Mohammed, that that military empire also be an effective instrument for commanding right and forbidding wrong—that it be God's Rule on earth. It was only because of the intersection of these two dynamics that philosophy found a home at all in Islam; either dynamic by itself would have excluded dialectics. But the requirement that the fantastically wealthy empire the Arabs were building also be a *just* empire posed problems which neither messianic preaching nor legal scholarship could resolve, and thus created a niche which the practitioners of *falasafa* tried, as best as possible to fulfill. In the end, however, with the ascendancy of the Turks, the twin dynamics of military expansionism and prophetic austerity took over and philosophy found itself marginalized.

More specifically, philosophy entered the Islamic world as one of the amenities which the early caliphs accorded themselves. Philosophers were also astrologers, alchemists, and physicians—functionaries which every Silk Road court required. And so beginning with the establishment of the *Bayt-Hikhmah* by the Caliph al-Mamoun, the Abbasids in particular subsidized the collection and translation of wisdom from every civilization with which the Arabs had come into contact, but most especially the Greeks, the Persians, and the Indians. Translation eventually gave way to elaboration, and soon the caliphs and the various other rulers who gradually took their place, were subsidizing extensive research in what might be called the Aristotelian physical and biological sciences, and in their practical application in alchemy, horticulture, and medicine. Metaphysics, and its extension into psychology, ethics, political theory, and spirituality, were something that the philosophers did, so to speak, on their own time. Even so, it was not at all unusual for a philosopher to be called to serve as *wazir* or to be appointed *qadi* or judge, and in this sense they had significant influence over public policy and the larger direction of development of Islamic civilization

The philosophy which entered *Dar-al-Islam* was an eclectic mixture of Aristotelianism, as interpreted by Alexander of Aphrodisias and Neo-Platonism, as represented in the misnamed *Theology of Aristotle*, which was really a paraphrase of sections of Plotinus' *Enneads* and the *Liber de Causis*, also incorrectly attributed to Aristotle but actually a summary of Proclus' *Elements of Theology* (Nasr 1964:9). The principal transmitters seem to have been dissident Christians—Nestorians and Monophysites who had fled East into Mesopotamia and Persia in the wake of the Christological controversies, as well as the few remaining pagan philosophers who fled after Justinian closed the last of the philosophical schools, Plato's Academy, in 529 (Rubenstein 2003: 75-77).

When philosophy began to be produced in Arabic by thinkers like al Kindi (801-866) and al-Farabi (870-950), it could hardly be called Islamic in any meaningful sense. It was, rather, simply a restatement, with perhaps some light rationalization and systematization, of the Platonized Aristotelianism of late antiquity. It was put forward as the rational or, in the case of those philosophers influenced by Shi'ism generally and the Ismailis in particular, the esoteric or *batin* content of the revelation made to Mohammed. It was, to be sure, necessary to credential it in the Islamic world, and this meant showing how it related to revealed or prophetic religion. Al-Kindi, took the first steps in this direction, making a distinction between *al-ilm al-ilahi*, which is given directly by God to the prophets, and *al-ilm al-insani* or rational knowledge, and argued that certain truths, such as creation *ex-nihilo* had to be accepted on faith, but there was no attempt to develop a philosophical doctrine of prophecy (Nasr 1964: 12). Al Farabi went further, and raised the status of philosophy, by arguing that religion (*milla*) and *falasafa* put forward the same truths, just in different forms: philosophy by means of demonstrative proofs (*burhan*), for those who could comprehend them, and religion by means of images and persuasion (*iqna'*), for the masses (al-Farabi. *Tahsil* 56, Crone 2004: 173). Philosophy comes first, grasps the truth in pure form, and is unchanging. Religions come about when lawgivers mediate philosophical truth to the masses in an attempt to found a just polity (Crone 2004: 173).

Al-Farabi was the first to define philosophically what is meant by prophecy—at least prophecy of the first rank. The prophet must *first* be a philosopher, and must be intellectually and morally perfect to such an extent that his intellect comes into contact with the Agent Intellect (*al'aql al-fa''al*) or intelligence of the sublunary realm, which is the agent of divine "revelation." Whether this is the result of a purely rational dialectic, as Crone claims (Crone 2004: 172), dismissing the claims that al-Farabi was a Sufi, or the result of a sort of mystical illumination which builds on philosophical speculation, as Nasr claims (Nasr 1964: 16) remains unclear. In any case this contact with the Agent Intellect not only perfects the potential intellect of the prophet but also forms his imaginative faculties, so that he becomes a great popular preacher, able to move the masses (Crone 2004: 178), thus establishing himself as paramount leader (*al-ra'is al-awwal*).

Al-Farabi further extends Plato's vision of the philosopher king by arguing that such a lawgiver could found not only a single city (*madinat*) but also a whole community (*umma*), that several such cities or communities could coexist, even if their religions were different, because the philosophers who governed them would constitute a kind of cosmopolitan elite who knew the real truth behind the differing imaginative forms embraced by the masses, and by specifying what happened after the lawgiver died—an issue which, as we have seen, was of fundamental importance for Islam. Ideally the lawgiver would be succeeded by one like himself. In practice, however, lawgivers seemed to appear only to found new communities: thus the long years between Moses, Jesus, and Mohammed. Generally speaking, the community would be governed instead by a *ra'is* or *malik al-sunna*, and new laws elaborated from those given by the prophet on the basis of *fiqh* or juristic science or by a group of philosophically trained individuals who did not rise to the level of prophecy: *riyasat al-afadil*. But where an outstanding philosopher did exist, he ought to rule directly if he could. If not, he remained *al-malik fi 'l-haqiqa*, the real, uncrowned king, and governed indirectly by advising the rulers as did the `ulamma and *mutakallim* who mediated philosophical truth to the masses (Crone 2004: 179–80).

It is only with ibn Sina (980–1037) that we really get what might be called an authentic synthesis between philosophy and Islam. Here the critical achievement was ibn Sina's analysis of being. Here he distinguishes between the essence of a thing (*mahiyah*) and its existence (*wujud*) and between its necessity, possibility, or impossibility. With respect to the first distinction, and contrary to the impression one gets from reading Gilson (Gilson 1952), it is existence which is principal (*asil*). Essence is a limitation on being. Beings are, further, divided into impossible (*mumtani'*), possible (*mumkin*) and necessary (*wajib*). Essences which, on analysis, are incompatible with existence are impossible. Those which are compatible with but do not require existence are possible. If, finally, the essence of a thing includes existence, then it is necessary. For such a thing, essence and existence are the same: it *is* Being. And this, for ibn Sina, is true only of God (ibn Sina. *Shifa'*, *Najat*, *Danishnamah*, Nasr 1964: 27.)

This understanding of God as Being as such sets ibn Sina apart from all earlier attempts at synthesis between the *way of the search for Being* and the *way of justice and liberation*, which had either primarily used philosophy as an apologetic tool, as was the case with most of the early Christian Neo-Platonists, or else treated philosophy itself as the real truth, and regarded prophetic religion as a means of popularizing it. Even the great Philo of Alexandria, who clearly appreciates both traditions, manages at best an eclectic synthesis, using the Jewish idea of God to find a "place" for Plato's ideas and using philosophical methods to interpret and argue for the superiority of Jewish law. Here, on the other hand, we have an integrated synthesis. On the one hand, an idea clearly drawn form the Jewish tradition is used to solve a core problem in the philosophical tradition: what is so attractive about the Unmoved Mover? Ibn Sina answers that the unmoved mover is attractive because it *is* Being, which is what all things seek in proportion to their nature. At the same time, philosophy militates against the concept of divine sovereignty which was emerging within Islam. God is, to be sure, radically transcendent. There can be no greater gulf than between possible and necessary being. But God is not arbitrary. He acts, rather, in accord with his nature, and his commandments are those which are written into the very nature of things, all of which, in the end, amount to one: *seek the power of Being as such.*

This said, it is also true that ibn Sina does not realize the full potential of his insight. He envisions the universe as a process of essentially intellectual emanation from God rather than as a real process of creative activity, and human beings as returning to God, again primarily by means of an intellectual ascent—completed by mystical union, if Nasr is correct, rather than sharing in God's creative activity by means of their own labor, with the intellect playing a leading and regulating role (Nasr 1964: 29–30).

This, in turn, shapes ibn Sina's psychology. Ibn Sina expands Aristotle's analysis of the intellect, defining four rather than merely two degrees of actuality. The material or potential intellect is the pure possibility of acquiring intellectual knowledge. When we exercise this capacity we develop the habitual intellect, which can receive knowledge, and the actual intellect, which can create it. When our intellect becomes, in effect, a copy of the universe, we have developed the adept intellect (Nasr 1964: 38–40).

As for al-Farabi, the prophet goes one step beyond this, his intellect actually becoming united to the Agent Intellect or Tenth Intelligence. But for ibn Sina, in addition to thus perfecting his intellect and forming his imaginative faculty so that he becomes a great poet and preacher as well as philosopher, the Tenth Intelligence also gives the prophet the power of making external matter obey his commands (Nasr 1964: 43). This union with the Tenth Intelligence represents the highest degree of development possible for human beings and the aim of all authentic spirituality. This is true even if one accepts as authentic his *Mantiq al-mashriqiyin* or *Logic of the Orientals* and the last chapters of the *Ishararat wa'l-tanbihat* (Nasr 1964: 43–44). Here he identifies his Aristotelian philosophy as exoteric and turns to an imaginative exposition of the soul's journey towards God. Even so, the journey in question is fundamentally an escape from the material universe, and terminates in liberation from physicality, not in connaturality with God. In this sense, Ibn Sina leaves the dialectical project incomplete.

Ibn Sina's political philosophy is similar to al-Farabi's except that he goes further in identifying Mohammed as, at the very least, the final and definitive lawgiver, and Islam as the final and definitive imaginative presentation of philosophical truth. He develops what amounts to an incipient sociology of religion, explaining how various Islamic laws draw attention to God and help to maintain social order (Crone 2004: 187–88).

It is important to point out here that Islamic *falasafa* advanced for the first time an ideal which would be further elaborated—and developed in two different directions—in dialectical materialism. On the one hand, full deification is ruled out—in the case of *falasafa* by the fact that it is logically impossible to cross the line between contingent and necessary Being, in the case of dialectical materialism for the individual even if for the collective political subject, it is held open. The pinnacle of human development is understood to be perfect knowledge of material world *and the ability to use this knowledge practically to control matter, physical, biological, and social.* In *falasafa* this is the role of the prophet. For dialectical materialism it is the role of the Communist Party, which becomes the "unique subject object of human history (Lukacs 1921/1971)." The technocratic strain of dialectical materialism focused on transforming social structure in order to unleash development of the productive forces (making external matter obey its commands); the humanistic strain focused on the transformation of social relations.

It was not long after ibn Sina produced his synthesis that the tide turned against metaphysics in the Islamic world. Here the underlying factor was the failure of the Islamic project itself: the effort to build a just social order presided over by a ruler who was not only just but himself actually the best and wisest man alive, and in some meaningful sense the heir of the Prophet. It was this common idea which united even the most literalist Muslims with the most rationalist practitioners of *falasafa*. And the ideal was resilient. It could survive caliphates and even whole dynasties which lacked even the most minimal qualifications for rule, whether by the standards of the jurists or those of the philosophers. It could even survive delegation of *de facto* political-military authority to a group of foreign invaders, so long as it was possible to argue credibly that real guidance was being exercised by the "best"—in reality the practitioners of *falasafa*, the *mutakallim*, and the *'ulamma*, and symbolically the *kalifah*. But when the Seljuks began blinding and dismissing caliphs at will, when it became apparent that *they* were the real power, the basis in experience for *falasafa* as a credible social force disappeared and Islamic Aristotelianism began to crumble, resulting in three main developments..

The first was the elaboration of a new Sunni orthodoxy which joined a *fiqh* which severely limited the role of *ijtihad* or independent reasoning, an Asharite *kalam* which stressed divine sovereignty, and a muted Sufism which is better understood as devotional than as mystical. Central to this process was the work of the theologian al Ghazali (d. 1111). Al-Ghazali had fully mastered the tradition of *falasafa* at Nishapur, where he studied, but turned against it, rooting himself instead in an emerging and unstable synthesis of Asharite *kalam* and Sufi mysticism. His most important work was his *Tahafut al-Falasafa*, the *Incoherence of Philosophy*. In this text, he undertakes a critique of ibn Sina's synthesis, arguing that on closer logical examination the philosophers core arguments fall apart. It is not possible to consider the work in detail in this context, but the key link in his argument is a critique of the idea of necessity, which he insists is a purely logical concept, which cannot be applied to physical and metaphysical relations—a position which many Western philosophers have themselves taken, following Hume. The realization of a possibility requires power and will—in effect it requires God. This was, in effect, a reflex of the political situation under the Seljuks and their great Persian *wazir* Nizam-al-Mulk, who was al-Ghazali's patron and who appointed him to the most eminent chair in *Dar-al-Islam*.

Such a God can, of course, be approached only by means of a personal relationship, and so after performing his great ideological service to the Seljuks, al-Ghazali renounced his chair and began a long search for mystical experience, which ultimately eluded him. Eventually he formed a small Sufi community (Collins 1998: 412–14, 421–23).

The second response to the collapse of Islamic Aristotelianism was the radically immanent turn taken by ibn Rusd and his followers. As Leaman points out, his revolutionary impact on the West notwithstanding, ibn Rusd was first and foremost a jurist, and a jurist of the conservative Maliki school which wanted to restrict the role of the Hadith, of consensus, and of independent reasoning in the application of the law and return to a more Quranically based Islam. He seems to have brought this same spirit to his reading of Aristotle. Specifically, he tries as much as possible to purge Aristotelianism from the Neo-Platonic accretions which had accumulated over the years. In the field of cosmology, this leads him to reject ibn Sina's emanationism in favor of an emergentist paradigm which, at least implicitly radically revalues the material world. Ibn Rusd seems to have rejected the idea that form came to matter from the outside, and argued instead that

> the primary, unformed matter contains potential forms as 'seeds'. Forms are therefore not extrinsic to but immanent in matter. If the forms were to come to matter from the outside, this would be a sort of *creatio ex nihilo*. The forms are as eternal and uncreated as is matter. God creates neither matter nor form. The task of the "prime mover" is to convert possible forms into actual forms, i.e. to develop the seeds contained in matter . . . Prime matter is universal potency that hides the seeds of the forms; the prime mover does nothing but turn potency into act (Trachtenberg 1957: 66 in Dahm 1987).

At the same time, ibn Rusd seems to have lost the realization that we see in ibn Sina of God as Necessary Being. Whether in the name of the same faithful if somewhat literalistic exegesis he applied in the interpretation of *sharia'* or in the name of more purely inner-worldly evolutionism, ibn Rusd reinstates the contradiction we saw in Aristotle's original formulation: we know that there must *be* an unmoved mover which draws things into being by attraction, but we do not know what is so attractive about it.

Ibn Rusd's position would seem at least to have laid the ground work for a more positive view human nature, and it did in the sense of putting greater emphasis on the human civilizational project by comparison with otherworldly salvation. At the same time, ibn Rusd seems to have radically devalued the individual human person and its prospects for anything like a full realization of our immanent drive towards divinity. This is because he reads Aristotle as upholding unicity of the not only the agent but also the potential intellect, with the result that human beings are reduced to the status of mere data collectors, with a single collective intellect doing our thinking for us.

This, in turn, has two consequences. First, it means that we have different ideas only because and to the extent that we have different experiences. This undercuts the role of difference and deliberation in political life and tends to accentuate the authoritarian dimension in dialectical political theory. Second, it means that there is no meaningful possibility of personal immortality, since there is no part of *us* which is immortal. We are, in effect, material instruments of the Agent Intellect for the collection of data and the transformation of matter—and no more.

This is reflected in ibn Rusd's political theory. On the one hand, ibn Rusd stresses the historic commitment of the dialectical tradition to the struggle for social justice. This is why he abhors democracy (*siyasat al-jama'iyya* or *al-hurriyya*), which he associates not with popular participation in decision making (something which, for reasons we will come to understand shortly, he seems not even to have considered) but rather a society in which everyone pursues their own aims (Crone 2004: 190).

The difficulty with this position is that it effectively forecloses the possibility of any "Jewish" solution to the "Greek" problem of deification, and leaves humanity at best in the first "philosophers'" circle of Dante's *Inferno* in which we are perpetual aware of a higher Good we can never fully know or enjoy. For the elaboration of such a synthesis, we need to look the Christianity. And it condemns the people to what amounts to a benevolent slavery from which their limited capacities do not allow them to escape.

The third development was the elaboration of a more profoundly mystical Islam, albeit one still deeply rooted in Islam's foundational commitment to *command right and forbidding wrong*, understood as the construction of a just social order. It is not possible to discuss this trend in depth here. We have already explored one of the better documented currents in another context" the so called *ishraqi* or illuminist school associated with Suhrawardi (1153–1191) and ibn Arabi (1165–1240). This first builds on the mystical dimension of ibn Sina's work, taking al-Ghazali's criticisms as a corrective to excessive rationalism and extending the philosopher's tentative overtures towards Sufism. But it also draws on and synthesizes two long esoteric traditions: that of Egypt and that of Persia (Nasr 1964: 64). The Ismaili tradition, which began by regarding Hellenic philosophy as the *batin* content of the *Quran*, eventually, at least in its Nizari expression, also syncretized significantly with Indian traditions, resulting in a highly developed mystical literature written in Gujarati, which draws extensively on concepts now regarded broadly as Hindu, but more properly understood as part of a complex intercultural engagement along the borderlands between India and *Dar-al-Islam* (Khan 2004).

What is distinctive about this trend is the fact that it has joined a syncretic, mystical spirituality with a profound historic commitment to social justice. This commitment has, to be sure, expressed itself in different ways at different times, from the broad based civilization building activities of the Fatimid Caliphate, through the revolutionary sectarianism of Alamut, up through what is currently one of the largest and most sophisticated global philanthropic networks on the planet today.

Christianity

Christianity represents a very different response on the part of the *way of justice and liberation* to the realities of life under *Empire*. Here the messianic path is embraced—and then radically transformed in its failure.

There continues to be considerable debate regarding the position of Jesus within the political-theological spectrum of first century Palestinian Judaism. One school understands him as, essentially, a radicalized Hillel school Pharisee. The Jesus we encounter in the synoptic Gospels was, clearly, a teacher of the oral Torah "reinterpreting the Hebrew Scriptures in a manner more in line with the social setting in which he found himself." Furthermore, the general pattern of his ministry "with its emphasis on teaching and healing" is characteristic of the rabbinic pattern for the period. "He likewise seems to have participated in Pharisaic-type fellowship meals, instituting the Christian Eucharist at the final one he attended (Pawlikowski 1982: 92–93)."

The *content* of Jesus' teaching also shows significant Pharisaic influence. This is evident in any number of places. Jesus' answers to the questions posed to him while teaching in the temple (Mark 12:13–34), and particularly the question concerning the great commandment, put him more or less squarely in the Pharisaic camp, marked as it was by a focus on love of God and neighbor (Mark 12:28–34) as the central aspect of Jewish life, a belief in the Resurrection (Mark 12:18–27), and internal division regarding such questions as the lawfulness of paying tribute to Caesar (Mark 12:13–18). The prayer which Jesus taught to his disciples—elements of which are preserved in the so-called "Lord's Prayer" (Matt 6:9–13, Luke 11:1–4)—also contains several characteristic Pharisaic elements—a sense of intimacy with God, who is addressed as "Father," a desire for the coming of the Kingdom, for the accomplishment of God's will on earth, a sense of the importance of forgiveness, etc.

Recent scholarship has, however, increasingly questioned this consensus, arguing that Jesus was the leader of one of the last revolutionary messianic uprisings (Eisenman 1997, Tabor 2006) and perhaps even the catalyst for the Jewish War. This thesis depends on a more skeptical reading of the synoptics, regarding them as not merely attempting to differentiate emerging Christianity from the Pharisaic Judaism of which it was originally a branch, but as actually falsifying events to hide the dangerous memory of one who understood himself, and who was initially accepted by many Jews, as the authentic Davidic messiah. We cannot engage here all of the evidence brought to bear by scholars like Eisenman and Tabor. Suffice it to say that even in the synoptics we also find significant support for this image of Jesus: the high note of eschatological expectation which characterizes what even the most critical scholars acknowledge as authentic sayings (e.g., Mark 4), the march on and messianic entry into Jerusalem, and the fact that he was executed by the Romans as a Jewish royal pretender.

Regardless of which of these two pictures turns out to be more accurate (and it is entirely possible that neither is, and that we will never really *know* the historical Jesus), already at the level of canon of the New Testament, Christianity represents a distinct departure from the Jewish variant of the *way of justice and liberation* in both its emerging rabbinic and its messianic variants. On the one hand, whatever the extent to which the historical Jesus was involved in messianic movements, Christianity embraces him as *mosiach*. On the other hand, it embraces messianism precisely in its failure, thus requiring a radical reinterpretation of the messianic event. *The struggle for justice leads inevitably to the cross and ends in Resurrection, the full meaning and significance of which remains at least partly hidden from us, but which becomes, as Christianity develops, a portal into the very* theosis *which Hellenism had sought but could not find.*

This is not quite to suggest that the struggle for justice is in vain and ought to be abandoned. On the contrary there is the possibility that, as for Judaism, the struggle for justice remains meaningful even in its global failure, pointing beyond itself to something which includes and transcends justice—though Christianity will define this meaning rather differently than Judaism. But it does mean that unlike earliest Israel (but perhaps very much like the Jewish people since then) Christians meet their God not in a victorious struggle for justice but in the failure of that struggle. Thus the synoptic infancy narratives, the many differences and contradictions between them, place the birth of Jesus at the time of a *defeated* insurrection.

Just what Christians do with this defeat depends on the way they handle the engagement between the originally Jewish encounter with the sacred in the struggle for justice and the Hellenic, Latin, Celtic, Germanic *ways* with which Judaism becomes syncretized.

Emerging Christianity

There has been a good deal of ink spilled in debate around the social composition of these Christian communities. Some, such as Kautsky and Weber, claimed that Christianity found its constituency among the exploited and lower-middle strata. Others, such as Dimitris Kyrtatas (1987), have suggested that Christianity, at least outside of Israel, was primarily a movement of the wealthy. Recent scholarship (Theissen 1982) has begun to bring some closure to this debate by pointing out the internal diversity of the Christian communities, and focusing attention instead on the political valence of Christianity within the complex social world of the Hellenistic city. Specifically, Theissen shows that early Christian communities included a broad range of the middle strata of Hellenistic-Roman Society, ranging from a small number of Equestrians occupying senior military and civilian positions in the colonial administration and a much larger number of decurions who had the unenviable responsibility of collecting the taxes owed to Rome, or making up the difference out of their own resources; through a middle stratum of merchants, artisans etc. some of whom were very wealthy and others of whom were poor indeed, to an urban plebianate of wage laborers and the marginally employed as well as slaves, some of whom would have been rather well off and secure, others of whom may have been severely exploited but whose conditions were better than those employed in agriculture and the mines (Theissen 1982: 69–119).

Within this context the story of Jesus began to take on a very different significance. The larger framework for this reinterpretation was given by the principal form of popular religion in the Mediterranean Basin—i.e. the mystery cult, which we discussed in the last chapter. These cults promised eternal life to anyone who went through a process of catechesis and initiation, leading up to revelation of the central mystery and a communion meal. The story of Jesus, as it was handed down by his followers, fit well in this framework. He looked like yet another dying and rising god and there was no reason why a format which had adopted Egyptian and Persian stories as well as Greek could not accommodate one from Israel, whose religion had acquired a certain mystique because of its rationality and focus on ethical conduct.

Just what this meant, however, varied widely depending on the social context and the other ways with which this already syncretic way engaged. Let us consider the principal variants of the Christian *way* prior to the Reformation.

Orthodox Christianity

Orthodox Christianity is intimately bound up with the Byzantine Empire, from which it was adopted by many of the Southern and Eastern Slavs. In order to understand Orthodoxy, therefore we must understand Byzantium.

Byzantine Civilization was one of several responses to the crisis of Hellenistic Roman civilization, a crisis which was, as we have argued elsewhere (Mansueto 201b) both structural and spiritual. At the structural level the crisis was a result of a sustained balance of trade deficit with India and China, due to the technological backwardness of the region, a shortage of slave labor due to the closing of the *limes*, and a crisis of legitimation as the *Empire* and the senatorial and to a lesser degree equestrian elites imposed the costs of sustaining *Empire* not only on the merchant, artisan, peasant and slave masses but on the *decuriones,* the local elites who formed the bulk of the "ruling" class. At the spiritual level the crisis was a result of the fact that the Empire itself had, from the beginning rendered meaningless a key aspect of the Hellenic ideal it was created to realize: life as a free human being and engaged citizen. But if *Dar-al-Islam* and Latin Christendom developed new structures in order to realize new ideals, then Byzantium embraced new ideals in order to save as much as possible of the old imperial structure.

This said, there were real differences between Byzantium and the Later Roman Empire at the level of social structure as well as of civilizational ideal. It is, perhaps, easiest to sum up these differences by saying that Orthodox Christianity provided a means for not only legitimating but also retheorizing and radicalizing the transformation of the Empire originally envisioned by Diocletian and Constantine. Let us see how this worked.

Like pagan Neo-Platonism, Orthodox Christianity was focused on liberating humanity from finitude and contingency and had, at best, a weak sense of sin. Where it differed was in offering an actual strategy for deification or *theosis*. This might seem, at first, simply to be a change at the level of anthropology and soteriology rather than at the ontological core of the system. The anthropological and soteriological changes required by the doctrine of *theosis*, however, required ontological changes as well.

These changes are, above all, concentrated on the doctrines of the trinity and the incarnation. Christianity needed a language in which it could speak of God as one in essence, but of three persons and of Jesus as at once truly God and truly human. The Platonic language of *ousia* (essence or nature) and *hypostasis* (person) provided a way to do this. Christian Neo-Platonism was, first and foremost, a theorization of the holy trinity and of the person of Jesus in terms of the successions of hypostases which emanate from the Neo-Platonic One.

By thinking God as Trinity rather than as the One while maintaining the underlying unity of the divine essence, Christianity began to think this essence in a new way: as something in which persons could participate in varying degrees. The divine persons of the Holy Trinity participate in it by nature: they *are* it; others share in it as a superadded quality, as a food becomes hot when cooked, without itself becoming heat. By thinking of Jesus as one unified person who is both human and divine, Christianity opened the road for human beings to take on the divine nature. Working out the details of all this was beyond the Neo-Platonists, and would have to wait the subtlety of the medieval Aristotelians, and of Thomas in particular, who applied to the problem the categories of substance and accident, potency and act. But the beginning of the process was here. And it was enough to provide an ontological foundation for the perfect mystery cult—one which conferred not just immortality (which is how the early Greeks had understood divinity) but divinity proper, as it was understood by the peculiar synthesis of dialectics and prophetic religion which was gradually replacing the Hellenic ideal. Only such a mystery cult could provide the ideal for an entire civilization.

This metaphysics of participation was systematized and passed on to the Latin Church in the work of Dionysus the Areopagite. In Dionysus the Christian Trinity and the various orders of angels replace the Greek and Asian gods and the hierarchy of the Church replaces that of the Empire, but the underlying logic of his system is little changed from that of his pagan teachers, except that here, in the Christian context, full divinization has become possible. The universe as a whole is sacred, an overflowing of God's creative power; we return to God by means of participation in the mysteries, ascetic purification, and meditation on, and infused contemplation of, a Divine Nature which radically transcends any possible discursive knowledge. As in the case of the pagan Neo-Platonists, the function of human society is to facilitate humanity's return to God. It is just that the society in question is that of the Church. Gradually Orthodox Christianity developed a complex theology which rationalized this process, theorizing the liturgy as a kind of "heaven on earth" participation in which, especially because of its beauty, elevates human beings above the earthly realm, lifting them towards heaven (Ware 1993).

This theology had, in turn, definite political implications. It led to a theorization of the whole society as a kind of liturgical system, in both the older sense of a system of public works undertaken for the common good and in the sense of the organized system of the mysteries themselves. Liturgy, in other words, which has always been a part of the civic life of the Hellenic and Hellenistic-Roman civilizations, effectively displaced public deliberation as the principal form of civic engagement. The empire existed in order to support the mysteries; the people existed in order to support the empire.

This political theology supported the transformation of the organization of labor in Empire. While antiquity had been characterized by a sharp distinction between slave and free, the Byzantine ideal made everyone into a servant of the sacral state. Slaves were transformed into *coloni*, settled on the land and bound to it but no longer subject to sale, but the same fate best free peasants as well, who found themselves subject to increasing burdens. Indeed, artisans and merchants were increasingly bound to their hereditary trades and required to meet the needs of the state, and the traditional senatorial order, which had been distinguished by its autonomy from the Empire, was merged with the equestrian order to form a unified service nobility (Jones 1974: 302, Anderson 1974: 100).

It is in this context that we must understand the patristic denunciations of private property and of the rich of which some liberation theologians have made so much (Miranda 1981). The Church Fathers were not, strictly speaking, advocates for the peasants or artisans, but rather for the public, liturgical economy as against the private economy of luxury consumption, which certainly persisted even among the somewhat chastened aristocracy.

At the pinnacle of this system was a sacral monarchic ideology which legitimated what was left of the Roman Empire for nearly another millennium.

> As the knowledge of one God and the one way of religion and salvation, even the Doctrine of Christianity, was made known

to all mankind, so at the self-same period, the entire dominion of the Roman empire was being vested in a single sovereign. Profound peace reigned throughout the world. And thus by the express appointment of the same God, two roots of blessing, the Roman Empire and the doctrine of Christian piety, sprang up together for the benefit of men . . . (Eusebius Or. Con 16: 4-7 in Ruether 1974: 142).

The emperor himself comes to be regarded in much the manner of a God-King,

> The emperor, like the rays of the sun whose light illuminates those who live in the most distant regions, enlightens the entire empire with the radiance of the Caesars as with the far reaching beams reflected from his own brilliance . . . Thus he is present everywhere, traversing the entire earth, being in all places and surveying all events . . . Having been entrusted with an empire, the image of the heavenly kingdom, he looks to the ideal form, and directs his earthly rule to the divine model and thus provides an example of divine monarchic sovereignty (Eusebius in Cunningham 1982: 51).

This strategy was, we should note, less demanding in what it required of the ruling classes than that of Julian the Apostate, whose claims to divinity were based on his actual virtue, and required that the emperor be at the very least a Platonic philosopher king. Here, it is emperor's office, magnified by the sheer extent of his realm—the reach of his laws and his intelligence service, in effect—which guarantees his sacral character. It also, furthermore, guaranteed the primacy of the royal (or rather imperial) office over the priestly office. The emperor is himself a kind of sacrament, a living image of what others might achieve; the priest is merely the maker of that sacrament. There is little or no integration of the Jewish understanding of the first principle as Being itself—and the prophetic office appears not at all.

This pattern persisted for some time in the Eastern Mediterranean. But Byzantium represented, in the end, a kind of rear guard action. The reasons for this are not hard to find. Orthodox Christianity rationalized the way in which surplus was extracted and the way in which it was used, but did not address the underlying structural problem of the Western economy: its backward position in the larger system of the Silk Road. The colonate replaced slave labor and more of the surplus really was used for public purposes than had been the case in the Hellenistic and Roman empires, but there was, in effect, no investment in developing new technologies and new products which might improve the balance of trade deficit with India and

China. The result was an underlying economic weakness and a tendency for the revenue needs of the sacral state to be met by increased rates of exploitation. In the end most of the people of Byzantium found the Islamic ideal more attractive.

Catholicism

As we have explained above the sort of conservative transformation of the Hellenic ideal carried out by the Byzantine Empire made sense only in regions in which imperial reform was working (after a fashion) and the imperial structure remained largely intact. In the West things looked very different, as Germanic warlords vied with Roman hierarchs and Celtic abbots for leadership of a new civilization.

This new civilization grew up on the basis of new technologies which made possible, for the first time, the emergence of true urbanization in Northern and Western Europe. Key developments include the alpine plow, which allowed cultivation of rocky soils resistant to the Mediterranean *ard* and the three field system, which more than doubled agricultural yields. These in turn were the product of a symbiosis between transhumant pastoralists and settled cultivators which ushered in the great era of animal powered development. Energy from streams and rivers was harnessed in new ways and specialized arts and crafts reached a new level of development.

The political-economic structures which organized this process of development, generally grouped together under the heading of "feudalism" allowed agrarian producers, who were generally required to work part of the time on land belonging to secular or ecclesiastical lords, to retain all or most of the produce of the allotments they were allowed to use in return, creating an incentive for innovation and improvement not present on the slave driven *latifundia* of the Empire. The emerging guild structure of the cities regulated prices, forcing competition based on quality, also pushing innovation.

Political authority in this period was fragmented, with people owing varying degrees of allegiance to lords secular and ecclesiastical, who wielded authority which came with the land they held (as in the case of the peasantry) in return for service, military or spiritual. While this sometimes led to what look like profound irrationalities from an industrial capitalist (or socialist) perspective, it created a new space for personal autonomy and for the emergence of the Church as a new form of society, still deeply flawed but ordered to the process of *theosis*.

It was on the basis of this new civilization that the Catholic variant of the Christian *way* emerged. Catholicism was itself the product of multiple and competing responses to imperial collapse and complex intercultural encounters. Let us trace these out briefly.

First, Catholicism appropriated and built on the system of liturgical *theosis* which defined Orthodoxy. The core Trinitarian and Christological formulae in terms of which this system was theorized and the sacramental system which was created became the theological and ritual core of the Catholic tradition.

This Orthodox synthesis was, second, transformed in context of a cultural encounter on the Northwest fringes of Europe with a Celtic culture in the context of which it took on a vastly different moral and political significance. Celtic civilization had, prior to the Roman conquests, hovered on the cusp of authentic urbanization. Land was owned collectively and parceled out to individual families. The lands of warriors and priests were worked partly by free producers and partly by dependent peasants, though the relative proportion between the two is not entirely clear. Kings were elected from among the warriors by a complex process which involved the kin network of the deceased king, which meant that the electoral college changed with each generation. The electoral process however, was controlled by the druidic priests, who also had to "make" the king by means of a series of rituals which left them with substantial control over him. These druidic priests were not so much ritualists as scholars, and were at the top of a complex priestly hierarchy which included bards of various kinds as well as ritualists and others. They mastered a complex lore which included, during the later period, material from the Hellenistic and Roman as well as their own traditions.

Christianity was appropriated in the Celtic regions in a way which reflected the historic Celtic emphasis on learning and on intellectual and moral virtue as the condition for leadership. Institutionally, it meant a Christianity centered on monasteries, which people went to pursue wisdom and to live in a just community. Ideologically, it meant a Christianity which, in addition to various traditional Celtic elements, fused Jewish Christianity with Neo-Platonism. Indeed, in the Celtic regions that we find more emphasis on Jewish Christian traditions than in any other part of Christendom. At the level of legend this is represented by the old story that Joseph of Arithemea brought the Holy Grail—whatever that may have been—to the monastery at Glastonbury. More substantively it is reflected in the teachings of thinkers like Pelagius, who taught that human beings are essentially good, that we have free will, and that salvation is the result of a long process of intellectual and moral development in which the savior, Jesus, plays the role first and foremost of guide.

This was reflected in a distinctive Celtic transformation of the Byzantine Neo-Platonism of Dionysus the Areopagite. John Scotus Eriugena, an Irish theologian of the ninth century, developed a powerful metaphysics of participation in which Creation replaces Unity as the defining characteristic of the divine. John divides Nature into four parts: that which creates and is uncreated, that which is both created and creative, that which is created and does not create, and that which is neither created nor creates. By the first division he understands God, from whom all things flow. The divine nature is so profoundly ineffable that not even God can understand himself. Were he to do so, he would place himself in a limiting category, something which would contradict the definition of God as infinite or unlimited. Creation is first and foremost a theophany, God's self revelation to the intellect and the senses. The second division in John's system corresponds to the Neoplatonic intellect. It is the realm of ideas which exist, in this case, first and foremost in the Word, or the second person of the Trinity, without in any sense being identical with it. From here God's creative power overflows in the realm of number, space, and time—the physical world in which the divine essence becomes visible, however, imperfectly, to the senses. The dimness of our vision of God leads, however, to become mired in sensation, something from which we are saved only by divine grace, expressed in the institution of the Church which, by means of the sacraments transforms the things of the senses into means of salvation. We thus rise from sensation through the various degrees of intellectual perfection—John distinguishes three (*dianoia* or internal sensation, *logos* or ratiocination, and *nous* or intellection), to the unity with God for which we were predestined. It is not just humanity, though, but the whole of creation which is ultimately restored to God. When God became incarnate he took on not only humanity's intellectual soul but also its animal and vegetable souls and indeed the very elements themselves which are thus joined forever to the divine nature of which they were always, in any case, a partial expression.

Here we see joined together the optimism of the Celtic tradition with the larger framework of Neoplatonic metaphysics. Christian elements—specifically the doctrine of the Trinity and the Incarnation—are mobilized to help flesh out the system and to articulate symbolically the return of all things to God. And for the first time we see God characterized as, first and foremost, *creative activity*. The existence of the material world is not the result of some error or accident but an expression of what God *is*—of God's *is-ness*—at the very deepest level. And we have a share in that creative capacity.

Third, Catholicism appropriated an Augustinian theology which emerged in a North African context over which the Church largely lost control with the advent of Islam, and which came to mean very different things in different cultural contexts. We have already analyzed this theological trend in depth elsewhere (Mansueto 2010b). Here we merely summarize the salient points.

Augustine's theology was a complex product born of a deeply personal spiritual quest but shaped definitively by the key political-theological struggles of his time. A member of the local landed elite, just short of decurial status, Augustine was trained as a *rhetor* and attempted to live the old Hellenic civic ideal in an Empire in which that was no longer meaningfully possible. This catalyzed a profound spiritual crisis, which both set him about searching for a higher ideal and led him to scrutinize his own character. He found the higher ideal, first in Neo-Platonism, which taught him *what* human beings want (to be God) and eventually in Christianity, which taught him how (and in what measure) that might be achieved. But in the process he became deeply aware of the extent to which his quest for God was held back by attachment to lower goods, something which led him to read the letters of Paul in a way which highlighted their focus on the problem of sin, and eventually to develop a theology in which the process of *theosis* was as much a matter of overcoming sin as it was of overcoming finitude and contingency.

The results of this personal journey, which in many way traces the interrupted *cursus honorum* of the Late Empire, were shaped by two of great political-theological crises of his time: the Pelagian and Donatist controversies. The Pelagian controversy concerned the question of original sin, and it was Augustine's doctrine on this question which became, at least nominally, normative for all of Latin and Germanic Christianity, Catholic and Protestant. Augustine's initial analysis of evil, as simply the privation of the Good, is fully in accord with a Platonic metaphysics of participation. "There is no such entity in nature as "evil;" "evil" is merely a name for the privation of good (Augustine, *City of God* XI:22). "Sin, furthermore, is simply a turning from the greater, immutable to the lesser, mutable good. "This failure does not consist in defection to things which are evil in themselves; it is the defection in itself which is evil (Augustine, *City of God* XII:8). "

Thus far there is nothing in Augustine's analysis which would suggest that human failure either merits eternal damnation or results in a fundamental inability to do good. The turn comes when Augustine asks about the *cause* of sin. The straightforward answer, and the one which would be coherent with the larger Platonic background of his analysis thus far, would be that we sin because of the relative weakness of our knowledge of higher goods, and especially of God, by comparison with our knowledge of lesser goods, which seem more vivid. But Augustine rejects this option, on the basis of a very thin argument, in favor of the view that our "defection" from

God to ourselves and other creatures is a product of willful disobedience (Augustine, *City of God* XII:8).

The weakness of human nature, which prevents us from doing what is right, is not so much a direct and natural consequence of original sin, as it is a punishment for our disobedience. As a result human beings can turn away from lower and towards the Higher Good which alone can set their hearts at rest only with the assistance of divine grace.

The Donatist controversy originally concerned the relationship between Christianity and the Empire. Many North Africans refused to accept the authority of bishops who had collaborated with the imperial authorities during the last persecution under Diocletian. The movement became a rallying cry for the oppressed masses of the region, and Donatist peasants raided the estates of the wealthy, wielding large clubs and crushing the skulls of the landowners while shouting *Deo laudes!* (Praise God!). Augustine stood in a unique position with respect this struggle. As a member of the exploiting classes he was no friend of the Donatists and looked to the public authorities to maintain order. As a member of an oppressed people he rejected the empire's claim to sanctity.

This is the context in which Augustine developed the political theology which defined Western Christianity. Humanity, for Augustine, is divided into two cities, the City of God, composed of those who love God, and the City of Man, composed of those whose love was disordered, and directed towards the creature rather than the creator. Augustine was, however, able to identify a certain limited order within the city of Man. Those who love honor, he argued, are generally more disciplined, and are able to prevail over, those who love pleasure. This, he argued is the foundation both of slavery and of the state, which derive their legitimacy from the capacity of lovers of honor to raise lovers of pleasure to a higher degree of order. Neither institution, however, really participates fully in the life of God. Nor can human beings depart of their own free will from the City of Man and return to God. This is because once we have sinned we are bound in sin until freed by divine grace.

The political valence of Augustine's theology in its original context is clear. On the one hand, he strips the Empire of any pretense to holiness. Its function is simple: to maintain order. Real authority belongs to the Church. At the same time, he saves the Church from the requirement that its clergy actually be virtuous. That is quite impossible, for they are drawn like everyone else from an impossibly sinful humanity. But their authority and their sacraments are, nonetheless valid; they are a means of grace even if they are not themselves personally just. The result was a spirituality of authority and submission which could legitimate both warlord and Church without demanding too much of either.

Christianity, to be sure, did not last long in Augustine's North African home—in no small part because of his efforts. Shorn of its anti-imperial valence, Christianity could no longer hold the interest of the North African people, who welcomed the invading Arab tribes of the seventh century as liberators. Augustinian theology did prove attractive to two other groups: the Germanic warlords who were gradually establishing their sway over Europe and the emerging hierarchy of what eventually became the Roman Church.

For the Germanic warlords it provided first a kind of limited legitimation of their authority as agents of order—if only that of the City of Man, and second a metaphor of salvation as a free gift bestowed by a victorious Christ on his loyal followers—a metaphor which resonated deeply with the warrior ethos of Germanic culture. Gradually these warlords began to revive the idea of the Roman Empire as a unifying framework for European society and to create "imperialist" theories which argued that while the spiritual power descended from God to the pope and the other bishops, the temporal power descended from God to the Emperor. Emerging monarchs outside the framework of the Holy Roman Empire—such as the Norman Kings of England—did the same. Thus Anonymous of York argued that the king was superior in every way to the priest because the latter represented Jesus, human nature, while the king represented his divine nature.

The Church countered these arguments with complex reasoning of its own. The early Augustinian acknowledgement of a limited but autonomous legitimacy of secular authority gradually gave way to the view that the warlords were no better than bandits unless their authority was confirmed by the Church, something which in turn required submission to the Church. Pope Gelasius put forward the view that all authority came from God—and through the pope—who handed the sword of secular power to the various kings of Europe, but always maintained his right to withdraw it.

This struggle between the temporal and spiritual authorities culminated in the investiture controversy of the twelfth century. Reforming popes such as Gregory the VII and Innocent III fought vigorously but not always successfully to wrest from the warlords and especially from the emerging monarchs the right to name bishops and thus to have in place local religious leaders who could challenge the warlords when their rapacity exceeded customary bounds. These reform bishops were, furthermore, encouraged to build and defend an independent economic and political base so as to be less dependent on the economic favor of the ruling classes. The difficulty of course is that while this gave bishops and abbots a measure of *relational* autonomy, it did not really give them *structural* autonomy. They became, in effect, great feudal landowners themselves. There is good reason to believe that their estates were administered less brutally and that the revenues generated were used in ways which better served the community than those of most feudal lords, but the fact remains that they were *structurally* quite similar, if not identical, to secular estates.

Fourth, Catholicism drew on the recovery and elaboration of Hellenic philosophy in the context of both *Dar-al-Islam* itself and the Jewish subculture which flourished wthin it. We have already considered Islamic appropriations and transformations of the Hellenic ideal in the previous section. Here it suffice to say that Catholic appropriation of this synthesis had two principal effects. First, it provided a much more complex philosophical apparatus than existed in the Neo-Platonism which survived in the West with which to theorize the process of *theosis*. Second, it reminded Christendom of its Jewish roots, and specifically of the centrality of the struggle for justice. This served to balance both the pessimistic anthropology which emerged from the Pelagian controversy and the Byzantine and Augustinian compromises with Empire. For Catholicism the struggle for justice would become constitutive of the process of *theosis*.

Finally, as the technological and political economic innovations which followed the collapse of *Empire* began to bear fruit, Catholicism worked its distinctive synthesis. This synthesis is most apparent in the work of Thomas Aquinas. We have considered in detail elsewhere Thomas' contributions to metaphysics (Mansueto 2010b). Here we focus on his formulation of the Catholic *way*. Thomas provides a new and distinctive way of resolving the problem of salvation which is faithful to the Jewish roots of Catholicism, but shows how a fuller and more complete divinization of human beings is possible than either Judaism or Islam allowed. The key here is the concept of connatural knowledge. The basic idea is simple: that like knows like. This is the basis of the whole the Aristotelian-Thomistic theory of sensation: that human beings and other animals know material things because being material ourselves we can be affected by material objects. But Thomas develops the idea further, and suggests that it is the key to a sort of intellectual knowledge as well. For example, there is a certain sense in which someone who is just or temperate knows what justice of temperance is, even if he has studied no philosophy at all. And this is true whether the justice in question is natural—acting in accord with the natural law, seeking God and the development or our neighbors because they are the condition of our own existence and development—or supernatural: seeking God and the good of others as ends in themselves. When we act with this latter, supernatural justice, which the Thomas calls *caritas* we act with God's own justice and love and thus have a direct, nonconceptual experiential knowledge of God. It is this "caritative wisdom" which constitutes the basis of Thomistic mystical theology and which is perfected in the beatific vision. But what we are seeking when we seek God, is of course Being, and what we promote when we act for the good of others—or for that matter for our own good, is nothing other than Being as such. This is, in effect, a philosophical and theological elaboration of the Jewish concept of *da'ath 'elohim*. Generally translated "knowledge of God," the prophets continually placed *da'ath 'elohim* in poetic parallelism with phrases denoting justice and ethical conduct (see, for example, Hosea 4:1-2, 6:3), something which essentially equates them (Thomas, *Summa Theologiae* II, Q 45, a2; Maritain 1937).

This, in turn, allows Thomas—without in any way diminishing the glory of the human intellect as our highest natural participation in the life of God, to overcome the hyper-intellectualism of the Islamic *falasafa* which seemed perpetually on the verge of denying any sort of salvation to those who are not philosophers. As we noted above, the closest we can come to a doctrine of salvation in ibn Rusd is identification of the potential intellect with the Agent Intellect—i.e. knowledge of the lowest of the angels. And this is something which comes about exclusively through philosophical study. Ibn Sina suggests something similar, but late in life elaborated an esoteric "oriental philosophy" which suggested the possibility of more, but again only for a select few who, *after* philosophical preparation, receive divine illumination. Thomas allows acquired philosophical and theological wisdom their rightful place. Only conceptual knowledge can be the basis for public discourse and thus leadership *in foro externo*. But it is quite possible to be illiterate and still be wise, in the sense of knowing God by means of the still higher caritative wisdom, the wisdom which even the philosopher and theologian need for salvation. Mystical theology is saved from esotericism and the elaboration of baroque theosophical landscapes, and made fully accessible to all who act justly.

Thomas' doctrine also allows him to speak meaningfully of the doctrine of the Incarnation without slipping into philosophical nonsense or theological absurdity. On the one hand, Thomas is quite clear that God cannot *become* flesh, for the simple reason that God, Being as such, is absolutely changeless, outside space and time. What Christians call the incarnation represents a change on the part of *humanity* which becomes joined to God in a qualitatively new way (Thomas Aquinas, *Summa Theologiae* III:1:1a2). While Thomas does not spell out the details—nor could he, for fear or reprisals from a hierarchy already turning away from his Aristotelian approach—this new way is just precisely that of caritative wisdom. The story of Jesus is an apt imaginative account of this joining precisely because of its ordinariness. Jesus was not a great philosopher or even a great prophet. He was not a priest and he was not a (successful) liberating king. All he did was to fulfill the law, consistently, to the very end. He represents Israel's fidelity to the covenants, a fidelity which, as was already painfully clear in Jesus time, was not ordered to Israel but to the development of humanity as a whole. And his resurrection represents God's vindication of Israel, God's promise that by acting beyond the demands of merely natural justice, by losing ourselves in the pursuit of Being, we do not perish but *become*, in ways we could not imagine, gradually growing towards God.

This distinctively Catholic *way* was at once a reflex of and served to reinforce the distinctive civilizational pattern which was emerging in Christendom. The advances in agricultural technology had made *materially* possible a flourishing of human civilization unprecedented in the region. On the other hand, the peculiar tension between the spiritual and temporal lords had created a social space in which that civilization could flourish: the autonomous chartered city. These cities, most often chartered by Bishops, but occasionally chartered by the Emperor or some other temporal lord, became centers in which ordinary human beings cultivated excellence in *techne*, in making—and thus in their a new sort of connaturality with God. This created a basis in experience for humanity to understand the possibilities of its autonomous participation in Being, quite apart from anything the Church might add and quite apart from the need for any sort of "baptism." At the same time, the presence of the Church—and especially of the monastic communities and later on the mendicant orders as distinctive communities within the larger human city pointed towards a still higher degree of participation in the life of God, one which was not in contradiction with, but rather completed that provided by ordinary labor and human civilizational progress. That is why, as the mendicant orders emerged, thousands if not millions of merchants, artisans, and peasants sought to participate in their ministry through third orders which recognized fully the sanctity of the lay state and sought to unlock the hidden potential of an authentically lay spirituality. But this remained an ideal and an attractor, not something that could be imposed or required. Where Islam could only wrestle with the problem of how best to "require good and prohibit evil," creating a just social order dedicated to civilizational progress, promising the masses a kind of earthly paradise and the philosophical elite a sort of mystical union not with God but with the least of his Angels, Christendom imagined a civilizational progress completed in full and complete enjoyment of God: the very divinization of humanity.

Thomas himself was a systematic rather than a mystical theologian, and never fully worked out what such a divinization would look like, and what its implications were for our life in this world. That task fell instead to a fellow Dominican, John Meister Eckhart,[1] who extended Thomas's ideas in important ways. Partly this was simply a question of drawing out more fully the implication of the insight, already implicit in ibn Sina, and Thomas, that God is Being as Such. If this is true, then our own being is in fact God's and we are, implicitly, already divine, not, to be sure, in *essence*, since our specifically human nature and individual characteristics represent a limitation if also the specific mode of our participation in the life of God, but in a way which is much more profound: the very fact that we are. This formulation clarifies considerably the proper term of human spiritual development, which is to know ourselves in and as God.

Second, however, unlike otherwise similar doctrines such as *advaida vedanta*, which regards everything as identical with *Brahman*, or the Higher Mahayana and Vajrayana schools, which regard everything as an expression of the already fully enlightened Buddha-Nature, but treat the world as illusion or covering over, the universe is understood by Eckhart to be an overflowing of God's creative power, the same overflowing which gives rise to the emanation of the persons of the Trinity from the Godhead. Eckhart is thus able to recover in the context of a metaphysics which "completes" the *way of the search for Being* the Jewish affirmation of the goodness of creation. Indeed, he goes much further than the kabbalists, who teach a similar doctrine of the universe as the overflowing of God, but one that went horribly awry at the metaphysical levels, "breaking the vessels" into which the divine power of Being flowed and leaving universe in a shambles. Eckhart's universe, while not by any means unmarred by sin and injustice, is far from being an illusion, a covering over, or sort of technical error in the creative process. Indeed, he qualifies the Thomistic insistence, technically correct in the language of Aristotelian metaphysics, that our human nature and specific individual characteristics constitutes "limitations" on our participation in Being as such, and suggests that we think of them instead as God expressing Herself in particular ways.

Finally, while clearly a teacher of contemplative practice and properly spiritual disciplines, Eckhart fully values these practices and disciplines without making them the driver of our spiritual progress. On the contrary, against those Buddhists who would argue that if we are to really be useful to anyone else we must first become a fully enlightened Buddha, and that any good works done before that are primarily merit making and a

---

1. For an in-depth consideration of Eckhardt's metaphysics, including its similarities to and differences from *Advaita Vedanta*, see Kelly 2010. For a discussion of the relationship between his teachings and Buddhist (primarily Zen) practice, see Merton 1968.

preparation for the hard work of meditation and yogic or tantric practice, Eckhart stresses that the struggle for justice—and even the simple demands of meeting the daily needs of our fellow human beings—takes priority over such practice. Indeed, what we meditate *on* even in the highest degrees of contemplation which are utterly beyond both image and concept and therefore beyond any memory of a specific act, is precisely that activity of doing justice, the activity which *is* God.

* * *

It would, in most Christian theologies, at this point be customary to consider the variants of the Christian way which emerged from the Reformation, even if those variants were then subjected to criticism. And it may, in fact, seem offensive to some that we do not. But it must be remember that at this point in our argument we are still considering the specifically *axial* ways of being human and the syncretisms between them which developed during the great Silk Road Era. It is central to our argument that Protestantism is not an axial but rather a secular *way*, centered, as Weber demonstrates (Weber 1920/1968) on innerworldly activity. So by not considering Protestantism here we are not claiming that it is not Christian, but rather that the division of *ways* by genealogy is less useful for our current argument than a division by metacivilizational project. It is for the same reason, that where in our previous works we treated the dialectical tradition, axial and secular with an emphasis on continuity here, without repudiating our earlier claims regarding that continuity, we emphasize the rupture constituted by the turn from a metaphysics of participation to a univocity of immanence.

At this point what remains is, simply to extract, summarize, and draw out the implications of what we have already said regarding the historic lessons of the *way of liberation and justice* and what a synthesis of its diverse variants might look like, a synthesis which, because Christianity stands between the *way of the search for Being* and the *way of justice and liberation*, already goes quite a bit of the way towards being a synthesis of the axial *ways* themselves.

We have already suggested that among historical representatives of this *way* prior to the advent of the secular ways, Eckhart remains the most advanced. Specifically, he at once fully develops the analogical metaphysics of *Esse* in a way which specifies the *telos* towards which humanity is ordered: Being as such, and shows how, in a very real sense, we are always and already this creative power and simply come to know it through struggle for justice and engaging in the contemplative practice which harvests the lessons of this practice. Later mystical theologians, especially in the Carmelite tradition, developed further insights into the spiritual side of these lessons—the doctrine of the dark nights of the soul—but Eckhart remains more advanced in his specification of our end not simply as mystical union but as knowing ourselves in and as God.

While Eckhart is already quite clear that this does not in any sense imply a substantive divinity, our engagement with Buddhism suggests ways in which this danger can be further averted and a deeper understanding of Being achieved. Specifically, the doctrine of dependent origination reminds us that Being cannot be substance or impassive self-subsistance, but rather pure generativity and that the desire to be God can be realized only when we cease to understand Being as that which preserves us from change and disintegration. To use Eckhart's words, as long as we love God the way we love a cow, we will be as disappointed in God as we are in created things and would be as disappointed were we somehow able to cheat logic and metaphysics and actually become that God. Being God means giving not receiving, creating, not clinging.

This said, while we have in a certain sense delivered a verdict in favor of the Christian as opposed to the Jewish or Muslim variants of the *way of justice and liberation*, our engagement with them contains important lessons. First, a correct understanding of what is unique and powerful within Christianity begins with a rejection of the claim that Jesus is the Jewish Messiah. Clearly his disciples thought he was. He might have thought he was. He might even have been a "legitimate" Davidic claimant to the throne of Israel, whatever that means. There were undoubtedly many. But Christianity as much as Judaism (even if neither are fully willing to recognize this) represents a stretching beyond messianism. Judaism—understood as rabbinic Judaism and its descendants—is based on an abandonment of the messianic project as hopeless and destructive. Christianity embraces messianism not because it believes it has or ever can succeed, but precisely in its defeat, which stretches us beyond humanity towards our true end, which is God.

This has further implications for any possible affirmation of the doctrine of the incarnation, which while perhaps less offensive to Jews than the claim that Jesus is their messiah, nonetheless appears to Jews and Muslims alike as idolatrous. This is because, if we understand the incarnation to mean that Jesus of Nazareth was in fact divine in essence, it *is* idolatry, as well as a metaphysical impossibility. But the truth is that most Christians who believe this version of the doctrine of the incarnation can do so only because they lack an adequate understanding of God, something of which Judaism and Islam, in both their prophetic and philosophical forms, remind us. Others, perhaps, affirm it precisely because it is absurd and a scandal "to Jew and Gentile alike."

Any correct understanding of the incarnation must begin with the concept of connaturality with God in the just act as something added accidentally to our human nature. It also, frankly, requires the revised doctrine of Being which, while implicit, I believe, in historic Christian negative theologies, becomes much clearer when we are able to draw on the Buddhist critique of the idea of inherent existence and their teaching of dependent origination. When we say that Jesus was in fact truly God as well as truly human we are saying something about God and about humanity as much or more than we are saying something either literal or figurative and symbolic about the historic Jesus of Nazareth. Specifically we are saying that what *most* makes God *divine* is *not* the necessity of divine Being as such, and therefore its exemption from suffering and change, which is something we cannot share and which can be affirmed of Jesus only at the expense of docetism, but rather Her limitless generativity and self-giving, which we *can* share, in gradually progressing degrees, as the struggle for justice stretches us towards and beyond full humanity, gradually making us more and more divine.

Beyond this it is also important to note that Judaism and Islam both serve as important reminders that the Christian focus on the spiritual fruits of the struggle for justice came at the expense of an effective abandonment of that struggle which is nothing short of shameful. The fact that the struggle for justice leads to the cross and beyond that to *theosis* is no excuse for abandoning that struggle, much less for legitimating *Empire*. Between them, Judaism and Islam also pose some challenging questions regarding just how to return to the active struggle for justice which, if they were unable to answer them, also remain unsolved by secular movements, such as socialism, which later took up that struggle. Do we, like the Jews, argue that there is no authority beyond a good argument? Certainly this protects us from the terror committed over the course of 150 years by history's most powerful attempt to build a just society. But it may also condemn us to political irrelevance. Or do we insist that doing justice requires an effective political-military leadership and a compact, disciplined organization, even if this leadership is less than perfect spiritually—the *Sunni* way? Can justice and power be authentically joined as the Shia generally claim they will be when the Imam emerges from occultation and as the Islmaili tradition (however modestly and cautiously) claims it already is in the living Imam of the age?

These are questions to which we prefer to offer answers only after we have considered the humanistic secular ways, which have also had to confront them. For now it is enough to insist that Christians return to the active struggle for justice as the condition of any possible spiritual growth and avoid formulations of their way which risk legitimating Empire.

With that said, we turn to the final axial way, the Chinese *way of harmony*.

5

The Way of Harmony

The third and final of the great axial *ways*—the *way of harmony*—is, in many ways the most conservative with respect to both its aims and its relationship to the primal and sacral monarchic projects against the background of which it emerged. On the one hand, it is in China that our claim that *humanity is the desire to be God* is, perhaps, most challenging to sustain. Only in the Higher Mahayana and Vajrayana Schools of Buddhism do we see anything like an attempt at *theosis* and then only in the distinctively Buddhist way which rejects inherent existence and thus strict divinity in favor of an enlightened embrace of dependent origination which is, to be sure, every bit as omniscient, omnipotent, and generative as the divine, but only on the basis of rejecting any claim at self-existence whatsoever. On the other hand, while the Chinese tradition is, like all of the other axial traditions, based on a critique of an (especially oppressive) sacral monarchy (the Shang Dynasty), China never fully rejected sacral monarchy as a cultural form, and instead chooses to reform and rationalize it. Finally, China represents one of humanity's two most powerful preindustrial experiences with the *Saeculum*, and specifically with *Empire* (the other being Rome), understood as a *way of being human* which is focused exclusively on innerworldly civilizational progress, with out any regard for the transhistorical or transcendental ordering of human existence, supported by an attempt to fully mobilize effectively all material and social resources in service to the *Saeculum*. This experience is brief, to be sure, in strict terms confined to the Qin dynasty, but the *way of harmony,* especially in its Confucian manifestations, tended to accommodate itself to this pattern, making it a defining influence on all of the Chinese *ways*—and indeed on the distinctively Chinese experience of the third, industrial capitalist and socialist iteration of the *Saeculum*.

Let us now explore the results of this distinctive civilizational path.

The Axial Age in China

The Axial Age in China was shaped, as in Israel, by the emergence, during the Bronze Age collapse, of a new *way* which challenged the dominant sacral monarchic structure and ordering of human society, but which remained, in certain aspects, pre-axial, in the sense that it preceeded the full flowering of religious problematization, rationalization, and democratization. Late Bronze Age China was ruled by the Shang or Yin dynasty (1600–1046 BCE), which was an especially exploitative sacral monarchy known for its practice of human sacrifice. It was overthrown towards the very end of the Late Bronze Age by the Zhou, who were originally a subject people and threw off the Shang yoke to become the new masters of China. Perhaps as a result of their experience as an oppressed people, the Zhou developed the view that effective and enduring rule depends on what they called the *tian-ming* or the Mandate of Heaven. Those who rule in a way which serves the common good obtain and keep this mandate; tyrants and oppressors do not. At the very center of the Zhou ethos was a land tenure system designed to extract sufficient surplus to support urban civilization, while limiting the rate of exploitation. Land in each village was divided into nine equal plots, eight private and one public, so that the peasants in effect contributed only 1/9 of their total product to support the ruling classes (*Zhou-li* in Nylan 2001).

At the same time, as in the case of the earliest traditions of Israel, we see only limited movement in the direction of a rational metaphysics or authentic religious democratization. The impersonal *Tian* (Heaven) replaced the anthropomorphic *Shang-di* (Lord on High) as the first principle and the object of the highest cult, but at no point did *Tian* become a *concept*. And there is even less evidence than in Israel or religious problematization (competing cults operating in a pluralistic public arena) or democratization (the extension of religious leadership beyond priestly lineages. And where earliest Israel rejected sacral monarchy and re-embraced it only grudgingly and as a geopolitical-military necessity, China chose instead to reform it and make it contingent on just governance.

In 722 BCE Zhou authority effectively collapsed, setting in motion a period of political fragmentation and warfare known as the Spring and Autumn and Warring States periods. This coincided roughly with the emergence of petty commodity production, which developed rather quickly in China which eventually emerged as one of the principal anchors of the Silk Road economy, exporting not only silk, but eventually porcelain, tea, and other commodities.

As elsewhere, one response to these developments was emergence of a skeptical and pragmatic trend—Legalism—which argued that order and progress depended on the development of a strong state. Some Legalists stressed the role of coercion in building a strong state, others the role of law, but all denied the existence of transcendental first principles and all upheld and essentially relativistic ethics (Collins 1998:148–53).

The other principal axial trends represent a reaction against this sort of skeptical relativism. Mo Tzi reintroduced the idea of a personal creator God who demanded of humanity an ethic of *bo ai*—universal love. Later Mohists moved in a more naturalistic direction, developing empirical and mathematical methods in the sciences (Collins 1998: 138–43). These developments were not unlike the simultaneous movement in Hesiod to emphasize the cult of Zeus as a god of justice, while naturalizing the other gods.

What the Confucian and Taoist traditions share is a common conviction that the universe is governed by a lawful *way*, the *Tao*, departure from which, through conquest and exploitation, has created inhospitable conditions for human development. Where these traditions differ is primarily with respect to the question of whether or not the *Tao* or the *Tian-ming* can be adequately articulated linguistically, comprehended conceptually, and embodied institutionally. The Confucian tradition answers that, by and large, it can. By means of careful "investigation of things" we can come to understand the *Tao* or *way* which governs them and which is conducive to their growth and development. This, in turn points us to *Tian* or Heaven which is the source and end of all things. "What Heaven imparts to man is called human nature. To follow our nature is called the Way. Cultivating the Way is called education. The Way cannot be separated from us for a moment. (*Chung Yung*). "

Confucius identified five virtues: *zhi* (wisdom), *li* (propriety or religion) *ren* (benevolence), *xin* (fidelity), and *yi* (justice). The main burden of cultivating wisdom is on the ruler, who must authentically be superior to those he would claim to rule. The *zhi, jen* and *yi* of the ruler together lead to the *xin* of the subjects and thus ensure social harmony. *Li,* or religion, plays a critical mediating role. By participating in the ancient rituals, the principal relationships which defined the social order were rectified and maintained, and thus brought into harmony with the larger order of the cosmos (*Li Ki* XXVII, in Lin Yu-tang 1938).

Confucius, like the Israelite prophets and the Hellenic dialecticians wants, in effect, to restore the archaic order undermined by the rise of the warlord state and of petty commodity production, but to do so on the basis of a rationalized understanding of the meanings behind and the social functions carried out by myth and ritual. The resulting system was hierarchical, making distinctions between the sage, the superior man, and the ordinary man, but its nobility was one of merit, not of birth (Confucius, *Lun-yu* IV:

15; VIII: 2,7; XIII:20; XVI: 8), and the task of the sage and the superior man was to promote the growth and development of the ordinary people. To this end, Confucius rejected the Legalist emphasis on force in favor of a strategy centered on rule by virtue (Confucius. *Analects* II.3)

Taoism shared with the Confucian tradition the conviction that the universe is governed by a first principle, but rejects the Confucian claim that this first principle can be articulated adequately in language or embodied in social institutions such as a sacral monarchy and scholar-bureaucracy or religious rituals. "The Tao that can be trodden is not the enduring and unchanging Tao. The name that can be named is not the enduring and unchanging name. Conceived of as without name, it is the Originator of Heaven and of Earth. Conceived of as having a name it is the Mother of All Things. (*Tao te ching* 1)"

Like the Confucian tradition, Taoism has a deep concern for social justice.

> Why are the people starving?
>
> Because the rulers eat up the money in taxes.
>
> Therefore the people are starving.
>
> Why are the people rebellious?
>
> Because the rulers interfere too much.
>
> Therefore they are rebellious (*Tao Te Ching* 75).

The emergence of a warrior aristocracy, which invested the surplus product in military conquests rather than in raising agricultural productivity, and of petty commodity production, which makes the generation of surplus a means of private profit, mark the departure of Chinese society from its natural course of development, its deviation from the *Tao*.

> When the Tao is present in the universe
>
> The horses haul manure.
>
> When the Tao is absent from the universe
>
> Warhorses are bred outside the city (*Tao Te Ching*: Forty-Six).

Taoist monasteries cultivated the martial arts as well as scholarship and meditation, and at certain points in Chinese history became centers of political-military resistance to the Empire (Deng Ming-Dao 1990: 13). The Taoist masters of Huainan were actively engaged in the process of reconstruction which followed the end of the period of Warring States (Cleary 1990: vii). The Taoist tradition in effect counsels a return to the communitarian norms of pre-tributary China which, they believed, represented a natural and healthy pattern of social development.

We have in the *way of harmony*, in other words, a common aim—restoring humanity's harmony with the *Tao*—and two very different approaches to realizing that aim. One attempts to reform the sacral monarchic way, redefining the sacred—and nobility—in terms of authentic virtue, and attempting to build a system of institutions which actually promote the full development of human capacities. The other—at least in its more radical form—regards not only sacral monarchy but perhaps human civilization, or at least urban civilization, as fundamentally a mistake. Harmony can be restored only by a radical simplification of life which reduces the level of surplus extraction and abandons complex institution building in favor of what amounts to village level organization informed by the wisdom of what amount to literate shamans who promote physical and spiritual health.

We need now to see how these two traditions interacted with each other. But that interaction was also shaped very profoundly by the Legalist tradition which was actually dominant in China, and by the growing influence of Buddhism on Chinese civilization. The first of these factors we will consider in some detail. The second we will discuss in a more limited way, since we have already discussed Buddhism in an earlier chapter. More specifically, we will focus on the ways in which interaction with Legalism and Buddhism shaped the Confucian and Taoist traditions and contributed to the eventual formation of a synthetic *way of harmony*: the *dao xue*.

Nalanda and Xian

The Chinese *Saeculum*

The First Empire

It is commonplace today to describe China as a "Confucian" society and to ascribe its legendary traditions of bureaucracy and meritocracy (as well as its disregard for individual liberties) to this Confucian heritage. The truth is, however, that neither the Confucian nor the Taoist tradition emerged from the Axial Age really dominant. The upper hand, rather, belonged to the Legalists, who came to power under the First Emperor and his Qin Dynasty, and who laid the foundation for a bureaucratic and meritocratic state structure which, while certainly modified and reformed by Confucian influence in later dynasties, remains the defining structural feature of Chinese society and the anchor of Chinese secularity (Gernet 1985, Fukyuama 2011, Bell 2015).

The early years of the Silk Road were a period of rapid technological progress for China, in a way that they were not in the West. This meant, first of all, improvements in agriculture, with the growing practice of crop rotation, and the increased production of soy, which helped restore depleted soils. We also see increased reliance on animal power, with the development of the ox-drawn plow, better methods of harnessing horses, a cart with two shafts, and the cultivation of Lucerne as fodder for horses. This is a sort of agrarian pattern that did not become widespread in Europe until the second half of the first millennium of the common era. But Qin and Han China was by no means exclusively agrarian. This was, among other things, the time when the Chinese made major improvements in the production of cast iron and developed a kind of steel technology. Indeed, there is some evidence that by the Qin or Han periods, iron and steel were, along with salt, China's most important nonagricultural economic products (Gernet 1985: 139–40)! Trade in silk, lacquer ware, and copper remained important (Gernet 1985: 139–41).

The Qin Empire was founded on an act of conquest by a state—the Qin—which was guided from the beginning by a Legalist ideology (Gernet 1985: 103–8). The first aim of this state was to break the old aristocratic families which had dominated China during the Warring States Period and found itself on the direct support—and control—of small peasant communities. The idea was to take the dependents of the old noble families and to transform them into free solider peasants directly dependent on the state—a goal which was to be pursued by many Chinese dynasties up through the Maoist era (Gernet 1985: 81). Old states and aristocratic domains were broken up and reorganized into 36 commanderies. A universal system of ranks was established, as well as standards for reward and punishment, promotion and demotion, based on service to the state. Everything imaginable was standardized: coins, weights and measures, characters, even the gauge of cart wheels. Old walls defining and defending historic states were torn down and a new wall built to protect a now unified China from the steppe, while an attempt was made to link China together internally with a system of roads and canals Gernet 1985: 103–8).

The Legalist empire had no use for knowledge which lacked an obvious practical application—or for wisdom which might challenge the authority or constrain the freedom of the Emperor. All books other than treatises on medicine, agriculture and divination were burned in 213 BCE and over 400 opponents of the dynasty were executed at Xien-yang. There were, no doubt, many Confucians among them (Gernet 1985: 109).

The Legalism which guided the Qin derived from the work of Xunzi (313–238 BCE) and his student Han Fei (280–233). Xunzi had been trained in the *ru xue* but understood the first principle in a radically naturalistic way and argued that, contrary to the teachings of Confucius himself and of Mencius, human beings are fundamentally selfish in character, though they can be restrained and cultivated through education and ritual (Yao 2000: 76–80). Han Fei took these teachings much further; he adopted a nominalist theory of knowledge and an extreme naturalism in cosmology and metaphysics. The world was, for Han Fei as for the Greek atomists and Epicureans and the Indian Caravakas, essentially just the play of material forces. Human beings are motivated by greed and the aim of politics is to satisfy that desire as much as possible by enriching the state (*fuo-kuo*). The state must be based on military might (*ch'iang-ping*), and must affect human beings by means of a system of rewards and punishments rather than relying on education and ritual to cultivate virtue. This said, the system of laws must be objective and impersonal and there is a sense in Han Fei, unlike some of the more radical Legalists, that they reflect natural laws understood in a materialistic sense. This doctrine, not surprisingly, found favor among the emerging class of great merchants, many of whom served as key advisors to the emperor under the Qin dynasty (Gernet 1985: 79, 90-93, 204-206, Collins 1998: 148-55).

This is, as we suggested earlier, one of humanity's most intense experiences before the Industrial Revolution of *Saeculum* and specifically of Empire. In many ways, it is even more intense than the Roman experience, which at least nominally understood itself as a means of supporting spiritual and civilizational idea—the Hellenic ideal of life as a free human being and engaged citizen—which it recognized as higher than itself. While China clearly never *fully* embraced the Qin project, something which is documented by the speed with which the Qin were overthrown, the First Emperor is still venerated and much of the what the West calls Confucian "collectivism" is actually a legacy of the Legalists and the Imperial apparatus they established, the basic form of which persists not only through the Silk Road Era but also under socialism, even if it is nominally or actually subordinated to a higher end.

China Between Sanctuary and *Saeculum*

Qin oppression lead to resistance across a broad spectrum of social strata—peasants, scholars and old nobility. This led ultimately to a rebellion led by Liu Pang, a minor Qin official of peasant origin who succeeded in 206 BCE in establishment of first the first Han Dynasty. The Early Han maintained much of the Legalist structure, including the ranking of essentially the entire population along a scale of 24 degrees of dignity, the system of rewards and punishments based on service, the organization of the country into centrally defined commandries and prefectures, and in general the policy of breaking down human communities into smallest possible units, moving large numbers of people, to wherever they could be used most effectively. The Han further undercut the aristocracy by eliminating primogeniture so that aristocratic domains would become subdivided and impoverished and limited rights of princes to the ability to tax grain in a certain territory (Gernet 1985: 110–16).

What changed is the civilizational ideal which these structures were increasingly mobilized to serve. It was under the early Han that we begin to see both the reassertion of the tradition of *ru xue*, now increasingly in synthesis with ideas from the *tao xue*, and the emergence of a more purely Taoist opposition.

The strategy on the Confucian side was simple. Even under the Qin there had been room for engaging the Emperor on the basis of materialistic arguments deriving from the five elements school and the yin-yang school, which argued that political events as well as physical and biological process were governed by the law-like behavior of material forces. It was also possible to engage him on by using ancient divination texts—texts which made reference to such core metaphysical concepts as T'ien (Heaven) and K'un (earth) and the Tao. Resurgent *ru xue* drew on these texts to set cosmology and politics—and thus imperial policy—in a broader metaphysical and thus moral context (Gernet 1985: 158). This was reflected at the religious level by the re-establishment of the core Confucian cult of Heaven (Collins 1998: 154).

An early stage in this process is reflected in the work of Tsou Yen (305–240) (Collins 1998: 153), who rationalizes divination by using the five elements theory as a cosmology and argues that the rise and fall of political power is governed by a natural succession of the five elements, in the order of earth, wood, metal, fire, and water (Gernet 1985: 158). Tung Chung-shu (179–104 BCE) (Collins 1985: 155, Yao 2000: 83, 88) made the link to *ru xue* explicit by treating the five agents as "ministers" or "sons" of Heaven, resulting in a fully moralized cosmology and sociology.

The precise political impact of these ideas is hard to gauge, but we know that they were influential in the later Han period and that this was a period characterized by *both* continued centralization *and* by a growing commitment to social justice and civilizational progress. Thus the great reformer Wang Ming (9–23), founder of the short-lived Xin Dynasty, systematically nationalized estates and slaves and attempted to reorganize agriculture on the basis of the Zhou-li. Unfortunately these reforms were never fully implemented and when the Han Dynasty was restored in 23

CE it relied for support on the large landowning families of Honan and allowed the emergence of an agrarian structure characterized by growing inequality, coupled with an increasingly specialized craft and mercantile sector centered on the production of salt, iron, silk, and local specialties such as lacquer ware, controlled by a mixture of private merchants and state monopolies (Gernet 1985: 149–57).

The failure of the centralizing reform strategies of the Confucians in turn created room for a more radical opposition inspired by ideas which are now generally regarded as Taoist, though the term is probably a bit anachronistic. Especially characteristic in this regard are the ideas reflected in the *Huainanzi*, which eventually inspired a rebellion led by the prince of Huainan in 122, which was put down, interestingly enough, by a disciple of Tung Chung-shu (Collins 1998: 157).

It is in this period that the principal metaphysical difference between *ru xue* and *tao xue* begins to emerge. Confucians generally opt for a positive understanding of the first principle, though they may understand this principle in more idealistic or more materialistic terms. Taoists on the on other hand, focus on the concept of *wu wei* or nonbeing, as a way of capturing the ineffability of the first principle and thus the impossibility of deriving definite moral principles and political norms from it.

> Vacuity gave rise to Tao, which gave rise to space and time, which in turn gave rise to material force, and then to the manifestations of the material universe. There was a time before yin and yang, Heaven and Earth, and even before non-being . . . (Collins 1998: 157).

This metaphysical doctrine implied a distinct approach to social justice centered on allowing things to follow their natural path of development, as against the centralizing reformism of the Han Confucians.

> The basic task of government is to make the populace secure. The security of the populace is based on meeting needs. The basis of meeting needs is in not depriving people of their time. The basis of not depriving people of their time is in minimizing government exactions and expenditures. The basis of minimizing government exactions and expenditures is moderation of desire. The basis of moderating desire is in returning to essential nature (The Masters of Huainan in Cleary 1990: 3–4).

The Taoist strategy was defeated, for the time being, by the victorious Han, but in the long run it had two effects. First, it paved the way for the Chinese reception of Buddhism, which radicalized the emphasis on nonbeing or emptiness and, even when it enjoyed imperial sponsorship, tended to favor development of a decentralized, monastery based social structure. Second, as China's economy center of gravity shifted from the North and West, with its wheat based agriculture, to the South and East with its wet rice cultivation, which required a higher level of investment in the land and thus tended to foster a stronger sense of ownership, this decentralizing impulse would begin to assert influence even in the Confucian camp, leading to resistance to centralizing reforms under the Song Dynasty.

We have traced out this process in greater detail elsewhere (Mansueto 201b). Here we merely summarize. The collapse of the Han dynasty was followed by a period of disunity. In the North, we witness at one and the same time, the emergence of a series of dynasties of nomadic origin and the large—scale settlement and sinicization of the nomadic peoples of the Northwest. This was also a period of intense debate between the *tao xue* and the *ru xue*, and perhaps the only period in Chinese history during which the former was dominant.

Of the various Taoist trends during this period, the most important was the Dark or Mysterious Learning (*xuan xue*), which became the focus of metaphysical speculations which essentially drove the future development of Chinese philosophy. The school was founded by Wei state officials, Ho Yun (d. 249) and Wang Pi (226–49). They took as their starting point the synthesis of yin-yang and five elements cosmology with Taoist ontology which had been formulated, for the Confucian side, by Tung Chung-shu (Collins 1998:171), but focused attention on the relationship between *wu* and *you*, nonbeing and being, emphasizing, for the most part, the priority of *wu* over *you* and developing much of the philosophical vocabulary in terms of which later debates were conducted, including the distinctions between substance (*ti*) and function (*yong*), one (*yi*) and many (*duo*), nature (*xing*) and emotion (*qing*), principle (*li*) and material force (*qi*) (Gernet 1985: 206, Yao: 2000: 89-90). The *ru xue*, for its part, resisted by developing for the first time in Chinese history a coherent doctrine of Being, represented by Pei Wei's (267–300) critically important treatise, the *chong you lun* or *Justification of Being*, which "argues that nature (*ziran*) is what is so (*ran*) by itself (*zi*) and that Nature is in "being" rather than nonbeing because nonbeing cannot create by itself (Yao 2000: 93–95).

This was also the period during which Buddhism penetrated Chinese culture, carried first and foremost by merchants who came first by land and then by sea, and later by pilgrims, who journeyed to India seeking manuscripts and studying at the great Buddhist centers such as Nalanda before returning home to undertake the work of translation and acculturation. In the North Buddhism was largely dependent on state sponsorship. Non-Han kings such as Shi Hu 334–349 invited Buddhist monks to court and eventually began endowing large monasteries. In the South, on the other hand, support came from the landed aristocracy who also began to endow monasteries which modeled themselves on large aristocratic estates (Gernet 1985: 220–221).

It was in this context that an increasingly sophisticated and distinctively Chinese Buddhism emerged. Paul Williams points out that the foundational development in this regard was the transformation of the concept of the *tathagatagarbha*, which in Indian and Tibetan Buddhism had been a soteriological idea, into the basis of a cosmological and metaphysical theory (Williams 1989: 109).

There were many variants of this philosophically sophisticated monastic Buddhism. The Tien Tai school, so called for its mountain home, argued for the centrality of the *Saddharmapundarkia* (Lotus) Sutra as the most complete revelation of *dharma*. Using the technique of *p'an chiao*, in which the teachings of various Buddhist schools are ranked in terms of their relative completeness, with the lower ranked schools treated as skillful means (*upayakausalya*), teachings directed at the less developed, The Tien Tai school essentially argued away centuries of Buddhist focus on emptiness as a way of helping the less developed get past their attachment to phenomena in order to prepare them for a future as advanced Bodhisattvas or fully developed Buddhas engaged in the work of "ripening being." They taught a complex cosmology of ten worlds, including numerous heavens and hells, as well as the persistence of Buddhas as agents for the cultivation of enlightenment, distinguishing between the eternal, cosmic Buddha and his various manifestations.

The Hua-yen (Collins 1998: 286) carried this process even further. Tsung-mi, whose *Treatise on the Origin of Humanity* is, perhaps, the most complete statement of the Hua-yen position, effectively rejects Madhyamika and Yogacara doctrine in favor of something new and distinct. Here it is neither emptiness or pure mind which defines the *tathagatagharba* but rather its underlying capacity for full enlightenment, which is clouded over by the illusion of inherent existence, giving rise to *samsara*. Once this illusion is overcome, the generative world building activity which defines the *tathagatagarbha* emerges in its true light: as the capacity to build an infinity of worlds each of which ripens the beings that inhabit it, cultivating their capacities, and leading them towards full enlightenment. What we have here, of course, is a Buddhism which has absorbed the cosmological and institutional generativity of the Confucian tradition—and the basis for a Confucianism which has an authentic answer to humanity's quest for *theosis*.

The Song Synthesis

This latter possibility was worked out largely in the context of the Song Dynasty. The new empire which grew up as China recovered from the crisis of the Tang system was radically different from its predecessors. Where the Tang Empire had been a relatively decentralized agrarian and aristocratic structure in which most of the progressive potential was lodged in the great monasteries, the Song Empire was commercial, democratic, and centralized—and effectively controlled by its Confucian intelligentsia.

This new system was made possible by a number of key technological developments. It is during this period that we witness the rapid expansion of wet rice cultivation throughout the South, making what had once been a hinterland the economic center of China, as well as the spread of such commercial crops as silk, hemp, cotton, and tea, (Gernet 1985: 319–320). We also see a massive development of complex handicrafts, including the emergence of large workshops in essentially all of the traditional areas of craft production (Gernet 1985: 320–322).

The underlying tendency towards latifundialization and towards the erosion of patriarchal relationships and their replacement by purely commercial forms of tenancy, which naturally accompanied the development of petty commodity relations, continued. We know that this was the case because only peasants, not large landowners, were taxed and only 30% of a total of 24 hectares of arable land was taxable in 1064-7 (Gernet 1985: 312–16).

There were a number of attempts to reform this system, the most important of which were the reforms of Wang An-shih (1069-1076), who proposed taxing landlords, imposing price controls, extending low cost credit to small farmers, and reforming the system of exams to include engineering and science instead of just the literary classics (Gernet 1985: 305–9, Collins 1998: 301–2) Somewhat later Chia Ssu-tao (1213–1275) tried to limit land ownership to 500 mu (about 27 hectares) and have the state buy 1/3 of the surplus to support the armies (Gernet 1985: 315).

The Song political structure represented a substantial rationalization and democratization of the imperial system. The Emperor presided over, ratified, and if necessary resolved differences in the Council of State but did not have and did not claim autocratic power. Policy was developed by the *xue-shih-yuan* or Court of Academicians who drew up documents based on consultation with broad ranks of the civil service and, through them, with the people. Appointment to and promotion within the civil service was based, at least nominally, on scholarship, though political considerations certainly also played a significant role (Gernet 1985: 303–5).

It was in this context that the Neo-Confucian synthesis, or what contemporaries called *dao xue,* finally emerged (Collins 1998: 299ff, Yao 2000: 98ff). *Dao xue* was, in effect, an elaboration of the earlier synthesis between Confucian ethics and Taoist metaphysics which had first emerged during the Han era modified by the debates of the Wei, Jin, Northern, and Southern dynasties and above all by the struggle with Buddhism. The foundational text was, in this regard, Zhou Dunyi's (1017–73) *T'ai-chi t'u shuo* or *Explanation of the Diagram of the Great Ultimate* (Yao 2000: 98–101). Given the centrality of this text, it is worth quoting from it extensively.

> The ultimate of nonbeing and also the Great ultimate. The Great ultimate through movement generates yang. When its activity reaches its limit, it becomes tranquil. Through tranquility the Great Ultimate generates yin. When tranquility reaches its limit, activity begins again . . . .
>
> By the transformation of yang and its union with yin, the Five Agents of Water, Fire, Wood, Metal, and Earth arise. When these five material forces are distributed in harmonious order, the four seasons run their course.
>
> The five agents constitute one system of yin and yang and yin and yang constitute one Great Ultimate. The Great Ultimate is fundamentally the non-ultimate . . .
>
> When the reality of the ultimate of nonbeing and the essence of yin, yang, and the five agents come into mysterious union, integration ensues. *T'ien* (Heaven) constitutes the male element and *K'un* (Earth) constitutes the female element. The interaction of these two material forces engenders and transforms the myriad things. The myriad things produce and reproduce, resulting in an unending transformation.
>
> It is humanity alone which receives the five agents in their highest excellence, and therefore is the most intelligent. The five moral principles of human nature (humanity, righteousness, propriety, wisdom and faithfulness) are aroused by and react to the external world and engage in activity, good and evil and distinguished, and human affairs take place.
>
> The sage settles these affairs by the principles of the mean . . . Thus he establishes himself as the ultimate standard for humanity. Hence the character of the sage is identical with that of Heaven and Earth; his brilliance is identical with that of the sun and moon; his order is identical with that of the four seasons, and his good and evil fortunes are identical with those of spiritual beings. The superior human cultivates these moral qualities

and enjoys good fortune, whereas the inferior man violates them and suffers evil fortune.

Therefore it is said that the yin and the yang are established as the way of Heaven, the weak and the strong as the way of Earth and humanity and righteousness as the way of man. It is also said that if we investigate the cycle of things we shall understand the concepts of life and death. (Zhou Dunyi. *T'ai-chi t'u shuo* 1, in Fieser and Powers 1998: 170).

This text is, clearly, extraordinarily condensed and obscure. There are, furthermore, debates over the original form of the text. The version quoted above begins, in the Chinese, "*Wuji ehr taiji*," but another version of the text beings "*Tzu wuji ehr taiji.*" The difference is significant. The longer version, which Julia Ching, among others, argues (Ching 2000: 22, 235–41) is original, gives more play to *wuji* as the source of *taiji* and thus emphasizes nonbeing over being.

It was, however, the ambiguity of this text which made it so fruitful as a *locus* for metaphysical speculation. On the one hand, it outlines a metaphysics, cosmology, and ethics in which a transcendent first principle gives rise to a hierarchy of cosmic forces, which in turn give rise to the physical, biological, and social universe. Human beings represent the pinnacle of what amounts to a cosmohistorical evolutionary process, and the sage, who understands and follows the laws which govern this process represents the most evolved form of humanity, and is thus the standard by which all others should be judged.

This said, fundamental ambiguities remain. Of these two were most important. The first was epistemological, and concerned the relative role of investigation and meditation in the search for wisdom. Do we know the *taiji* by means of a kind of rational dialectic which begins with the "investigation of things" and concludes to a transcendental first principle? Or do we know that first principle through a kind of intellectual intuition achieved through meditation? While most of the practitioners of *dao xue* engaged in both scientific investigation and meditation in a broadly Ch'an tradition, the tradition diverged sharply around this question.

Second, what is the relationship between *wuji* and *taiji* and what is the nature of the *taiji* itself. The first question defines one's position in the broad Chinese intellectual spectrum which extends from Buddhism on the one side through Taoism to the more rationalistic and materialist variants of Confucianism. The second divided Confucians between those who emphasized *li* or principle, those who emphasized *xin* or mind/heart, and those who emphasized *qi* or material force.

We have discussed the full range of positions which emerged in the context of this debate elsewhere (Mansueto 2010b). What interests us here is both the model of spiritual and religious syncretism and shared substantive vision which the *dao xue* creates. We have here at least a *formal* synthesis between not only the Confucian and Taoist variants of the *way of harmony*, but, at least implicitly, a synthesis with Buddhism as well, in that the ideal of the *sheng* or Sage increasingly took on the characteristics of the fully enlightened Buddha, and if advocates of the *dao xue* pulled back from drawing out this conclusion explicitly it was, in large part, because they remained anxious to stress the importance of a *civilizational* as well as a *spiritual* ripening of Being. Which points, of course, to the substantive vision, which focuses precisely on *ripening Being*. The term itself appears first in a Buddhist context, but it is a better characterization of the Confucian and Taoist ethic than either could have achieved by themselves. And it defines what it means to be human in a way which leaves room for the disputed questions which define the *way of harmony*. Once we understand that our calling is, fundamentally, to tend the garden of Being, it becomes understandable that we will have to draw on both the universal principles of gardening and our understanding of the needs of each and every plant. And while we might debate the relative importance of each, soil and water, air and light, root and trunk, branch and leaf and fruit all matter.

This said, China never really settled accounts with sacral monarchy or with its more radically *Saecular* successor, *Empire*. Wave after way of Chinese scholars and monks attempted to make *Empire* serve the higher civilizational ideals of harmony, enlightenment and later, in the secular era, of communism. But that is not what *Empire* is about. *Empire* is fundamentally a way of mobilizing the energy of a social formation whole and entire in service to its own power. This power can—and in the case of the Han, Tang, and Song often was—wielded for good. But ultimately the criterion of success is the power wielded and not the end to which it is ordered. The West errs when it sees in this phenomenon the legacy of Confucius. It is, rather, the legacy of the Legalists and of the First Emperor which is at issue. But the result, that China is the most *Saecular* of the great axial civilizations, the most *Saecular* on the planet until the time of the Reformation, nonetheless holds.

This does not mean, however, that China has nothing to contribute to the resistance to *Saeculum* or to the construction of a new spiritual and civilizational ideal. On the contrary, the *dao xue* is a powerful model of intercultural synthesis which integrates a concern for seeking wisdom and doing justice in the context of a commitment to ripen *Being*, both by promoting the spiritual development of the individual and the construction of a just social order. We will draw significantly on this tradition when we propose our own synthesis in the final chapter.

* * *

The crisis of this whole wave of civilizational development—of centralizing empires taxing the Silk Road trade and significantly rationalized by engagement with the axial project—came as a result of a long series of invasions. In Christian Europe these invasions were partly constitutive of the civilization in question, and expressed their full impact only gradually, with the formation of modern sovereign states as a result of the Norman Conquests (which completed the Germanic migrations), the Crusades, and the Reconquista. In India the invasions were carried out by the relatively mild Turks as opposed to the more ruthless Mongols and allowed traditional Indian civilization to largely persist under Islamic rule. But the two most advanced regions of the planet—*Dar-al-Islam* and China, felt the full force of the Mongol invasion and as a result found their global leadership significantly compromised to say the least. And when the underlying civilizational traditions eventually recovered—under Turkish rule in the Islamic world and under the native Ming Dynasty in China, what was restored was a formalized version of that tradition which had largely lost touch with its creative sources and which was not really prepared for the confrontation with the third and final interation of the *Saculum*.

We need now to explore the world created by these conquests.

6

God's Work of Redemption

We need, at this point, to address what will undoubtedly seem like a deeply troubling and confounding question for our liberal Protestant readers, and indeed for many who are accustomed to engaging them in interfaith dialogue, deliberation, and organizing. Is Protestantism meaningfully part of the *way of justice and liberation*, and specifically its Christian variant, the *via crucis*, or is it a fundamentally new *way* more closely allied with the *Saeculum*? We have, obviously, already tipped our hand on this question, simply by the way in which we have organized our discussion, engaging Protestantism in the context of our discussion of *secular* rather than *axial* ways. But we will, in fact, want to temper this answer significantly, partly because Protestantism a sociologically and theologically diverse phenomenon and partly because even to the extent to which Protestantism has been part of the *Saeculum*, its contribution to finding meaning in the secular project and to advocating for justice cannot simply be ignored.

Our question has historical-sociological, philosophical, and theological dimensions. At the sociological level the question is ultimately that raised by Weber. Was Protestantism, and the Reformed tradition, especially in its Puritan variant, ultimately just a form of transition to industrial capitalism, a way of religiously legitimating a mobilization (and instrumentalization) of human energy hitherto unseen in the course of human history, a transition which terminates precisely in the Iron Cage of the *Saeculum* (Weber 1920/1968)? Or is the actual record of the relationship between historical Calvinism and capitalist development so complex, with significant evidence that many Calvinists, especially on the evangelical side, vigorously resisted capitalist development, that any thing like Weber's *Protestant Ethic* thesis is simply untenable (Heimart, 1966, Lockridge 1970, Hatch 1977)? At the philosophical level, the question turns around the claims made, in somewhat different form by John Milbank (Milbank 1990, 2014) and myself

(Mansueto 201a,b) that secularism is defined by a univocal metaphysics which is, in fact, shared by Protestantism.

Theologically, the question is rather more complex. On the one hand, there is a good case to be made that however transformed their meaning may be in the Protestant context, the language of liberation and justice remains central to the Protestant project. How else would the tradition be *defined* theologically by debates around *The Liberty of a Christian* (Luther 1517/2015) and the problem of justification? (Diet of Augsburg 1530/2015)? There is, on the other hand, a strong case to be made that most of what Protestantism actually hopes to *realize* is quite secular. If the question of our spiritual state has already been settled by the cross and or by God's inscrutable decree "before the foundation of the worlds" then there is nothing left except the working out of God's will in the world. And whether this is understood in postmillenial terms largely as a matter of renewing the fallen orders of creation and building a Holy Commonwealth, an authentically just city on a hill, or in premillenial terms as a worldly rule of a returned Jesus from Jerusalem followed by a new creation, we are still talking about events that unfold within the phenomenal world which we experience with our senses. Thus the insistence of the fundamentalists on a literal—and of liberals on a nonsymbolic, moral, secular—reading of the scriptures.

Understanding Protestantism as a purely *Saecular* movement, however, does not take into account tendencies which, while resolutely Protestant, have emphasized incarnation, sacrament, and *theosis*. What, for example, do we do with the long history of Catholicizing movements within Protestantism, such as the Oxford Movement (Brown and Nockles 2012), the Mercersberg Theology (Schaff 1844, Nevin 1846/2012; Graham 1995, Borneman 2011) and contemporary developments in Finnish Lutheran theology which are attempting to reground a Lutheran doctrine of *theosis* (Mannermaa 2000)? What all of these trends share is a commitment—developed furthest in Manneraa, perhaps because of his engagement with the Orthodox tradition, to the think Protestantism as a meaningful process of *theosis*, in which God is really and truly incarnate and in which this incarnation has as its issue an authentic transformation of humanity towards the divine, and not merely an instrumentalization of a humanity which, however "justified" or "sanctified" still participates not at all in the actual *life* of God. While Anglo-Catholicism has sometimes been comfortable with Arminian theological formulations, the other tendencies within this trend have tried to do this in a way which is compatible with historic Protestant commitments to the priority of divine agency and with as little concession as possible to scholastic theological categories (generally preferring patristic to scholastic sources). In this regard this trend may be seen as convergent with tendencies in Catholic theology which go back to the Tubingen school in the nineteenth century, and which are represented the *nouvelle theologie* (de Lubac 1938/1988, 1944/2007, Congar 1962), the *Communio* trend (von Balthasar 1968; Ratzinger 1984, 1986), and Radical Orthodoxy (Milbank 1990, 2005, 2014).

Our approach to this question will attempt a middle road. Specifically we will argue that Protestantism is the complex of *ways* which derive from the Germanic migrations into and conquests of Europe, the interaction between the Germanic peoples and the Celtic, Latin, and other peoples already in the region, and of a "second wave" of Germanic conquests which began with the Normans, extended through the Crusades and *Reconquista* and terminated in the European conquests of Asia, Africa, and the Americas. As such, it is part of a spiritual and civilizational trajectory which is deeply bound with the *Saeculum* and which clearly terminates, as Weber argued, in the Iron Cage we currently inhabit. From this point of view the key events in the Reformation were not Luther's 95 *Theses* or Calvin's *Geneva*, but rather Henry VIII's *Act of Supremacy*, and the *First* and *Second Suppression Acts*, which represent the definitive turning point in the *Saeculum*'s struggle against the Church (an authentic if imperfect expression of *Sanctuary*) and in the creation of sovereign state structures and the catalysis of primitive capitalist accumulation.

That said, Protestantism and the peoples whose project it has been are complex and diverse and Protestantism embodies many dissident tendencies which have significantly resisted the *Saeculum*, and others which have worked diligently, often within the framework of a univocal metaphysics of transcendence and a theistic secular *way*, to find meaning in the *Saeculum* or to hold it accountable to higher standards of justice.

We will proceed by giving an account of this trajectory, which we began in our account of the Catholic tradition, which we will trace all the way from the Germanic conquests through the current, increasingly fragile, *Pax Americana*, showing out it is intimately bound up with the specifically Protestant *way*. We will show how the dominant forms of the Protestant *way* are fundamentally secular in character, and catalysts for and forms of legitimation of *Empire* and *Capital*. At the same time we will also show how even from within this trajectory alternative projects emerged, questioning the very structures which historic Protestantism was helping to create, affirming their meaningfulness as part of "God's work of redemption," while holding them accountable to a higher standard of justice. If Liberal Protestantism struggles it is precisely because this task, which it has made its own, is more and more difficult to realize. And while an in-depth engagement with "Catholic" movements within Protestantism remain beyond the scope of this work, we will at the very minimum sketch out what we think they contribute and how we see further dialogue with them progressing.

The Germanic Conquests

Background

It is quite impossible to understand Protestantism apart from the Germanic matrix from which it emerged. While it is not possible to provide a fully historical-sociological account of the development of Germanic society in this context, we can provide a broad outline (Bucholz 1968, Russel 1994, Ewing 2008).

Germanic society first emerged out of a broader Indo-European context in southern Scandanavia and northern Germany. Like most Indo-European peoples, the Germanic tribes combined agriculture with pastoralism, but privileged pastoralism sufficiently for the Romans to take note of this preference, perhaps because of the relatively harsh climate in the region they initially inhabited. Second, the society was largely tribal, with small settlements of no more than ten households living in scattered clearings in the woods. There is very little evidence of any significant level of urbanization. Priestly functions do not seem to be strongly differentiated from royal functions, with the king being an elected war leader, judge, and high priest.

Central to the functioning of Germanic society was the relationship between the war leader and his retainers. Warriors legitimated themselves by winning and distributing the spoils of war among their followers, a process which led to the development of a loose and informal hierarchy of warrior nobles ruling over a peasant population which they at once exploited and protected. The central relationship within this system was the pledge of fealty which bound a man to his lord and a lord to his overlord. In return for this fidelity in service the lord was bound to share freely what he won for his men. Germanic war leaders performed sacrifices on behalf of the communities they led, and if there were separate priests involved they were very much in the background.

This said, it is worth noting that among the Germanic deities there is one who stands out has being more nearly a god of wisdom than of warfare, though he is in some measure both. This is Odin, who is said to have discovered the wisdom of the runes after sacrificing himself by hanging on the world-tree, or *Yggdrasil*.

The Germanic tribes gradually expanded across a broad area just to the North and East of the *limes* of the Roman Empire. They were engaged by the Romans both as adversaries and allies, and the old model of a "barbarian conquest" of Rome has gradually given way to a more nuanced picture in which Germanic tribes, gradually moving west and south as a result of population pressures and competition from other groups migrating west from Central Asia were sometimes resisted but also sometimes called upon to govern border areas which the Roman state, during its period of decline, was no longer able to effectively occupy.

The precise form of the Germanic appropriation of Christianity follows quite naturally from both the underlying nature of Germanic society and from what we said in an earlier chapter about the development of the Pauline and Augustinian theologies. On the one hand, as we have noted, the Germanic warlords appropriated the Augustinian theology which legitimated their authority as agents of order without imposing severe religious obligations (as Jews or Greeks or Romans or Celts would have understood them, in terms of seeking wisdom or doing justice) on them in order to maintain that legitimacy. At the same time, Germanic culture provided a context in which the Pauline and Augustinian theologies of grace found a ready reception. According to this theology Jesus is first and foremost a warrior who does battle with Satan much as Beowulf does battle with Grendel, and binds him deep in hell. He then bestows his booty, which is salvation, as a free gift to those who have been faithful too him. Similar themes are evident in the *Dram of the Rood*. To the extent that wisdom plays a role in the emerging Germanic spiritual ideal, it is not the acquired wisdom of the Greeks, achieved by means of rational dialectics, but rather the supernatural, almost shamanic wisdom of the dying and rising god Odin, who learns the runes while hanging on the tree.

It is interesting in this regard to note that early Germanic Christianity was largely Arian. While Arianism is not Germanic in its origins, the underlying spiritual problematic of Germanic pagan society was not focused on *theosis*. There is thus little need for thinking God in a way which allows the divine being to be shared by more than one person. And there is a case to be made that much, if not most, later Protestantism remains crypto-Arian in character, with Jesus understood as "the man of God's own choosing" rather than as the first born of many brothers, all participating fully in the life of God. And to the extent that the divinity of Jesus becomes important, it is largely as matter of explaining how Jesus' death is redemptive for the rest of humanity.

The Norman Conquests, the Crusades, and the Reconquista

The civilization which emerged out of the synergy between Latin, Celtic, and Germanic patterns after the middle of the first millennium of the common era was extraordinarily progressive and dynamic. The alpine plow, transhumant pastoralism, and the three field system led agrarian production to more than double in less than half a millennium (Anderson 1974) while the fact that peasants, even when bound to the land and obliged to perform *corvée* on their lord's land as well as paying rents, fines, and taxes of various kinds, were able to keep part of what they produced for themselves led to rapid economic growth and development. Increased production in the countryside made possible and expansions of crafts production in the cities, and Europe joined the Greater Silk Road Economy as an exporter of dyed wool cloth and other crafts products.

There were, however, limits to the Christian regime of accumulation. The expansion of the areas under cultivation led, by the middle of the twelfth century if not earlier, led to land shortages. These were not so much *absolute* shortages in the sense that the carrying capacity of the land was being pushed, but rather relative shortages engendered by feudal landholding patterns. The law of primogeniture, followed in varying degrees by most European warlord families, meant that nearly the whole of a lord's land was bequeathed to his eldest son. Dowries were provided for daughters and perhaps for a second son who chose to enter a monastery or who was able to obtain a senior clerical post. The other sons were sent to be trained as knights and to serve as retainers for other lords. The lived in their lord's castle as "knights bachelor" until such time as their lord was able and saw fit to grant them a fief, after which they could settle down, marry, and have children. The difficulty is that as the land under cultivation was extended so too was the land which was already enfoefed. This meant more knights bachelor—and what amounted to a sort of aristocratic gang problem, as these armed, unmarried young men did what such men have always done, preying on women and peasants and generally undermining the social order.

Many aspects of medieval culture can be traced to efforts to address this problem. The codes of chivalry were, no doubt in part, at least, an attempt to control armed men by ideological means. But a shortage of land and a surplus of armed men in the long run could only mean one thing: pressure for conquest. This dynamic was overdetermined by the last of the great Germanic migrations: the Norman conquests. While some of the pressure for conquest was played out within Christendom—the Norman conquest of England, for example, for the most part it resulted in pressure for expansion. From the end of the eleventh century on, Christendom adopted a far more aggressive posture towards *Dar-al-Islam* (and the Byzantine Empire), with the "the crusades" in the narrower sense of the effort to conquer the land of Israel and the Reconquista of Sicilia and *al-Andalus* flowing into each other and ultimately into the conquest of Africa, Americas, and Asia.

These conquests had two results. First, they gradually improved the position of Europe in the global trade networks and provided the "first installment," as it were, in the primitive accumulation of capital, which led eventually to the emergence of an authentic bourgeoisie and to the industrial revolution. Second, wars of conquest helped bring into being strong monarchies which gradually put forward claims to sovereignty which were hitherto unheard of in Europe. Indeed, it is *only* in those regions of Europe which were touched significantly by these conquests that we see early developments in the direction of the sovereign nation states: England, which was formed by the Norman Conquest of Britain, France, where the monarchy played a leading role in organizing the crusades, and Spain, which was the product of the *Reconquista*. Elsewhere state formation lagged, sometimes well into the nineteenth century.

It was the process of state formation which first had an impact on Christian theology. The link is, in fact, startlingly simple. As long as Christendom knew nothing like sovereignty, and the public authorities, temporal and spiritual functioned more like ideals or attractors than as coercive authorities, people thought of God as an ideal or attractor as well. But the emergence of absolutist monarchies created both a *basis in experience* and a *social interest* in thinking of God as a heavenly sovereign. On the one hand, the experience of emerging political sovereignty provided a model for thinking about God. On the other hand, the emerging monarchies sponsored intellectuals who not only argued for the superiority of the king to the priest and prophet, but also sought to undercut the emergence of a natural law ethics which might constrain royal imperatives.

The result was the series of condemnations of Aristotelian philosophy and theology and a resurgence of Augustinian theology which ultimately culminated in the Reformation. A whole host of "corrective" strategies, from Anselmian formalism and Bonaventurian exemplarism to Scotist voluntarism and Occamist nominalism was employed to reign in metaphysics and safeguard revelation and divine liberty.

In Anselm this impulse is still relatively weak and the connection between a univocal metaphysics and royal imperatives is only implicit. Defining God as "that than which nothing greater can be thought" clearly marks the difference between God and the universe in quantitative terms, but it does not directly magnify divine sovereignty. Anselm's account of the fall, and the ethics implicit in it, stress God's demand for obedience and human over-reaching, but they do not stress God's *arbitrary* power.

Bonaventura goes further. Exemplarism is the notion that everything in creation reflects in some way the divine nature. For Bonaventura this meant specifically the Holy Trinity. This may, at first, seem like a rather positive outlook on the material universe, but for Bonaventura this reflection of the divine nature is wholly and completely the product of God's creative activity. The active potency of matter and secondary causes such as human labor play little or no role. The beauty of the natural world is simply an occasion for praising the greatness of God, the recognition of which seems to be the principal function of the human intellect. Thus the insidious link, in all Franciscan spirituality, between the romantic adulation of nature and the rigid repression of the whole upward drive of complex organization, life, and intelligence (Bonaventura, *Quaestiones disputate de Scientia Christi*).

John Duns Scotus and William of Occam go even further. God is defined for Scotus as the infinite, and his proof for the existence of God is essentially an analysis of the concept of infinity. (John Duns Scotus, *De Primo Principio*).

Augustinian ethics draws out the conclusions from this metaphysics quite neatly. For an analogical metaphysics there is, quite simply, no contradiction between the full development of my capacities *properly understood* and the full development of everything else in the universe. This is because what all things seek is, quite simply, the undivided and inexhaustible power of *esse* as such. Ethics is all about understanding properly what we seek. For a univocal metaphysics, on the other hand, the universe is a zero-sum game. While it is *possible* for me to grow and develop in ways that do not take away from others, it is also quite possible for the development of two systems, even when rightly understood, to come into conflict. Ethics is more about containing human over-reaching than it is about combating ignorance.

This reasoning led Scotus—who advanced the most complete and consistent form of this ethics—to make a distinction between the *affectio commodi* and the *affectio justiae*. The first seeks its own development, the second what is right. When my development comes into conflict with that of another, I am obliged to do as God commands, loving my neighbor as myself and God above all. Some contemporary thinkers (MacAleer 1996) see in this line of reasoning the basis for a postmodern ethics of *caritas* understood as respect for the radical otherness of the Other, not unlike that elaborated by Levinas. The more straightforward reading though, is that is an ethics of obedience: to God and to his earthly representatives.

On the question of just who those earthly representatives are, the thinkers of the Augustinian reaction are nearly unanimous: it is the king or

Emperor, depending on the precise geopolitical allegiance of the thinker in question. We have already noted the early apologist for the Normans known only as Anonymous of York who entered the struggle between the spiritual and temporal lords by arguing that the King was superior to the priest because he represented Jesus' divine nature and the priest his human nature. It was Stephen Tempier, the Bishop of Paris, who was essentially a creature of the French monarchy, who undertook the purge of Aristotelianism from the University of Paris in the 1270s. And it was in Oxford, in what was the most advanced absolutist state of the late middle ages, that the Augustinian reaction reached its peak in the works of Scotus and Occam.

The Reformation

The Lutheran Project

The Reformation was fundamentally an extension of these processes which were already at work within Christendom. It is important here to recognize both the relative autonomy of spirituality, religion, and theological discourse and the fact that it forms an integral part of a materially situated and constrained civilizational project. Ideas which developed as the result of what were initially very personal spiritual struggles transformed the world forever because they coincided with the needs of the emerging absolutist state and emerging *Capital*.

Nowhere is this more apparent than in the work of Martin Luther. Luther's personal spiritual struggle was very much a product of the Augustinian theological problematic in which he had been formed. As we noted above, in the context of a univocal metaphysics the universe is understood as a zero sum game. Seeking our own development, and especially our own *theosis* is not only a threat to our neighbors; it is an assault on God Himself. And yet our own *Being* is indeed what we seek. Much as the Franciscan way might respond to this dilemma with a call to an *imitation Christi* centered on poverty and the *via crucis*, Luther was quite right that such attempts will end only in failure and frustration. As finite beings we are incapable of the perfect sacrifice, which is what the Law requires. Faith alone, which joins us to the perfect sacrifice—that of Christ Crucified—can render us just. There is, furthermore, no way to build a new social order on the basis of this perfect sacrifice. Make it a requirement of the Law and the message of forgiveness and the offer of free grace implicit in the sacrifice are deformed; let the Law go into abeyance and injustice goes unpunished and ultimately triumphs.

It is an open question whether or not this theology allows for an authentic doctrine of *theosis*. Historically justification within the Lutheran tradition has been read in a purely juridical sense, as a covering over of the sinner by Christ, so that we are left as *simul justus et peccator*, justified but also still sinners. This is by contrast not just with Catholic or Orthodox doctrines of *theosis* but even with Reformed doctrines of sanctification which put rather more emphasis on the transformative power of divine grace. Tuomo Mannermaa, on the other hands, working out of dialogue with the Orthodox tradition, has argued that Luther actually argues for a real presence of Christ in us, indeed a real transformation of the believer, through faith *into* Christ, so that it is no longer we who live, but Christ in us (Mannermaa 2000), a position which implies authentic *theosis*. Indeed, one might argue that such a view is quite consistent with the broader German mystical tradition which reaches back to Eckhardt, for whom our being is always and already God's. It is just that in the context of the Franciscan understanding of Being and of love which Luther inherits. The demands of the Law, the problem of sin, and the penetrating character of divine grace are all rather more sharply drawn, resulting in what might be called a rather different *erotic*: God penetrates and transforms us rather than we being lured by the incredible beauty of God to become what we actually have been all along.

This said, significant issues remain at the level of political theology. If Luther's spirituality has been historically misread, his political theology is more difficult to overcome. While there is certainly room for an ethics of love rooted in the spiritual transformation which faith and grace bring about, it is difficult to see, given his sharp opposition between Law and Gospel, how this might ever be institutionalized. And this ultimately undercuts the Catholic idea of the Church as a different and higher form of social life. Like his Augustinian and Franciscan predecessors, Luther ends up legitimating emerging absolutism even if he does so in the name of what is still an authentic ethics of love and spirituality of *theosis*.

The Reformed Trajectory

The Lutheran Reformation represents a logical working out of the problems inherent in Franciscan spirituality and politics. What began as a tactical alliance between a sectarian movement committed to a radical *imitatio Christi* centered on absolute poverty, a poverty which would have destroyed the Church as an effective civilizational power, and an Empire (and eventually other emerging monarchies) which aimed at just precisely this destruction, became a strategic alliance between a piety which had come to recognize the impossibility of any authentic *imitatio Christi*, for the simple reason that finite beings dependent on self-interested behavior for their own survival *cannot* imitate the radically self-sacrificial love modeled by Christ on the cross and the emerging monarchies which this liberated from the demand that their form of rule be shaped in any manner whatsoever by the Gospel. The Calvinist Reformation on the other hand represents a spiritual and civilizational project in which both the Church and the State are merely instruments, vanishing moments, which are eventually transcended entirely by the Power of which the Calvinist God is the ideological reflex: that of *Capital*.

Understanding Calvinism and its role in the larger project of secular civilization is, of course, a *locus classicus* for modern social theory. Weber (Weber 1920/1958) argued that Calvinism created an ideological and psychological situation uniquely favorable to industrialization and capitalist development. On the one hand, Calvinism regarded all useful work, not just specifically religious work, as an expression of God's will in the world. On the other hand, the fact that such work was a probable—but only probable—sign of election created a profound psychological tension which favored hard work, investment, and accumulation. If I work hard, then I *might* be among the elect; if I am lazy I know I am damned. If I save and invest, so that my work serves the common good, I *might* be among the elect; if I consume what I produce then know that I am damned . . .

As our thesis suggests we are inclined to be broadly favorable towards Weber's claims. There are, however, certain aspects of the broad historical context and of the internal diversity of Calvinism as a movement which Weber missed, and which we believe are fundamental to a correct understanding of "actually existing Calvinism" as an historical project. First, Weber fails to take adequately into account the complex relationship between Calvinism, state creation, and capitalist development in the two most important centers of Calvinist spirituality: England and the United States. Second, drawing as he did on a single text by a middle of the road English Calvinist, Richard Baxter, Weber misses the internal diversity within the Calvinist tradition around the question of just how, precisely, one knows whether or not one is among the elect.

The first point concerns the role of the English monarchy and of secularization. In a very real sense, neither the demands which Henry VIII made of the Church nor the actions he undertook and the processes those actions set in motion were especially unusual. They represent part of a process of the emergence of sovereign state structures which flowed out of the original Germanic conquests and more especially of the "second wave" of conquest we discussed above, which included the Norman Conquests, the Crusades, the Reconquista, and the European conquests of the Americas, Africa, and much of Asia. That the Holy See was unwilling to meet Henry's demands was more a function of geopolitics, and of Rome's alliance with England's adversaries than of any especially strong commitment to theological principle. Rome frequently compromised the very principles it upheld in Henry's case when it was advantageous for it so to do.

This said, we should not underestimate either the *political economic impact* or the *political theological significance* of the formal break with Rome. On the one hand, dissolution of the monasteries was an integral part of a much broader process which included the enclosure of the commons (sometimes, in fact, resisted or retarded by the Crown), which transferred wealth from both the peasantry and the church to the emerging bourgeoisie (including the landed gentry). The break with Rome accelerated this process and allowed England to accomplish by the end of the eighteenth century what other countries, such as Italy and Mexico (Sereni 1958, Zitara 1971; Wolf 1969) only began in the nineteenth. On the other hand, the Act of Supremacy effectively *ended* the Church as a form of society distinct from and higher than the *Saeculum* and instead made it effectively an institution *of* the *Saeculum*, without its own organized material resources or its own distinct authority. This does not mean that it ceased to offer a broader theological and moral perspective, even sometimes a critical one, but its function was hitherto to reflect and reform, not to offer a fundamental alternative.

This same pattern was played out in North America, where the process of enclosure took the form of the expropriation of the lands of the indigenous communities and where there was never a separate sphere which could offer *Sanctuary* from the forces of emerging capitalism. This was true, again, even in the Holy Commonwealths. While membership in the Church may have been a condition of political participation up until the time of the Half-Way Covenant, the church itself was controlled by lay elders whose presence in the Americas was fundamentally a part of the whole process of the primitive accumulation of capital, even if they were not themselves personally always meaningfully members of the gentry or the bourgeoisie.

Our second correction to Weber concerns the way in which Calvinists sought clues about their spiritual state. Broadly speaking, Calvinists divided on this question between those who stressed "usefulness to the community," something which some, in turn, understood to mean productivity in the economic arena and others to mean a concern for religion and social justice, and those who stressed the need for a convincing narrative of a personal conversion experience. The New England Puritans were marked by, among other things, the requirement that such a narrative of personal conversion be presented to the existing members of the Church as a condition for admission to membership, something which in the Massachusetts Bay and

New Haven colonies was in turn a condition of suffrage. It is not possible in this context to trace out in detail the complex internal struggles of the Holy Commonwealths.[1] Suffice it to say that after the English Revolution in 1640, radical Puritans were more inclined to stay home, where the action was, and that the children of the original colonists, as well as many newcomers, saw the colonies first and foremost as commercial ventures and were more interested in making money and in advancing their social position than they were in building Holy Commonwealths. Many of the children of the early colonies' leading lights were unable to fulfill the requirement that they give a convincing narrative of their conversion experience, and were thus unable to qualify for membership in the church and thus for the franchise. The result was the "Half-Way Covenant," which admitted the children of church members to baptism and thus to the franchise, though not to communion, and eventually, the reorganization of Massachusetts Bay as a royal colony. Accompanying this gradual process of secularization was the strengthening of what eventually emerged as "liberal" Calvinism, which stressed usefulness to the community rather than personal conversion as evidence of election. At its far end, liberal Protestantism gradually evolved away from many of the historic tenets of Christianity, including the divinity of Jesus, and gave birth to Unitarianism.

Liberalism did not, however, mean abandoning the sense of "election" which had characterized the founders of New England. It is just that being among the elect now meant a sense of moral superiority based on greater productivity (and thus prosperity) or on a sense that the new society being forged in the Americas was free of many of the social injustices which characterized old England and especially the Continent, rather than a radical conversion experience.

The Great Awakening of the 1730s was, first and foremost, a response to this growing liberalism and to the growing wealth and privilege of those who espoused it. The poor, especially in the more remote regions still focused on subsistence agriculture could not give any great evidence of their "usefulness to society," especially when this was interpreted to mean productivity and wealth; but they could provide a convincing narrative of personal conversion. North American Evangelicalism was, in other words, from the very beginning, a movement of those who had been "left behind" by the *Saeculum*. At least to begin with this "evangelical" trend in American Protestantism did not reject the struggle to build a better society. It was, rather, anxious to point out the hypocrisy of the liberals, many of whom were involved in

1. This account of Puritanism, of the development of New England society, and of the impact of Puritanism on the larger American project is indebted to, among others, Heinmart 1967 and Hatch 1977

the slave trade or in grabbing land from the Indians, and who were in general more concerned with enriching themselves than with advancing God's work of redemption. Indeed, up through the Civil War, most evangelicals upheld what is known as a postmillennial eschatology, which teaches that Jesus will return only *after* the millennium, i.e. only *after* humanity, by means of personal conversion and social reform, as created a just social order. Very early on, however, the evangelical trend itself began to experience differences between those who stressed the purely subjective character of the conversion experience, and placed relatively little emphasis on transformed personal conduct or social reform, and those who, such as Jonathan Edwards and his followers in the New Divinity movement, regarded ethical conduct as the natural consequence and best indication of authentic conversion and who were actively engaged in efforts to combat the evils of American society, such as slavery and land speculation (Heimart 1966, Hatch 1977).

By the middle or end of the eighteenth century, in other words, New England Calvinism had developed from a relatively compact ideology into a complex ideological ensemble containing at least four distinct trends. There was, on the one hand, a liberal trend, which was less and less focused on historic Christian doctrine and which regarded usefulness to the community as the best indicator of election. The liberals in turn were increasingly divided between those who regarded economic prosperity as the best evidence of usefulness to the community and those who focused on efforts at social reform. These two tendencies eventually gave birth to the Gospel of Wealth and the Social Gospel, both of which remain important poles in the liberal Protestant spectrum. The evangelicals, on the other hand, while united in stressing the importance of personal conversion, were, in turn divided between the high Calvinists (and especially the New Divinity movement) who believed that conversion had to bear fruit in ethical conduct and social reform and what was originally a relatively small group of back country revivalists who stressed a more purely emotional conversion experience—and, for the most part, gradually abandoned, at least in practice, their adherence to Calvinist distinctives such as limited atonement and double predestination.

Anyone who is familiar with the political and religious history of late colonial North America, or with the period during and immediately after the Revolution knows that these various trends despised each other and saw themselves locked in what many regarded as mortal combat over the soul of the new "nation." What they all shared in common, however, was the idea that they were building something qualitatively new and fundamentally superior to anything which existed in Europe or elsewhere. They had united unquestioningly in supporting England, which they regarded as the capital of True Christianity, in her struggle against "papist" France during the Seven Years War, but they saw themselves as building something nobler and purer than old England could ever hope to be. Freed from the bonds of tradition and the accumulated weight of medieval corruption and tradition, they would build a society which was truly capable of advancing God's work in the world, whether that work was understood as personal conversion, social justice, or capitalist accumulation—or some combination of all three. They were intensely aware of the moral failings of the new nation, especially the guilt of slavery, but regarded this consciousness of guilt as itself a mark of election, something which set them apart and promised to bear fruit in a future more glorious than that of the planet's grandest empires. It would be the last and the best empire, and while some understood this literally and others more figuratively, it would be the empire of Jesus Christ.

The extent to which the liberal form of Calvinism served as a form of transition to the development of an ideology centered on inner-wordly, decidedly capitalist, but still morally and spiritually meaningful activity is especially apparent in the work of economist Henry Carey. For Carey the laws of political economy revealed the wisdom and benevolence of the creator. What labor did was to increase the level of organization of the material world. This, in turn, required progressively more complex forms of social organization, or "association." The development of human society toward higher levels of association at once reflected and realized the divine love which ordered the cosmos as a whole.

Against the individualism of the Manchester school, Carey argued that human societies were governed by a law of association, which played the same role in organizing human affairs that the law of gravitation played in the organization matter generally.

> The more [man's] power of association, the greater is the tendency toward development of his various faculties; the greater becomes his control of the forces of nature, and the more perfect his own power for self-direction; mental force thus more and more obtaining control over that which is material, the labors of the present and the accumulations of the past (Howe 1979: 114–15).

Because of this

> economic development was a means to human redemption. Addressing himself to women in particular, he argued that economic diversification held out the promise to them of liberation from the role of farmer's wife . . .

By bringing people into ever higher degrees of association, economic development helped to realize the creator's plan for the cosmos.

Carey was firmly committed to capitalism, but not to the doctrine of *laissez faire* promoted by the Manchester school. (Howe 1979: 111–12). The marketplace could be a catalyst for development, but it could also become an obstacle. This was particularly true in the arena of international trade. Colonialism, furthermore, destroys the social fabric and undermines the traditions which are the precondition for the economic development of any people. In this sense Carey was ". . . a now forgotten spokesman for peoples who felt their communal identity threatened by economic colonialism . . ." He found that his message was welcomed wherever nations were industrializing and British economic hegemony resented (Howe 1979: 118–19).

This kind of thinking had definite political implications. First of all, the tendency of capital to redeploy itself towards low wage, low technology activities such as plantation agriculture, and the whole dynamic of colonial expansion which grew out of this tendency had to be restricted. Slavery had to be abolished. Second, the state had to act as an agent for centralizing and investing resources in the development of the kind of physical and social infrastructure required by an advanced industrial society. Not only roads, canals, bridges, and railroads, telecommunications lines, and the like, but also schools, libraries, museums, and universities were necessary if human beings were to fully realize their potential. Finally trade had to be regulated—encouraged when it opened up new opportunities for human development, and restricted when it undermined those opportunities.

Formation of a political alliance capable of implementing these sorts of policy was a protracted process. Neither of the two main political parties which emerged after independence were really parties of the industrial bourgeoisie. The Federalist party had its principal base among the merchants of the great port cities, while the Democratic Party, while it incorporated many radical farmers and artisans, was first and foremost the party of the Southern planter elite. Alexander Hamilton was able to win Federalist support for a sophisticated strategy of state led industrialization, but his plan offered too little to the workers and farmers to make it politically credible. Aaron Burr, similarly, made a bid to transform the Democrats into a revolutionary democratic party, but was beaten back by the slave owners, who were able to keep the masses in line with promises of cheap land stolen from the Indians.

By the mid-1820s, however, a new party, the Whigs, began to link together the emerging industrial bourgeoisie, the evangelical intelligentsia, and the more commercially oriented farmers. The Whig program included a commitment to a national bank, internal improvements, and high tariffs. The Whig party had close ties to the evangelical united front which was leading the Second Great Awakening. While less overtly hostile to the working class than the Federalist program, the Whigs were still unable to unite around the need to halt the expansion of, and eventually abolish slavery, which had become an increasingly serious brake on development. And the Whigs still offered too little to the working class and the farmers to make themselves a strong majority party. Specifically, there was nothing in their program which pointed towards higher wage levels, and no promise of access to cheap or free land in the West.

It was not until the 1850s, with the formation of the Republican party, that the industrial bourgeoisie was able to advance a program which united all of the progressive *Saecular* forces in U.S. society. To industry the Republicans promised a reform of the national financial system, a commitment to federal investment in infrastructure and high tariffs. But they joined to this program, which they had taken from the Whigs, a firm position against the further expansion of slavery, a promise of free land for settlers anxious to move West, and a commitment the development of human capital. The Morrill Land Grant College Act of 1862, for example, set aside some 30,000 acres of federal land for each state for each senator or congressman that represented it in Congress. This land was to support the establishment of agricultural colleges, which eventually became the cornerstone of the state university system.

It was this alliance which was finally able to defeat the southern planter elite and to set create the conditions necessary for the emergence of a strong, industrial capitalist system in North America. The achievements of the Republican Party during the 1860s are impressive indeed, and rank alongside those of other revolutionary parties of the period. The Republicans

- abolished slavery, and thus slowed the flow of capital into unproductive low technology activities,
- raised taxes and state expenditures in order to create the infrastructure necessary for rapid industrial development, including federally subsidized railroads, and the land grant college system which became the cornerstone of the country's land grant state university system, and
- raised tariffs in order to protect U.S. industry from foreign (primarily British) competition.

It is the victories of 1860-1865, rather than those of 1776-1800, which made possible the emergence of and advanced industrial economy in the U.S.

The Crisis of the Puritan Ideological Ensemble

Up through the Civil War and the early stages of Reconstruction, then, the Reformed project in the United States was fundamentally one, even if there were significant differences between liberals and evangelicals. Both understood the process of industrialization and capitalist development, modified by state intervention to correct abuses and include as many as possible in the rising tide of productivity and prosperity, to be an integral, even constitutive dimension of God's work of redemption. And the emerging centrality of the struggle against slavery to this project gave the it a moral force which was absolutely compelling. One need only think of the Battle Hymn of the Republic to understand the power of this vision.

But as was the case with other "bourgeois revolutions," the full promise of the Republican program of 1860 was never realized. A complete capitalist transformation of the United States would have involved not only an end to slavery but expropriation and redistribution of the lands of the southern plantation owners. This was, in fact, the program of the Radical Republicans, who represented the emerging steel and railroad industries, but the proposal won only 37 votes in the House of Representatives. The older section of the bourgeoisie based in the New England textile industry, was still too deeply dependent on cheap cotton to liquidate entirely the southern plantation system. Indeed, after 1876, the Union withdrew its troops from the South and allowed the southern landed elite to reconstitute itself on the basis of tenant rather than slave labor. Between 1876 and 1908 the industrial bourgeoisie ruled, in effect, in coalition with the Southern landed elite in what Barrington Moore has called an American version of the Prussian alliance of iron and rye (Moore 1966: 141–55). The United States emerged from the Civil War as a dynamic, rapidly industrializing contender for great power status and effective control of the entire middle section of the North American continent. And it soon developed imperial ambitions which extended to Latin America and Asia. But it was a far cry from the Holy Commonwealth envisioned by its Puritan founders.

The disillusionment which resulted from the failure of the bourgeoisie to complete the promised redemption of the "nation" cannot be underestimated. As we noted above, most American evangelicals up until the Civil War were postmillennialists and regarded the creation of a just social order as the essential precondition of the second coming of Christ and thus an integral part of God's work of redemption. The struggle against slavery was seen as the leading edge of that process. God really was sifting out the nations beneath his judgment seat—and the Union armies were to be the agents of that judgment. When the promised redemption failed to take place the old

Evangelical United Front began gradually to dissolve, with some drifting towards the liberal gradualism which eventually became the Social Gospel movement and others abandoning their postmillennial eschatology in favor of what eventually emerged as modern fundamentalism (Marsden 1980). This new, fundamentalist evangelicalism was based on a dispensational premillennial eschatology. According to this view, God deals differently with humanity during different periods. The ministry of Jesus, up until the time of his crucifixion, was part of the dispensation of the Law, and Jesus' moral teachings with their profound social implications are essentially part of a superceded Judaism. Humanity is living now in the age of grace, when salvation is by faith, not works. What is more, rather than leading naturally to moral uplift and social reform, personal conversion has no really visible moral or social effects. Far from looking forward to the creation of a just society, the new fundamentalism expected the world to get worse and worse until Jesus came to "rapture" the elect and redeem it.

This new fundamentalism had a social base very different than that of the old Evangelical United Front. While evangelicalism had always spoken to those who were "left behind," it did so at least in part because it promised a better world, and not only in the beyond. Evangelicalism had, been, in other words, an ideology of those who hoped to make America keep its promises. In this regard it overlapped very substantially with liberal Protestant reformism. Now, increasingly, it spoke to those who recognized that the *Saeculum* (they never said "America" or "capitalism") had no use for them and their way of life and who felt, furthermore, that the proposals of liberal reformers and socialists, far from offering a more humane secularism, simply promised a more vigorous effort to extinguish their way of life. For broad layers of the rural population in the South and West and for the petty bourgeoisie and even small capitalists of the smaller cities and towns, "progress," whether understood in the capitalist or the socialist sense, meant only further attacks on their way of life. And so they dug in their heels and resisted and waited for Jesus. They are still waiting.

The one politically significant exception to this pattern was the African American people who, alone among the members of the old Evangelical United Front have retained both their evangelicalism and their commitment to social reform. Black evangelicalism has, to be sure, always been different from its "white" counterpart. As Eugene Genovese pointed out long ago, African Americans never really bought into the doctrines of original sin and double predestination (Genovese 1974). The Black community has, however, always had a deep sense of the degrading effects of oppression on personal morality. Personal conversion in this context means getting your act together and learning to live productively and creatively in "the world as it is" while struggling to create "the world which could and should be."[2] The result has been that African Americans, while more than willing to point out the shortcomings of the United States are, perhaps more than any other group in the country, true believers in "America," and are so in more nearly the classical Puritan sense than any other ethnoreligious community. As anyone who has attempted to organize in the African American community has discovered, it is one thing to call "America" to task for her sins; it is quite another to attack the American ideal. It is interesting to note however, that when African Americans *have* called the American ideal into question, this has usually involved an explicit break with Christianity, something which could be made fully explicit only by opting for another, and historically opposed religion—Islam.

Well before the end of the nineteenth century, in other words, the American Dream as it had been understood by both its Puritan and its Enlightenment advocates was dead. The United States would be neither a Holy Commonwealth the Christian commitments of which would be reflected in a just social order nor a petty bourgeois utopia of self-cultivation in which yeoman farmers and master craftsmen studied the arts and sciences and philosophy in the evening and sent their sons to public universities which allowed the best the rise to the top while permitting everyone to develop as far as they could. It was, rather, a developing industrial capitalist power with a continental empire—and a voracious appetite for cheap labor.

Liberalism and its Discontents

What, given this analysis, is the significance of Liberal Protestantism in the post Reconstruction period? It is worthwhile in this regard to be clear what we are talking about. Historically, we are referring to at least four distinct theologies: the older liberalism which persisted from the Antebellum period, the Social Gospel, Neo-orthodoxy, and the Radical or Death of God Theologies of the 1960s and beyond. These were and are, however, fundamentally distinct attempts to mobilize and orient the same basic demographic during its period of historic triumph, crisis, and imminent decline.

We begin with the demographic. Ethnicity is a challenging social concept to define. On the one hand, any attempt to reduce it to shared genetics, language, religion, culture, or history quickly collapses. These phenomena

---

2. The phrases "world as it is" and "world as it should be" are part of the stock in trade of the Industrial Areas Foundation, an organizing institute which challenges people in oppressed communities to take seriously the need to build power. The language seems ultimately to derive from Nietzsche.

are overlapping rather than corresponding and are constantly shifting. On the other hand, ethnicity is nonetheless real, in the sense that people embrace, share, and reject identities which, however fluid, are meaningful to them and to others not just in the moment but over moderately protracted historical periods.

The Puritan core driving the Reformed project in North America derived from a very specific region. They were not merely English: they were from East Anglia, a region which included Suffolk, Lincolnshire, and Cambridgeshire, and New England culture was marked especially by the influence of this specific region. There was a time when immigrants even from other parts of England would have been perceived as ethnically different. The long process of nation-state formation which culminated in the Civil War, together with the successive waves of immigration from across Europe changed this, forging a common identity shared by Protestants from across the British Isles and indeed from across Northern Europe including, even, though to a lesser degree, Germans and Scandinavian Lutherans. This identity was defined in large part in distinction to four other groups: the growing numbers of Jewish, Catholic, and Orthodox immigrants from Ireland and from Southern and Eastern Europe, the African American population, the annexed Mexican population of the Southwest, and the South which, defeated though it may have been, came out of the Civil War with a quasi-national identity as strong as that of the North.

At the same time, this Protestant *ethnos* was internally differentiated and stratified. The highest status elements remained—and to some extent remain—those descended from the Puritan elite of New England and to a lesser extent New York and New Jersey and the (distinct) Episcopalian and Dutch Reformed elites of New York and the other Mid-Atlantic states. Elsewhere, moving west, Presbyterian and even Methodist or Lutheran elements dominate. While this *ethnos* cannot be regarded as ruling *class*, since most of its members are quite proletarian or petty bourgeois in their economic situation, and because the sense in which even its wealthiest members are still *ruling* is seriously open to question, it *can* be regarded as a high status *caste* or quasi-caste, the principles and values of which long defined what it means to be American and which long attracted imitation by groups trying to rise in status.

What this *ethnos* shares is a common *way* of being human, a *way* centered on making useful contributions to society, contributions which are understood—but ever more dimly—as being part of God's work in the world. This *way* is Liberal Protestantism understood as a spiritual movement or tendency.

The *theological trajectory* of Liberal Protestantism is fundamentally a series of attempts to find (religious, Christian, Protestant) meaning in the North American variant of the capitalist project—or to come to terms with the growing difficulty in so doing, and in the process to ground Liberal Protestantism as a *way* of being human. For the older liberalism which emerged before the Civil War and which persisted for some time after it (and which continues to be the *de facto* theology of many Liberal Protestant churches populated by members of the bourgeoisie and upper petty bourgeoisie who consistently vote Republican) there was no contradiction between a moderate gospel of wealth and a broad commitment to moderate social reform. As the realities of industrial capitalism became more apparent, though, those more strongly committed to the idea that they were doing God's work in the world found themselves attracted to more radical reform projects which brought into conflict with Capital and even led them to question capitalism as an economic system (the Social Gospel).

From this point of view Neo-Orthodoxy and the Death of God movement are not the radical break with liberalism that they understood themselves to be. The horrors of the first world war, the rise of fascism, and disillusionment with actually existing socialism all required significant qualifications to the idea that the secular project, as it was actually being played out, was in any sense "God's work in the world." Neo-orthodoxy responded by emphasizing themes in Reformation theology which stressed the *limits* to which sinful human beings could actually do God's work in the world. Thus their emphasis on divine transcendence, the priority of revelation over reason, the seriousness of original sin, etc. But they did this without calling into question the basic assumption that Christian faith should be expressed in *trying* to do God's work in the world. A classic "high" theology, it could never have mass appeal, because it required of its adherents a very high degree of spiritual maturity and a willingness to persist in undertaking a work in which they knew they could never succeed, renouncing spiritual pride and triumphalism, and making difficult decisions in morally ambiguous situations. It remains attractive, however, to liberal Christian political leaders, such as Barak Obama, as way of finding meaning in the their efforts to promote social reform under extraordinarily difficult conditions, all the while making decisions (such as those required by the conflict with al-Qaeda and Daesh) which they would probably rather not have to make.

Radical and death of God theologies, as we noted in an earlier chapter, can mean three very different things. On the one hand, for thinkers such as Altizer and Hamilton (Altizer and Hamilton 1966), we are looking at a reaffirmation of the Christian meaningfulness of the secular project in the wake of the new hope which emerged during the post-WWII period. This trend, we should note, vanished with the crisis at the end of the 1960s. In the case of Vahanian (Vahanian 1961) the death of God, refers to a loss of the sense of the sacred in society, a perspective which might be read as within the neo-orthodox camp. For Rubenstein (Rubenstein 1966), finally, the term "death of God," is a response to the Shoah and to the sense that it is obscene to talk about God in the wake of the attempted and nearly successful extermination of His people. This is a Jewish, not a Protestant insight, though it has raised important questions for Protestants and other Christians.

If Liberal Protestantism is experiencing a crisis, then it is because the Liberal Protestant project has proven itself to be ultimately untenable. On the one hand, the long term tendency of the process of capitalism is toward the constitution of Capital as an autonomous power which leaves even the bourgeoisie unable to organize and direct the course of human history. On the other hand, the project of fully mobilizing and instrumentalizing human labor turns out to be rather difficult to reconcile with the Christian *way of liberation and justice*, to which Protestantism remains connected. In the end this affects not just Liberal Protestant support for capitalism but also for actually existing socialism which, as we will see, found itself forced to engage in a similar degree of mobilization and instrumentalization.

This said, Liberal Protestant churches have played an absolutely critical role in the development North American civilization and they will continue to be a place to which the broad *ethnos* constituted by the process of capitalist development in North America will turn for meaning. Because of this it is important for them to find a road forward—a road which, we will argue, of necessity leads beyond both liberalism and Protestantism, but which is still meaningfully connected with their heritage. In searching out this road two seemingly disparate trends—the New Thought and New Age movements and Catholic movements within Protestantism—require at least brief consideration.

Post-Protestantism

New Thought and New Age

We have already considered the New Thought and New Age movements from a methodological perspective, as forms intercultural engagement, in a previous chapter. What we hope to do now is to show both the profound continuity of this trend with Reformed Protestantism and its role as a response to the increasing difficulty of finding meaning in *Capital* from a Christian vantage point.

This trend (Albanese 2007) probably has its immediate origin in the teachings of healer Phineas Quimby and has taken both Christian and post-Christian forms. On the one hand, Mary Baker Eddy, while departing from anything like Christian orthodoxy on a number of key questions, including trinity, creation, and the nature of sin, nonetheless insisted that her doctrine was (yet another) restoration of primitive Christianity. At the other end of the spectrum, Theosophy (Godwyn 1994) drew on emerging scholarship regarding Hinduism, Buddhism, and Western Esotericism to proclaim that "there is no religion higher than truth," a truth which ultimately amounted to a sort of subjective idealism. Religious Science, Unity, and other such movements stood somewhere in between.

What all of these movements shared was the conviction that one's life situation—including everything from one's health to one's economic situation to one's usefulness to society—is dependent on one's spiritual state. While sometimes articulated in *language* deriving from Hinduism or Buddhism (e.g. ideas about *karma*) the spirit is decidedly Calvinist. It is just that "enlightenment" has replaced "election" and the illusion of finitude and contingency has replaced sin as the problem to be solved.

This was originally the ideology of the *rentiers* who regard the world from what is quite literally a speculative point of view and which is convinced that reality is what you make of it. Those who suffer, whether from illness or economic distress, do so in large part because of the choices they have made which in turn derive from a fundamental misunderstanding of reality.

More recently this trend has been embraced by the "new global elite" analyzed by Paula Freeland in her January 2011 *Atlantic Monthly* article by that name. Much of what Freeland discusses is, to be sure, "old news." The rich have been getting richer while the working classes and middle strata, at least in the developed countries, have lost ground. The new rich have benefited from globalization, and especially the liberalization of capital flows and the emergence of new information technologies in ways that the vast majority have not. And the new rich are increasingly global in their allegiances and outlook, with little loyalty or investment to any one nation state.

This all sounds a great deal like the analysis advanced by Robert Reich (Reich 1992) two decades ago in *The Work of Nations,* and elements of it, at least, simply represent a working out of tendencies identified nearly a century ago by Lenin. But Freeland describes the contours of the "new global elite" in a very distinctive way which merits further analysis. It is especially important to understand this sector because it is concentrated in the information, technology, and investment banking sectors which form an integral part of the base of the Democratic Party in the United States. Freeland's analysis also has some profound implications for our "civilizational crisis" thesis.

First, Freeland argues, the new global elite is composed almost entirely of *nouveaux riches* who, while rarely of working class origin, derive mostly from relatively modest "professional middle class" or "new petty bourgeois" backgrounds. The have enjoyed access to good, often elite schools but have not generally benefited from inherited wealth or aristocratic social capital. Freeland does not address this point, and it needs to be tested empirically, but the tendency seems to be for technology entrepreneurs to have "dropped out" of an elite institution at some point in their education (though often at the doctoral rather than the undergraduate level, like Bill Gates). Those in the financial sectors are more likely to be top graduates with outstanding quantitative skills and an appetite for risk taking, often validated by membership in secretive, elite organizations such as Skull and Bones which have initiation rituals centered on taboo-breaking. They are, in this sense, the polar opposites of their cousins in the academy, which values conformity, collegiality, and "fit" even more than it does intellectual brilliance and has zero tolerance for those who break its rules. Technology and information sector entrepreneurs generally "make it" by coming up with a great new idea—Google, Facebook, Groupon—and building a team and raising the money to make it happen. Recruits to the financial sector "make it" by developing ever more exotic financial instruments which allow them to meet "tenure" criteria which would make most academics (as well as their priors in the industry) tremble with fear—e.g., earning the firm staggering profits during their first years on the job.

Economically, this stratum is distinguished from the bourgeoisie proper by the fact that it draws most of its revenue from nominal salary. Freeland quotes a study by Emmanuel Saez showing that while in 1916 the wealthiest 1 percent of the US population derived only 20% of its income from wages and salaries, in 2004 that number had risen to 60%. And this is in spite of the fact that it is more advantageous from a tax standpoint to report income as capital gains than as wages and salaries. What we are looking at here is a social stratum constituted by monopoly rents on skill. Economically, they are more like athletes or movie stars than like the financial, industrial, commercial, or agrarian capitalists of the past.

To the extent that they have engaged the political arena, they have leaned Democratic and were, in fact, among the most important funders of Barrack Obama's 2008 campaign. Many, though not all, appear to have pulled away over his attempts to raise taxes on the wealthy and regulate the financial industry, reigning in the ability of its superstars to find ever more creative ways to capture surplus created elsewhere. But with the exception of a few outliers they tend to be social liberals.

There is little evidence, furthermore, that this stratum has advanced a global civilizational agenda. They have, rather, invested most of their money instead in what Matthew Bishop and Michael Green have called "philanthropocapitalism." In short, they look to replicate in the philanthropic arena their success in business, introducing the next big, world transforming idea. While a few, like George Soros, have actually built real institutions, most have not. Nor have they supported existing artistic, educational, charitable, and religious institutions. Their projects are almost all directed either at ecological issues such as climate change or at the very poor, especially in Africa. The "new global elite" tends to believe that if one comes from a solid working class or professional middle class background and fails to achieve global elite status it is due either to mediocrity or poor choices. There is a strong bias towards the view that the working classes and middle strata in the Europe, North America, and Japan are overpaid relative to the value added they create and need to take a "pay cut" to world market levels. They are, in effect, *advocating* the leveling down to world market wages which Robert Reich *predicted* but offered no strategies to *prevent*, in *The Work of Nations* two decades ago.

These programmatic limitations are matched at the level of institution building. The new global elite (the conspiracy theorists notwithstanding) do not have a political party. While they have tended to dominate the Democratic Party in the US in recent years they appear not to be sufficiently invested in it either to make sure that the candidates they support follow policies they can live with or that they retain the congressional majorities they need to govern effectively. They are, in short, political dilettantes. The elite conference circuit which attracts much of the intellectual and organizational energy of this elite is not really a potential instrument of rule.

Situating this trend within the broader context of Anglo-American religious history, we should see it as what happens when Liberal Protestant elites lose faith in both the Protestant narrative, in which the industrial, democratic, and scientific revolutions are all unambiguous engines of social and spiritual progress, and also begin to lose their status as an authentic ruling class. Economically successful, they retain their sense of "election" or at least spiritual superiority. Imperial cosmopolitans, they make the world's spiritual traditions their own, but interpret them as variants of their own subject idealism. Where they can have an impact for the better (as they understand it) they do, but they interpret their marginalization as *Capital* emerges as a fully autonomous, impersonal power as a movement to a higher, less material and political, spiritual plane.

This said, the New Age might also be regarded as a reflection of yet another feature of the Germanic and Norman ethnogenetic trajectory. While the Normans in England were quite brutal and repressive, elsewhere, especially in Sicily, they actively engaged and to some extent even imitated and took on the culture of those they conquered—in this case the complex syncretism of North African, Italic, and Greek, Jewish, Catholic, and Muslim cultures which defined Sicily. Indeed, even in Britain, the Normans made the Celtic history of that land, in the form of the Arthurian cycle, their own. The Norman conviction in their inherent superiority has always been joined by a profound curiosity.

The New Age represents a significant part of the actually existing spirituality of the United States and, to a significant extent and perhaps with some subtle differences which are not fully understood, the rest of the developed world. It is therefore vitally important that it be engaged, that its contributions be acknowledged, its limitations challenged, and that it be helped to grow into something more mature. We will consider what this might look like later.

Catholic Movements in Protestantism

We need, finally, to consider the potential of a cluster of what might be called "Catholic" movements within Protestantism. By this we mean movements which have attempted, in one degree or another, to recapture elements the Catholic (and/or) sometimes the Orthodox traditions while remaining faithful to what Paul Tillich called the "Protestant Principle." These elements include a stronger emphasis on what we have called the *theotic* project, or at least on the doctrine of the Incarnation and the possibilities it opens up for humanity, a stronger doctrine of the real presence, a more liturgical approach to worship, more emphasis on the Church as an institution, and often a "conservative critique of capitalism" as both unjust and disruptive of the social fabric. We include here Anglo-Catholicism generally and the Oxford movement in particular, the Mercersburg theology, the Finnish school in Lutheran Theology, and Radical Orthodoxy

It is not possible to consider each of these movements in detail in this context. Each certainly merits at least a chapter and perhaps a book in its own right and each, of course has been the object of in-depth studies by others. Our aim here, rather, is to consider the impulse as a whole, to analyze its social basis and political theological valence, and to consider what it contributes both to a possible future for the Protestant project and more broadly to the ongoing deliberation among the *ways* of wisdom.

The entire trend of Catholic tendencies within Protestantism can, in many ways, trace its roots to Richard Hooker (Hooker 1621/1970), the sixteenth century English theologian who attempted to find theological meaning in the Tudor project of a Reformed but still meaningfully Catholic Church not in communion with Rome. On the one hand, Hooker took for granted both the necessity of Reformation and core Protestant principles, such as justification by faith and the break with Rome. On the other hand, he argued that reason, redeemed by faith, was fundamental to religious knowledge and that justifying faith expressed itself necessarily in good works. He rejected the idea that any specific form of ecclesiastical government was required by scripture but made instead an argument that authority is necessary for the good order of church and society, but that authority in turn depends on the intellectual and moral quality of the leaders.

This tendency within the Church of England was strengthened further when, in the nineteenth century, Whig governments threatened to secularize Church lands in Ireland. The response was a reassertion of Catholic elements still present in the Anglican tradition and a revival of others, such as religious orders. Many members of the movement served parishes in poor communities and began to develop a sharp critique of capitalism, at least in its more radical forms, a critique which flowed both into what eventually became the Red Tory and the Labour traditions. Many members of the movement, including John Cardinal Newman, eventually became Catholic, but others remained within the Church of England and integrated significant elements of Catholic tradition with a theology which retained an evangelical and Protestant character. Both the Inklings movement and Radical Orthodoxy are essentially extensions of this movement. The latter makes the critical contributions of pointing to the centrality of an analogical metaphysics of participation to the Christian project of *theosis*.

Similar movements have emerged at various points within the German Reformed and the Lutheran Traditions. We have already mentioned two of these. The Mercersberg theology, which developed in Pennsylvania in the middle of the nineteenth century, argued that the atonement was a product more of the Incarnation itself than of the death of Jesus Christ and argued for a stronger doctrine of the real presence, mystical but not substantial, of Jesus in the Eucharist. The movement was a North American expression of a broader trend in the German Church which read Protestantism through a Hegelian lens, and looked for a synthesis between Catholic and Protestant positions. Expressions on the Continent are ordinarily referred to as Neo-Lutheran. The Finnish Theology, which we mentioned earlier, is more profoundly engaged with the Orthodox than the Catholic tradition but arrives at similar conclusions. Christianity is not merely about forensic justification—a free choice on the part of God to overlook our sins—but is, rather, an authentic transformative process which creates a new human being, stretching us beyond mere humanity, towards the divine.

All of these tendencies have attractive features. They show deep roots in the Christian tradition and an ability to make nuanced judgments regarding disputed questions, possibilities which were often ignored by both the Reformers and the theologians of the Counter-Reformation. The latitudinarian approach pioneered by Hooker and further developed by the Oxford, Mercersberg, and Neo-Lutheran restores to Protestantism a sense of the sacred and mounts a defense of the centrality of the public spiritual authority of the Church as a challenge and corrective to the *Saeculum* without making indefensible claims on behalf of the ontological character of ordination or the unique value of apostolic succession, which become symbols of the presence of priestly and prophetic authority in history rather than the sole legitimate claimants to it.

This said, there are some real limitations to the project these tendencies share. On the material society this limitation derives from their acceptance of the secularization of church property and of ecclesiastical authority (of which the Oxford movement resisted the extension, but accepted in principle), the inevitable result of which is to make the Church dependent on *Saecular* patronage, whether that of the Crown or, more prominently, of Capital itself. This, in turn, severely circumscribes the extent to which the Church can exercise an authentically prophetic voice. Only when it is authentically autonomous, with its own organized material resources (which are not themselves either feudal lands or *Capital*) and radical autonomy from lay (capitalist) elders can the Church really and truly be prophetic. This judgment must be balanced, of course, by a recognition that the Catholic solution—the constitution of the hierarchy as a closed clerical corporation and a sovereign state under the law of nations—does not solve the problem either. From the theological side, the limitation is the failure, prior to the work of John Milbank, to recognize the centrality of an analogical metaphysics of participation to a restoration of the sacred and of *Sanctuary*.

Radical Orthodoxy is a powerful and compelling attempt to address just precisely these limitations by restoring an analogical metaphysics of participation, showing its profound importance to but also dependence on theology, and by rejoining the argument for the Church as a distinctive form of society and not just as one social institution among many. This said, Milbank is at once too harsh on Protestantism and far too much of a Christian exclusivist. And he makes these errors, we would like to argue, precisely because he remains, at core, a Protestant, however "catholicizing."

The issue fundamentally is that Milbank fails to recognize that a metaphysics of participation rules out Christian exclusivism. It is quite possible to argue for the unique and even superior contributions to Christianity to the ongoing problem of advancing humanity's *theotic* project. But a metaphysics of participation by its very nature means that *all* ways participate in some measure in the truth. Milbank misses this point and is thus too harsh in his judgment of Protestantism, of the *Saeculum*, and of non-Christian spiritual traditions.

Where we differ from Milbank is in our insistence that all *ways* seek the same end, even if they understand and pursue it differently and sometimes in disastrously destructive ways. This work reflects, of course, the value we have found in essentially all of humanity's great spiritual traditions. We need here to recognize the truths discovered by the Protestant project as well.

The historic process set in motion by the Germanic conquests is, for better or worse, now an integral part of the human spiritual and civilizational project. It must be understood and criticized, but also appreciated. It may well be spent. But the broken shards it has left behind are thinking and acting shards wrestling with the same fundamental questions of meaning and value as the rest of humanity. And they are thinking hard and struggling hard to find meaning in a very dark time. They must be listened to, respected, and answered.

From this vantage point it is possible to draw out the following conclusions regarding what might be conserved from the Protestant project, and in what form:

Revelation is indeed the principal and indeed the only source of knowledge but only in the sense that the universe itself reveals the glory of God. And this revelation is always and only mediated through human reason—reason which itself is socially conditioned and situated.

Spirituality is never about propitiating a God or gods or about earning salvation. Luther and Calvin were quite correct that salvation can never be merited. Against *Being as such* there are no valid claims and we are always constitutively defective. The possibility of spiritual progress, whether understood as Enlightenment or Justice or Harmony is always and only a free gift of Being itself, indeed it is *the* gift of Being itself, in the form of our finite and contingent participation in Being. And the limits of this participation are themselves gifts and a form of grace, as they are the catalysts for the *dark nights* which propel us forward spiritually.

There is indeed a priesthood of all believers in the sense that we all *are* and all make God really present. And our ordinary work in this world, in so far as it is ordered to the Good, is in fact God's own work. Ordination confers no ontological difference and the forms of life of monastics, mendicants, clerks regular, and apostolic "religious" are no more "religious" or "consecrated" in and of themselves than those of people living a married life "in the world." This said, there is also a compelling need for conscious leaderships which can guide humanity along the *ways of wisdom*. This includes both those learned in their *ways* and able to teach (and innovate) within those ways, order the life of their communities in accord with their respective *ways*, and ripen *Being* along those ways. There is, in other words, a need for a clergy. And this clergy must have the organized resources, social networks, and *mana* to build and exercise real power. There is also a place for communities of people who, regardless of whether their members are called to public leadership or not, want to follow their *ways* with particular intensity (religious communities or institutes of consecrated life). These communities also need the material resources and autonomy to carry out this calling.

The experience of the New Thought and New Age movements, with all the limitations they bring as a result of their class basis, carries these lessons into our engagement with humanity's great spiritual traditions. And the Catholic movements within Protestantism suggest ways in which such commitments might be carried forward, even if their movement in the broadly Catholic direction does not go far enough.

While I write as Catholic deeply formed by engagement with humanistic secularism, Judaism, Islam, and Buddhism, I write as well as the son of a Protestant mother and, as a North American, part of a Protestant project. The Protestant project and its discontents are, therefore, inevitably part of my own project and my own discontents. In what follows, and especially in the conclusion to this work I hope to join these broken shards together in a synthesis which is as meaningful to and respectful of the Protestant project as it is of all of humanity's other *ways* of wisdom.

But first we need to consider the two remaining secular ways: the technocratic and humanistic secular paths.

7

The Engine of Divinity

The State of the Question

We have now reached the crux of our argument. We have seen that the arc of spiritual and civilizational development set in motion by the Germanic and especially the Norman conquests unleashed processes which altered fundamentally the tentative stalemate between *Sanctuary* and *Saeculum* which had prevailed during the Silk Road Era. The *Saeculum*, to a degree not seen since the late Bronze Age, began to understand itself as God's work in the world. The conquests, furthermore, set motion not only the formation of sovereign nation states but also in the industrial revolution and capitalist development. This was an extraordinarily disruptive and oppressive process for the vast majority of humanity, but it also unleashed an unheard of degree of human productive, if not always creative, power.

From the vantage point of the *Saeculum,* as we have seen, God (or the gods) exist, if at all, in precisely the same way we do. He/they is/are just vastly—even infinitely—more powerful. This is integral to the project of the *Saeculum*, which consists of building God, and thus overcoming finitude, by means of innerworldly civilizational activity. We have seen, furthermore, how this understanding of the nature of God was further refined and how it achieved greater influence in the context of Augustinian Christianity and especially within the context of Protestantism.

It was inevitable, under these circumstances, that the question would once again be posed whether or not we might actually be able to push back the boundaries of finitude so far as to become effectively divine. Rarely explicit, often, as in the case of liberal Protestantism, and some forms of liberalism, democracy, and socialism, subordinated to or articulated with another secular project, theistic or humanistic, technological godbuilding nonetheless became the dominant spiritual and civilizational *way* from the eighteenth century on. We call it technocratic secularism and it is nothing less than an *engine of divinity*.

Even considered purely on its own terms, from the vantage point of the mathematical physics of *cosmogenesis*, this *way* faced profound challenges. This is because, after a brief period of youthful optimism, the science on which the industrial revolution and the entire technocratic project became, after 1848, increasingly pessimistic in terms of its outlook on the long term prospects for complex organization, life, and intelligence. Malthusian demographics, the Second Law of Thermodynamics, the Poincaré Recurrance Theorem, and Big Bang cosmology all presented, at the very least, serious challenges for technological godbuilders to overcome (Mansueto 2012). And yet our entire civilization remains, without fully knowing that it is, or believing that it should be, ordered to this single end.

Is technological god building a viable spiritual and civilizational path? The current state of this question is, in many ways, a bit confusing. On the one hand, it is possible to read the entire trajectory of philosophy over the course of the past 200 years as critique of this project. Humanistic secularisms such as those of Hegel, Marx, and their interpreters, even when they have taken a very positive view of technology, have insisted that technological progress be subordinated to and serve the end of a specifically human development which centered not on the quantitative accumulation of technological capacity or wealth (Hegel's "bad infinite") but on making humanity the master of its own destiny (overcoming contingency rather than finitide in the context of a univocal metaphysics of immanent *Being as Such* rather than a univocal metaphysics of transcendent common Being). And the philosophical trajectory which begins with Schopenauer, Kierkegaard, and Nietzsche, passes through Heidegger, Levinas, and the phenomenologists, and which terminates in deconstruction, while rejecting the socialist "metanarrative" of the "definitive solution to the riddle of history" also, even more fundamentally, rejects the metanarrative of technological godbuilding. Add into this the widespread recognition of impending ecological crisis and the enduring salience of quite radical ecologistic trends, often synergistic with various feminisms and the fact that much of the Right also rejects at least some "science" and it would seem the question has been settled. Indeed, for anyone trained in the humanities or humanistic social sciences in the latter part of the twentieth century, mounting a critique of technological godbuilding would seem like trying to get one last spark out of already incinerated straw man.

This said, the debate has recently taken a new turn. On the one hand, we have witnessed a broad transhumanist trend which echoes at the level of the high tradition the technological solutionism which is the official ideology of the increasingly powerful high technology (information and biotechnology) sectors of Capital. At its most radical this takes the form of a quite explicit godbuilding, such as that advocated by Frank Tipler. But even in its more moderate forms it is a *way* which finds what meaning it can primarily in a technological assault on human finitude. On the other hand, the New Atheism, which we have already discussed, while reading the philosophical implications of the physical and biological sciences in a far more sober and even anti-utopian way, rejects the forms of knowledge behind humanistic critiques of science as much as it rejects traditional religious epistemologies.

At the same time, recent developments in both the history of science (Eamon 1996) and in philosophy and theology (especially the criticism which John Milbank and I have mounted of univocal metaphysics), coupled with the growing recognition that fundamentalism is an integrally modern, secular movement (Marsden 1980) closer in its epistemology and metaphysics to modern science than to any kind of traditional spirituality, has suggested new ways of understanding the contemporary "culture" wars, i.e. as a struggle *within* the *Saeculum*.

Finally, we should note that the longstanding "religion and science" debate cuts across this question and addresses issues which are important to its resolution. Before proceeding it is worth considering the state of this debate in some depth. If one reads current accounts of the current "state of the question" regarding the relationship between religion and science one generally finds four principal alternative positions identified. The first of these is the conflict hypothesis, which holds that religion and science make conflicting and incompatible claims about the same questions. This view is held by most religious fundamentalists (Marsden 1980) on the one hand, and by advocates of the New Atheism (Harris 2004, Dawkins 2006, Dennett 2006, Kraus 2012) on the other. The fundamentalist position is actually a bit more nuanced for very few reject all secular science, but only those fundamental theories which they believe conflict with the revealed truth contained in the sacred scriptures. Generally this means the theory of evolution by means of random variation and natural selection and, for some, the "big bang" cosmology associated with the Standard Model in physics. For these they substitute, depending on the the extent of the commitment to biblical literalism, either "intelligent design" or something they call "creation science." The claim that the creation stories in Genesis constitute a science may seem outrageous from the vantage point of outsiders, but it is really integral to the fundamentalist claim that being and truth are univocal, the first consisting of a single set of "beings," one of whom is infinite, omniscient, omnipotent, etc. and the second consisting of a set of facts which are all ultimately empirically verifiable, if only through the "reliable witness" of the scriptures.

We reject this approach for a number of reasons. Religion and science don't ask the same questions and their objects have a fundamentally different epistemological and ontological status. Literalist readings of the scriptures are anti-traditional and unjustified by what the formal characteristics of most scriptural texts tell us about their nature. But we should note that this argument extends as much to the New Atheist as to the fundamentalist variant of the thesis. Both equally misunderstand the analogical sense in which the term Being is used and miss utterly the distinction between contingent and necessary Being and between truth and mere fact. Indeed, the New Atheism is ultimately little more than a farcical parody of fundamentalism and one that— vividly if accidentally—illustrates the fact that fundamentalism and technocratic secularism are ultimately of just two sides of the same coin.

The second approach to the relationship between religion and science is the idea of "nonoverlapping magisteria" advanced by Stephen Jay Gould (Gould 1997). This approach begins from the quite correct observation that religion and science ask two different kinds of questions. This difference might be summarized best by saying that science asks "how?" while religion (and philosophy) ask "why?" where "why? is understood in a fundamental sense, as demanding both an irreducible first cause and a purpose for whatever system is the object of the inquiry or a demonstration that such a cause and purpose do not exist. From this correct observation, however, Gould and the other partisans of this view conclude that religion and science have nothing to do with each other. This is a fundamental mistake. How the universe works has profound implications for what it all means and for whether or not we can conclude to a first principle (Mansueto 2005, 2012). And our understanding of what it all means can in turn generate new questions with scientific implications. A conclusion, for example, that there is no strict causality, as in some readings of quantum mechanics, affects our ability to employ something like the cosmological argument to demonstrate the existence of God. But philosophical verification of such a conclusion also has profound implications for sciences which retain classical understandings of causality, which must then be revised.

It is for this reason that the dominant position in the academic debate between religion and science is the position of dialogue (Barbour 2000, Haught 1995). Religion and science do indeed ask different questions and their answers have different epistemological and ontological status, but these answers are nonetheless relevant to each other, requiring an open ended dialogue in which science and religion may affect each other's conclusions in profound ways. For the most part this impact has been one way, with liberal and other secularizing religious trends accepting, for example, that scriptural accounts of creation must not be taken literally and that even classical philosophical arguments for the existence of God may need to be re-examined and re-formulated. Only a handful of scientists have returned the favor, taking seriously the questions which religion might raise for science.

This by itself ought to be enough to suggest that the position of "dialogue" is inadequate if not actually dishonest. This is not to suggest that the lessons which theologians and philosophers have taken from secular science are not valid. Nearly all of them almost certainly are. But a one-way discussion is not a dialogue, but simply an accommodation.

More broadly the position of dialogue does not deal adequately with fact that questions of "how?" and questions of "why?" while both important and valid, are not simply equal. Either we acknowledge the priority of knowing why over understanding how or we conclude that ultimately we can only know how. The latter position, which is ultimately that not only of technicist secularism but of theistic secularism with its high doctrine of divine sovereignty, essentially eliminates philosophy from the field and reduces theology to biblical hermeneutics. It is just that liberal advocates of dialogue use a nonliteralist hermeneutics compatible with secular science, even if they lack the metaphysical foundation (an analogical metaphysics) necessary to ground such a hermeneutics. They leave the ontological status of the sacred and the epistemological status of claims regarding the sacred unresolved even as they elucidate the many meanings of the sacred with great subtlety. This cannot but have contributed to the crisis of the liberal, and especially liberal Protestant churches, since it becomes unclear to even the unschooled (perhaps especially to the unschooled) exactly what they teach and believe.

The fourth position usually identified in accounts of the current state of the question in the relationship between religion and science is the position known as the "integrative" approach, which attempts to join the conclusions of science and religion into an integrated worldview, generally one which ultimately answers religious questions and sets the conclusions of secular science in a context compatible with such answers. The classic example of such an integrative approach is Teilhard de Chardin's *The Phenomenon of Man* (Teilhard 1959) and associated works. More recent attempts include Frank Tipler's *The Physics of Immortality* (Tipler 1994) and the work of spiritually inclined scientists and cultural theorists such as Bryan Swimme and Thomas Berry (Swimme and Berry 1992).

The integrationist position takes seriously the fact that real dialogue means real learning and thus real change. This means a willingness to challenge prior understandings of both scientific results and religious dogmas. The position also takes serious the need of human civilization for an integrated worldview which takes into account the contributions of different forms of knowledge. At the same time, most integrationist projects have left themselves vulnerable to an opportunistic reading of the scientific evidence in the interests of a religious agenda. In effect, aware that some readings and possibly even some fundamental results of secular science challenge *any* attempt to find meaning, they simply re-read these results in a way that eliminates the problem. This issue has been raised with respect to the work of Teilhard, Swimme, and Berry. Frank Tipler, one of the few physical scientists to attempt a comprehensive integrationist project, in addition to being only modestly informed philosophically and theologically, has, to all appearances, simply ignored the experimental results disconfirming his prediction that, if his Omega Point Theory is true, the Higgs Boson will weigh in at around 220-240 GeV. It its, apparently, terribly underweight.

There is, however, an additional problem with the integrationist position. It almost always simply ignores, or treats in a cursory fashion, the contributions of the discipline which was historically the link between scientific and religious interests, i.e. philosophy. This is no doubt partly due to the fact that much philosophy in the *Saeculum* has either retreated into "underlaboring" for the sciences (Bhaskar 1993) or avoided engaging the sciences at all, as is the case with much of the existential, phenomenological, and broadly continental tradition. There are, however, philosophers who have taken seriously the contributions of secular science and asked what they mean for questions of meaning and value. Most of these have come from the Thomistic tradition (Maritain 1936) or the Hegelian tradition (Harris 1991, 1992). Essentially these thinkers argue, albeit in somewhat different ways, that scientific results are of use to theology only when mediated by philosophy, that is only when their implications for epistemology, the philosophy of nature (including human nature), metaphysics, and ethics have been identified. The result has generally been both more respect for the integrity of secular science than we get from integrationist scientists-theologians, while at the same time generating or contributing significantly to the creation of an integrated worldview which authentically answers fundamental questions of meaning and value.

In what follows we will show that the Scientific Revolution of the seventeenth century and the Industrial Revolution of the eighteenth and nineteenth century were part of the same process, set in motion by the Norman Conquests, the Crusades, the *Reconquista*, and the Conquest of the Americas as the Augustinian Reaction and the Reformation. They are, in fact, simply the further extension of this process, the Iron Cage for which the *Protestant Ethic* is ultimately just an (admittedly rather austere) bait. In the process we will document the process by which older institutions such as guilds (including both craft and academic guilds) which served to nourish human creativity were destroyed and gave way to the bare power of *Capital* and *Empire*. And we will show that contemporary expressions of the technocratic project, from transhumanism and technological solutionism on the one hand to the New Atheism on the other are just the contemporary forms of legitimation of a project which can never give humanity what it seeks (*Being as Such*). Transhumanism represents what Lukacs (Lukacs 1953/1980) would have called a positive apologetic, selling us on what still fundamentally industrial technologies can do for us; the New Atheism operates in the tradition of what he would have called "negative apologetics," undercutting alternative forms of knowledge which suggest other *ways*.

This said, in accord with our commitment to the view that a metaphysics of participation excludes the possibility that any *way* is wholly outside the truth, we will identify aspects of the technocratic project which have enduring value. Specifically, we will argue that most secular science does in fact provide a broadly accurate, if still radically incomplete and still fundamentally changing, picture of how the universe works. Second, we will argue (as we did with respect to the *Protestant Ethic*) that while scientific, technological, and economic progress are not purely and directly either "God's work in the world" or a process of "godbuilding" they are *participations* in the work of God. This is particularly true if science and technology can transcend the mechanical and industrial mode they entered after the Augustinian Reaction and the Scientific Revolution and integrate the discipline of mathematical formalization which they have cultivated with that of teleological explanation, which they rejected for understandable but ultimately untenable reasons and, in the process, create a new alchemical *techne* which focuses on unleashing and cultivating the potential latent in matter rather than breaking down existing forms of organization in order to release energy and do work.

A Short History of Science as a Spiritual and Civilizational Discipline

Axial Science

Science as a distinctive enterprise based on empirical observation and systematic rational analysis of the phenomenal world, was one of the innovations of the Axial Age, the period between 800–200 BCE which witnessed a combined problematization of meaning, and a process of religious rationalization and democratization. It was, more specifically, an integral part of the process of religious rationalization. As we noted above, we can trace a direct line from Homer, for example, for whom the gods are characters in a story with real personalities, through Hesiod, for whom they have become personified natural forces, through the natural philosophers, for whom they have become merely natural forces, up to the pre-Socratics, for whom they are represented mathematically as "the One" or "the Infinite." This process reaches its culmination in the dialectical tradition with its teleological physics in which matter is drawn into Being and towards God. Similar processes occurred in the other major axial centers (Mansueto 2012).

Within this context, we should note two points. First, in essentially *all* major axial civilizations we see the emergence of theoretical perspectives which are, in some sense, predecessors of secular science. These generally take two forms. The first is a whole series of atomisms which reduce everything in the universe to indivisible material particles, sometimes of varying structure and thus with different properties. This outlook is characteristic of the doctrines of Democritus and the Epicureans in Hellas, of the Vaishsikas in India, and of the Mohists in China. Generally speaking these schools did not explicitly deny the existence of gods, but treated them as superior beings also composed of atoms. The Mohists in particular, however, and later Vaisheshikas, tended towards a monotheism which they supported with eutaxiological arguments, using the idea of a divine sovereign (though not necessarily a creator *ex nihilo*) to explain the ordered character of the universe (Chaterjee 1954, Radhakrishnan 1957: 386, Collins 1998: 234ff).

The second "secularizing" tendency was a radical skepticism which questioned the possibility of knowing much of anything. This view was upheld by the more radical Sophists in Hellas and the Skeptics in the later Hellenistic-Roman World, by the Caravakas in India and by the Legalists in China. Skepticism of this sort was closely bound up with state building projects and its proponents both acted as teachers and advisors to both wealthy families in republics like those of Greece and Rome and emerging monarchs in India and China.

These two tendencies taken together can be understood as part of the "second *Saeculum*" which brought into being the great Iron Age Empires, the Qin, the Romans, and (pre-Ashokan) Mauryans in particular.

The broader tendency of Axial Age science, however, tended towards a rationalization rather than a negation of preaxial mythologies. Generally speaking this took two forms: mathematical mysticism and teleological physics. The best known example of mathematical mysticism in the West is that of Pythagoras, who taught that number was the foundation of the universe. But as we noted before, mathematical concepts are fundamental to the rationalization of the idea of God and the development of a philosophical as opposed to a prophetic monotheism in the West. Of particular importance here are the claims of Xenophanes that God is One and of Anaximander that God is Infinite. A similar emphasis on the centrality of number appears in India in the tradition of *jyotisha* and *vastu* or Vedic astrology and architecture, in which the ratios between numbers plays an important role. In China, this trend was less developed, but by the Song dynasty Shao Yong developed a strongly mathematical and numerological interpretation of the *dao xue* which focused on achieving sagehood by decoding the mathematical structure of the great ultimate.

The most fully developed form of teleological physics is that of Aristotle. Matter for Aristotle was the possibility of organization, form its actuality. Motion was the gradual realization, over the course of time, of the latent potential of matter as it moved toward the perfection of form. The explanation of particular forms of motion involved an understanding of the matter in question, of the form that was being perfected, and of the efficient cause—that by which the change took place, as well as the end toward which the change was ordered. Ultimately, however, the whole process of change was grounded in the attractive power of the first unmoved mover, the incredible beauty, truth, goodness and integrity of which drew all things to itself (Aristotle, *Metaphysics* 12.7). Thus, minerals tend toward stability or the conservation of their own forms, plants toward nutrition, growth, and the reproduction of their forms. Animals actively pursue the goods they need for nutrition, growth, and reproduction by moving themselves toward these goods that they know by sensation. Human beings, being rational animals, seek the cultivation of the intellect and the will as well as the perfection and reproduction of the body. Everything in the sublunar realm is, furthermore, driven by the motions of the heavenly spheres. Celestial influences lead to the combination of various qualities (hot and cold, wet and dry) to form various minerals, a process which in turn affects the underlying material substratum out of which living systems emerge. This was the basis for the development in the medieval period of the disciplines of astrology and alchemy. The stars, with their perfectly regular motions, also draw the human intellect upward toward the intelligible. Each of the celestial spheres is, in turn, moved by emulation for the one above it. But there cannot be an infinite regress. There must, therefore, be some first unmoved mover, the beauty, intelligibility, and goodness of which moves all the others without itself ever being moved. This, for Aristotle, is God (Aristotle *Physics, Metaphysics*, Lindberg 1992).

From this point of view physics, while not the study of God in Herself (that is the object of metaphysics) is clearly the study of divine action, or of the progressive spiritualization of matter. It is a sacred science.

Similar tendencies developed in India and China. Thus the Samkya tradition in India developed a doctrine of cosmic evolution in which *prakriti*, or matter, understood precisely as limit, gradually trained *purusa* in its independence and infinity. These doctrines were supplemented by an element cosmology and ayurvedic disciplines which cultivated both health and spiritual development. In China five element physics merged with the doctrines of the *yin-yang* and the emerging concept of the *tao* to suggest that nature has its own ultimately inscrutable way which can, however, be partially deciphered. By understanding and following the way we can achieve health and, ultimately, sagehood (Collins 1998).

What this means is that aside from the atomistic and skeptical trends, Axial Age science presented little difficulty for religion. Indeed, it formed part of the larger dialectical foundation on which axial and postaxial religious doctrines rested. And the *techne* they promoted, which might broadly be characterized as "alchemical" in character, focused on cultivating the latent potential in matter in order to catalyze growth and development, the higher levels of which were, in effect spiritual. As James Elkins points out "alchemy rehearses and often speeds up process that the earth does naturally by brewing metals underground. The work was God's and it was the ongoing perfection of the world. (Elkins 1999: 73)"

This is not suggest that there were not conflicts between teleological physics and postaxial religious traditions. Among other things, as we have noted above, Aristotelian physics provided at best a limited ground for doctrines of creation *ex nihilo* and personal immortality. But until the time of the Augustianian reactions these concerns were very much in the background.

Teleological physics ultimately ran into serious scientific problems. This is because it was unable to advance a unified theory of motion. How does one explain teleologically a decaying corpse or a thrown javelin? These processes do not seem in any sense ordered to the perfection of form. Thus the distinction between natural and violent motion. This in turn led to a distinction between the celestial realm, where all motion is natural, and the sublunar realm where both kinds of change occur. Second, teleological science had considerable difficulty coming to terms with the growing evidence that even the heavens were not ordered in the perfect manner required by theory. This was a problem long before Copernicus and Kepler. There are sharp differences between Aristotle's cosmology and the formal, mathematical models of his near-contemporary Eudoxus. Refinement of these models by Ptolemy and others involved a departure from the perfect spherical motion which was central to Aristotle's system long before Copernicus opted for heliocentrism or Kepler displaced the circle with the ellipse (Murdoch and Sylla 1978, Grant 1978, Pedersen 1978, Lindberg 1992).

There were two ways to resolve this problem. One would have been to generalize the concept of teleology in such a way as to accommodate the reality of violent motion, and to abandon the particular cosmological models developed by Aristotle in order to save the principle of teleological ordering. There were powerful reasons to take just precisely this approach. Aristotle and his interpreters had, after all, already implicitly shown that the only complete explanation is a teleological explanation. This is because a complete explanation must terminate in a principle which (directly or indirectly) explains everything else while being self-explanatory. Such a principle must be necessary, infinite, and perfect (and thus divine), and it must cause exclusively by the attractive power of its own perfection (otherwise it would be in motion itself and would thus require some other explanatory principle, resulting in an infinite regress) (Aristotle, *Metaphysics* 1071b–1076b, Thomas *Summa Theologiae* I, Q2).

Secular Science

This was not, however, the road taken. Teleology was abandoned altogether, and (though this was never acknowledged, or perhaps, even really recognized) the possibility of a complete explanation along with it. Instead, an attempt was made to develop increasingly general mathematical formalisms which describe motion (now conceived exclusively as change in place over time). Thus the whole history of mathematical physics, beginning with the special theories of Galileo and Kepler, up through the "first unification" by Newton, and each of the successive generalizations and unifications: Hamiltonian dynamics, Maxwell's equations, relativity, quantum mechanics, and most recently quantum cosmology.

The reasons for this choice against teleology were as much political-theological as scientific. Teleological physics presented specific problems for the doctrines of divine sovereignty which emerged as a reflex of the strong state structure in *Dar-al—Islam*, especially after the Turkic invasion, and in Christendom as a result of the Norman conquests, the crusades, and the *Reconquista*. The idea that the universe was eternal, whether an emanation from or a spontaneous response of prime matter to the attractive power of God, the rejection of extracosmic void space, of the plurality of worlds, and of the possibility that God could move the universe rectilinearly, as well as the affirmation of the unity of the Agent Intellect all undercut Asharite and Augustinian doctrines of divine sovereignty and personal immortality. Stephen Tempier, the reactionary Bishop of Paris condemned a number of "Averroist" thesis, including the eternity of the university and the impossibility of moving the universe in a straight line, on the grounds that they conflicted with the emerging idea of divine sovereignty (Duhem 1909).

What this suggests, of course, is that the emergence of secular science and mathematical physics, far from representing a turn away from sacred to the secular was, at least to begin with, a rejection of one theology for another. Specifically, it was a rejection of an Aristotelian theology which regarded God as a teleological attractor and spiritualization as an immanent property of matter itself, for an Augustinian theology which regarded God as a an absolute sovereign and matter as inert and dependent. And this remained *explicitly* the case up through the eighteenth century. Newton (Newton 1700) Paley (Paley 1802/1986) and the like took for granted the fact that the wonderful order which they were describing had a divine author in terms of whom alone its beauty and harmony could be adequately explained. Indeed, they regarded the motion they described as, in effect, divine action and their science as no less sacred than the old Aristotelian physics.

What this new discipline *did* contribute was a way of formalizing the efficiency of our work on behalf of God's plan in history. The equations of Newtonian physics include one for work:

$$W=fs$$

where W is work, f is force and s is distance. This allows us to measure the quantity of work done per unit of time, energy, money, etc. The more work we do the more efficiently, the better we carry out God's work in the world. In this sense Weber was quite correct that Protestantism and capitalism (indeed industrial production in general) are intimately bound up with each other.

The further development of mathematical physics, to be sure, complicated this relationship somewhat, but it did not change it. The generalization of Newtonian mechanics into a universal dynamic theory in which the position and velocity of every particle could be accounted for in terms of that of every other particle made it possible, at least in principle, to "account for" everything in the universe without reference to any immaterial or metaphysical principles (Laplace 1799–1825). Thus Laplace's claim that God is "an hypothesis of which I have no need." But all that this did was to create a more rigorous distinction between science and theology. Science didn't need theology in order to provide a complete mathematical description of the universe, but nothing in the descriptions it provided contradicted the foundational claim of the Augustinian tradition: that of a sovereign creator. Later scientific results (the second law of thermodynamics, the Poincaré Recurrence Theorem, inflationary cosmology) may have called into question the idea that God's plan for the universe is focused on the creation of an innerworldly kingdom of God, but then most conservative Protestantism also abandoned this idea during the same period. And the implications of these results for the secular ideal are even more devastating. How does one have unlimited progress in a universe structured by the Eternal Return or destined for a cosmic heat death?

The most recent fundamental theories, from relativity through quantum mechanics to the various attempts at unifying them have not really changed this situation. While the occasional fundamentalist may rail against the "Big Bang Theory," the fact remains that this theory is quite friendly to theism, especially the a univocal theism with a doctrine of creation *ex nihilo*. And the more subjectivist interpretations of quantum mechanics mesh quite well with neo-Berkeleyan attempts to articulate a subjective idealist metaphysics which reconciles theism with secular science (Tipler 1994).

The situation with biology is very different. Mathematical physics from Newton through string theory has created more problems for pagans anxious to find an immanent divine principle than it has for Jews, Christians, or Muslims convinced that the universe is the work of a divine sovereign. Biology, on the other hand, has challenged the idea of divine sovereignty much more seriously. In order for us to understand this we need to trace out in greater depth the archeology of biological theory.

It is easy to read biology as simply an application of mathematical physics to living systems, and much biology (especially molecular biology and genetics) does, in fact, aspire to this status. But the real challenge to the doctrine of divine sovereignty has come not from this sort of physical and chemical reductionism, which can be read as simply an explication of how the product of God's free and sovereign act of creation works, but rather from the theory of evolution by means of random variation and natural selection. Interestingly enough, the roots of this theory can be traced not so much to biology proper as to the demography and economics. Indeed, it might be properly understood as a theory in the subdiscipline of *ecology*, understood as the discipline which analyzes the way in which organisms and populations of organisms interact with each other in a larger physical and biological environment—including interactions which are technological or which involve the centralization and allocation of resources as well as their production (i.e. what is ordinarily understood as economics). The development of this theory must be seen to begin with the work of

Adam Smith, who shows how individuals pursuing their own self interest spontaneously allocate their resources in whatever way leads to the highest rate of return. This is, in effect, a theory of natural section, Next comes the Malthusian demonstration that if food production grows arithmetically and population grows geometrically (we say if, because it is not entirely obvious that either claim is always true) the result will be widespread shortages of food and mass starvation. This intensifies the pressure to innovate and thus strengthens the process of natural selection. Darwinian evolutionary theory simply draws out the implication of this larger paradigm for the "origin of the species."(Smith 1776, Malthus 1798, Darwin 1859/1970).

Given this background, it is no accident that the most complete statement of evolutionary theory in recent years has come not from a biologist but from an economist, F.A. Hayek (Hayek 1988), who theorized human orders (he disliked collective terms such as societies) as systems of individuals seeking to maximize their self interest under conditions of scarcity. In the process they develop new practices. Those which are effective survive and become part of an ongoing tradition; those which are not are discarded. Among the evolutionarily successful practices he identified are language, technology, the family, the market, and religion. Centralized systems of rational redistribution, on the other hand, have, in his mind, demonstrated their lack of survival value and are being discarded.

The spiritual and civilizational imperative, from this point of view, is either, as Hayek seems to prefer, to act in accord with practices which have demonstrated their survival value and profitability, or to act in such as way as to develop as many new practices which promote survival and profitability as possible.

Hayek, whose ideological as opposed to scientific mission was to help provide a sound theoretical framework from the neoliberal-social conservative alliance which dominated politics in the US and the UK in the years between 1978 and 2008 and which remains influential, is quite explicit in linking his scientific results with divine imperatives: "be fruitful, multiply, and fill the earth (Genesis 1)." But he also makes it clear that his argument for religion is based on its survival value, not its truth claims. Here we are on the cusp of the transition between theistic and technocratic secularism.

There are, as we have noted (Mansueto 2012), significant *scientific* problems with this paradigm. Specifically, random variation turns out not to supply anything like the level of innovation necessary to explain evolutionary change. Complex systems theorist Ilya Prigogine has shown that

> the time necessary to produce a comparatively small protein chain of around 100 amino acids by *spontaneous* formation of

structure is much longer than the age of the Earth. Hence, spontaneous formation of structure is ruled out ... according to the modern theory of self-organizing systems, classical arguments concerning the "coincidental" realization of a complex living system cannot be employed (Zimmerman 1991).

Molecular biologist Barry Hall, similarly, has found that the bacterium E. coli produces needed mutations at a rate roughly 100 million times greater than would be expected if they came about by chance. Nor can random variation and natural selection account for the fact that evolutionary changes often seem to occur rather suddenly, rather than in gradual increments, as the theory of natural selection would suggest. A retina or a cornea, after all, without the rest of the organ, would have no survival value by itself, and would be unlikely to be preserved in future generations.

None of this should be taken as requiring an external, supernatural principle to drive or direct evolution, but it does suggest that there are natural processes which are at work which we have not yet adequately theorized and which operate in ways that operate in tension with, even if they do not contradict thermodynamics.

The new discipline of complex systems theory and associated developments in biology (which should not be confused with intelligent design theories, much less creationism, which actually pull in the opposite direction) are trying to theorize the self-organizing dynamism of matter. This work is only beginning, but it suggests at least a partial return, on firmer empirical and mathematical ground, to old Aristotelian and vitalist perspectives.

This said, the challenge to theistic secularism is the same. Evolutionary theory, whether in its Neo-Darwinian or complex systems form, shows that it is quite possible for complex organization to emerge apart from the action of an intelligent designer. This still leaves, of course, the question of why there is something rather than nothing. But theistic secularism with its univocal metaphysics cannot answer that question anyway. This is apparent in its recourse to the ontological argument, when it attempts a rational proof of the existence of God, which we have shown to convertible with Zorn's Lemma, which cannot be proven (Mansueto 2002b), or (more consistently) to blind faith.

What happens, of course, when the theistic veneer drops away is that theistic becomes technicist secularism: a god building focused on scientific and technological progress. It is interesting to note that this kind of godbuilding only emerges when scientific results such as the Poincaré Recurrence Theorem and the Second Law of Thermodynamics are already calling it into question. And it is rarely articulated explicitly, with a handful of exceptions such as the left Bolshevik Alexandr Bogdanov (Bogdanov 1928/1980) and astrophysicist Frank Tipler (Tipler 1994). For the most part, however, godbuilding has functioned as a kind of secret religion, hidden even from itself, upheld by people who already know it to be false and hopeless, but who hope nonetheless in the limited temporal goods which scientific and technical progress can offer.

John Milbank (2014: 81ff)[1] has recently demonstrated the effective convertibility of theistic and atheistic possibilisms. From Duns Scotus on, he argues, the defense of divine sovereignty involved postulating hypostatized "possibilities" along side the actual world decreed by divine will. As the internal logic of this position was worked out, especially, by Leibniz, it became clear that, because everything is dependent on everything else, this implied an infinity of hypostatized "possible worlds." This, in turn, leads to the idea, now widespread in physics, that all possible worlds exist actually, somewhere, somehow, in some sense. The fact that ours seems fine tuned for us is simply the result of a selection bias, in that only a world which can support the emergence of complex organization, life, and intelligence, can be known to exist. It is a very short step from this meaning of "selection," though, to the idea that selection operates across possible worlds, with those permitting the emergence of intelligence also, ultimately, permitting intelligence to become pervasive, omnipotent, and omniscient, constructing Tipler's Omega Point. And of course there can be only *one* being which is infinite, omnipotent, omniscient, etc. because all such beings would be identical with each other and the existence of multiples would imply limit.

1. Milbank also argues that possibilism can be given a "Western Buddhist" cast by reading the manifold of possible worlds as a kind of void of virtuality. This may be true, provided that the qualification "Western" is both emphasized and properly understood to mean that Buddhism is *re-interpreted* to accomodate a univocal metaphysics. Such Buddhisms might include both the very austere reading of the Madhyamika suggested by Kalapuhana (Kalapuhana 1992) and the subjective idealism which passes for Buddhism in the New Age movement. Authentic Buddhism, however, is based on a sharp distinction between conventional reality, the world of facts and events which we experience through the senses and formalize through concepts and reality as it actually *is*, i.e. the process of dependent origination. This is a more "negative" characterization of the first principle than we find in other axial traditions (in the specific sense of reflecting an option for the *via negativa*) but the result is still an analogical metaphysics. It is just that it is an analogy of nonbeing rather than of Being, where nonbeing is understood conventionally as finitude, contingency, and thus suffering but ultimately as pure relationality and generativity beyond any claim to substance or any claim for self, a realm in which we live not only in but as each other's embrace. It will be fundamental to our argument that engagement with this way is essential if we are to break through to the highest degree of spiritual development in which we know ourselves in and as Being, for the simple reason that any accidental *theosis* or union with Being prior to this remains tainted by the desire for self-subsistence.

So radical theism becomes radical atheism and them becomes theism again all without any change in the underlying univocal metaphysics.

Thus we can, in a very real sense, say that while Tipler's science is almost certainly wrong, it *is* the only correct interpretation of the internal logic of the possibilism which began with the assertion of divine sovereignty during the Augustinian reaction, giving birth to both the Reformation and the Scientific Revolution, theistic and technocratic secularism which ultimately turn out to be the same thing. This suggests that even from the vantage point of a science, metaphysics, and theology we reject, the integrationist approach to religion and science is the only fully consistent option. Mathematical physics, including thermodynamics and statistical mechanics, evolutionary theory, and its chronologically earlier but logical subsequent twin, political economy, are the *theoria* of the *Saeculum*.

We need, finally, to assess where the New Atheism (Harris 2004, Dawkins 2006, Dennett 2006, Kraus 2012), fits in this analysis. We have already considered the significance of this trend from an epistemological and methodological perspective. Here we focus on its social basis, substantive claims, and political-theological valence. In a certain sense the New Atheism (Harris 2004, Dawkins 2006, Dennett 2006, Kraus 2012) appears by comparison with transhumanism to be sober and sane. The New Atheism is defined above all by the claim that the idea of God is scientifically testable and has been disconfirmed by the emergence of more economical theories of the origin of the universe and the emergence of complex organization, life, and intelligence. While they tend to remain optimistic (for good reason) about what science can do for humanity, they avoid the unsubstantiated optimism of the transhumanists and counsel humanity to come to terms with the ultimate meaninglessness of its existence.

The reality, however is more complex. Politically, the New Atheists argue against toleration of religion and for active efforts to combat it. The New Atheism shares the empiricism and univocal metaphysics of the fundamentalists and transhumanists. Everything that exists exists in the same way and that everything that is true is a fact which can be empirically verified. It differs from fundamentalist Christianity regarding what both treat as a simple matter of fact: the existence of an infinitely powerful Being to whom submission is the only possible response. In the absence of such a Being we are free to seek as much technological power, rooted in scientific understanding of how the universe works, as possible. It differs from transhumanism primarily in not making such radical claims regarding what science and technology can do for us.

Or does it? Identifying the social basis and political valence of the New Atheism is challenging. It is no accident, however, that many of its advocates are biologists and that the largest single funder of atheism as a social movement (if not precisely of the New Atheism as an ideological trend) is Todd Stiefel (Dan Merica, The money man behind atheism's activism, CNN 2013.03.23), scion of a pharmaceutical industry family. This is hardly surprising. Fundamentalist mischief is felt most directly in attacks on the teaching of evolutionary theory and on important medical research, such as stem cell technology and genetic engineering. Neo-Darwinian Evolution is the fundamental theory behind the biological sciences and biotechnological research promises both real if perhaps also morally ambiguous solutions to serious human problems—and handsome profits for those who undertake it.

There is, however, more at issue here. Understanding the affinity at this level implies that the biotechnology and the larger healthcare sector of which it is a part should be classed with other high technology and information sectors as part of the more "progressive" wing of Capital, something which appears to be sustained by the political donation patterns of the biotechnology sector, if not of healthcare generally (Open Secrets). This is misleading. The link between biology and the New Atheism is both deeper and more sinister. Biology remains fundamentally an empirical science in a way physics can no longer really claim to be. It is not surprising that it would share with fundamentalism an empiricist approach to knowledge and become locked in a battle to the death over "the facts," as though establishing matters of fact resolved everything. Darwinian theory, furthermore, while it undercuts fundamentalist theism in fact shares with it a rather harsh view of the universe as dominated by amoral forces which select and elect without respect to substantively rational considerations of merit. What this suggests is that despite what is fundamentally a *tactical* decision to support the Democratic Party and comparable center parties in the electoral arena, the New Atheism and the biotechnological sectors which support it lean *fundamentally* and *strategically* to the *right*. If fundamentalism counsels submission to a celestial tyrant, the New Atheism counsels submission to the invisible hand of evolutionary and market selection, with the *fit* standing in for the *elect*. To this must be added the consideration that in a civilization driven by the biotechnological sector *fitness* will be determined in part by access to biotechnological treatments and enhancements which in turn depend on market position.

It is also possible to regard transhumanism and the New Atheism as distinct but complementary apologetics for the *Saeculum*. Transhumanism proclaims proudly everything that the *Saeculum* can and will do for us, if only we endure another generation or two as batteries; the New Atheism disarms alternative perspectives which might appeal to those skeptical of these claims, while protecting the transhumanist research agenda. This is the distinction between what Lukacs, comparing the optimistic liberal democratic defenses of emerging capitalism with the pessimistic ideologies which capitalism began to generate after it became established, called the direct and indirect apologetics (Lukacs 1953/1980).

What makes all of these empiricist and univocal approaches radically inadequate as a way of answering questions of meaning and value is their failure to distinguish between explaining *how* (the task of science) and explaining *why* (the task of the various wisdoms). The existence (or nonexistence) of an omnipotent Being, while strategically significant for humanity, does not by itself have any direct ethical or spiritual consequences. Might does not make right and power, unless it is understood as the power of Being as such, something of which empiricism in both its fundamentalist and technocratic varieties is incapable, is not the same thing as meaning or value. *Indeed, it would not be possible to identify a question with less ethical or spiritual relevance than the existence of nonexistence of God as most fundamentalist Christians and most New Atheists understand the concept.* Claiming otherwise is tantamount to arguing that if only Hitler or Stalin had managed to become powerful enough, they would have, *ipso facto* ceased to be icons of evil and become absolute moral and spiritual authorities.

Fundamentalism is a secularism; transhumanism and its sober twin, the New Atheism are, for all intents and purposes, fundamentalisms.

Towards a New Science and a New *Techne*

All this leads to the inescapable conclusion that, if we are to handle the relationship between religion and science correctly, we must recognize that we are dealing with an encounter, or rather with multiple encounters between *ways* of being human, and not just between disciplines. The only consistent approach to the relationship between disciplines is the integrationist approach, since only such an approach results in a worldview which is consistent within a particular *way*, and that this integration must be philosophically mediated, paying attention to philosophical presuppositions and implications. Indeed, if Duhem (Duhem 1909), Milbank (Milbank 2014), and I (Mansueto 2012) are right, then it must also be *theologically* mediated since the option for possibilism and thus for mathematical physics was ultimately driven by theological concerns.

In this context it is possible only to map out in the most preliminary way what such an integration looks like. Elaboration will have to await later volumes of this work which, I hope, will include a complete theology of the cosmos, including, physical, biological, social, and suprasocial degrees of being. But the map itself tells us a lot.

First, it should be clear that, given the way in which we have characterized theology, as always beginning with *theoria,* with looking and listening, with seeing and hearing, and thus with the *world,* theology and indeed philosophy must build on the firm foundation not only of empirical observation but of *science* of some kind. The conclusions of science must, furthermore, within their own sphere be taken as final and serve as the basis for higher order philosophical and theological abstraction and superabstraction. Otherwise we have no firm foundation in reality (Maritain 1937).

Second, we are in very good position, based on the foregoing analysis, to specify exactly how much of this science modern secular science provides, and where it is lacking. The science which emerged from the Augustinian reaction and the Scientific Revolution of the seventeenth century provides a rigorous, formal, mathematical description of how the universe is structured.

What this means is that there is no need, in order to challenge the hegemony of theistic and technocratic secularism, to challenge the facts with which secular science presents us, or even the analysis of those facts in the sense of the basic mathematical formalisms which make up most of secular science. While it must be remembered that one of the strengths of this science is its commitment to revisiting and revising earlier conclusions, it is unlikely that the main results of relativity, quantum theory, thermodynamics, statistical mechanics, evolutionary biology, or political economy will be overturned, at least any more than relativity and quantum mechanics overturned Newtonian dynamics. Facts, while *merely* facts, are in fact factual.

Where our perspective differs is in the conviction that knowledge (and Being) do not *stop* with the facts. We must proceed to *explain* them and to ask what they *mean.* As we have argued at much greater length in another context (Mansueto 2012) what the *Saeculum* calls science is actually a preliminary or auxiliary to science, specifying in a mathematically rigorous way what must be explained and interpreted. This is nothing to be scoffed at. We don't want to spend our time interpreting what it means that the sun and the other planets revolve around the earth when, in fact, the earth and other planets revolve around the sun. But it is not enough.

In my earlier works (Mansueto 2010, 2012) I have argued for the restoration of a teleological paradigm in science, as the condition for any possible unification of physical theory, much less of a unification of physical, biological, and social theory. The model which I have proposed is frankly Aristotelian, even if to attempts to incorporate into the Aristotelian framework the role of contradiction and decay in what I see as ultimately a process of cosmohistorical evolution ordered towards transcendental ends. More specifically, I have argued that any process, physical, biological, or social can be analyzed as a result of the interaction of 1) a material base, i.e. whatever is given at the lower level of organization (the structure of pure possible beings given by mathematics generally, the structure of space time, the fundamental physical forces, the laws of statistical mechanics, thermodynamics, and complexity, evolution and natural selection, a resulting ecosystem, technologies, economies, polities, cultures, etc.) 2) structures which define how the process under analysis works, and 3) a transcendental end, Being, to which everything is ordered, but which may be represented at various levels of organization by lower order ends (thermodynamic stability, survival and reproduction, a civilizational ideal, etc.)

This approach, I think, represents a fundamental advance over the division between philosophy and "science" which has existed since the seventeenth century, in which science asks how the world works and philosophy asks why, as though the two had nothing to do with each other. This said, model persists in allowing the sacred to be segregated at the level of the *telos* or transcendental end, and does not explain fully how the material base and the structures by which it is ordered to Being are themselves sacred.

In order to overcome this limitation we must move from explanation to interpretation, asking what it *means* that the universe is structured in a specific way and thus ordered to Being in one way rather than another. Specifically, I propose to take the fundamental theories of physics, biology, and sociology and bring them into dialogue with ancient sacred sciences in a way which will allow terms like sacred geometry make sense in a post-Euclidian world, and which will endow the use of terms like "energy" by certain religious traditions with scientific rigor, and which will explain just how various forms of matter, such as minerals, life forms, and civilizations have sacred significance even as they operate in accord with establish physical, biological, and social law.

We have already done some of this in *Knowing God: The Ultimate Meaningfulness of the Universe* (Mansueto 2012) pointing out, for example, that something like the Second Law of Thermodynamics can be understood as operating both to make room for the emergence of more complex forms of organization by limiting the ability of any finite and contingent form to establish and maintain its hegemony and, for intelligent life, to teach us by means of the hard lessons of our finitude and contingency the infinite and necessary Being which is our true end.

Along with this new teleological science, we have argued for a restored "hortic" or "alchemical" *techne*, not in the sense of a literal return to the specific technologies of the horticultural era or the middle ages, much less an attempt to transmute "base" matter into either gold or the philosopher's stone (which our analysis of Being and Dependent Origination above suggests is quite impossible) but rather in the sense of a *techne* which, based on an understanding of the dynamic by which matter becomes spirit, cultivates and releases the potential latent in diverse forms of matter and helps them grow and develop. We have outlined what such a *techne* might look like in more detail in *The Death of Secular Messianisms* (Mansueto 2010a).

We will have more to say about the spiritual significance of such a *techne*, but before we can we need to consider one last encounter: with the humanistic secularisms which derived from the Averroist countereaction and which found expression in the attempt to create a collective political subject—the rationally autonomous individual, the *demos*, the party, or the *ethnos*—which might make humanity the master of its own destiny.

8

The Solution to the Riddle of History

Central to the argument of this work is the proposition that, while deeply and profoundly flawed, the humanistic variant of secularism is both distinct from the technocratic variant at the core level of its metaphysics and its spiritual aim and, in the end, an integral part of the emerging movement to take *Sanctuary* from the instrumentalizing power of the *Saeculum*. What we are calling humanistic secularism is, fundamentally, a development of Hellenism formed and transformed by its encounter with Judaism, Islam, and Christianity and later by reaction to the Augustinian Reaction, the Reformation, and the Scientific, Industrial, Democratic, and Socialist Revolutions. It shares with this tradition a metaphysics of *Esse*, of Being as the causative power of existence, as opposed to the metaphysics of beings which characterizes the later Augustinian strain in Christianity and technocratic secularism, but it understands Being not as Substance, but rather as Subject, and treats it as radically and fully immanent in the phenomenal world and most especially in human consciousness. It aims at deification by constructing a political subject—whether the rationally autonomous individual, the people as *demos* or *ethnos*, or the proletariat, which will make humanity the master of its own destiny and thus the effective "subject-object" of the cosmohistorical evolutionary process. We will include in this trend its autocritical tendencies, from critical theory and romanticism through deconstruction and the new "atheology" represented by the late Derrida and Agamben.

It is the aim of this chapter to demonstrate that our characterization of humanistic secularism is, in fact, correct and that it is, as we have claimed, both radically inadequate, but not at this point in history the principal threat to the human spiritual and civilizational project, but rather an ally of the axial traditions in resistance to the instrumentalizing *Saeculum*. This will entail not just philosophical critique, but analysis of the trend as a social movement, with a definite social basis and soteriological strategy and trajectory (or multiple but related strategies and trajectories). More specifically, we will argue that the trend is an expression of the aspirations of the humanistic intelligentsia which emerged as the old Masters of Arts were marginalized from the Catholic Church by the Augustinian reaction, and then organized to achieve state power in alliance, at various times, with the peasantry, the aristanate, the proletariat, and the petty bourgeoisie, usually—though not always—in opposition to the aristocracy and Capital. We will show that it is to this trend that we owe the enormous gains of the past 500 years with respect to personal freedom and democratic participation. But we will also have to come to terms with grave crimes against humanity, including the Shoah and the excesses of Stalinism and the Cultural Revolution, committed by advocates of the trend and in its name. We will show that synthesis between axial trends and humanistic secularism is, in fact, possible and indeed essential if the axial project is to be completed. But this synthesis must take place on rather different terms than those envisioned by earlier liberal or liberation theologies, religious socialisms, etc. Specifically this will entail taking more seriously both feminist critiques of the axial traditions and "conservative" axial critiques of humanistic secularism of the kind advanced by Radical Orthodoxy and its predecessors. On the feminist side, we will argue—with Mary Daly—that even the most ruthlessly critical criticism in the dialectical tradition has failed to address the original expropriation which was constitutive of the *Saeculum*: the expropriation of female creative power by men. On the conservative side we will affirm, with Milbank, that because humanity is naturally ordered to and end which transcends our capacity—that of full deification—the rigid separation between reason and revelation, nature and grace, philosophy and theology, *polis* and *ecclesia* suggested by some forms of Late, Second, and Third Scholasticisms is untenable (and contrary to the teachings of Thomas). We will also affirm with him that historical materialism or other forms of social theory cannot simply be annexed to Christian theology as "methods of social analysis" as many theologies of liberation suggest, because these theories are, in fact, the carriers of distinct and organically secular spiritualities. At the same time, against both Daly and Milbank, we will affirm that humanity can find an authentic path to deification only by exploring fully the blind pathways forged by patriarchy and Promethean secularisms. It is only by understanding why and how deification by means of patriarchal expropriation, conquest and exploitation—and even inner worldly revolutionary struggle directed at the construction of the "unique subject-object" of human history—are all misguided and impossible that we can, in fact arrive at the "way of ways" we will map out in the final chapter of this work, a way which integrates seeking wisdom, doing justice, and ripening being in the context of a cosmohistorical process which is a participation—but always and only a participation—in the life of God. Another way of putting this is to say that the critical functions of humanistic secularism and especially its historical materialist and critical theoretical and even deconstructive forms cannot be simply jettisoned. Alienation, including religious alienation, is real. The historical-dialectical critique of religion must be revised, but it cannot be discarded.

We will proceed largely by means of a philosophically critical comparative social history of the trend, beginning with Latin Averroism and reaching forward through the trend's liberal, democratic, socialist, populist, and critical/deconstructive moments. This will in turn make possible an opening to the synthesis we envision.

A Critical History of Humanistic Secularism

From Averroism to Liberalism

Our first task will be to demonstrate the underlying metaphysical and soteriological continuity of humanistic secularism from its point of inception in the Averroist Counter-Reaction to the Condemnations of 1270 and 1277 up through its transmutation into (a certain form) of Liberalism in the seventeenth and eighteenth centuries.

By comparison with Thomas Aquinas and John Meister Eckhardt, the "Radical" Aristotelians -Almaric of Bena, David of Dinant, and Siger of Brabant-as well as later "Latin Averroists" such as Marsiglio di Padova, are all conservatives. They are not, to be sure, conservative *Christians*. They represent, rather, an importation into Christendom of the cautious spirit of Islamic *falasafa*: cautious in the sense that they limit what reason can achieve -at the outside we can know everything the Agent Intellect knows- and thus what humanity as a whole can achieve. We have also noted that this entailed a shift in the principal locus of meaning from the pursuit of beatitude towards innerworldly civilization building activity.

In order to understand this claim it is necessary first to clarify the principal doctrines of the Radical Aristotelians. First, they upheld, along with Aristotle and most of his non-Christian commentators, the eternity of the world, a conclusion which flowed quite naturally from the Aristotelian doctrine of the unmoved mover. If the unmoved mover was eternal, and drew the world into being by its attractive power, then the world must naturally have been in existence as long as the unmoved mover itself—forever. Even Thomas conceded that this claim could be rejected only on the basis of revelation. Second, however, they upheld the unity of the Agent, and in some cases the Potential, Intellect. As we have seen above, in our analysis of the Islamic commentators, this doctrine radically undercuts human individuality and undermines the philosophical basis for belief in anything like personal immortality. Individuation comes exclusively as a result of our materiality, which is precisely what are charged with overcoming. For followers of Ibn Sina, we might obtain a kind of union with the Agent Intellect in—a very imperfect—contemplation of the divine as it is reflected in the material reality of the sublunar realm. For followers of Ibn Rusd, even that seems difficult to imagine. Material civilizational progress represents not only our natural *telos* but the outer limit of our potential. Human beings are, in the end, simply information collection devices and manual laborers for the Agent Intellect, sharing in its work of creation, and then dying. As individuals, we mean nothing. We will see this spirit replicated in modern dialectics—both that of Hegel and that of Marx, Engels, and their interpreters.

Finally, the conservatism of the Radical Aristotelians is reflected in their doctrine of God. We see little evidence here of any assimilation of the innovations of Ibn Sina and Thomas Aquinas. Indeed, they even seem to retreat from Aristotle's own identification of God as first and foremost the *final* cause of the universe—an identification which Ibn Rush had sustained, as we noted above (Trachtenberg 1957 in Dahm 1987).

Among the Latin Averroists, this position is documented for Siger of Brabant, and later by Giordano Bruno. Most, however, developed interpreted Aristotelianism in a much more radically pantheistic way. For some this meant idealism. Almaric of Bena, for example, reasoning that it was form, not matter, which characterized actual being, Almaric argued that in a very real sense everything is form, and thus implicitly, at least, everything is God (Dahm 1987: 94). David of Dinant, on the other hand, argued that since God is the source of all things, God must *be* prime matter.

> The philosophy of David of Dinant is .. a materialist pantheism . . . The basic ground of this philosophy is the pantheistic unity of the material, spiritual, and divine principles . . . this unity lies not in the empirical world, and not in the reason of the individual, and not in the matter of single things, but in a higher realm, where reason *as such* melds into God and "prime matter (Trachtenberg 1957: 96–97 in Dahm 1987)."

As in the Islamic context, Radical Aristotelianism—here often called Latin Averroism—points forward toward dialectical materialism. Lacking a way to theorize the deification of humanity, it focuses its attention instead on civilizational progress. Lacking a coherent doctrine of connatural knowledge it cannot trust that ordinary people can achieve wisdom, and so casts itself in the role of an esoteric truth reserved for the elite—or revolutionary vanguard—while the people are led to an approximate truth by means of the imaginative language of religion. Ultimately, however, this would prove a dead end. Civilizational progress which does not point beyond itself toward deification is not the work of philosophers, but rather of scientists and technologists on the one hand or organizers on the other. The philosopher is reduced the role of under laborer.

The interests represented by the Averroist or Radical Aristotelian Counter-Reaction did not disappear as a result of the Augustinian Reaction. While Latin Averroism gradually died out as a leading philosophical trend, many of its concerns were translated into the Neo-Platonizing Humanism of the Renaissance. And we will show that there was, in fact, a direct line between the Jewish Aristotelianism of Moshe ben Maimon and the rationalism Benedict Spinoza, who conserves and advances the concerns of this trend in a new ideological context. And ultimately, of course, Spinoza's project leads to that of Hegel, Marx, and their interpreters.

Initially, however, the focus within this trend was simply to counterpoise to the Augustinian spirituality of authority and submission one of meaning and human self-cultivation without clearly defining the relationship between human self-cultivation and humanity's ultimate spiritual aims, and above all to make a case for rational autonomy against the competing claims of divine and monarchical sovereignty. This is, in effect, the first step in the political trajectory of the humanistic secular intelligentsia, as it emancipates itself from the bishops and the supervision of the theological faculties (including those allied with the emerging absolute monarchies) and before it articulates an alliance with the popular classes in the struggle against *Capital* and mounts a contest for state power and cultural hegemony.

Let us now trace out this process step by step.

As we noted above, the concerns of the Averroist counter-reaction were, in significant measure, driven underground by the ascendancy of Augustinian philosophy and theology in the late Middle Ages. Latin Averroism persisted as an independent philosophical trend only at the University of Padova, in the work of thinkers such as Cesare Cremonini. But many of its broader themes were taken up by the Renaissance humanists. This is true first of all with respect to method. Like ibn Rusd, the humanists of the Renaissance devoted themselves to careful textual scholarship, and developed an "originalist" hermeneutic which privileged the author's meaning over that of commentators. On the one hand, this tended to diminish the importance of ibn Rusd himself, and of the other Islamic and Jewish Aristotelians, as a source for understanding Aristotle. But it represented the first step towards the development of the historical-critical method which has dominated religious studies in the modern era and which has certainly favored rationalizing interpretations with a broadly Averroist flavor.

But the substantive concerns of the Averroists also found expression, albeit in a very different philosophical vernacular, within the context of Renaissance humanism. Specifically, Renaissance philosophers such as Pico della Mirandola and Giordano Bruno translated the Averroist focus on human self-cultivation and civilizational progress into the language the Neo-Platonic revival. This represents, in many ways a development parallel to the reorientation of scientific activity towards mathematical formalization following the Condemnations of 1270 and 1277 which set the stage, as we have argued, for the Scientific Revolution.

This survival of Averroist concerns was made possible, in large part, due to the unusual cluster of social conditions which existed in Renaissance Italy. The stalemate between the Papacy and the Empire had created a context in which networks of autonomous city states could develop governed largely by powerful merchants and bankers but sometimes with significant participation of the artisan class. These cities were inserted into the Silk Road trade networks in a fairly privileged way. The papacy maintained its legitimacy in this context in large part by positioning itself as a patron of human self-cultivation and civilizational progress (especially when viewed against the background of the darker visions of Luther and Calvin). Renaissance humanism, furthermore, unlike Latin Averroism, did not propose a globally rationalizing hermeneutic which called into question the legitimacy of the Church or reduce it to a mechanism for social control in system in which philosophers were the sole legitimate rulers. Even so, those Renaissance humanists who pressed crypto-Averroist themes most consistently -e.g. Giordano Bruno-did not fare well in spite of the support of powerful secular patrons.

The most direct line between Radical Aristotelianism and modern dialectics, however, by-passes Christian philosophy entirely. Idit Dobbs Weinstein (Dobbs Weinstein 2001, forthcoming) has traced out the lineage linking Spinoza to the Radical Aristotelians by way of Gersonides. Yirmiyahu Yovel (Yovel 2001), for his part, has stressed the *converso* milieu as the context which nurtured this tradition. It is not hard to see how the cross fertilization of Jewish inner-worldliness and the Christian focus on divinization would trace a pathway from ibn Rusd through Spinoza to Hegel and beyond.

It is, furthermore, clear that Spinoza, despite his fascination with the results of the scientific revolution, had deep roots in the medieval Aristotelian and specifically Averroist tradition. Spinoza frames the question of God not quantitatively, as perfect being, in the manner of Descartes, but rather qualitatively, in terms of the problem of substance, which for Spinoza is that which can exist on its own -i.e. Necessary Being. At the same time, he makes a very subtle move which opens up the way for a secularist transformation of the Aristotelian tradition. Human beings are but modes of this one substance, the product of intersecting networks of relationships. Our only hope for beatitude consists in identification with the whole, i.e. with God. This can be read in the manner of a very sober philosophical spirituality in the manner of Maimonides or ibn Rusd, for whom human beings found fulfillment in identification with the Agent Intellect, simply adapted to the realities of a post-Copernican cosmology, in the context of which the idea of the Agent Intellect no longer made much literal sense. But it can also be read as a challenge: to develop to or at least towards the point at which we are in fact identical with the single substance.

What happens, in effect, is that for both an inner core of Radical Aristotelians (many of them Jews, *moriscos* or *conversos* operating in the shadows of a world in which they are no longer intellectually at home) and a broader periphery of thinkers working in other traditions (e.g. the Neo-Platonism which became prominent during the Renaissance) the developments of the late medieval and early modern era -the scientific revolution and later the democratic revolutions—are read as actually raising humanity to the a higher ontological level. At first this is simply a new spin on the old Radical Aristotelian soteriology, which terminates (when we understand fully how the sublunar realm works) in identity with the Agent Intellect. But ultimately it pointed, by way of Spinoza's more ambiguous doctrine of the intellectual identification with Nature = Substance = God, toward the Hegelian doctrine of innerworldly divinization.

Let us see how this transformation plays itself out in Spinoza's metaphysics. Spinoza begins with a number of definitions and axioms and—skipping over the *cogito* entirely—proceeds through analysis of the idea of substance (something which can be conceived in and through itself, independently of any other conception) to a proof of the existence of God and of the identity between God and the universe. All particular systems are simply modifications of God; thought and extension are those two of the infinite divine attributes of which we are able to conceive (Spinoza 1675/1955). This is, in effect, an attempt to draw out fully the implications of the Avicennist and Thomistic distinction between Necessary and Possible Being for the Aristotelian concept of substance. Ultimately only Necessary Being -i.e. God- exists in and through itself.

How do we know that 'substance' exists at all? In one place (Proposition VII of Part One of the *Ethics*) Spinoza seems to depart from the Aristotelian tradition, which argues from existence and motion, and presents instead an analytic argument which reflects the spirit of modern rationalism—that existence belongs to the notion of substance. Later, however, in

Part Two, Proposition XVIII, he acknowledges that we know that something exists because our bodies are modified in certain ways by other bodies. Our knowledge of the universe, in other words, derives from sensation of finite particulars, from which we infer the existence of God.

Though Spinoza sometimes uses mathematical language which conceals this fact, his metaphysics is analogical—i.e., the distinction between substance and modes, or God and universe is qualitative and turns on the attribute of necessity.

Spinoza's Ethics is first and foremost an ethics of seeking Being. "To act absolutely in obedience to virtue is in us the same thing as to act, to live, or preserve one's being (these terms are identical in meaning) in accordance with the dictates of reason on the basis of seeking what is useful to one's self (Spinoza. *Ethics*, Part IV, Proposition XXIV)."Lest we read this as a kind of hedonism or ethics of power, we should note that the highest expression of this drive is the intellectual love of God. "The highest endeavor of the mind, and the highest virtue, is to understand things by virtue of the third kind of knowledge (Spinoza. *Ethics*, Part V, Proposition XXV). " By the "third kind of knowledge" Spinoza means an intellectual intuition in which we grasp the very essence of God. "The intellectual love of the mind toward God is that very love of God whereby God loves himself . . . (Spinoza, *Ethics*, Part V, Proposition XXXVI).

This is, of course, very close -at least in the language used—to the Thomistic concept of connatural knowledge of God. But for Spinoza this is possible on the base of natural reason alone. We will see that this sets the stage of a distinctive strategy for innerworldly divinization -one which bears fruit, ultimately in the modern communist movement.

There has been considerable debate regarding the political implications of this vision—and this in spite of the fact that Spinoza left not one but two political treatises (Spinoza, Benedict. *Theological-Political Treatise* and *Political Treatise*; Eckstein 1944, Den Uyl 1983, Feuer 1987, Negri 1991, Prokhovnik 2002, Garrett 2003, Rosenthal 1998, 2003, Miller 2012). This confusion is largely because the political context within which Spinoza wrote was rather different from those which informed most liberal political philosophy. Spinoza wrote in the context of the exiled Sephardic community of the Low Countries and more specifically in the context of his own excommunication from that community, which coincided with the brutal repression of the Arminian or Remonstrant Party by the Calvinist majority there after the Synod of Dordt. Within this context, his fundamental concern is the same as that of the Latin Averroists who sided with the Holy Roman Emperor (a monarch but not their own) against their local bishop (an ally of the French state) in an effort to secure the freedom *of the philosopher* against the authority of the clerical intelligentsia (in this case the Calvinist clergy of the United Provinces).

The result is a political philosophy which is often compared to that of Hobbes, with perhaps a bit more opening to democracy and a stronger argument for religious toleration. But Spinoza himself is clear that his politics differs from that of Hobbles in at least one important respect.

> With regard to political theory, the difference between Hobbes and myself, which is the subject of your inquiry, consists in this, that I always preserve the natural right in its entirety [*ego naturale jus semper sartum tectum conservo*], and I hold that the sovereign power in a State has right over a subject only in proportion to the excess of its power over that of a subject. (Spinoza, Benedict. *Epistle 50*)

This position is dictated by Spinoza's metaphysics.

> By the right and order of nature I merely mean the rules determining the nature of each individual thing by which we conceive it is determined naturally to exist and to behave in a certain way. For example fish are determined by nature to swim and big fish to eat little ones, and therefore it is by sovereign natural right that fish have possession of the water and that big fish eat small fish. For it is certain that nature, considered wholly in itself, has a sovereign right to do everything that it can do, i.e., the right of nature extends as far as its power extends ... since the universal power of the whole of nature is nothing but the power of all individual things together, it follows that each individual thing has the sovereign right to do everything that it can do, or the right of each thing extends so far as its determined power extends. (Spinoza, *Theological-Political Treatise*, 16, 195; cf. TP 2/4).

One might also add that when Spinoza defends the right of every being to build and exercise power to the full extent of its capacity, he is does not envision as a result of this a Hobbesian war of all against all, but rather an imperfect approach to and ideal in which everyone realizes to a greater or lesser degree their potential for the intellectual love of God. But it *is*, above all, for Spinoza, the freedom of the philosopher, who most closely approaches this ideal, which matters most. Religious authorities are to be subordinated to the civil authorities, and the civil authorities counseled to respect the freedom of conscience, not so people can get on with the business of making money unhindered by spiritual concerns, but so that the higher spirituality of the philosopher can be defended against interference by backward and superstitious clerics.

This is, clearly, an ultimately untenable position. Philosophy, which is always and only a minority movement, has no hope for autonomy unless it is able to find allies, either within the clergy or among the people (or both). The next step in the development of humanistic secularism will be precisely this search for allies.

This said, we should note that it is Spinoza, more than any other philosopher, who makes the strongest claim for *rational* autonomy. There are others who claim more for reason, and others who claim more for individual autonomy, but no one claims that the rationally autonomous individual on the road to full realization through intellectual love of God retains full sovereignty in proportion to their actual power.

Kant, who is generally celebrated as *the* philosopher of the rationally autonomous subject, is cautious by comparison. At issue, of course, is another century and half of the unfolding project of the *Saeculum*. In the middle of the seventeenth century it might have been possible, even for a victim of religious persecution—and a witness to the persecution of a trend far closer to the mainstream than his own (the Arminians) to believe that a market economy and an enlightened and constitutional monarchy with significant aristocratic and democratic checks and balances might secure the full freedom of the philosopher and create a society which actually nurtured the philosophical potential of all its citizens. By the end of the eighteenth century this claim was increasingly untenable. It was increasingly clear that what a rationally autonomous will could require of itself—morality—and what it could legislate for others—right or law—were quite distinct, at least in an emerging capitalist economy.

Kant begins by making a distinction between two types of judgments: analytic and synthetic. In analytic propositions the predicate is already contained in the subject; analysis merely draws it out. Synthetic propositions, on the other hand, join ideas which were previously separate.

Prior to Kant, it was taken for granted that analytic arguments are *a priori*, and that synthetic arguments are *a posteriori*. The judgment that all triangles have three sides requires no observation; we conclude directly from the definition. The judgment that the chair is red, on the other hand, is possible only after we have observed the chair and determined its color. What Kant proposes is that there is another sort of synthetic argument, the synthetic *a priori*, which provides the solution to his problem. Synthetic *a priori* judgments join two ideas prior to any observation, by showing that they are the condition of any possible experience. Kant claims that we make this kind of judgment all the time in mathematics. The idea of '7' is not, he claims, contained in the ideas of '3' and '4', nor is the idea 'shortest distance between two points' (which is quantitative) contained in the idea 'straight line' (which is qualitative). The same is true of physics. The conservation of matter for example involves not an analysis but rather a synthesis of ideas. But in none of these cases are the judgments based on observation. We make the judgment prior to any observation whatsoever.

What Kant concludes from this is that knowledge is not so much a matter of conforming our minds to objects as it is of conforming objects to our minds. He did not mean by this that the object is created by the mind, and therefore exists only within it, but rather that we know the object only as it is structured for us by the operation of the intellect. What the mind does is to take the manifold data of experience and impose on it a unified structure which makes thought possible. The forms of intuition, space and time, structure our actual sensory experience; the categories of the understanding—quantity, quality, relation and mode—structure the way we relate experiences to each other and form them into a unified whole.

What this does for Kant is to establish a sort of foundation for mathematics and science. Universal and necessary knowledge is possible in these disciplines because everyone organizes and unifies the given data of the senses in the same way. The same is not, however, true for metaphysics. Because the intellect unifies rather than abstracting, we cannot conclude to anything supersensible. Concepts such as the self, the cosmos and God, which Kant calls the transcendental ideals, reflect nothing more than the drive of the intellect to unify our experience perfectly. These ideas do not, however, correspond to any possible object of experience and we thus have no basis on which to claim that they correspond to anything outside the mind. Indeed, when we try to treat the transcendental ideals as if they were objects of experience, reason runs into contradictions or antinomies from which it cannot extricate itself. Thus the interminable debates regarding freedom and necessity, the finitude or infinity of the universe and its infinite divisibility or reducibility to simple parts (atoms), and the existence or nonexistence of God.

It is on this basis that Kant rejects the historic arguments for the existence of God. The ontological proof he rejects out of hand. Being, he points out, is not a real predicate which can be deduced by analysis of some other predicate, such as 'than which nothing greater can be thought' or 'perfect.' We know something actually exists only by observation. But he goes on to reject the cosmological and teleological arguments as well. The cosmological argument, he points out, turns on extending the category of causality, by which the understanding orders sensible experience, to the supersensible realm—a move he claims is illegitimate. Similarly, the teleological argument argues from the presence of cosmic order to the notion of an orderer who is, however, beyond any possible experience.

Unable to conclude to a first principle, Kant had to seek some other way in which to ground ethical judgments. Here, too, Kant turned to *a priori* reason. Like science, ethics is grounded in the *a priori* structure of human reason. Just as the mind unifies experience under the forms of the intuition and the certain definite categories of the understanding, so it seeks to unify our action under a single, internally consistent and universal principle, the categorical imperative: 'Act only on that maxim whereby you can at the same time will that it should become a universal law.' From here, Kant goes on to argue that in order to follow this principle through consistently, we must assume (though we cannot prove) freedom of the will, immortality and the existence of God.

But within this context Kant is forced to make a distinction between the demands autonomous reason makes on itself and those which it can make on others. From the internal, subjective vantage point of conscience, we can consistently will only those actions which treat rational beings as ends rather than as means, for the simple reason that we reject our own instrumentalization. But society itself—or at least capitalist society—is quite impossible apart from such instrumentalization. Imposing such a morality as law would precipitate brutal repression and civilizational collapse. And so law, for Kant, must allow the maximum freedom which is consistent with similar freedom for others: essentially the norm of what Marx would later call bourgeois right, the norms of the market order.

Shortly we will see Hegel and later Marx searching for a solution to this problem. But first we need to consider another stream of humanistic secularism, that which flowed into—and out of—the French Revolutionary experience.

The Democratic Moment

Democracy is a profoundly problematic concept. In the Hellenistic tradition and those traditions which it influenced it referred to a form of rule in which the *many* as opposed to the *few* or the *one* exercise the preponderance of power and authority. It has retained this sense for some political philosophers for whom the terms of debate continue to be set by Aristotle, and John Milbank (Milbank 2014) has recently tried to mobilize this use of term in a more creative way, making a case for the idea that a metaphysics of participation requires a mixed regime in which the role of the few, in the sense of the spiritually excellent, is conserved. In the US political tradition the term tends to be used in a way profoundly influenced by Lockean notions that only broadly accountable government will respect natural rights.

This is modified to some extent by popular sovereignty doctrines mediated through the discourse of *founders* such as Jefferson and Lincoln. But in the US it is taken for granted that liberty and democracy go hand in hand.

Here we use the term in neither of these senses, but rather in the sense of the stronger popular sovereignty tradition which comes out of France. Here the classical political thinker most often associated with the idea is not French at all, but rather Swiss and Calvinist by extraction, though he did much of his work in France: Jean Jacques Rousseau.

For Rousseau the "state of nature" is characterized by absolute moral neutrality. The law of nature commands nothing more than self-preservation. This is, however, quite impossible apart from civil society. Because of this human beings come together to form a social compact in which they alienate their natural liberty in return for the security of the political order. In the process, however, they bring into being a new collective being, a General Will which is the authentic arbiter of the moral. Human beings, on entering into civil society, are transformed from amoral individuals into moral beings and citizens dedicated to whatever the General Will commands.

A full understanding of the French democratic tradition, however, requires that we consider not only Rousseau but also his traditionalist critics—and the functionalist sociology which, in turn, emerged out of traditionalism.

Traditionalism was a reaction against the Enlightenment, and specifically against the Enlightenment ideal of rational autonomy. Thinkers like de Maistre and de Bonald, the principal theoreticians of reaction in the wake of the French revolution, focused attention on the role of religion generally and ritual in particular, in constituting and maintaining the social order. They regarded the social order, including language and religion, as part of a primitive revelation that provided humanity with the tools it needed in order to think—and indeed survive (Milbank 1990). The central social category for the traditionalists was that of violence and especially the ritualized violence of sacrifice which, they believed, *constituted* the social order. In this sense, they put forward not only a *critique* of the French Revolution, but also a kind of hidden *reading* of that revolution, which was nothing if not a reconstitution of the social order through violence.

Traditionalism runs like a secret thread through postmodern social theory. In its original "rightist" form, it represents, of course, simply another way of theorizing history as a kind of theomachy and a fully developed sociology in this vein (which we do not have) would complement Weber's interpretive sociology, which is distinctively Protestant in its understanding of religion as "word" with a Catholic focus on religion as liturgy and sacrament. But there is also a left traditionalism—or perhaps many different left traditionalisms—and a "center" traditionalism. John Milbank (Millbank 1990: 69) has, for example, recently called attention to the work of Pierre Simon Ballenche, who argued that the Axial Age represented a radical democratization of the religious arena as the popular classes struggled to gain full access to the cult and thus claim their full humanity. But any theory that regards the spontaneous dynamism of the people, especially as expressed in revolutionary upheavals, as somehow constitutive of social order, is ultimately a leftist inflection of the traditionalist emphasis on violence as constitutive of social order.

Alexis de Tocqueville, finally, is an example of "centrist" traditionalism. De Tocqueville shared traditionalist concerns about the violence of the French revolution but responded not by rejecting democracy as such, but rather by looking for an alternative form of democracy, something he found in the complex, pluralistic civil society of the young United States.

This whole history has been obscured somewhat by the refraction of the original insights of the traditionalists through the lens of positivism. Auguste Comte and the other positivists turned traditionalism on its head, arguing that society was not a divine creation, but rather that God was a social creation, and that it is human society itself that is the real object of worship, something that Comte attempted to make explicit with his system of socialatry. It is in Comte, of course, that we see the most explicit form of modern secularism, with science actually replacing not only theology but also philosophy.

Durkheim took the ideas developed by this already contradictory tradition and developed them in new and far more subtle ways. A Jew and a man of the republican and socialist left he celebrated the victory of the Third Republic and began his career by attempting to define for the Republic a secular and modern approach to moral education. Increasing demographic pressure, he reasoned, gradually forced humanity to develop new technologies, something that lead ultimately to first the social division of labor between various trades and occupations and eventually to the technical division of labor within trades characteristic of modern industry. This, in turn led to a change in the way human societies maintained their cohesion. Preindustrial societies, in which most people did the same thing, relied on a "mechanical solidarity" based on shared beliefs and values. But as peoples lives diverged so too did their beliefs and values. Mechanical solidarity gave way to an "organic solidarity" based on material interdependence. This was, he argued, basically a positive development, since it permitted an unprecedented degree of ideological pluralism. In this sense, he clearly affirmed the Enlightenment ideal of rational autonomy. But he also noted the existence of serious contradictions in the economic system: what he called the "anomic" and "coercive" forms of the division of labor. The anomic form derives from insufficient economic regulation, and results in a loss of meaning. The forced form results from the existence of inequalities between contracting parties, and leads to exploitation (Durkheim 1893/1964). These contradictions were further reflected in rising suicide rates in the most advanced industrial countries (Durkheim 1897/1951), which he attributed to a deepening moral crisis. People seemed to find less and less meaning in their lives, and to feel less and less connected to each other and to society as a whole. While capitalism had increased the level of material interdependence, it was also undermining our ability to understand the social significance of our work and to feel like members of a cohesive social group.

In response to this situation Durkheim advanced a far reaching proposal for the development of occupational groups or "corporations." This proposal amounts to a comprehensive attempt to adapt the tradition of the medieval guilds and journeymen's associations to the new and much more complex conditions of an industrial society. These corporations were not only to regulate wages, hours, and working conditions; they were eventually to collectively control the means of production, and connect them to the "directing and conscious centers of society." They were, further, like the guilds, to serve as the center of a rich social life, and the locus of new moral forces that would combat the egoism and anomie that was gradually eating away at the social order (Bellah 1973: xxxi).

Durkheim argued, furthermore, that the social basis for the implementation of his proposal lay in the popular religious traditions of the people themselves. His study of Australian religion had convinced him that religious symbols were "collective representations" of the structure of human society. Indeed, God *is* the community, in transcendent form, binding the individuals together into a social being that is greater than themselves, to which their ties are stronger than any tie of self-interest, and which has the moral authority, but also the compelling beauty, to command self-sacrifice. In ritual gatherings he found a "collective effervescence" that catalyzes the formation of a sense of unity and oneness that transcends the existing empirical forms of social order and that opens up the possibility for the emergence of radically new social forms that later on become embodied in new economic and political institutions.

> In such moments of collective ferment are born the great ideals upon which civilizations rest. These periods of creation or renewal occur when men for various reasons are led into a closer relationship with each other, when reunions and assemblies are most frequent, relationships better maintained and

the exchange of ideas most active. Such was the great crisis of Christendom ... in the twelfth and thirteenth centuries. Such were the Reformation and the Renaissance, the revolutionary epoch and the Socialist upheavals of the nineteenth century. At such moments this higher form of life is lived with such intensity and exclusiveness that it monopolizes all minds to the more or less complete exclusion of egoism and the commonplace. At such times the ideal tends to become one with the real, and men have the impression that the time is close when the ideal will in fact be realized and the Kingdom of God established on earth (Durkheim in Bellah 1973: l)

Durkheim hoped fervently for the renewal of such collective effervescence in his own time, and had little doubt concerning its probable source.

Who does not feel ... that in the depths of society an intense life is developing ... We aspire to a higher justice which no existing formulas express ... One may even go further and say with some precision in what region of society these new forces are forming: it is in the popular classes (Durkheim in Bellah 1973: xlvii).

What Durkheim has done, in effect, is to gradually and partly rescue left traditionalism from its positivistic captivity, while developing a more complex and subtle account of the dynamism that earlier traditionalists of the left and the right saw in sacrificial and revolutionary violence. Even if Durkheim's analysis of the internal contradictions of capitalism is rather undeveloped and schematic, his theory nonetheless captures better than Marx the actual dynamics of mass socialist movements. It is now well established that the principal social base of the socialist movements of the late nineteenth and twentieth centuries was not the urban proletariat, but rather the peasantry, that these peasants were struggling not so much to transcend capitalist modernity as to resist it, and that they did so by drawing on popular communal institutions and religious traditions (Wolf 1969, Lancaster 1987). But even in the cities, socialism found its base in popular communal institutions and religious traditions. William Sewell (Sewell 1980) has argued at great length that French socialism emerged out of the struggle of the *compagnonages*, associations of journeyman artisans, against the penetration of market relations into French society, in the years following the revolution of 1789—long before *socialized* industrial forces of production had become important in the French economy, which retained an agricultural and artisanal character. Some of these guilds maintained traditional Catholic cults centered on patron saints; others were Masonic and neopagan, but nearly all were, in some sense, religious. And the development of urban working class socialism incorporated showed similar patterns even in countries such as the United States where there was no formal guild structure (Mansueto 1985, 1995, 2002a). John Milbank's recent (Milbank 2006a) attempt to retheorize socialism as a movement of resistance to the enclosure of the sacred and in defense of a "general economy" that orders material production to higher and ultimately transcendental ends, falls clearly within the theoretical space created by Durkheim, even if Durkheim himself retains too much of the taint of secularism for Milbank's tastes.

This said, there remain serious difficulties with Durkheim's theory. Indeed, Durkheim's own trajectory might well be read as a self-criticism of the French democratic tradition—a critique which never fully transcends that tradition. First and foremost, Durkheim's work is an acknowledgement of the fact that however much he may *value* the insight into higher truth which emerges out of both revolutionary and ritual collective effervescence, the dominant trend in the *Saeculum* is that of industrialization, the division of labor, and collapse into egoism and anomie. For democracy as for socialism (something we will see shortly) entails mastery over nature and this in turn sets in motion the technological and economic processes which dissolve solidarity and undermine the generation of collective effervescence. His proposals for guild socialism and secular moral education were never fully taken up by any mass social movement and Durkheim's late turn to the study of religion can only be read as a covert acknowledgement that the sociological power of collective effervescence derives at least in part from the conviction that the higher truth it discovers is actually both higher and true. And when we take this step we depart from the *Saeculum* and begin to develop and authentic theory of *Sanctuary*. This is why Durkheim is both so indispensible for postsecular religious thought, but also ultimately inadequate.

It is, above all, in Hegel, finally, that we find both the fullest expression of the democratic humanistic project—the aim to create, in the democratic state, a political subject which could make humanity the master of its own destiny—and the beginnings of a recognition that this project was running up insuperable obstacles. It is also in Hegel that we discover the hidden social basis of the *way* which succeeded and attempted to complete, the democratic project: socialist humanism. Hegel is *the* philosopher of the humanistic intelligentsia as it approaches its historic attempt to become the ruling class. Let us consider each of these claims in turn.

Hegel is quite clear that his aim is nothing other than the deification not only of humanity but of the entire secular realm.

> The divine spirit must interpenetrate the entire secular life: whereby wisdom is concrete within it, and carries the terms of its own justification. But that concrete indwelling is only ... ethical organization (Hegel, *Encyclopaedia of Philosophy: Part Three: Philosophy of Spirit:* Paragraph 552).

Here the analogical metaphysics of the dialectical tradition is saved, but with the—extraordinary—difference that the qualitative distinction between contingent and necessary Being is overcome by means of revolutionary practice, which elevates humanity to the status of conscious subject of the cosmohistorical evolutionary process and confers on it what amounts to a divine status.

Concretely, the institutional form which Hegel proposes for this divinized *Saeculum* looks rather like a moderate constitutional monarchy. Many commentators have seen in Hegel's *Philosophy of Right* a profound accommodation with the Prussian state and even with the semifeudal aristocracy and with Evangelical (Lutheran) Christianity. Bhaskar (Bhaskar 1993), for example, argues that after an early infatuation with the democratic revolutions, Hegel resigned himself to the status quo and became a *de facto* apologist for Prussian absolutism, mapping out a strategy by means of which it might hegemonize the revolutionary intelligentsia. This verdict is not, however, really fair. His own pretensions to the contrary, Hegel was, after all, finite and a person of his time. The wave of democratic revolutions which began in France in 1789 crested and receded early in his career and the next wave did not come until after his death. It was already becoming clear that the new world which these revolutions had ushered in was far from perfect—something which Hegel acknowledged implicitly in his critique of the limitations of the market order. Indeed, Hegel is quite clear, very much in the vein of later social democrats, that it is one of the principal functions of the state to resolve the contradictions created by the market order. It would be more accurate to say that Hegel sought an accommodation with the Prussian monarchy in order to leverage influence for the intelligentsia, which he called the universal class. Despairing of establishing the intelligentsia as the ruling class, he opted, in other words, for a classic Confucian solution. Hegel's position with respect to religion, furthermore, was hardly fideistic or irrationalist. On the contrary he reproduces within a Protestant context what amounts to a moderate (Arab) Averroist position on the religious question, apparently without even being aware of it. Religion is, for Hegel, simply an imaginative statement of truths grasped more completely and more profoundly by philosophy and above all by his own system.

Hegel's standpoint was, in any case, fundamentally unstable. Hegelianism soon disintegrated into right and left wings. The right wing *did* devote itself to polemics on behalf of the Prussian state (Lukacs 1953/1980). The left wing, on the other hand, cultivated the revolutionary insight that human beings create their own institutions and ideas to mount an increasingly revolutionary critique of religion, the state, and eventually the market order.

Socialism

The challenge, of course, was to find a strategy by means of which the secular humanistic intelligentsia could actually come to power. By the middle of the nineteenth century the answer was becoming clear: the intelligentsia could rule only in alliance with the working classes, and above all with the emerging proletariat, the size and potential power of which was rapidly increasing as Europe industrialized and which seemed to have nothing to bind it to the old order. Thus Marx's claim that "philosophy is the head of the revolution and the proletariat is its heart (Marx 1843b/1978: 65)."

That the aims of communism are every bit as metaphysical as they are economic or political is apparent from Marx's formulation in the *Paris Manuscripts*, where he calls it :

> . . . the definitive solution of the contradiction between man and nature and between man and man, the true solution of the contradiction between existence and essence, between objectification and self-realization, between freedom and necessity, between the individual and the species. Communism is the solution to the riddle of history and knows itself to be that solution (Marx 1844/1978: 84).

The question, of course, is how one arrives at this "solution." It is to this problem that Marx devoted his later work and to which the subsequent history of the socialist and communist movements have been devoted. Historically this problem has been considered under two distinct but related aspects: that of socialist strategy and that of socialist construction. In reality, however, the two are the same. The problem is that of constructing a subject which can make humanity full the master of its own destiny, i.e. *Esse as such*.

Understood in this context, and the claims of Althusser (Althusser 1965/1977, 1968/1970) and his followers notwithstanding, there is no contradiction between this metaphysical and "humanistic" concern for transcending contingency and the focus in Marx's later works with the development of the productive forces. Like ibn Rusd and Levi ben Gerson (and like Hegel) Marx regarded *all* knowledge and *all* mastery as contributing to a human self-realization which, even though the religious language has dropped away, still amounts to a kind of divinization. Indeed, communism can realize its metaphysical aims *only* if humanity masters cosmic history as well as its own.

There have, broadly speaking, been two competing strategic lines within the socialist and communist movement, with the basic distinction between the two reproduced within the communist movement. The first approach is the gradualism of the social democrats. While there were thinkers, such as Eduard Bernstein, who theorized gradualism in moral terms, drawing especially on the Kantian tradition, most looked to Engels' *Dialectics of Nature* (Engels 1880/1940) and his *Socialism Utopian and Scientific* (Engels 1880/1978). Engels argues in the first work that quantitative changes throughout the material world gradually become qualitative. In the second work he theorizes the transition to socialism in precisely this way. Industrialization gradually increases the size of the proletariat, eventually giving them a majority and the ability to win elections.

The difficulty with this strategy was that it effectively subordinated the *humanistic* secular project of constructing a political subject which could make humanity the master of its own destiny to the *technocratic* project of the industrial revolution. With industrialization (including later proletarianizing dynamics such as the information technology revolution) driving development, social democracy effectively consented to the process of capitalist development with all that it implied, and simply worked to ameliorate the condition of the working classes within the broader industrial regime. This was reflected first in social democratic support for imperialist projects leading into the First World War and ultimately in the effective liquidation of any revolutionary aims in favor of the creation of a welfare state. Ultimately, however, social democracy tends to liquidate its own base because, contrary to Marx's expectations, proletarianization, precisely because it alienates humanity from its essence or species being, which is creativity, tends to erode first metaphysical, then political, and ultimately even economic, trade union class consciousness.

The alternative *communist* approach builds on Marx's undeveloped idea of a revolutionary vanguard which understands the "conditions, line of march, and ultimate general result" (Marx and Engels 1848/1978) of the cosmohistorical evolutionary process. This vanguard, which for Marx was emphatically *not* a distinct party, becomes for Lenin a disciplined cadre organization which deploys a complex, *longue durée* strategy first for winning state power and then for creating a communist society. For the most part the struggle for state power involved leveraging what Lenin called "transitional" and later communist leaders called "democratic" demands, such as national liberation, land reform, peace, democracy, etc. which bourgeois parties were unable or unwilling to meet, to build support for a communist movement the ultimate aims of which the majority would never fully understand or embrace. Socialist construction, on the other hand, as "the resolution of the contradiction between freedom and necessity, between the individual and the species" (Marx 1844/1978) required either actually overcoming scarcity, so that everyone can do what they want to without it conflicting with the desires of anyone else, or overcoming selfishness, so that they want only what serves the Common Good. The first alternative, like social democracy, chained socialism to the technocratic project, as reflected in the strategy of primitive socialist accumulation and rapid industrialization supported by Trotsky and Stalin. While this strategy produced extraordinary results from a purely technological and economic vantage point, it liquidated the broader humanistic aims of socialism as fully, if not more so, than social democracy, and, after it became clear that the structures and strategies of Soviet socialism were not well adapted to more advanced stages of industrialization (the information technology revolution) ultimately led to rapid de-legitimation and collapse of the Soviet system. The attempt to overcome selfishness, a theme throughout Mao Zedong's thought (Mao 1938/1971) and something attempted with great intensity during the Cultural Revolution, showed itself to be both civilizationally destructive and radically incompatible with classic humanistic values of rational autonomy.

Given this record—and given the fact that the whole idea of effecting a metaphysical project such as "the resolution between existence and essence" by means of a political process is not intrinsically any more reasonable than the idea that such a transformation might be effected by ritual means, it might be wondered why insist on continuing to engage this tradition at all. Our reasons are two. First, Marx's work taken as a whole provides a compelling statement of what humanity *is* and *wants to be*. Sartre's later crystalization of the insight that *Humanity is the desire to be God* (Sartre 1943: 556) may state the truth more baldly, but Marx's elucidation of what this entails, and especially his analysis of the metaphysical status of human labor—or rather creativity—is far more developed and provides much better insight into the secular project in both its humanistic and technocratic forms. That our *desire* might, at least in the more obvious senses in which it might be understood, be in vain, does not mean that it ought not to be recognized, named, and understood. Second, Marx's political economy provides a powerful critique not only of capitalism, but ultimately also of actually existing socialism, which never found a way to transcend the wage relation, which is the economic expression of alienation within the context of the *Saeculum*.

Marx, in other words, asks questions which cannot be evaded and provides specifications for any possible satisfactory answer to those questions, even if his own answers and those of his interpreters remain inadequate.

Populism

The final form of humanistic secularism which we need to consider is what I have chosen, with some trepidation, to call populism. This term is, of course, used in many different senses and it will be used here to name a range of spiritual and civilizational tendencies which fall at diverse points on the conventional political spectrum. Specifically, by populism, I mean that strain of humanistic secularism which looks to the people as *ethnos* or nation (as opposed to *demos* or *laos*) as the political subject which, once constructed, will make humanity the master of its own destiny, and carries from the realm of contingent to that of necessary Being.

The original social basis of this tendency was in the disintegration of the great multicultural "world" empires of the Silk Road Era and the formation of nation states. It has continued as a struggle against the imperialist metropoles created by global Capital. But in each and every case it integrates within itself *both* popular *and* imperialist aims. This is because the nation, as a people sharing a common language, culture, history, and territory, with the right to self determination, is itself a social construct. There simply *are not and never have been* significant regions capable of sustaining a viable national market and an effective sovereign state apparatus in which all inhabitants actually share a common language, culture, and history. *Every* process of nation building, whether it was prosecuted in the context of a national liberation struggle or more or less transparent conquest and empire building has involved the removal or forced migration of ethnic minorities, the imposition or even the creation of a shared national language, generally based on the dialect of the capital or an important cultural metropole (such as Firenze) and a complex negotiation between the axial and secular ideologies with salience among the people to forge a shared national identity. The position of diverse populisms on the conventional political spectrum is largely a function of the extent to which they understood themselves (and persuaded others) that they were national liberation struggles as opposed to attempts at creating an empire and the extent to which the popular elements (peasants, artisans, workers, petty bourgeoisie) as opposed to Capital played a role in the ruling bloc.

It should, therefore, not be surprising, that we find in Martin Heidegger, *the* philosopher of populism as I have defined it *par excellence*—both an apologist for the NAZIs and a darling of the postmodern, multicultural, deconstructionist Left. It is also why the internal dynamics of populist regimes look so much alike, even when their relationship to global Capital is vastly different.

That Heidegger is indeed *the* theorist of populism as a spiritual project is apparent from his writings immediately after "the turn." Being, for the later Heidegger, manifests itself in a people only through the voice of the few who help it to discover its "god," a sort of mythos under which Being is revealed.

> ...the essence of the people is its "voice." This voice does not, however, speak in a so-called immediate flood of the common, natural, undistorted and uneducated "person." The voice speaks seldom and only in the few, if it can be brought to sound...
> (Heidegger >1934/1989: 319)
>
> A *Volk* is only a *Volk* if it receives its history through the discovery of its god, through the god, which through history compels it in a direction and so places it back in being. Only then does it avoid the danger of turning only on its own axis...
> (Heidegger >1934/1989: 398–99).

Heidegger sees humanity as a passive instrument of Being rather than an active creator of meaning. After the "turn" in his thought, however, Heidegger also becomes more interested in analyzing the historical process by which Being is unconcealed—or by which it "withdraws" leaving the world subject to τεχνη and to the will to power—than he is in the existential analysis of *Dasein* (human being or literally "being-there") as an opening to Being. While the historical process is treated here simply as a product of Being's unconcealments and withdrawals, the effect is, nonetheless, to reinstate the Nietzschean focus on the nexus between power and meaning, while endowing this nexus with an ontological legitimation which makes the forcible irruption of meaning in history no longer the product of finite human organizing activity, but rather an epiphany of Being itself. It is this notion of the historical destiny of the people as an unconcealment of Being, by Being, which made Heidegger vulnerable to the appeal of Nazism, which appeared to him as the possible occasion of just such an unconcealement.

Populism is, in this sense, also always theomachy. For Heidegger, in effect, one "unconcealement" of Being vies with another, without any underlying onto-logic which relates them as aspects or progressive revelations of a single truth. Through the medium of national myths or "gods" these unconcealements of Being constitute nations which are then locked in what can only be a mortal combat.

What makes a populism lean to the right or the left? Michael Millerman (Millerman 2013) argues that the difference between the Heideggerian Right and the Heideggerian Left is that while both are «postfoundationlist» in rejecting the idea of a rational metaphysical foundation for the human spiritual and civilizational project, the former privileges the «event» while the latter privileges «difference.» What this means in practice is that the Heideggerian Right treats the unconcealment of Being in a particular «god» or comparable cultural event as a quasifoundation for the constitution of the people as a political subject, while the Left regards identity as something constituted by difference, so that the constitution of one people is always the constitution of Others. This makes Left Heideggerianism less susceptible to fascist appropriation than the Right.

The question remains why some populist movements lean more towards fascism than others Here the social analysis developed by another group of populist thinkers is critically important. The Russian *Narodniki* argued that capitalism is impossible apart from imperialism because the dispossession of the peasantry drives demand down so low that it is impossible to sustain growth (Radkey 1958, 1962; Lewin 1968). Later, dependency/world system theory developed this idea further, arguing that capitalist development was dependent on imperialism from the beginning, because it was imperialism which made possible the primitive accumulation of capital which made the industrial revolution possible.

From here, of course, the populist project can move in either of two directions. It can conclude that the construction of the *ethnos* as a political subject capable of making humanity the master of its own destiny requires *Empire*, and that this is possible, and then leverage the emerging national identity to legitimate a global militarization of the society in order to facilitate global conquest. This is the strategy of the NAZIs and of fascism generally. Or it can conclude that empire, being either impossible or immoral, capitalist development is also impossible, in which case populism tends to ally itself with socialism, generally of a peasant oriented and somewhat autarchic strain. But in the end these are ideal types. The two largest socialist polities of the last century, the Soviet Union and China, emerged out of struggles which were in part national liberation struggles (for Russia against the ambitions of the Germans and for China against the Japanese). But both polities were already empires before their revolutions and remained so afterwards and not only pursued objectively imperialist policies towards ethnic minorities, but experienced "fascistoid" political dynamics at various points in their history: the Great Purges which dominated Stalin's rule and the Cultural Revolution.

There is, to be sure a theory which attempts a populism of the center. This is Weber's interpretive sociology (Weber 1920/1968). For Weber, as for Heidegger, history is fundamentally a *war of the gods* (Weber 1918) or, to use more contemporary language, a *clash of civilizations* constituted by distinct and ultimately incommensurate ideals. And like Heidegger, he bemoans the fact that the technocratic secular ideal has left us trapped in an *iron cage* of instrumental rationality. At the same time, he believes that this instrumental rationality is so powerful that it will ultimately give those peoples that adopt it a critical comparative advantage. Because of this he favors a liberal democratic and capitalist polity to an authoritarian one which attempts to restore or establish and alternative national or popular ideal by force. At the same time, it must be pointed out, Weber offers us no way out of the iron cage. His liberalism and commitment to moderation is ultimately built on despair. The most that he offers is a commitment to seek mutual understanding of diverse ideals or «unconcealments» or «advents» of Being, a theme further developed by Heidegger's disciple Gadamer.

What this suggests is that the populist project is flawed at its core. This is not because there is no such thing as a "people." As we have suggested elsewhere (Mansueto 2013) peoples represent particular ways of being human, ways which, because they are socially constructed are fluid and defined both by the substantive ways they understand what it means to be human and by the ways in which they draw and redraw boundaries. The historical constitution of peoples (ethnogenesis) and, under certain circumstances, their struggle for liberation and self determination as collective political subjects is a real participation in Being as such. In this sense, even Heidegger's characterization of peoples as unconcealments of Being contains some truth. But the critical term here is *participation*. And participations are always partial and incomplete. The danger of populism—as with other forms of humanistic secularism—is that it claims an ontological status for its favored subject that it lacks. The result is particularly dangerous because, within the *Saeculum*, autonomous peoplehood as a sovereign state with an effective national market requires Empire, and where the state constituted is powerful enough the temptation is irresistible. It is not that all manifestations of populism end up where the Nazis did. But there is pull in that direction.

From the Criticism of Religion to the Religion of Criticism

It remains for us to consider the situation of humanistic secularism in the present period. Here it is possible to distinguish three tendencies. First, there is a trend which is more or less direct continuity with the socialist project, but understands itself as more faithful to that project's humanistic aims therefore willing to criticize "actually existing socialism" as vigorously as capitalism. This tendency is, itself, quite diverse and amorphous and includes elements which identified more nearly with social democracy than with communism as well as many, such as Bogdanov and the godbuilders who Lenin rejected as "left-wing communists," though most have ties, however loose, to the Right Opposition which supported Lenin but rejected both Trotsky and Stalin. What binds these diverse tendencies together is an understanding of the role of the humanistic intelligentsia as the locus in which humanity becomes conscious of itself—of both its nature and aspirations on the one hand, and of the obstacles to realizing those aspirations on the other hand—which more or less fully conserves the Hegelian and young Marxist understanding of philosophy and the "universal class." These are what Konrad and Szelenyi, in their brilliant work *Intellectuals on the Road to Class Power* (Konrad and Szelenyi 1979) call "teleological intellectuals" committed to the allocation of resources in accord with *substantively* as opposed to *instrumentally* rational norms.

What this trend lacked is a viable strategy. There have, to be sure, been *elements* of a strategy. Bogdanov (Rowley 1987) supported Lenin's call for a revolutionary vanguard, but argued that it should devote itself to organizing and education rather than leveraging transitional demands in order to claim state power as quickly as possible. Gramsci developed a sophisticated analysis of class rule centered on hegemony and opened the way for later theorists to both understand the role of popular ethnoreligious traditions as forms of transition to socialist consciousness (Gramsci 1949c, Portelli 1974, 1975, Lancaster 1987, Mansueto 1995, 2010a). This in turn suggested both ways to build a mass movement towards socialism as well as alternative ways of theorizing the struggle to overcome selfishness which do more justice to the historic contributions of the axial spiritual traditions (Mansueto 1988, 2005, 2010a). Taken together these strategic contributions helped us to understand why it was, in fact, most often the peasantry, especially peasantries with strong village community and popular religious traditions, and not urban proletariats, which provided the most reliable allies for the humanistic intelligentsia (Hobsbawm 1958, Wolf 1969), and even created an opening to the clerical intelligentsia through the medium of liberation theology and other religious socialisms during the period from 1945–1989. But these insights came just as what may be the last great wave of peasant revolts in human history were ending as the population became increasingly urban and proletarianized and the socialist project itself was increasingly discredited, especially from the vantage point of consumerist urban populations.

This tradition has, broadly speaking, contributed two key insights. First, critical theory makes it clear that what Marx was criticizing was not simply or even primarily private property, but rather the commodification of labor power. The commodification of labor power, furthermore, has profound consequences for the entire socialist project. On the one hand, it results in an alienation of humanity from its species being which is far more profound than that reflected in religious consciousness. In religion, humanity's creative, transformative generativity is projected onto a wholly other Divine; in a fully commodified society this transformative generativity is actually dissolved and human beings become, or at least fully imagine themselves to have become, the consumers which Capital requires that they be. This means, on the one hand, that the creation of a mass socialist movement is effectively impossible. On the other hand, where socialism has been established as the result of the effective application of a communist strategy of transitional demands, commodification remains and the people become, especially as their basic needs are satisfied as a result of socialist reforms, a constituency for the restoration of capitalism, which they believe will result in richer opportunities for consumption.

Second, critical theory realizes the potential latent in the early Marx, for the socialist project to understand itself as a *self-criticism of religion* and thus generates, increasingly, both a revolutionary atheistic spirituality, in which the *values* of various religious traditions are separated from their metaphysical claims and embraced openly as guides both for spiritual development and political action. We see this already in thinkers like Fromm (Fromm 1941, 1947, 1966) who understood profoundly the continuity between Marx and the broader inconclastic Jewish tradition. It has reached a new stage of development in thinkers like Zizek and Baidou for whom Paul has remeerged as a key revolutionary figure (Zizek 2009, 2012, Baidou 1988, 2006). This has also resulted in ran argument that the codes of the *Saeculum* were already embded within Christianity, a thesis developed at length by Giorgio Agabmen (Agamben 2007, 2011, 2012,).

The principal limitation of this tendency is that precisely because of its closer approach to honesty regarding the metaphysical nature of the communist project and its impossibility, critical "third way" socialisms and communisms tend inevitably to have an air of nostalgia for what they themselves have already proven to be impossible. Such nostalgia may be productive starting point for spiritual and political progress, but it cannot be where we end. And in the increasingly secular climate which prevails especially in Europe, it is not at all clear what the future of religion might be in an atmosphere in which the principal advocates of its *values* are critics of the metaphysical foundation on which those values rest.

The second tendency within contemporary humanistic secularism is deconstruction. This tradition has dual roots, understanding itself at once as an extension of critical theory which turns the criticism of religion back, in a more rigorous and complete way than critical theory, on the socialist metanarrative itself. Just as Marx extended the Hegelian dialectic to expose its internal contradictions and residual essentialism to reveal it as an apologia for an intelligentsia anxious to reach an accommodation with the rising Prussian state, so deconstruction exposes the residual essentialism in Marx and shows how it became an apologia for rising statist elites. But the deconstructionist postmodernism of Jacques Derrida (Derrida 1967/1978) can also be seen as developing dialectically out of Heidegger's position. Derrida accepts Heidegger's critique of metaphysics but rejects his continued use of the language of "Being" and of gods which, he suggests, reinstates the "violence" of metaphysics. What Derrida suggests is that violence is unavoidable: there is no escape. The best that we can do is to unmask the violence embedded in our own discourse and that of others in an effort to contain the damage.

As a political theology this position differs from a nihilistic theomachy primarily in its decision to retire from the *agon* or struggle. By exposing *all* ontologies as bids for what amounts to divinity, deconstructionism claims to make room for a properly human life, freed from the totalitarian delusions of the past century. Deconstructionists set themselves the task of of unmasking claims to universality and showing them up for what they are: claims to power. More specifically, deconstruction for the conservation of "difference" and are thus at the forefront of struggles for multiculturalism, gender equality, etc.

This position is, however, characterized by profound internal contradictions. If values are purely and simply the product of human social action, and lack any ground in the structure of being as such or the nature of the universe, then any claim to universal authority on the part of a particular moral vision (including a critical, emancipatory vision) must be regarded as a claim to power on the part of the social class, ethnic group, or gender group which developed the vision. If, however, there is no universal standard outside of the array of competing moral systems developed by different cultural traditions, then on what basis can we argue with moral authority that diversity, the preservation of difference, and "multiculturalism" are values? The matter is complicated by the fact that many, if not most, of the cultural traditions which deconstructionists are anxious to defend against the totalitarian hegemony of "Western Civilization" in its Christian-conservative, market-liberal, or secular-socialist forms in fact differ very sharply with deconstruction regarding the fundamental question of the meaningfulness of the universe.

More generally, we should point out that deconstruction gives us neither a positive vision of the Good nor any method of adjudicating the competing claims of rival individuals, social classes, ethnic groups, gender groups, etc. As such, we must say that it fails as a political theology.

This said, certain aspects of the deconstructionist and related analyses have demonstrated their power. Two points are in order here. The first is that the deconstructionist critique of the rationally autonomous subject, whatever one may think of it from a normative perspective, is in fact accurate as analysis of postsecular humanity. The criticism of religion, it turns out, with or without revolutionary practice, did not constitute an autonomous subject which bears in itself the full divinity which, in the "unhappy consciousness" of Christianity remained alienated and projected on an alien power. Divinity, rather, *even for those show regard themselves not only as spiritual, and not only as religious, but even as classically theistic* has largely evaporated. This dissipation of the divine is not a product of the criticism of religion as such, but rather of the advancing process of proletarianization and commodification, which dissolves the human subject of which the divine was supposedly a project (or, from a vantage point more friendly to religion, the human subject which served as the basis in experience for thinking the divine). Another way of putting this is to say that the axial traditions were narratives at once symbolic and conceptual and higher and truer than fact, and of which the facts of our lives were merely metaphors or analogies. Secularism substituted a single innerworldly narrative (or actually two, that of scientific, technological, and economic progress on the one hand and that of the rationally autonomous subject on the other). Religious narratives, such as that of Reformed Protestantism or Liberal, Democratic, or Socialist readings of the axial traditions in general were read as metaphors for this narrative, with the criticism of religion being the form of transition from the first to latter. Deconstruction abandons unified narratives entirely so that people—even as they continue to live lives more or less completely subordinated to the instrumentalizing power of the *Saeculum*—flit back and forth between narratives which no longer stand in any meaningful relationship to each other. They are *Star Trek* or *Harry Potter* fans, militant atheists or evangelical Christians, practitioners of Bikram Yoga or the latest health fad, "crunchy" or "techie" all without being, in any meaningful sense, integrated human beings. The narratives are, from the standpoint of the organization and mobilization of their life energy, mere distraction, mere entertainment. This is the true opium of the people, the true abandonment of the *desire to be god* which constituted all earlier humanities primal, sacral monarchic, axial or secular.

It is no accident then, that deconstruction, which began as one development of the criticism of religion, a criticism then extended to the humanistic secularisms of which it was born, should end in the rediscovery of the undeconstructible, as Derrida calls it (Derrida 2002), which is Justice or (for those able to read the "twilight" language of this unreconstructed kabbalist) God. This is not just any God to be sure. It is the God of Israel, the bitter enemy of all other gods, be they devic or asuric, the breaker of idols, the one whose name may not be uttered lest it, too, merit deconstruction. In this sense deconstruction rejoins critical theory as form of atheistic revolutionary spirituality, fully conscious of its religious roots, and indeed understanding itself as a *religion of criticism.*

A third, and quite distinct tendency within humanistic secularism is reflected in the philosophy and social theory of Roberto Magnabeira Unger. Like others who have attempted to revive the humansitic secular project, Unger engages religion directly and positively. Humanity, he argues, is constrained by our mortality, our groundlessnes, in the sense of our inability to explain adequately why there is something rather than nothing, our insatiability, in that being conscious of the possibility, at least, of the infinite and necessary, we can never be satisfied with the finite and the contingent, and what he calls our susceptibility to belittlement: the fact that our daily lives place us constantly in situations which remind us of these larger predicaments.

Historically humanity has confronted these challenges in one of three ways: by overcoming the world, in the Buddhism and Hellenism, by means of rational and/or mystical ascent which renders the struggles of the phenomenal world irrelevant, by humanizing the world, in the manner of the Confucians, or by a struggle with the world which is aimed at making us more nearly divine. This final way he associates with Judaism, Christianity, and Islam on the one hand, and secular movements of liberation on the other.

Unger locates himself firmly within this last way. The problem, he argues, echoing the Marxist critique of religion, is that historic religions have accepted too much of the world as it is, accommodating themselves to class structures which limit the possibilities of development for the vast majority. This accommodation is intimately bound up with their embrace of "feel good" spiritualities which promise that the constraints of human existence in this life will be overcome in the beyond.

Secular movements of liberation, on the other hand, have been guided by social theories which fail to fully realize the implications of their own principal insight: that human society is, in fact, an artifact. He rejects, in this regard, the attempt of historical materialism and other forms of secular social theory to identify an underlying structural dynamic which simply plays itself out through the mechanism of human historical action. For Unger, in other words, human beings really do make their own history, and while they may confront constraints, these are metaphysical or physical and biological and not social. Indeed, even natural laws evolve over the *tres longue durée* of cosmic history.

Unger concludes to a position which represents the full development of the internal logic of humanistic secularism, including it own self-criticism at the metaphysical and political levels. He is quite clear that humanity is the desire to be God. He is also quite clear that this is impossible. And yet we must try. "The goal is not to humanize society but to divinize humanity." It is "to raise ordinary life to a higher level of intensity and capability (Unger 2014)."

There is much to commend this view. Indeed, Unger's argument makes it clear why we cannot simply dismiss a self-critical humanistic secularism as part of the instrumentalizing *Saeculum* which currently dominates the planet, as Milbank tends to. A revolutionary secular mysticism must clearly be a constitutive element of any future *way*. This said, there are a number of difficulties with Unger's position. On the one hand, he seems to take too nearly at face value the secular humanistic critique of religion as "feel good" metaphysics. It is not at all clear that there is anything "feel good" about either a Buddhist or Hellenist metaphysics which fully understands the origin of suffering or the fact that in order to become divine or enlightened we must cease to be ourselves. The purifications of the dark nights and of the *via negativa* change forever one's perception of spirituality, making it no longer possible to regard it as a refuge of comfort in a frightening world. It is, rather, the most frightening and the most challenging in that it suggests that not only can't we have what we want, but that simply resigning ourselves to this fate will do us no good. We have no choice, in the long run, but to wake up and go "where we do not want to go" (John 21:18).

At the same time, Unger dismisses too easily the "deep structure" social theory of historical materialism and the rest of the sociological tradition. It is certainly true that the deterministic element of historical materialism was often exaggerated for ideological purposes by the Soviet Union in particular in order to legitimate oppressive structures as "necessary" at the current stage of development. But the option for voluntarism is no guarantee against abuse, as China discovered at its peril.

Ultimately these two failures are related to each other. Humanity is not incapable of full self-determining divinization not because we just aren't up to the task physically or metaphysically and may never be. We are incapable of such divinization because understood in this way divinization is impossible. It is not just that there *isn't* such a God and the we can't build one. Rather, such a being would not in fact be divine. It would lack the relational, transformative generativity which is fully realized only once we have given up for ever the aims of both impassive self-subsistence and autonomous self-determination. It is this realization which is the authentic term of the criticism of religion, realized as a criticism of humanistic secularism. And it is to the construction of a spirituality and a politics based on this realization that we now turn.

9

The Way of Ways

Humanity is the desire to be God. But we are also, ultimately, the product of the realization that this is an impossible desire, at least in the sense that what we at first seek in God is, in fact, impossible and a contradiction. There is no impassive self-subsistence, no infinite, self-determining subjectivity. The causative power of Being as such is neither substance nor subject, but rather pure relationality, generativity, and creativity. Deification, therefore, cannot possibly consist in either a self-subsistence immune to suffering and change or a self-determining agency free from all overdetermination by other actors. It consists always and only in the generative and transformative self-giving relationality which we sought, in our quest for deification, to avoid in the first place.

Seeking deification in the wrong form—as self-subsistence or self-determining subjectivity—leads inevitably to seeking deification in the wrong way: through the patriarchal expropriation of female creativity, through conquest and exploitation, and through the accumulation of Capital. This, in turn leads to tyranny and injustice. And yet we cannot know that this is the wrong way until we have traveled it. And, being intelligent and thus aware of the possibility of God, we cannot rest content in our finitude and contingency. Indeed, the *ways* by which we seek God, even when they are flawed and lead to unjust and even monstrous deformations are, in fact, God's own showing forth. It is only by traveling these *ways* that we can comprehend their limits and approach, ever more closely, to the *way of ways*, the *way* which recognizes that Being is neither substance nor subject, but rather relational transformative generativity. It is only by traveling these *ways*, that we *know* Being most fully *doing Justice*, and that our only possible hope of realization is in an endless journey along a *way* which can never be fully mapped or named, the way that leads, along an infinite asymptotic approach, towards fully enlightened connaturality with Being as such. This is the *way* which *ripens Being*.

What is this *way of ways* which, whenever we attempt to name it, vanishes? Clearly this is a matter which is beyond language—as far or further beyond conceptual language as concept is beyond image. And yet *Ripening Being* must find its path. What follows is but an approximation, written by someone still very early on the journey as a humble gift to those who follow, and presented for correction by those further along, if I can find them.

Being, Dependent Origination and the Triune Nature of Enlightening Being

Our way begins with the simple fact that things exist, or at least appear to exist. And, as the tradition which reaches from Socrates through Hegel, Marx, and their interpreters tells us, nothing can exist without a cause. There must, therefore, be something which *causes* things to exist, or at least to appear. And there cannot be an infinite regress of causes, because this would result in there being no first cause, and thus nothing at all. But for something to be a first cause it would have to have the power of Being in itself. It would thus appear that God *is* and is, in fact, *isness*. And God's causative power is, first and foremost that of a teleological attractor. Indeed, that is the *only* form which God's causative power can take, because otherwise God would in some sense be in motion, and thus not perfect, and thus lacking in the perfection of Being which the causative power requires.

This simple form of the cosmological argument can be elaborated at far greater length, something we have done in earlier works in dialogue with recent developments in the physical, biological, and social sciences (Mansueto 2012) and with deconstructionist and related critiques of metaphysics (Mansueto 2010b). Ultimately, however, we must recognize that it is at once inescapable and profoundly unsatisfying. It is inescapable because, behind all our myriad perceptions and inferences lies the bare fact of *Being itself*, at once the implicit condition of any possible predication (Rahner 1957) and the hidden lure buried within all of the myriad objects of our desire. It is unsatisfying for the simple reason that it does not tell us what it is that we must presuppose or what it is that we seek.

Thus the *via negativa* and thus the beginning of all our *dark nights*. It is, in fact, quite possible to evade the problem presented by the cosmological argument entirely by rejecting the claim, which Aristotle and Thomas took as obvious, that there could be no infinite regress of causes. Perhaps there is nothing with the power of Being in itself. Perhaps things exist not as expression of some creative power which lies behind them, but rather as nodes in a complex network of interdependent relationality? Perhaps we all live, not as participations in the life of the Living God, but rather in each other's embrace? And if this is true, perhaps our initial qualification that things *appear* to exist turns out not to be just a technical hedge at all, but something profoundly important. Perhaps all things hover in the twilight between being and nothingness, existing in the sense that they have *effects*, but not in the sense that the have a first and final *cause*. And if this is true, then our quest for Being is in vain and our lives—at least as long as we continue this quest—unavoidable suffering.

And yet by taking this *via negativa* we have resolved at least one of the fundamental problems with the cosmological argument and the metaphysics of *Esse*: that it cannot tell us what Being is, at least not without falling into simple tautology. In opening ourselves to the possibility that there is no *Being* behind beings we have discovered something profound about what it means to exist: to be related and to contribute to, if perhaps not to exhaustively cause, the existence of other beings. Being, in other words, reappears along the *via negativa* (which is, of course, also the Buddhist way) as relationality, generativity, and self-giving which is, in fact, the way in which the bare power of Creation appears to us.

This opens up extraordinary possibilities in terms of the way in which we understand the source and goal, the font and summit of our existence. We have already sketched out the conclusions at the level of metaphysics. Here we merely summarize.

Being, I would like to suggest, is organization. Imagine for a minute something which is stripped of all organization: it has no purpose, no structure, and no relation, either internally or externally. Then the thing, quite simply, doesn't exist.

In order to illustrate the usefulness of this idea, we begin with some distinctions. First, we should note that both "being" and "organization" are used in a variety of different ways. It is important, on the one hand, to distinguish between mere existence (what Thomas calls possible being and most modern philosophers contingent being) and *Esse* as such, the actual power of Being, which no finite, contingent system has in itself. On the other hand, it is important to distinguish between the various dimensions of the concept of organization:

- relation,
- form, order or structure, and
- purpose, end or telos.

Drawing on this set of distinctions, we can say that *to be* in the sense of contingent being is *to be related*, i.e. to be an element of a larger whole.

Any system which has a definite structure, however can be said to have its own distinctive identity, and thus to exist in the much stronger sense of being something of which other things can be predicated. For a system to be organized, however, the structure must be ordered to some end or purpose. "Organization," finally, may mean

- being organized, in the sense of being ordered to an end,
- having the capacity to organize, and thus create, or
- being the end to which things are ordered, either relatively or absolutely and finally.

With these distinctions in place, it is easy to show the power of our approach. Relationship implies both unity and difference. Being realized as relationship consists neither in simple, undifferentiated unity nor in pure difference. Without difference there is nothing in particular, but only a One which is at the same time Nothing. Without a prior, underlying unity, difference is mere disintegration: the absence of any capacity to connect, to relate, and therefore potentially to act, have properties, etc. Being consists precisely in the capacity to unite things which differ—in the self-differentiating unity which we call "system." The word "system" comes from the Hellenic roots *sys-* and *histanai* meaning "to put together." At the very simplest level, therefore, system refers to the radical interconnectedness of all things, an interconnectedness so profound that the existence of the tiniest subsystem abstracted from the whole implies the system in its entirety. The most minute alteration at any point in the system affects the system as a whole. The fact that I am sitting here at my tablet, thinking and writing, requires and implies, with iron clad logical necessity, everything else in the universe—not only the existence, but the precise disposition of every particular system along every possible world trajectory in the cosmos, from the most intimate thoughts of a young woman on a corner in Bukhara or Bangkok waiting for her lover to the precise disposition of the atoms and molecules in some remote nebula in a galaxy far too distant for its light to ever reach me during my lifetime.

Some important conclusions follow from this analysis. First, it should be clear that it is not really possible, given our scheme, to conceive of being as substance—as something that exists in itself. Finite systems clearly derive their being from each other; the first principle, on the other hand, while it clearly is the Power of Being, exists precisely in drawing others into being. Because of this both Aristotelian pluralism and Spinozist monism (while each grasping a part of the truth) are fundamentally inadequate. Neither really understands that Being is quite the opposite of self-possession.

Nor should we really think of being as subject. Subjectivity, as a way of being ordered to others and to the infinite, is incipient and emerging in contingent being, but it hardly makes sense to regard merely physical systems as subjective. But clearly such systems exist and thus share in being. Necessary being, on the other hand, while it can be shown to exercise an unlimited subjectivity and inwardness,[1] does not exist in this subjectivity but rather precisely in its creative power, which is always and only directed outward, as the power of teleological attraction. Rising to subjectivity—even becoming the unique subject-object of the cosmohistorical evolutionary process, in other words, is *not* an authentic divinization.

Being realized as relationship, on the other hand, has the merit, first of all, of grasping the interconnectedness of being without negating difference. Indeed, it makes it fully possible for us to meet the objection of existentialists and deconstructionists who are concerned that any philosophical doctrine of God—or indeed any other totalizing metanarrative which attempts to describe or explain the universe as a whole—inevitably submerges difference into identity. And this is, indeed, a danger for both Spinozist and Hegelian monisms. When being is conceived as substance, and we assert (as we must, once we have taken this first step) that there is only one substance, one system which exists in and through itself, and that that is the whole, we are, in effect, saying that particular systems don't exist and that the rich difference which makes life interesting is, in fact, a mere difference of location in a single system—in effect, an illusion. When being is conceived as subject, similarly, one ends up reducing individuals to mere vanishing moments of the One subject, Absolute Spirit, which develops itself and becomes conscious of itself through them—and then casts them aside. Aristotelian pluralism—and more especially Thomism—avoids this problem only at the price of a certain inconsistency, arguing on the one hand that there are many substances, and that difference is therefore real, while at the same time arguing their dependence on the teleological attraction of the Unmoved Mover (for Aristotle), and on the Single Pure Act of Being which is God (for Aquinas), an argument which is tantamount to admitting that they are not really substances at all. By conceiving being as relationship we unify in a way which not only conserves, but in fact presupposes difference.

---

1. This can be demonstrated quite easily. Personality or subjectivity consists in the full possession of one's faculties. This requires intellect. Now intellect consists in taking on the form of the things known, including things which are purely intelligible, such as intelligible essences or even Being itself. But Necessary Being *is* those forms—it is the form of forms—and thus knows all and is therefore pure subjectivity. To put the matter in an other way, Necessary Being knows things because it creates them and thus has infinite subjectivity.

One cannot, after all, be meaningfully ordered to something, in the sense we have defined it, without being different from it.

At the same time, we avoid the fall into an infinite expanse of difference, without horizon or point of reference, which the deconstructionist philosophy of difference celebrates but which in fact is nothing less than a willful option for death and loss. The difference of being is always and only a difference of relationship, a difference of being ordered to, a difference of sensing and imagining, of knowing and judging, of desiring and hoping and willing, which are never possible for the same, but which nonetheless make difference a principle of unity rather than of division. And this series of differences, even if it is itself infinite in the sense of extending without limit through space and time (and there are good reasons, both scientific and philosophical to believe this) nonetheless terminates in a principle which unifies (because it is the common *telos*) but does so precisely by creating "infinite diversity in infinite combinations."[2]

Thinking of being as relationship has profound implications for the way which we think about essence. It is no longer possible to understand the universe as a composite of immaterial forms and a passive material substrate, or as a set of interacting atoms which sometimes come together to constitute systems. On the one hand *essence*, which Aristotle understood as form imposed on passive matter, and in some places as what gives things their being, must be radically retheorized. At the same time, the atomism dominant since the eighteenth century, for which *what* things are is purely accidental, the product of random interaction and natural selection, must also be rejected. The universe generally, and its various subsystems, *appear* to us as things possessing various properties. The underlying essence or nature of a system or subsystem, however, (what it is), is determined by its internal and external relationships, of which its appearance is merely the expression. *Essence*, in other words, is nothing other than *structure*, both a system's internal structure and its place in the larger structure of the cosmos as a whole, which defines both its own trajectory of development, and its contribution to the development of the cosmos generally.

Understanding essence in this way allows us at once to acknowledge the relative and partial meaningfulness of the world we know by means of the senses and the lower or analytic intellect, without assigning to it any absolute or autonomous existence. This is what the Hua-yen doctrine of the three natures is intended to capture. The discriminated nature (*parikalpita-svabhava*) consists in the way things appear to us, i.e., as really existing independent

---

2. This phrase is put in quotations because it is a favorite slogan of Star Trek fandom. I am unsure of the origin. It does, however, speak of just what sort of popular ontology underlies this uniquely hopeful vision of humanity's future.

things. The dependent nature (*paratantra-svabhava*) is the underlying nature of the thing as merely a node in a network of relationships and thus lacking any inherent existence. Finally, the perfected nature (*parinispanna-svabhava*) is "the real nature of this object as it is apart from our suppositions. We may say that this is its Suchness (*tathata*) divorced from concepts superimposed on it . . . (Cook 1977: 57)." But what is Suchness if not Being as such, or at least the share or participation that a thing has in Being?

This is how matters look at the level of metaphysics. But a properly theological discourse which has integrated the cataphatic and apophatic *ways*, and even more so one which has engaged the primal ways, the three principal axial *ways*, and the various modalities of the *Saeculum* suggests even more extraordinary possibilities. Consider the fact that, understood in the light of the foregoing metaphysics, while Being is *the most formal*, it is itself empty of form or inherent existence, *Being* the pure potential for all things, necessary but without limit, *materia* or matrix, the Mother of all things. We find here the metaphysical trace of the teaching at the heart of all of the primal *ways*, a truth preserved in Hellenism, in Taoism, and in the Kabballah and the Tantra in particular, and in essentially all forms of popular religion. This is the teaching of the duality of the divine, as *Magna Mater* and *Dyaus Pater*, as *Tien* and *Kun*, *wu qi* and *tai qi*, and as the masculine and feminine branches of the tree of life. But we find it as well in Buddhism, even before the full flowering of the *tantra*:

> The *prajnaparamita*
> Is a real dharma, not an inverted view . . .
> The Buddhas as well as the Bodhisattvas
> Are able to bring benefit to all.
> *Prajna* serves as mother to them.
> It is able to give birth to and raise them.
> The Buddha serves as father of beings.
> *Prajna* is able to give birth to the Buddha.
> This being so, it serves for all
> As the grandmother of beings . . .
>
> The *prajnaparamita*
> Is comparable to a great fiery blaze.
> It cannot be grasped from any of four sides.
> There is neither grasping nor not grasping.
> All grasping has already been relinquished.
> This is what is meant by being ungraspable.
> It is ungraspable and yet one grasps it.
> It is just this which is meant by "grasping."

> *Prajna* is characterized by indestructibility.
> It goes beyond all words and speech.
> Fittingly, it has nothing upon which it depends

(Nagarjuna. *Treatise on the Great Perfection of Wisdom Sutra*).

It is not surprising that *prajnaparamita*, personified as a sort of wisdom goddess, became the center of powerful popular cults in Nepal and Kampuchea!

This theme is carried further in the *tantra*, in which the maternal feminine is complemented by the *yogini, dakini*, and the feminine *yidams* who (for the heterosexual male practitioner) awakens and channels a desire which carries him through and beyond *samsara* towards an enlightenment which, transcending form, subsumes death within itself and transmutes it into infinite creativity.

Even Christianity, which remains so resistant to the feminine dimension of the sacred, teaches a God who cannot reveal Himself fully, as he actually *is* (as relational, transformative generativity) apart from the *fiat* of an illiterate peasant girl who, the protestations of the official *magisterium* to the contrary, is recognized by the *sensus fidelum* as not only *co-redemptrix* but as an integral and indeed constitutive dimension of the doctrine of the incarnate God, and thus as Herself a modality of the divine. This is because it is precisely as the radically dependent fruit of our mothers' wombs that we first learn that we live in each other's embrace and that *Being* is not, in fact, impassive self-subsistence, but relational transformative generativity.

And Islam, which insists most vigorously on the patriarchal appropriation of female generativity (even as it also insists on actually creating a just society, and not just instrumentalizing the struggle for justice as a spiritual discipline) cannot help but venerate the Prophet's *daughter*. The Shi'a, in fact, derive the whole line of Imams, who understand the hidden, *batin* meaning of the Quran in a way that even the Prophet himself did not, from *her* line: Fatima who reappears as a name of the Blessed Virgin.

The realization of Being as neither substance nor subject, but rather relational, transformative, generativity has, further, profound implications for the way in which we understand such difficult, historic doctrines as the Trinity. It is not possible to consider this question fully in this context, but some preliminary indications will be useful. According to Thomas, the Trinity shares one common divine essence across three distinct persons defined, above all, by their relationship to each other (Thomas, *Summa Theologiae* I.39.1). If we think essence as substance, as Thomas himself still *partly* does, then we are left, in his theory, with an elegant but still less than fully satisfying solution to an impossible dogmatic problem: elegant because it does, in fact work; unsatisfying because it then becomes very difficult to see why there should not be 4, 777, or an infinity of divine persons. But if this were true, then the entire structure of Catholic theology, centered on the uniqueness of the Incarnate Word as the only possible and only full revelation of the divine nature, would collapse. But understanding the One *Being* of God precisely as relation, while it may stretch Catholic doctrine, does not entirely disrupt it. The One *Being* shared by the persons of the Trinity is, precisely, the relational transformative generativity which is the font and summit of all things. Relationality, in turn, implies persons as its only fully satisfactory term. We can, of course, relate to prime matter, qualities, elements, minerals, plants, or animals, but it is only when the object of our relations has the full possession of its capacities and responsibility for its own actions and development that relationality can become truly reciprocal. Otherwise we would be satisfied with gardens and dogs, which are certainly less trouble, and never bother with spouses or children or friends.

Thomas however, avoids this problem only by arguing that in God *substance* is in fact identical with *relation* (Thomas, *Summa Theologia* I.29.2). The specific relations which define the Trinity can then be understood as at attempt at a "highest order" ontological taxonomy of possible modes of relationality. Thomas identifies four real relationships within God, or what is the same thing, four primary forms of relationality: paternity, filiation, spiration, and procession. These relationships then define three and only three distinct persons: the Father, the Son, and the Holy Spirit.

We would correct Thomas in the following ways which, I think, are wholly consistent with Catholic doctrine and with the spirit of his system. First, we eliminate entirely the whole notion of *substance* as of something self-subsistent, as we have discovered that the power of Being as such consists not in self-subsistence but rather of generativity. Second, of we would argue that *paternity*, which Thomas understands as the relationship of generation, must be supplemented by *maternity*. Generation is the primary mode of relationality because apart from other persons relationality cannot, as we have demonstrated, be complete. But this involves, at least as it can be perceived by human beings, both paternity and maternity. And these are, in fact, distinct modes of relation as the mother's relationship to the child is different from that of the father and, at least in some ways more fundamental, even if it is not self-sufficient.[3] Similarly, filiation is therefore also understood as constituting the person of Daughter.

---

3. Of course the Catholic tradition also teaches *parthenogenesis*, which is a *topos* which merits both deconstructive and constructive attention. It would have been possible to represent Mary's maternity as the product of divine/human intercourse, something quite ordinary across the history of religions. Perhaps the insistence on her

Maternity and paternity are the primary forms of relationality because unlike all others they can be fully realized and healthy without the demand of full reciprocity. Pure, unrequited self giving in a father or a mother creates loving, generative children. The same unrequited self-giving in a friend or spouse generates what pop psychology calls co-dependency.

What this does is to preserve the uniqueness of the Trinity without in any way diminishing the possibility of extended deification behind the person of the Son/Daughter or Word. Those who, through seeking wisdom, doing justice, and ripening *Being* actually achieve connaturality with the relational transformative generativity which is God are in fact deified to the full extent of their connaturality. In so doing, however, they actually *become* the Son or Daughter of God, not merely in a relative sense, but absolutely. As they long as they cling to some element of their self-subsistence their connaturality is incomplete and so is their deification.

The historic distinctiveness of the Incarnation consists not only in the fact that we do not perceive among us persons who have achieved this level of connaturality with the divine, which might imply either that it was impossible or simply that no one had yet done so, but rather that we *cannot* perceive such individuals because their self-subsistence recedes as their connaturality with God advances. The greatest saints, like the Jesus of the stories in the New Testament, must *always* vanish.

This is why, in the *Avatamska Sutra* it is written that all the Buddhas in all the myriad oceans of worlds, and all the Enlightening Beings in those oceans of worlds, are ultimately the same Buddha and the same Enlightening Beings, who can be distinguished from each other only as lines of asymptotic approach to the *telos* and not as authentically distinct substances. And this is why even the most advanced schools of the Mahayana and Vajrayana, in spite of the fact that they have all far transcended the early Buddhist impulse to escape from suffering through extinction, nonetheless continue to depict the passing into *paranirvana*, consummate nothingness, as a constitutive dimension of Buddhahood.

Our perspective also allows us to recognize the value of other doctrines of the Trinity, such as that which emerged in Puranic Hinduism, without compromising the integrity of the Trinitarian relations and persons. Brahma, Vishnu, and Shiva and their consorts, Saraswati, Lakshmi, and Parvati (and their tantric equivalents) are not, strictly speaking, persons of the Trinity constituted by the internal relations implicit in a complete process of relationality. They are, rather, imaginative names for various

---

maternity as *parthenogenetic* fecundity suggests that maternity, unlike paternity, at least *can* be autonomous.

aspects of the cosmogenetic process which the Trinity sets in motion, a process which inevitably involves creation, nurture and preservation, and transformative violence and destruction. They are, in effect, ways in which the divine can be experienced. The same is true of the great tradition of the Triple Goddess who, as Maiden, Mother, and Crone complement the masculine paternal and filial imagery of the historic Christian doctrine of the Trinity while at the same time marking the phases of any individual participation in cosmogenesis.

Nontrinitarian doctrines of procession, on the other hand, fall short of the doctrine of the Trinity as ways of capturing the transformative generativity which is constitutive of the divine. This is because they require that, in order to actually engage the Other, an emmanation be less than whatever the particular system regards as highest (generally Being or the Good or the One). This preserves the illusion that impassive self-subsistence is the highest state and the aim of our existence.

One exception to this pattern is the Kabbalistic doctrine of the *sephiroth*. While clearly a product of a Hellenized Jewish identification of the transcendent unnamability of the Divine with Neo-Platonic ideas about the self-subsistent One, fully developed Lurianic Kabbalism (Sliverman 1998) makes it clear that *Keter* or the *Ein Soph* remains radically transcendent not out of impassivity but rather in order to quite literally create space for other beings to exist. The *sephiroth* are not strictly emmanations but rather the structural trace of the Divine Withdrawal from *h'a olam* without which the beings would be obliterated by the divine glory and never have the opportunity to grow and develop. The result is an inevitably fractured *olam*. It is fractured because there can be only *one* being with the *power of Being it itself* and all others are necessarily defective. But it is also an *olam* which we can mend (*Tikkun*), and in which, through the just act, know (and thus become connatural with) God.

What is left when God withdraws is simply the prime matter, the shadow of the divine but also its presence or *Shekinah*, which is the first form in which we meet the sacred.

Cosmogenesis

Thinking the divine as transformative generativity, in other words, means thinking the divine as *cosmogenesis*. We have already considered the problem of what the universe looks like from the vantage point of a *critique of mathematical physics* which extends Marx's *critique of political economy* and demonstrates the need to complete mathematical formalization with teleological explanation (Mansueto 2012). Here we will only summarize as much of this as is necessary to carry out what is really a subsequent task: assessing what, if anything, those aspects of the axial traditions that clearly *cannot* be rationally demonstrated might still *mean* if we accept secular mathematical physics, as completed by a teleological physics, as a broadly adequate description and explanation of the phenomenal universe.

This is clearly a vast terrain. We will, therefore, confine ourselves to four questions. First, what does our principal thesis—that Being is neither substance nor subject but rather relational, transformative, generativity—tell us about the debate between the various axial traditions regarding whether or not the phenomenal world is, in some sense, real and a good thing, or whether it represents instead the result of an emmanation which amounts to a falling away from authentic Being or an appearance which is the result of our own deluded consciousness. Second, what are we to make of the language of *many worlds* shared by some forms of axial theology and secular physics, though abhorred by others? This includes, among other things, the discourse about heavens and hells. Third, how much of the phenomenal universe participates in the process of deification? Aside from a few quotations by mystics like Rumi the consensus among the axial traditions seems to be that only sentient beings are part of this process and perhaps, for those traditions without a strong doctrine of reincarnation or rebirth, only rational beings. And yet much of what we now recognize as physical was once considered rational, such as the heavenly bodies. And it seems like a residue of a substantialist understanding of essence to distinguish radically, in a way which excludes much of the universe from *theosis,* between degrees of Being (plant and animal for example or animal and rational). Fourth, what are we to make of the extensive language of angels and demons, *devas* and *asuras*? We have already broached this matter by discussing names of God which reflect the way in which we experience the divine as active in cosmogenesis, but somewhat more needs to be said.

We have already, in fact, staked out our position on the first of these questions in our consideration of the problem of less-than-divine-emmanation. Being understood as relational transformative generativity already *is* the world, at least implicitly, in that it is the *Mater/ia* out of which all things emerge. Matter, as the shadow of Being, while just the pure possibility of the universe, represents the first sense in which the full power of Being as such is already immanent in everything. And because Being as such acts as an inescapable lure, matter seeks *Being,* and this, in turn generates forms of all kinds, giving rise to distinct physical constants, fundamental forces, elements, and degrees of organization, and thus of *Being*. We have already considered the basic characteristics of matter as the pure possibility of Being elsewhere: they are the realm of what is mathematically possible, or the realm of possible beings, so that matter itself is, at first, purely formal (though not *most* formal, which it becomes only when it achieves the relational trans*form*ative generativity which defines Being as such).

Because of this the *cosmoi* of matter of many, infinite in the diversity of the laws which govern them, their fundamental forces and physical constants, their forms and degrees of organization.[4] All partake in Being to some degree, but some *are* more than others. Some, in fact, are simply *real possibilities* which could exist but do not. Others are structured in such a way as to make possible only the most minimal degrees of organization and exclude anything even remotely approaching life or intelligence. Still others are structured in such a way that life and intelligence flourish, achieving rationality and more.

Let us be clear here that we are *not* affirming a plurality of worlds in the sense advocated by the Many Worlds interpretation of quantum theory (Tipler 1994). Nor are we arguing that these world are, in any sense, distinct *universes*. The concept of the universe: as the whole material world or the whole ensemble of material worlds, allows the possibility of only *one universe*. These other worlds are simply evolutionary attempts at Being as such, like various crystalline formations, plant and animal species, or human civilizations. That some may be currently or perhaps permanently inaccessible to us, or to any beings like us, does not mean that they are not ultimately unified in the complex organization draw into Being by the incredible Beauty of the divine. And there may well be ways to access the realms which of current technology is simply unaware, just as it was once thought impossible, in this life, to ascend even to the "sphere of the moon." And now we have, albeit only through the medium of our robotic proxies, actually left this solar system entirely. These technologies of access, furthermore, many be recognizable as developments of our own secular *techne* or they may represent more advanced developments of other trajectories, axial or otherwise.

What this means is that the various worlds, while all fundamentally real and good in some sense, since they are all participations in the causative power of *Being itself*, are real—and good—in differing degrees. In some cases this difference is simply quantitative, in the sense of representing a greater or lesser development of certain potentials implicit in a particular *cosmos*, in the way that certain ecosystem is more favorable to the development of life and intelligence or a certain civilization has realized more nearly the ideal

---

4. I owe this understanding of "many worlds," as well as some elements of my use of the term *Saecular*, to Neal Stephenson's *Anathem*, in which he presents alternate timelines as hierarchically ordered, with some participating more fully in reality than others (Stephenson 2009).

to which it is ordered. In other cases the difference is qualitative, so that it permits the presence only of participations in Being which are either qualitatively less or more advanced than others. This is the significance of the whole axial discourse on "heavens" and "hells," of which some traditions, such as Hinduism and especially Buddhism, have developed rather detailed typologies, based on the sorts of beings which can inhabit them.

How would we answer the argument that such other worlds, to the extent that they remain inaccessible to us, must be mere fantasy and that belief in them is contrary to a proper scientific mentality? *Images* of these worlds are, to be sure, fantasies. And its quite impossible to demonstrate their material existence apart from the common criteria which we human use to identify the material: that it we can experience them through our senses. But it is important to remember that material existence is not the highest degree of Being by any means, but rather simply the beginning of Being's emergence. And, as we will see, these "worlds," as long as we recognize that our images of them are just that, and not facts or concepts or transconceptual knowledge, can be useful in explaining the larger phenomenon of *cosmogenesis* and *theosis* as they are actually playing themselves out in our broader experience.

The same dynamic that unfolds among the many *cosmoi* of matter also unfolds within our *cosmos*. The forms and degrees of organization and thus of Being are many. Out of the pure potential of matter emerge dimension, force, element, thermodynamic stability, nutrition, growth, reproduction, sensation, locomotion, and intellect. All partake in Being to some degree, but some *are* more than others.

There is a tendency among the axial traditions to allow that only intelligent or at least sentient being participates in the quest for the divine. Thus for the *way of justice and liberation*, with its focus on ethical categories, only intelligent beings can be meaningful participants in the process of *theosis*. For the *way of seeking* Being, the net is cast somewhat more broadly, but there is still a tendency to speak of the quest of enlightenment for all *sentient* beings, and to regard it as only sentient beings which are caught in and seek to escape the cycles of *samsara*. One of the rare exceptions to this pattern is the Sufi poet Rumi:

> I died as a mineral and became a plant,
> I died as plant and rose to animal,
> I died as animal and I was Man.
> Why should I fear? When was I less by dying?
> Yet once more I shall die as Man, to soar
> With angels blest; but even from angelhood

> I must pass on: all except God doth perish.
> When I have sacrificed my angel-soul,
> I shall become what no mind e'er conceived.
> Oh, let me not exist! for Non-existence
> Proclaims in organ tones, 'To Him we shall return.'

(Rumi <1273/1914)

With respect to this question, we give our judgment on Rumi's side. This is for the simple reason that we know that life, sentience and intelligence does, in fact, evolve out of inorganic forms of organization, and that inorganic forms of organization are, in fact part of the process of *theosis* which, to be sure, becomes conscious only with intelligence. The Buddhist insistence on limiting enlightenment to *sentient* Beings is largely a result of a residual substantialism (or perhaps subjectivism) within the Buddhist tradition, specifically the insistence that while there is no such thing as inherent existence, that there is a continuity of mindstream between the various rebirths of sentient beings. This idea developed to solve the problem of just what could be reborn if there is no soul, but of course simply recreates the idea of soul on a somewhat more refined level. It is not really consistent with the idea of Being as transformative generativity. On the one hand, to the extent that this is an attempt to reassure ourselves that there is something of "us"—as opposed to anything else—left beyond death or at the point of enlightenment it represents a retreat from the full force of the Buddhist critique of the concept of *atman*. Clinging to self is the source of suffering. If, on the other hand, it is an attempt to theorize just how there might be continuity of memories between lives, as some advanced practitioners claim (without insisting that the one doing the remembering is really "us") or to capture the value of each individual experience even as we recognize its transience, there are other ways to accomplish this. The fact that we experience ourselves as coming into Being and passing out of Being is the ineluctable result of our degree of development. We can think time, but not really eternity. When we develop to the point that we can think eternity, we will no longer be ourselves and in this sense we really do pass away. But that will not be at some point in the distant future, but rather outside of space and time entirely so that we are now Being's cognition of a particular aspect or dimension of its existence, and only seem to our current, phenomenal selves to be something else. In this sense the *advaita* Vedanta doctrine has merit even if it clings still more vigorously to something like a doctrine of substance. Our individual experience is fully conserved in Being from the vantage point of eternity and it cannot pass away. And yet we can access this experience only by ceasing to be our finite, contingent, phenomenal selves.

Memories of past lives are not the result of some continuity of mindstream but rather of a gradual approach towards this higher point of view, so that we begin to recognize that our lives and those of others are part of a complex process in which some are so proximate to our own that they appear, at this level of development, as our own past, future, or "alternate"/parallel reality.

Being finite and contingent, all of these forms come into *Being* and pass away. From the vantage point of the causative power of *Being* and of the Mother nothing is ever lost, but for particular forms change and death are real. It is only by ceasing to be what they have been that beings become what the are and will (to) be. But the animal is always afraid.

Angels and Demons, Powers and Principalities?

Intelligent entities are, at least potentially, aware of their aim. We are the desire to be God. We are also aware of our finitude and contingency, and suffer from the impossibility of becoming God while remaining our*selves* and on the basis of the natural powers associated with our form and degree of organization. We nonetheless seek *Being*, proliferating through *cosmoi*, galaxies, star systems, planets, ecosystems and biomes, creating technologies, economies, polities, and cultures and material and spiritual artifacts, mobilizing resources and engaging in patterns of activity ordered to diverse inflections of our common aim of *theosis*. We create civilizations. Each civilization is an attempt, under definite material conditions, using definite structures, to realize an ideal which represents an authentic but always and only partial vision of *Being*.

These too are finite and contingent. No ideal is adequate to our true end, no structure to the particular civilizational ideal to which it is ordered. Matter, which makes us possible, also constrains us. The result is contradiction and change, whether by reform or revolution, decadence or collapse. We are forced to try again and again we fail.

Integral to the way in which we have analyzed both the process of *cosmogenesis* generally and human civilization and spirituality in particular is the recognition that, just as *substance* and *subject* are themselves ultimately illusions, supra-individual, collective or structural actors are fully as real as individual actors. When we speak of *Sanctuary* and *Saeculum*, and of *Empire* and *Capital*, we are not speaking purely metaphorically. While these are not "real entities" in an absolute sense, neither are we, and they *are* every bit as real as we are.

It is in this context that we must understand the axial discourse around angels and demons, *devas* and *asuras*. Just as it is meaningful to analyze life-process at the level of biochemical interactions, cellular processes, organismic processes, or ecosystems, social processes may be analyzed at the level of individuals, organizations, institutions, and higher order forms of organization which may be difficult for us to do much more than name. These higher order forms act just as surely as we do, with effects which are every bit as significant historically—and spiritually. Like minerals, plants, animals, and individual human persons, peoples, civilizations, and metacivlizational projects are *also* the desire to be god.

Within this context it is possible to distinguish between two broad *ways* of seeking *theosis*. We may, on the one hand, seek divinity as infinitely powerful self-subsistent being or subjectivity which allows us to enjoy the good of creation completely and forever. Or we can seek divinity as relational, transformative, generativity the realization of which requires, as we have argued, radical self-transcendence. These two broad ways, which in the human historic context we have called and *Sanctuary* and *Saeculum,* might in the larger spiritual context be called *devic* or *angelic* and *asuric* or *demonic*.

There is nothing intrinsically evil about the asuric alternative. It is, in fact, the natural response of emergent intelligence to the possibilities of *Being* which are only just beginning to come to consciousness and which are only very dimly understood. At the same time, it is also predicated on a fundamental misunderstanding of what *Being* is, and thus leads those individuals and organizations and civilizations that pursue it down a blind alley. Specifically, it might seem possible that by patriarchal expropriation of female creativity men might enjoy the pleasures of sexuality and the incipient continuity of being offered by paternity without full reciprocity towards the women on whom these goods actually depend. It might seem to emerging warlords that by conquering and laying tribute on a cluster of villages they can participate in Being more fully than by cultivating their land or, more likely, pasturing their flocks on the less desirable land to which history has relegated them. Or perhaps we don't have to actually conquer, but can simply exploit comparative advantages to accumulate enough Capital that the *cosmos* becomes, in effect, our own (though history gives little evidence of such primitive accumulation apart from prior conquest and exploitation). And for a time this may seem true. It is even possible for the protagonists of such projects to do great good, in the sense of making authentic contributions to human development and civilizational progress, contributions which in turn contribute to *theosis* properly understood. But in the long run the internal contradictions of these exploitative projects become intractable and they die.

On the other hand, seeking God in the right sense and in the right way does not guarantee either that we will succeed or that we will avoid grave evil.

On the contrary, it is quite possible to advance significantly along this pathway and achieve a measure of spiritual progress, and then imagine that we have "arrived," either at divinity itself or at the closest approach to divinity of which we are capable. This is most common among advocates of a return to innocence and a simple life who reject entirely the whole irascible and agonistic dimension of Being and *cosmogenesis*. In this case the progress is quite modest and dogmatic defenders of such "right ways" can do a great deal to hold back human development and civilizational progress. They may even avail themselves of the repressive force of practitioners of the first way to protect their private sanctuaries. It is one thing to appreciate the spiritual achievements of "simple folk." It is quite another to insist that everyone remain simple.

These two ways also become entwined with each other and generate their own opposites. Specifically, as we have argued, the entire *axial* project on this planet reflects a realization of the error of the sacral monarchic way, and more broadly of all attempts at deification by means of conquest and exploitation, but does not turn back and reject the patriarchal expropriation of female generativity. The result is most often a correct understanding of deification as a participation in Being, but a misunderstanding of Being as impassive self-subsistence. This is clearly the case with Hellenism and most of the dialectical tradition which emerges from it. It is also reflected in the Yahwistic rejection of not only the cult of *ba'al* but also of his female consorts, so that any sense of the divine feminine is driven underground and committed to the authority of male esoterics. But clearly we see something similar in Buddhism, which has been historically quite resistant to female monasticism, quite apart from the fact that Buddhism rejects the concept of substance. Perhaps the idea of a mindstream moving in and out of bodies plays the equivalent role here. And Taoism, while it celebrates the *yin* and the female, did little to catalyze a feminist resistance in China.

Humanistic secularism represents another intertwining of the ways. Here there is a recognition of the mistakes of not only the sacral monarchic project and its persistence in the great Iron Age empires, with which the axial traditions often decided to collaborate, but also of *Capital*, at least where it is allowed to operate as the hegemonic force in human society. Being is understood as generativity, creativity, or labor, but the category of subjectivity remains paramount, so that it is the struggle to create a political subject which can make humanity the master of its own destiny which is regarded as the key to deification or of the closest approach thereto which is possible for us. Here, too, we would argue, the underlying problem is the failure to transcend the patriarchal expropriation of female generativity, which creates the illusion that some sort of self-subsistence of self-determination is really possible, or actually constitutive of divinity.

We have attempted in this work to set out a new path which transcends these errors and which, specifically, understands Being as relational, transformative generativity. No doubt our own effort to transcend patriarchy is still only partial and incomplete. And we also want to warn against attempts which make that transcendence complete at the risk advocating a return to innocence, a common mistake of mystics (Merton 1968) *and* something which seems to have made its appearance in Mary Daly's final work (Daly 1998). The agonistic, asuric dimension of cosmogenesis is not only unavoidable. It actually adds something.

Thus far our discussion of *devic* and *asuric* has been limited to a human historical context. But it is quite possible that such projects might advance much farther than they have here—that there are whole stellar/planetary systems or even entire *cosmoi* dominated by *asuric* or *devic* forces. This possibility dovetails with our earlier consideration of the axial language around heavens and hells, though it is quite important to note that Hinduism and Buddhism do not consign the *asuras* to hells but rather to realms which are at once more advanced and more profoundly deluded than our own. Chitra Banerjee Devakaruni (Devakaruni 2009) has an interesting gloss on this in her novel *Palace of Illusions*, portraying the *asuras* as masters of some poorly understood technology.

If such realms exist, we reject the claim on the part of most Buddhists that enlightenment is possible for *devas* and *asuras* only when they die and fall from their higher realms to that of the humans. And there is an extensive tradition of both *devas* and *asuras* seeking out and defending dharma. While such realms might radically transcend space and time as we experience them, existing in what Thomas called *aeveternity* (Thomas, *Summa Theologiae* I.10.5), there *is* in fact still change, at least in the sense of reasoning. This in turn makes it possible for the limitations of their projects to be demonstrated and transcended.

That said, our own interest is not in purely asuric or devic paths, but in the path of the *tzadik* or saint, the *bodhisattva*, and the sage, and of the postsecular humanistic revolutionary dedicated to helping human beings achieve enlightenment and *theosis*. It is that way which we must now explain.

The Way of Ways

Cosmogenesis and history are the school of matter and by learning matter becomes spirit. Through our failed attempts at deification by means of patriarchal expropriation, conquest, and exploitation, we learn that *Being* is neither substance nor subject. Learning that *Being* is neither substance nor subject, we cease grasping at self-existence. Ceasing to grasp at self-existence we act justly. Acting justly we become the *Being* we sought all along. This is the *way of ways,* the path of wisdom, justice, and harmony, the "mountain road" of the *bodhisattva,* the prophet and *tzadik,* and the *sheng or* sage.

Ultimately this *way* is One, but as we have seen, as it traverses the complex terrain of *Being* it appears as an infinitely branching and intertwining lattice. As we resume the *way* at this point in cosmic and human history, we do so with a deepened understanding of the complex topology which defines the relationship among its strands.

As it should be apparent by now, this work originates within one of these strands: the *way of the search for Being.* It is, in other words, written by a Gentile who asks Greek questions and engages other *ways* looking for answers to *those* questions. More specifically, it is written from the vantage point of someone for whom the *search for Being* has led through the humanistic secular passage which seeks to construct a collective political subject—in my case the Communist Party—which might make humanity, finally, the master of its own destiny, resolving the "contradiction between existence and essence (Marx 1844/1978). But it is also written from the vantage point of someone who has been grafted on to the *stock* of Israel through the medium of the Catholic Church, which joins the *way of the search for Being* with the *way of justice and liberation.* And it is written from the vantage point of someone who has been adopted into the *way of harmony* through the medium of the two children which I have, in turn adopted from the homeland of that *way,* which is China.

And so the strands become One, but only in one of the many ways in which their underlying unity becomes manifest.

This particular unity is characterized by the intertwining of both *asuric* and *devic* notes. The *way of the search for Being* emerges, we will recall, when some among the *masters* recognize that the sacral monarchic project, which seeks deification by means of conquest and exploitation, is doomed to failure. We are among those who, recognizing our own unquenchable thirst for *Being,* left our villages behind, having bound the women to care for what we imagined to be our land and our children, and set out to *become God* in the only way we knew. We returned, chastened, to the discipline of Wisdom, only after more than two millennia of failure had taught us that the *way of conquest* is a dead end.

Wisdom has been gentle with us, more gentle than we deserve. She showed how, by means of a rational dialectic, we could ascend to a first principle by means of which the universe could be explained and human action ordered. She restored meaning and value to the battlefield we had littered with the bodies of our brothers and sisters and the slave quarters we had made of our homes. But she could not show us a way to *become* this first principle. Indeed, while there were other penances she imposed, the greatest was to lead us to the antechamber of *Being as such*, only to inform us that we could not pass beyond that point, not because our particular sins rendered us unworthy, but because *Being is One* and our very existence implies plurality. There, reflecting on what we had learned, we arrived at a Noble Truth indeed: that life is suffering, at least as long as we understand it as a quest for inherent existence. Indeed, the prize we sought, first through warfare and then through *theoria,* is not merely unattainable. *It does not exist.* There is no freedom from relationship, change, transformation, and death.

It was then that those we had enslaved became our teachers. It was then that, believing ourselves at the end of the road, found an opening onto the *way of justice and liberation.* Those who never imagined that *theosis* was possible, who were concerned simply with surviving the catastrophe of our attempts at becoming God: it was *they* who found a *way.* Doing what they had to do, fighting to protect themselves and their children from the predations of the *ba'alim,* from those who would be gods, they entered the battlefield of revolution. And they were met there by the only true God, a God who detests all other gods (because their attempts at the divine instrumentalize everything else in the universe). They were met by *'el yahwi saboth yisrael,* the God who brings into being the armies of Israel, the armies of the poor. And joining the battle, they realized that *this* God, unlike any other, really is *the causative power of Being as such.* And this power shows itself not to be impassive self-subsistence, but rather action, revolutionary action, action on behalf of justice. This God entered a judgment on behalf of his people Israel, and against the *ba'alim,* and through Israel he entered a judgment for all those who had been instrumentalized by the attempt of others to become gods and against those who would be gods forever.

This judgment did not, to be sure, simply condemn the rest of us to wander, forever restless, unable to find what we sought. Rather, God's judgment on behalf of Israel, became an "ensign for the peoples (Isaiah 11:10)," and many of us gathered to it. But Justice, it turns out, is a harsher mistress than Wisdom. She leads us further, but only by leading us *where we do not want to go* (John 21: 18). Action, revolutionary action, action on behalf of justice does not, it seems, find its term in a peaceful, settled life "each under his own vine and fig tree" in a land of milk and honey. It leads, rather to death and genocide: death on a cross, genocide in the gas chambers of Auschwitz. There are many ways to explain why this is true. Historically and sociologically it is because building and exercising power, even power in service to the Common Good, involves the instrumentalization of the Other. It is just that failing to build and exercise power also instrumentalizes: it sacrifices Justice for the Other to our own peace of mind. Cosmologically it is because the transformation of forms of organization is also always their death. The asuric dimension of our existence is, in other words, inescapable. There are only so many options. We can resign active struggle and live as witnesses to a Justice which always wholly Other, God's justice and not our own, waiting for the day, which we eventually realize lies infinitely far into the future (otherwise we would have to resume the struggle), when this God will act and redeem us. We can treat the whole struggle for justice as a kind of spiritual exercise which reveals the true nature of God and defines for us a path for connaturality with Her, but which leaves the oppressed largely where they are. Or we can continue the struggle, joining Justice to Power, and accept the fact that the more nearly just society we create will be imperfect and that we ourselves, in the process of creating it, will become, little by little, more like the *ba'alim*.

This final alternative was, in a certain sense, that chosen by Islam, especially in its Sunni form, as an alternative within the *way of justice and liberation*. But it is also, above all, the alternative which defines humanistic secularism, and especially the communist movement albeit, if we read Marx correctly, as a solution to a Gentile (metaphysical) and not primarily a Jewish (ethical) problem. For Islam, the problem was one of creating a leadership which was both effective, at the political-military level, in a world still dominated by *Empire* and authentically capable or *commanding right and forbidding wrong*. For the communist movement, it was a matter of overcoming selfishness or overcoming scarcity or, preferably, both, and doing so without compromising rational autonomy or instrumentalizing other human beings or our ecosystem.

This turned out to be impossible. The great Caliphates did the justice they did because they did not hesitate to be *Empire*. The Imamate, in its present form, avoids instrumentalization (and even now not completely, for the Imamate is also a major instance of *Capital*) only by renouncing the struggle for global hegemony. Historic socialism, on the whole, opted for the *way* of overcoming scarcity, prioritizing technological and economic progress on the assumption that as concerns around survival receded, so too would selfishness and the a materially enriched humanity would devote itself in equal measure to intellectual, moral, and spiritual self-cultivation and to service to the Common Good, without any contradiction between the two. This was clearly Stalin's expectation as late as the early 1950s (Stalin 1952). As it turned out, well clothed and well fed workers with growing ruble bank accounts wanted instead expanded opportunities for consumption. And the unwillingness of the Soviet Union to sacrifice civilizational progress for consumer satisfaction ultimately doomed Soviet socialism.

More broadly, however, the option for *overcoming scarcity* chained socialism to the technocratic secular project and led it to lose sight of its fundamental humanistic commitments, so that it ceased to be judged even as a failed attempt to do something different than capitalism was attempting, and instead appeared as a failed attempt to do what capitalism had already achieved.

Overcoming selfishness was a theme in Chinese communism from the 1930s on (Mao 1938) and by the early 1960s Mao and his faction recognized that the Soviet strategy was not actually leading towards communism. While it is certainly true that the policies of the Cultural Revolution were overdetermined by factional political considerations, there is also no evidence that study and "struggle" (public criticism and self criticism), both of which have a long history as spiritual disciplines, could by themselves, in short order, accomplish what the entire axial project had struggled, with only occasional and very limited success, in the form of the great *tzadikim*, *bodhisattvas*, and *sheng*, to achieve for millennia.

It is little wonder that, looking at the world in the wake of the Shoah and the Great Purge, many partisans of this *way* concluded that we were all victims of some kind of cosmic joker. This is why those who continue to embrace the values of the communist tradition have settled into a revolutionary atheistic mysticism which, whether Jewish (Derrida) or Catholic (Zizek) in its heritage, is essentially a retreat to the rabbinic position: arguing about, bearing witness to, and acting in limited ways on behalf of a Justice which we know will never be fully realized in this world, because it is the Justice of a God who, Beyond Being, never comes.

But this is not the only alternative. And it is here that Buddhism, Hinduism, and the *dao xue*, which have loomed so large in this work but which we have barely mentioned, thus far, in our conclusion, rejoin the debate. Buddhism is above all a technology for not just accommodating ourselves to (the Theravada) but actually thriving and being creative in (the Mahayana and the Varjayana) the realities of a contingent being which we have realized is inescapable. It is one thing to learn the lessons of our failed attempts at *theosis* and our failed attempts to rectify the damage cause by our attempts at *theosis* intellectually. It is quite another to actually *live* those lessons. From a purely conceptual vantage point, the *journey of the dialectic* would appear to teach precisely what revolutionary atheistic mysticism has learned from it: that God not only does not exist but cannot be built, and that we need to live the Justice for which that God was a code without priest or sacred pillar (Hosea 3:4). But transconceptually, from the vantage point of a connaturality with Being, realized as relational transformative generativity, a connaturality cultivated in the struggle for justice but experienced through contemplative practice, we really do, objectively and subjectively, by small degrees, over an infinite period of time, actually become God (or, if we prefer the Buddhist terminology which rejects the language of theism because of its association with false doctrines of divine substance and divine subject), we become Enlightened. And the life which was suffering, inescapable suffering, becomes incomparable joy, a journey through oceans of worlds in which, as we grow, we learn to create and liberate and enlighten even as we realize that we never remain ourselves, that we are always dying and always giving birth.

Other spiritual traditions have, to be sure, addressed this set of questions. It is of the essence in the Christian *via negativa* and in the Catholic mystical tradition of the "dark nights" of the soul. It is part of the warp and woof of Sufism. And Vedanta, which developed in dialogue with the Mahayana (Collins 1998) has its own ways to address it. But it is Buddhism's specific contribution to human mystical theology to take the purely negative realization that *Being* is neither substance nor subject, which by itself results in atheism and which is pregnant with the potential for nihilistic rage and despair, and transform it into a spiritual discipline which (admittedly beyond actually existing historic Buddhism) yields a new understanding of what God might be.

Puranic Hinduism and the *dao xue* add still another, essential element to this synthesis, albeit with slightly different notes. Arjuna's dilemma is real. We need to stand up to injustice. We need to build and exercise power. Sometimes we even need to kill. (In fact, we *always* need to kill, at least plants, if we are to survive). And if we embrace the claim advanced earlier this chapter that even minerals and other lesser forms of organization participate the cosmogenetic process of *theosis*, when we mine and build we "kill" them too. And we actually bear this *karma*. We are, in some measure deformed by it. And going off to a monastery, while it may be the proper calling for some, isn't going to solve our problem. Monasteries become large landowners and they instrumentalize the peasants that work their land. In the process they have become great technological and economic engines of progress, doing great good. But the taint of instrumentalization, the *asuric* dimension of our existence, is quite impossible to avoid.

Without embracing the specific claim that there are four well defined *varnas* or broad degrees of development, or much less that membership in these *varnas* is hereditary, the Hindu claim that there are diverse degrees and forms of spiritual development and understanding our calling means understanding where we are on the journey is vitally important if we are not to yield too much to any one of the legitimate aims of life—*kama, artha, dharma,* and *moksa*—leaving the others shortchanged. And when we do approach the task of *moksha*, from whatever degree of spiritual development, there are different paths which are appropriate to different people.

Hinduism also contributes the vitally important element of the concept of *ashrama* or stage of life. While acknowledging that some may be called to bypass the stage of householding and that some may never pass beyond it, this doctrine allows different responsibilities for *brahmacaryns* who are called to devote themselves to what can be learned from dialectics and formal spiritual discipline—or to revolutionary warfare—and for householders who learn from a form of generativity which enmeshes them into the limitations of our material existence and who have an obligation (and inclination) to conserve. And it suggests that most, if not all, eventually ought retire from householder responsibilities not to live out their last days as petty *rentiers* but to resume, with the benefit of a life's experience, the formal study, civic engagement, and more intense spiritual disciplines of their youth, perhaps eventually becoming full renouncers.

From the *dao xue*, finally, we learn that integrating these diverse elements of the *way* both benefits enormously from the formal structures of human civilization: languages and concepts, institutionalized communities and their rituals, but can also never be fully captured by those them. There is an element of flexibility and unknowing which must complement our progress along the structured paths of our *way*, whether it is one we have inherited or one we have carved out for ourselves. There are rules which one must master to tend a garden well. But one must also pay attention to the plants. The *way of ways* is, ultimately, about *Ripening Being*.

Finally, however, this work would be neither honest nor internally consistent without acknowledging the contribution of those who have historically remained largely invisible in accounts of humanity's struggle for *theosis*: women. Our entire effort to retheorize Being as neither substance nor subject but rather relationship, generativity, and transformation, while it draws on sources and traditions which have been officially authored and dominated by men, is ultimately a return to the archaic wisdom which was once the common heritage of men and women, but which men expropriated when we began our quest for *theosis* through conquest and exploitation, and in the process, without entirely destroying it, deformed it beyond recognition. Unlike Mary Daly (Daly 1978, 1984, 1998) who has nonetheless shaped my outlook profoundly on this question, I have argued that this fault or fall was inevitable, necessary, and ultimately enriching. But it was still a fault and fall and still needs to be confessed and still requires that penance be performed. For men especially, it is only when we recognize our always and only fallen and penitent state that we can begin to grow—and to lead spiritually in a way which, while conserving the asuric, irascible, agonistic element of humanity avoids the collapse into *Empire* and *Capital*.

* * *

What then does this *way* look like from the vantage point of one who journeys along it? In its early stages this *way* is simply the ordinary way of life as a rational animal. As we enter this human life, we *all* bring with us the capacity not only for sensation and locomotion, but also an intellect which is aware of our finitude and contingency and thus of the possibility of the Infinite and the Necessary, which is God. At first our intellectual capacities are relatively undeveloped, confined to the exercise of what we have elsewhere called *totalization* (Mansueto 2002b), which abstracts from things *what* they are, in the sense of identifying specific differences which define them, an activity which results in taxonomies which may, at least initially, be *ad hoc*, overlapping, and even contradictory. Similarly, we have the ability to understand and embrace rules of practical reason, which govern the will. Initially, during earliest childhood, we are—regardless of what prior development we bring with us from "previous lives"—concerned primarily with our survival and thus with getting what we want. This means developing our sensiormotor capacities, as Piaget noted, and a tendency to regard ourselves as the center of the universe, without respect to any moral characteristics. Later we discover that things have names and that our relentless effort to satisfy ourselves often results in "push back" from others. We move through the long, preoperational transition to employment of a rational taxonomy and begin to internalize moral rules primarily as things for which we will be punished, or at least elicit a negative reaction, if we violate them. Finally, at the end of this process, sometime in middle childhood, we emerge with the full command of natural language, including the ability to use more or less complete by not yet fully rationalized taxonomies and the ability to operate logically on concrete objects (as in performing basic arithmetic and other simple logical operations). We also emerge with an internalized conventional morality shaped by the culture in which we grow up, which gives us a sense of which ways of pursing our own interests will be successful and which will not. In the process we learn to become interested in others as well and discover the joys of friendship and giving and are stretched beyond the narcissism of infancy and the tyranny of toddlerhood.

Because we are rational *animals* we have a tendency to always return from reason to the image, a tendency which is even stronger at this stage than it is later. We thus engage the our realization of the possibility of the Infinite and the Necessary, our experience of the sacred, by means of image and story. At this point sacred art, sacred stories, and ritual are fundamental to our spiritual progress. What these images and stories do is to situate our secular taxonomies (the system of categories we use to make sense out of the world around us in order to survive) and our conventional morality in the context of a larger story which gives them meaning, especially in light of our realization of the possibility of God and the reality of our own finitude and contingency.

It is entirely possible for someone, while remaining intellectually at the stage of totalization (or what Piaget calls concrete operations) and embracing what seems to be a largely conventional morality, to demonstrate a much higher level of spiritual development, and we hope, in what follows, to say something about how this is possible, whether on the basis of what was achieved in previous lives or on the basis of an otherwise challenging and even heroic life which is simply rather limited from an intellectual vantage point. But if such development does *not* take place, our spiritual stage remains one largely of regarding the sacred images and stories, the conventional morality with which we were raised, and any specifically sacral activities, such as rituals in which we participate, primarily as a way of solving the problem of our finitude and contingency. It is unlikely that we will rise to the level of seeking *theosis*, at least not explicitly, but we will want to live forever. We will, in other words, as Eckhardt said, love God as we love a cow—except that the milk we seek is the nectar of immortality and unending pleasure, sensual, social, and spiritual.

Some traditions, especially the more Augustinian strain in Christianity, look at the limitations of this state and see its selfishness, and concludes that it is sinful and that humanity is radically depraved. Others, such as the Buddhists, recognizing that what we desire at this stage is quite impossible, will tell us that it is a stage of profound illusion and deep suffering. We prefer to say that this is simply a state of relatively modest spiritual development. But it can never make us happy or allow us to make each other happy.

We may fully believe that by doing what we are supposed to do we can achieve authentic happiness or we may doubt the stories and what we imagine they promise. We may do what we are supposed to or not. If we simply discount the stories and fail to do what we are supposed to we will likely make little progress, remaining mired in sensuality and a despair regarding our long term future softened by a failure to reflect very profoundly, if at all, on our condition. If, on the other hand, we embrace the stories and make an effort to do what is right and to be good within the limits of our understanding we will eventually begin to discover both that the stories, while meaningful, don't quite hold together, and that conventional morality, while it works much of the time, is nowhere near sufficiently complex to meet the challenges of even a life of very ordinary complexity. At this point we are on our way to the next stage, according to the various *ways* we have defined: the stage, on the one hand, of formalization, critical rationality, and the dialectic, the stage of *political* action on behalf of justice, and of a rational, critical search for harmony.

It is here that the articulation of a unified *way of ways* becomes a bit more challenging. On the one hand, the full development of human capacities *requires* the cultivation of our intellect beyond the stage of totalization and through the stage of formal and transcendental abstraction (Mansueto 2002b). On the other hand, such cultivation has been, and remains, our progress in extending access to liberal education notwithstanding, the province of a relatively small minority. And our analysis has shown that the spiritual gains which result from this cultivation are, in fact, accessible by other means, specifically by engaging in action on behalf of justice which *formally presupposes* principles which would normally be accessible only at this level but which has been arrived at in some other way. Specifically this means action which is ordered not just towards reciprocal interpersonal care and nurture but a also to the structural requirements of organized human social existence, the rectification of injustices in such structures, and the creation of new, higher forms of organization which more fully *ripen Being*. Progress is possible, in other words, along the *way of Justice and liberation* as well as along the *way of the search for Being*. Let us look now at what this passage looks like along each pathway.

For those traveling along the *way of the search for Being*, progress begins with a recognition that the images and stories and the simple moral rules we grew up with at once conceal and convey higher formal principles. Thus the anthropomorphic God of childhood will be recognized as a metaphor for a rational first principle in terms of which the universe can be explained and human action ordered: the One, the Infinite, or "that than which nothing greater can be thought." The common sense moral rule that we ought to treat others as we would like to be treated ourselves is recognized as an informal statement of the requirement that moral principles be universalizable and order action towards the good of the systems which promote human development as well as to the good of those immediately around us. For those traveling along the *way of justice and liberation* it is, rather, a matter of taking responsibility for the welfare a larger community, beyond the family, something which requires connatural if not theoretical knowledge of universal principles of justice as well as their prudential application. Here God is known not through the medium of the *concept* but rather of the *Law*. Religious stories are important as a way of mediating and providing a context for interpreting this law, more so than as either statements of fact or symbols pregnant with a higher conceptual meaning. This is the level of development typically achieved by conscientious local community leaders who take responsibility for carrying out the work of the institutions which ripen Being.

Those who follow the *way of harmony* travel somewhere in between these two paths. The degree of rationalization and formalization is higher than it is along the *way of justice and liberation* but not so high as along the *way of the search for Being*. Conceptual and connatural knowledge are balanced.

Ultimately, along any of the *ways* this stage is unstable. Attempts to theorize the divine using purely formal reason are, as Kant demonstrated, ultimately doomed, a transcendental ideal which might orient action but not a sound framework of meaning. The institutions which *ripen Being* are themselves in need of cultivation and it soon becomes apparent to those most dedicated to justice that to the extent that they are nurtured at all it is only in order to instrumentalize them, making them tools in the project of deification by means of conquest and exploitation which is the *Saeculum*. Rationalistic hubris gives way to critical skepticism and the ordinary work of *ripening Being* to a "ruthless criticism of everything existing" Marx 1843a/1978) not only including but actually beginning with religion itself (Marx 1846/1978). The *way of harmony*, which seemed to be embodied in the cycles of nature and the rituals of ordinary social life suddenly seems at odds with these structures and beyond naming.

It is quite possible to become trapped at this stage, in which case there is a further danger (though by no means an inevitability) that we will fall into nihilism and despair. This is clearly the dominant mood of those who arrive at this stage along the *way of the search for Being*, but it is also quite common, especially in the wake of the Shoah and the crisis of socialism to end up in such a state as a result of political setbacks along the *way of liberation and justice*. It is also important to recognize that ideas which emerged as a result of higher degrees of spiritual development, such as the Buddhist recognition that all things are empty of inherent existence, can be mobilized at a lower level of development such as this as a way to at once legitimate and soften or regulate the consequences of what amounts to a global existential despair (Kalapuhana 1992). The same is true of certain forms of Taoism, such as the *xuan xue* or Dark Learning School (Collins 1998).

Passage beyond this stage can come in either two ways. The ordinary way is by completing the journey of the dialectic or its practical equivalent by passing beyond critical to a fully dialectical reason, or beyond despair at the failure of political action to yield the desired justice to a recognition of reason, theoretical and practical, as the self-organizing principle of a cosmohistorical evolutionary process which extends, perhaps infinitely, towards a degree of development which we can comprehend only in principle and fully know only over the *longue durée of* its progressive realization.

Here despair is only partly overcome. As Lukacs points out (Lukacs 1921/1971), for the individual alienation (we would say finitude and contingency) remain. It is only by identification with the larger cosmohistorical process that we transcend this alienation, and then it is not *for us* but for a future which we will never live to see.

This is the degree of development represented imaginatively by Dante in his *Comedia* (Alighieri, Dante. *Commedia* 1:4) as the "first circle" or the hell of the philosophers, where in one enjoys the full development of the intellect and the full development of the moral virtues, but nonetheless remains deeply dissatisfied. It is, in general, the stage represented by Radical Aristotelianism as identity with the Agent Intellect. Dialectical materialism achieves this degree of development when it finds reason to hope that the cosmohistorical evolutionary process extends infinitely into the future (Mansueto 1995, 2010b, 2012). When it fails to do this and claims that communism can by itself resolve the "contradiction between existence and essence (Marx 1844/1978)" it either cycles back into the despair of critical rationality or becomes idolatrous and an asuric, *Saecular* deformation.

The other way forward from the despair engendered by critical rationality is by *faith* and *grace*. This *way* proposes, in effect, to skip over the stage of the full development of human capacities and, with divine assistance to achieve what humanity alone could not. As long as it is recognized that some potentials are being left unrealized and that the faith required cannot be either fully justified or commanded (otherwise it becomes submission) this is a permissible route, though not one that leads to full enlightenment or *theosis*. But it is also an extremely dangerous route. Its partisans tend to slide from a sober recognition of reason's limits (which are real but which they have not yet fully explored) to an irrationalism which regards reason as "the devil's" whore (Luther 1546/1914)." Lukacs and Fromm (Lukacs 1953/1980, Fromm 1941) were quite right to see this path as leading potentially, if not inevitably, to fascism, as reason's limitations become an alibi for irrational submission to equally limited spiritual realities such as the "gods" of particular peoples (Heidegger 1934/1989), something which always seems to entail the rejection, oppression, and even annihilation of peoples who do not embrace the (asuric) deity in question. While the *locus classicus* for this phenomenon lies on the Right (Nazism and fascism generally) and it is distinct and ultimately a more serious deformation than the idolatrous forms of communism, it is possible for this same phenomenon to occur on the Left, in the form of a cult of personality associated with a populist or nationalistic deformation of communism, of the sort encountered in the more extreme manifestations of Maoism.

Authentic passage beyond nihilism and despair requires that one achieve a fully dialectical rationality, or its practical equivalent, which is a full dedication to and identification with the struggle for Justice. It then requires, further, that we embrace our dissatisfaction with this state but refuse idolatrous or "feel good" remedies of any kind, and instead enter into the dark nights of the soul in which we begin to learn at last what *Being* and *Justice* are and what it means to *Ripen* them.

This stage of the spiritual life, which, following the "first conversion" and the beginner's path, Juan de la Cruz and the tradition which followed him called the "first dark night" (de la Cruz 1578/2002, Garrigou-Lagrange 1938, Merton 1951/2002) corresponds roughly to what Buddhism calls the lower Bodhisattva stages, during which we have finally recognized the emptiness of the phenomenal world and embrace *bodhicitta*, or the desire for enlightenment. This stage is characterized by a radical realization that we are not and can never be the center of the universe, that deification in the sense of self-subsistence or subjective rational autonomy is in fact impossible, and that there is no power on heaven or on earth which can remedy our condition. Our only road forward is to live through our finitude and contingency, embracing it as the mountain road along which we discover the authentic nature of the divine, which is always and only relational, transformative, generativity.

This is, to be sure, not really the first dark night, and it is only a spirituality which retained significant monastic elements, as both Catholicism and Buddhism do, which could imagine that it was. The realization that Santa Claus does not exist, at least in the sense that we do, and is more nearly a social obligation than a Cappadocian Bishop turned gift giving elf dressed up as a boreal shaman, is a dark night for the children who pass through it and this passage may have both fruitful and barren resolutions. The stage of critical rationality, in which we recognize that the rational content which thought we had rescued from the discarded images of our childhood is in fact empty as well is also, surely, a dark night and a very dangerous one, as it most often issues in radical despair. But this dark night is different. It is about the recognition that there is no exit from our suffering and a demand that we find in that suffering a joy which conquers all.

Living through this dark night, we eventually emerge on the other side, able "once again to see the stars (Dante, *Commedia* 1:33). In point of fact, we see them authentically for the first time. Before they were ornaments of a universe which revolved around us; now they are unfathomably distant worlds which at once beckon and terrify, calling us to evolve beyond our humanity towards something different and greater, and thus no longer ourselves. It is at this point that we begin the *understand*, in the sense Thomas used this term to name one of the Gifts of the Holy Spirit, revealed and mystical wisdom. This is what the Carmelite tradition calls the illuminative stage and corresponds to what Buddhism regards as the middle Bodhisattva stage, when real progress has been made on the cultivation of *bodhicitta* and the perfection of spiritual practices, but before we achieve the status of *arhat*. We begin to be able to dwell in the phenomenal world in a way which is authentically fruitful and generative for ourselves and others, undertaking difficult missions which stretch us, and to integrate and interpret the suffering which is inevitably a result of the fact that these missions are not about *us* in a way which contributes to our own growth and helps enlighten beings at all stages of development.

It is, however, easy at this stage to imagine that we have become wise and just indeed and that we can handle all manner of crises, spiritual and material. But in reality our journey has only begun. Being contingent, living in each others embrace, is always and only material existence and, in spite of the dawning of intelligence and higher spirituality retains an animal element. And the animal is always afraid. If it wasn't we wouldn't last long enough in this world to learn or accomplish anything. And even to the degree that we authentically realize that we lack inherent existence and are ultimately nothing we congratulate ourselves on this recognition. Spiritual pride is a great danger at this stage. And because we are authentically more developed, and far more powerful, we are also far more dangerous. Many great *asura* are born in the illuminative stage.

Ultimately, however, we recognize that our pretense is in vain, and the we are, ultimately, just animals destined to die. No matter how highly developed we become, there is nothing we can achieve which merits permanence or which endows us with the power of *Being as Such*. This is a power which can be given, but which cannot be possessed. And so we enter into yet another dark night, the final one for most Christian mystics, in which we yield definitively any and all claims to self-subsistence or subjectivity. This is the most difficult night by far, though I cannot describe it in detail, finding myself at best only at the twilight which precedes it. I know only that beyond it lies the ecstasy of the mystical union, the realization that in giving and yielding fully and completely we are utterly known and loved and find our joy in participation in the *causative power of Being itself*.

For most spiritual traditions this is the last and highest stage of development. That is certainly true of most classical theisms, including Judaism, Christianity, and Islam, for whom the divine must always be recognized as the source and summit of action and for which the return to source—understood as full participation in its creative activity—represents the highest possible degree of development. Buddhism, however, challenges to look over this horizon, and the *Mahayana* and *Vajrayana* in particular challenge us to regard the enlightenment achieved by the *arhat* (which is simply the mystical union understood from the vantage point of the *via negativa*) as in fact just a starting point for a new cycle of spiritual development. The rationale for this is that *union* still implies multiplicity and *liberation* is liberation from . . . something, and is thus not yet fully complete. For the *Mahayana* the subsequent stages of development are understood as a combined purgation of residual impurities and the cultivation of vast powers to teach and enlighten. The *Vajrayana* proposes sophisticated ways by means of which we can pass through this purgation and cultivate these capacities more quickly. At the end lies the full enlightenment of Buddhahood in which all duality and multiplicity is overcome and in which we live fully and completely by giving.

The one Christian writer who proposes something beyond the mystical union seems to propose something beyond this final purgation as well: John Meister Eckhardt, for whom, beyond all dark nights and beyond any possible mystical union, beyond any cultivation of incredibly advanced powers to enlighten and liberate, there lies the reality—and the knowledge—of ourselves in and as Being, what he calls *Breakthrough* (Fox 1980).

From our vantage point, still traveling along the illuminative path and perhaps entering the dark night of the spirit in which we prepare for the mystical union, these *look* like traces of a perhaps infinite process of continued development which extends so far beyond our current degree of development that language becomes inadequate to the task of marking specific differences. I suspect that that is how it looks to those who reach these higher stages as well.

It might be argued that in tracing out this path I have, ever so subtly, revealed that my own *way* is always and only that of the *way of the search for Being*. But then I admitted that at the outset. But it is a search for Being which has been deeply enriched and profoundly transformed not only by encounter with its internal other, which is Buddhism, but also by its encounter with the *way of justice and liberation*. And it is so not simply because it was this encounter which originally made clear to us that the struggle for deification could lead to the exploitative instrumentalization of others, or that authentic deification required the willingness to give up everything, even to the point of death, death on the cross. It is so because the *way* we have charted is fundamentally a way of *living* in which the cognitive dimension, while fundamental and constitutive, does not operate independently. The way we have charted, in other words, is not just a way of dialectical ascent to a first principle followed by contemplative practice which carries us where concepts dare not tread. Nor, for that matter, does it merely supplement the cognitive with the affective (or substitute the affective for the cognitive), as does the Augustinian tradition and as do many devotional mystical traditions, including certain strains of Sufism and *bhakti yoga*, though clearly the *Being* we seek is as much an object of desire as of knowledge, apart from which we "wander forever restless." What we have done, rather, is to stress that it is life itself which is our teacher and our mistress. It is by creating that we actually participate in Being. This creativity involves both knowledge and love, but it is not reducible to knowing and loving. It is an actual bringing into Being, a bringing into Being which, as ultimately unameable, is beyond knowledge and beyond our capacity for fully informed and reciprocal caring.

We have also shown that our teacher is both Beautiful and incredibly demanding. She nurtures us when we are small and gradually demands more of as us as we grow. But the nurture is always there and as we grow we are able to appreciate its more subtle forms. Ultimately, however, it is Her responsibility to teach us that we are not, and so she is the harshest of disciplinarians. Life lures us, gives to us, and then takes away. And it does this at every stage along the *way* from our first days at our mother's breast, through the days of our toil and achievement, labor and loss, our "years of rice and salt" (Robinson 2001), until the days of our passing.

Cognition, whether sensual, intellectual, or contemplative orients us in this journey and we can proceed more rapidly if we understand where we are and where we are going, so long as we also understand that our map of the *way* is not the *way itself,* and may sometimes mislead us. The same is true of affection. It is the desire to be God which leads us on, and our desire for God which sustains us. And affective practices, both devotional and tantric, including those which appeal to the senses, can help us progress more quickly. But they do not, by themselves, produce spiritual progress. We have to actually live life and travel the *way.*

I stand now at a critical juncture on my journey. I have devoted this lifetime in great measure to regrounding and revitalizing the dialectical tradition in dialogue with both the sciences (physical, biological, and social) and with other spiritual traditions (including technocratic as well as humanistic secularism) and have found myself forced to recognize the limits of dialectics. I have struggled against *Empire* and *Capital* only to discover that those who have succeeded better than I in these struggles did so only by becoming, in significant measure, what they struggled against. But it is precisely these failures which have allowed me to understand what the journey is all about. I believe as passionately as ever in the power of the dialectic. But I know that ultimately it teaches us only what we—and what God—are not, leaving us poised for still higher cycles of growth and development. I remain as dedicated as ever to the construction of a classless and communal society which promotes the fullest possible development of human capacities. I no longer believe that the construction of such a society can ever resolve the contradiction between existence and essence. There are no solutions to the riddle of history.

I have been gazing at the stars, lured and terrified by them for some time now. I have even journeyed to some of those which are near and have some modest conquests to my name. And I know that the journey is only beginning.

I submit this map as a guide to those who follow behind me and as a report to those who have gone before so that they may correct me and help me find my next steps along the way. May we all participate fully in the *causative power of Being as such,* knowing that we live in each others' embrace, and thus *do justice* and *ripen Being.*

Bibliography

Agamben, Giorgio. 1995/1998. *Homo Sacer: Sovereign Power and Bare Life.* Trans. Daniel Heller-Roazen.

———. 2003/2005. *State of Exception.* Trans. Kevin Attell. Chicago: University of Chicago Press.

———. 2007/2011 *The Kingdom and the Glory: For a Theological Genealogy of Economy and Government.* Trans. Lorenzo Chiesa with Matteo Mandarini. Palo Alto: Stanford University Press.

———. 2011/2013. *The Highest Poverty: Monastic Rules and Form-of-Life.* Trans. Adam Kotsko. Palo Alto: Stanford University Press.

———. 2012/2014. *Opus Dei.* Trans. Adam Kotsko. Palo Alto: Stanford University Press.

Albanese, Catherine. 2007. *A Republic of Mind and Spirit.* New Haven: Yale University Press.

Al-Farabi. 10th C CE/1983. *Tahsil al-sa'ada,* edited by Ja'afar al-Yasin. Beirut: Dar al-Andalus.

Alighieri, Dante. 1300–1318/1969. *De Monarchia.* Indianapolis: Bobbs-Merrill.

———. 1300–1318/1969. *Commedia.* trans. as *The Divine Comedy* and with commentary by John D. Sinclair. New York: Oxford University Press.

Althusser, Louis. 1965/1977. *For Marx.* London: Lane.

———. 1968/1970. *Reading Capital.* London: New Left.

———. 1966–1969/1971. *Lenin and Philosophy.* New York: Monthly Review.

Amin, Samir. 1978. *The Law of Value and Historical Materialism.* New York: Monthly Review.

———. 1979/1980. *Class and Nation, Historically and in the Current Crisis.* New York: Monthly Review.

———. 1988/1989. *Eurocentrism.* New York: Monthly Review.

Altizer, J. J. and William Hamilton. 1966. *Radical Theology and the Death of God.* Bobbs-Merrill.

Anaxagoras. c. 450 BCE. *On Nature,* in *Classical Greek Reader,* edited by Kenneth Atchity and Rosemary McKenna. New York: Holt.

Anaximander. c. 560 BCE/1996. *On Nature,* in *Classical Greek Reader,* edited by Kenneth Atchity and Rosemary McKenna. New York: Holt.

Anaximenes. c. 545 BCE/1996. *Air,* in *Classical Greek Reader,* edited by Kenneth Atchity and Rosemary McKenna. New York: Holt.

Anderson, Perry. 1974a. *Passages from Antiquity to Feudalism.* London: New Left Review.
———. 1974b *Lineages of the Absolutist State.* London: New Left Review.
Aquinas, Thomas. 1272/1952. *Summa Theologiae,* Chicago, Encyclopaedia Britannica.
Athanasius. 325. *On the Incarnation of the Word of God.* Accessed at http://www.spurgeon.org/~phil/history/ath-inc.htm.
Asvagosha. 2nd C CE/1964. *Awakening of Faith in the Mahayana.* Surrey: Shrine of Wisdom.
Augustine. 426/1972. *The City of God,* trans. Henry Bettenson. New York: Penguin.
Aristotle. c. 350 BCE/1946. *Politics,* trans. Ernest Barker. Oxford: Clarendon Press.
———. c. 350 BCE/1952. *Metaphysics,* trans. Richard Hope. New York: Columbia University Press.
———. c. 350 BCE/1973. *Physics,* trans. Richard McKeon in *Introduction to Aristotle,* Chicago: University of Chicago Press.
———. c. 350 BCE/1973. *De Anima,* trans. Richard McKeon in *Introduction to Aristotle,* Chicago: University of Chicago Press.
Avineri, Shlomo. 1981. The Making of Modern Zionism: The Intellectual Origins of the Jewish State. New York: Basic.
Badiou, Alain. 1988. "L'*Etre et l'événement.* Paris: Seuil.
———. 2006. *Logiques de mondes.* Paris: Seuil.
Barbour, Ian. 2000. *When Science Meets Religion.* SanFrancisco: Harper.
Bellah, Robert. 2011. *Religion in Human Evolution.* Cambridge: Belknap.
Beyer, S. 1977. "Notes on the vision question in early Mahayana," in Lancaster, L. ed. *Prajnamaramita and Related Systems.* Berkeley: University of California Press.
Bhaskar, Roy. 1989. *Reclaiming Reality.* London: Verso.
———. 1993. *Dialectic: The Pulse of Freedom.* London: Verso.
Bogdanov, Alexander. 1928/1980. Tektology. Intersystems Publishers.
Boler, John. 1993. "Transcending the Natural: Duns Scotus on the Two Affections of the Will," in *American Catholic Philosophical Quarterly* LXVII:1
Bonaventura. c. 1274/1970. *Quaestiones disputate de Scientia Christi,* in Fairweather,
Borgen, Peder. 1987. *Philo, John, and Paul.* Atlanta: Scholars.
Brooks, Douglas Renfrew. 1990. *The Secret of the Three Cities: An Introduction to Hindu Shakta Tantrism.* Chicago: The University of Chicago Press.
———. 1992 *Auspicious Wisdom: The Texts and Traditions of Srividya Shakta Tantrism in South India,* Albany: State University of New York Press.
Brown, Stewart J., & Nockles, Peter B., ed. 2012. *The Oxford Movement: Europe and the Wider World 1830–1930,* Cambridge: Cambridge University Press.
Buchholz. Peter. 1968. "Perspectives for Historical Research in Germanic Religion, *History of Religions,* vol. 8, no. 2, 111–38.
CNN. Dan Merica, The money man behind atheism's activism, CNN 2013.03.23.
Campbell, Colin. 2007. "The General Depletion Picture," in *The Association for the Study of Peak Oil and Gas Newsletter,* #76, April 2007.
Capriles, E. 2003. *Buddhism and Dzogchen: Volume One: Buddhism A Dzogchen Outlook.* Merida, Venezuela: Universidad de Los Andes.
———. 2007. *Beyond Being, Beyond Mind, Beyond History: Dzogchen, Western Philosophy and Transpersonal Psychology* (3 vols.). Merida, Venezuela: Universidad de Los Andes.
Cardenal, Ernesto. 2000. *Cantico Cosmico.* Managua: Trotta.

CERN. 2012. *The Higgs Boson,* accessed at http://home.web.cern.ch/topics/higgs-boson.
Chandler, David (1992). *A History of Cambodia.* Boulder: Westview.
Chaterjee, Satischandra and Datta, Dhirendramohan. 1954. *An Introduction to Indian Philosophy.* Calcutta: University of Calcutta.
Coedès, George. 1943. *Pour mieux comprendre Angkor.* Hanoi: Imprimerie d'Extrême Orient
———. 1968. *The Indianized States of Southeast Asia.* Honolulu: East West Center.
Chiesa, Lorenzo and Toscano, eds. 2009. *The Italian Difference.* Melbourne: re.press.
Childe, V. Gordon. 1851. *Man Makes Himself.* New York: Mentor.
Cleary, Thomas. 1990. *The Tao of Politics.* Boston: Shambala.
Cline, Eric. 2014. *1177 BCE: The Year Civilization Collapsed.* Princeton: Princeton University Press.
Clooney, Francis S. 2011. *Comparative Theology.* New York: Wiley Blackwell.
Collins, Randall. 1998. *The Sociology of Philosophies.* Cambridge, Massachusetts: Belknap Press
Confucius. [c. 500 BCE] 1963. *Chung Yung (The Doctrine of the Mean).* In Wing-Tsi Chan. *A Sourcebook in Chinese Philosophy.* Princeton, NJ: Princeton University Press.
———. [c. 500 BCE] 1979. *Lun-yu (Analects),* Translated by D.C. Lau. New York: Dorset.
Congar, Yves. 1962. *The Mystery of the Temple, or the Manner of God's Presence to His Creatures from Genesis to the Apocalypse,* trans Reginald Frederick Trevett, London: Newan.
Cook, Francis. 1977. *Hua-yen Buddhism. The Jewel Net of Indra.* University Park: Pennsylvania State University Press.
Cook, Michael and Crone, Patricia. 1977. *Hagarism: The Making of the Islamic World.* Cambridge: Cambridge University Press.
Crone, Patricia. 2004. *God's Rule: Government and Islam.* New York: Columbia University Press.
Coomaraswamy, Ananda Kentish. 1987. *Metaphysics.* Princeton: Princeton University Press.
Cruz, Juan de la. 1578/2002. *The Dark Night of the Soul,* translated and with introduction by Mirabai Starr. New York: Riverhead.
Cunningham, Agnes, ed. and trans. 1982. *The Early Church and the State.* Philadelphia: Fortress.
Dahm, Helmut. 1988. *Philosophical Sovietology: The Pursuit of A Science.* Dordrecht: Reidel.
Daftary, Farhad. 1992. *The Isma'ilis: Their History and Doctrines.* Cambridge: Cambridge University Press.
———. 1994. *The Assassin Legends: Myths of the Isma'ilis.* London: I.B. Tauris.
———. 1998. *A short history of the Ismailis.* Edinburgh: Edinburgh University Press.
———. 2004. *Ismaili literature.* London: I.B.Tauris.
———. 2005. *Ismailis in medieval Muslim societies.* London: I.B.Tauris.
Daftary, Farhad; Hirji, Zulfikar. 2008. *The Ismailis: An Illustrated History.* London: Azimuth Editions.
Daly, Mary. 1978/1990. *Gyn/Ecology: The Metaethics of Radical Feminism.* Boston: Beacon.
———. 1984. *Pure Lust: Elemental Feminist Philosophy.* Boston: Beacon.

———. 1998. *Quintessence.* Boston: Beacon
Darwin, Charles. 1859/1970. *The Origin of the Species,* in *Darwin: A Norton Critical Edition,* ed. Philip Appleman. New York: Norton
Dawkins, Richard. 2007. *The God Delusion.* San Francisco: Black Swan.
Delph, Ronald K. 1994. "From Venetian Visitor to Curial Humanist: The Development of Agostino Steuco's 'Counter'-Reformation Thought." Renaissance Quarterly 47: 102-39.
———. 2006. "Renovatio, Reformatio, and Humanist Ambition in Rome." In *Heresy, Culture and Religion in Early Modern Religion.* Edited by Ronald K. Delph, Michelle M.Fontaine, and John Jeffries Martin, pp. 73-92. Kirksville, Mo: Truman State University Press.
Den Uyl, Douglas J. 1983. *Power, State and Freedom: An interpretation of Spinoza's Political Philosophy,* Assen, The Netherlands: Van Gorcum.
Dennett, Daniel. 2007. *Breaking the Spell: Religion as a Natural Phenomenon.* New York: Penguin.
Derrida, Jacques. 1967/1978. "Violence and Metaphysics," and "From a Restricted to a General Economy: For an Hegelianism Without Reserve," in *Writing and Difference,* Chicago: University of Chicago Press.
———. 2001. *Acts of Religion.* London : Routledge.
Devakaruni, Chitra Banerjee. 2009. *Palace of Illusions.* New York : Anchor.
Diet of Augsburg. 1530/2015. *The Augsburg Confession,* accessible at http://bookofconcord.org/augsburgconfession.php.
Dobbs Weinstein, Idit. 2000a. "Gersonides : The Supercommenator on Aristotle : The Decisive Forgotten Link Between Averroes and Spinoza," in Maroth Miklos, ed. *Problems in Arabic Philosophy.* Berlin: Klaus Schwarz.
———. Forthcoming b. "Necessity Revisted: Spinoza as a Radical Aristotelian," *Spinoza by 2000.* Vol. 5, Yirmiyahu Yovel, ed. forthcoming.
Duhem, Pierre. 1909. *Etudes sure Léonard de Vinci.* Paris.
Duns Scotus, John. 1301/1965. *A Treatise on God as First Principle (De Primo Principio).* trans Allan Wolter. Chicago: Franciscan Herald.
Durkheim, Emile. 1911/1965 *Elementary Forms of Religious Life.* New York: Free Press
Eamon, William. 1994. *Science and the Secrets of Nature.* Princeton, New Jersey: Princeton University Press.
Eckstein, Walter, 1944. "Rousseau and Spinoza: Their Political Theories and Their Conception of Ethical Freedom," *Journal of the History of Ideas,* 5 (3): 259-91.
The Economist. 2104. "The Power of Xi Jinping," in *The Economist* 2014.09.24.
Empedocles. c. 500 BCE/1996. *On Nature,* in *Classical Greek Reader,* edited by Kenneth Atchity and Rosemary McKenna. New York: Holt.
Engels, Frederick. 1880/1940. *The Dialectics of Nature.* New York: International.
———. 1880/1978. *Socialism: Utopian and Scientific.* in *Marx-Engels Reader.* New York: Norton.
———. 1884/1948. *The Origins of the Family, Private Property, and the State.* Moscow: Progress.
———. 1895/1978. "Introduction to Marx's *Class Struggles in France. 1848-1858,*" in *Marx-Engels Reader.* New York: Norton.
Eisenman, Robert. 1997. *James, The Brother of the Lord.* New York: Penguin.
Elkins, James. 1999. *What Painting Is.* London: Routledge.
Evola, Julius. 1995. *Revolt Against the Modern World.* Rochester, VT: Inner Traditions.

Ewing, Thor. 2008. *Gods and Worshippers in the Viking and Germanic World*. Stroud, UK: Tempus.
Feuer, Lewis. 1987. *Spinoza and the Rise of Liberalism*, New Brunswick, NJ: Transaction.
Firestone, Shulamith. 1970/2003, *The Dialectic of Sex*. New York: Farrar, Strauss, and Giroux.
Fox, Matthew. 1980. *Breakthrough*. New York: Image.
Frank, Andre Gunder. 1998. *ReOrient: Global Economy in the Asian Age*. Berkeley: University of California Press.
Fromm, Erich. 1941. *Escape from Freedom*, New York: Holt Reinhart Winston.
———. 1947. *Man For Himself*. New York: Holt Reinhart Winston.
———. 1966. *Ye Shall Be As Gods*. New York: Holt Reinhart Winston.
Garrett, Aaron. 2003. "Was Spinoza a Natural Lawyer?" *Cardozo Law Review* 25 (2): 627–41.
Garrigou-Lagrange, Reginald. 1932. *La principe de la finalité*.
———. 1938. *Les trois ages de la vie interieure*. Paris: Cerf.
Genovese, Eugene. 1974. *Roll, Jordan Roll*. New York: Random House.
al-Ghazali. 10th C CE/2001. *The Incoherence of the Philosophers*. Trans. Michael Marmura. Salt Lake City: Bringham Young Univeristy.
Giambutas, Marija. 1991. *Civilization of the Goddess*. San Francisco: Harper.
Gilson, Etienne. 1968. *Dante and Philosophy*. Gloucester, MA: Peter Smith.
———. 1936. *The Spirit of Medieval Philosophy*. New York.
———. 1952. *Being and Some Philosophers*. Toronto: Pontifical Institute of Medieval Studies.
Godwyn, Jocelyn. 1994. *The Theosophical Enlightenment*. Albany: State University of New York Press.
Gottwald, Norman. 1979. *The Tribes of Yahweh*. Maryknoll: Orbis.
Gould, S. J. 1997. "Nonoverlapping Magisteria," in *Natural History* 106: 16–22.
Graham, Stephen R. 1995. *Cosmos in the Chaos: Philip Schaff's Interpretation of Nineteenth-Century American Religion*. Grand Rapids: Eerdmans.
Gramsci, Antonio. 1948. *Il materialismo storico e la filosofia di Benedetto Croce*. Torino: Einaudi.
———. 1949a. *Il Risorgimento*. Torino: Einaudi.
———. 1949b. *Note sul Macchiavelli, sulla politica, e sullo Stato Moderno*. Torino: Einaudi.
———. 1949c. *Gli intelletualli e l'organizzazione di cultura*. Torino: Einaudi.
———. 1950. *Letteratura e vita nazionale*. Torino: Einaudi.
———. 1951. *Passato e presente*. Torino: Einaudi.
———. 1954. *L'Ordine Nuovo*. Torino: Einaudi.
———. 1966. *La questione meridionale*. Roma: Riuniti.
Griggs, Richard. 1992. "Background on the Use of the Term Fourth World," *Center for World Indigenous Studies*, accessed at http://cwis.org/GML/background/FourthWorld/.
Guenon, René. 2007. *The Crisis of the Modern World*. Varansi: Indica.
Gösta, Hallonsten, 2007. "*Theosis* in Recent Research," in *Partakers of the Divine Nature: The History and Development of Deification in the Christian Traditions* (ed. Michael J. Christensen and Jeffrey A. Wittung); Grand Rapids: Baker Academic, 2007

Grant, Edward. 1978 "Cosmology," in David Lindberg, editor, *Science in the Middle Ages*. Chicago: University of Chicago Press.

———. 1996. *Planets, Stars, and Orbs: The Medieval Cosmos, 1200–1687*. Cambridge: CUP.

Hardt, Michael and Negri, Antonio. 2001. *Empire*. Cambridge: Harvard University Press.

———. *Multitude*. New York: Penguin.

Harris, Errol. 1965. *Foundations of Metaphysics in Science*. London: Allen & Unwin.

———. 1991. *Cosmos and Anthropos*. Atlantic Highlands, NJ: Humanities Press.

———. 1992. *Cosmos and Theos*. Atlantic Highlands, NJ: Humanities.

Harris, Sam. 2004. *The End of Faith: Religion, Terror, and the Future of Reason*. New York: Norton.

Hatch, Nathan. 1977. *The Sacred Cause of Liberty: Republican Thought and the Millennium in Revolutionary New England*. New Haven: Yale University of Press

Haught, John F. 1995. *Science & Religion: From Conflict to Conversation*. Mawah, NJ: Paulist.

Hayden, Brian. 1986. "Old Europe: Sacred matriarchy or complementary opposition?" in A. Bonanno (ed.), *Archaeology and fertility cult in the ancient Mediterranean*. Amsterdam: Gruner, 17–30.

———. 1998. "An Archaeological Evaluation of the Gimbutas Paradigm," in *The Pomegranate* 6: 35–46.

Hayek, F.A. 1973. *Law, Liberty, and Legislation, Volume One: Rules and Order*. Chicago: University of Chicago Press.

———. 1988. *The Fatal Conceit*. Chicago: University of Chicago Press.

Hegel, G.W.F. 1807/1967. *Phenomenology of Mind*. trans J.B. Baillie. New York: Harper.

———. 1817/1990. *Encyclopaedia of the Philosophical Sciences (Outline)*. trans Taubeneck, Steven. New York: Continuum.

———. 1830/1971. *Encyclopaedia of the Philosophical Sciences*. Trans. William Wallace. Oxford, UK: Oxford University Press.

Heidegger, Martin. 1928/1968. *Being and Time*, New York: Harper & Row.

———. >1934/1989: *Beitrage sur Philosophie* ("Contributions to Philosophy"). Frankfurt-Main: Klosterman.

———. >1941/1979–1987 *Nietzsche*. San Francisco: Harper & Row.

———. 1977. *The Question Concerning Technology*. New York: Harper & Row.

Heimart, Alan. 1966. *Religion and the American Mind: From the Great Awakening to the Revolution*. Cambridge: Harvard University Press.

Heraclitus. c. 500 BCE/ 1996. *On Nature*, in *Classical Greek Reader*, edited by Kenneth Atchity and Rosemary McKenna. New York: Holt.

Hesiod. c. 750 BCE/1988. *Theogony*, translated with an Introduction and Notes by M. L. West. Oxford: Oxford University Press.

Higham, Charles. 2001. *The Civilization of Angkor*. Berkeley: University of California Press.

Hobsbawm, Eric. 1959, *Primitive Rebels*. New York: Norton.

Hooker, Richard. 1612/1970. *A Learned Discourse of Justification*. in Hooker, Richard, *Works* (Three volumes). Edited by John Keble, Oxford: Oxford University Press, 1836; Revised by R. W. Church and F. Paget, Oxford, 1888. Reprint by Burt Franklin, 1970 and by Via Media Publications.

Houtart, Francois. 1952. *Sociologie de la Catholicism Americaine*. Louvain.

———. 2000. *Sociología de la religión*. Mexico: Plaza y Janes.
Howe, Daniel Walker. 1979. *The Political Culture of the American Whigs*. Chicago: University of Chicago Press.
Hubbert, M.K. 1956. "Nuclear Energy and the Fossil Fuels" Paper presented before the Spring Meeting of the Southern District, American Petroleum Institute, Plaza Hotel, San Antonio, Texas, March 7-8-9.
———. "Oil: The Dwindling Treasure," in *National Geographic*, June 1974.
Ingham, Mary Elisabeth, CSJ. 1993. "Scotus and the Moral Order," in *American Catholic Philosophical Quarterly* LXVII:1.
Intergovernmental Panel on Climate Change. 2007. *Climate Change 2007" The Physical Science Basis: Summary for Policy Makers*. Paris: IPCC.
Jaspers, Karl. 1953. *The Origin and Goal of History*. New Haven: Yale University Press.
Kalupahana, David. 1992. *A History of Buddhist Philosophy*. Honolulu: University of Hawaii Press.
Kant, Immanuel. 1755/1968. *Universal Natural History and Theory of the Heavens*. New York: Greenwood.
———. 1781/1969a. *Foundations of the Metaphysics of Morals*, trans. Lewis White Beck. Indianapolis: Bobbs-Merrill.
———. 1781/1969b. *Critique of Pure Reason*. trans. Lewis White Beck, Indianapolis: Bobbs-Merrill.
Kelly, C.E. 2008. *Meister Eckhart on Divine Knowledge*. New Haven: Yale University Press.
Khan, Dominique Sila. 2004. *Crossing the Threshold: Understanding Religious Identities in South Asia*. London: Institute of Ismaili Studies.
Kierkegaard, Soren. 1846/1941. *A Concluding Unscientific Postscript*. trans Lowrie, Walter. Princeton: Princeton University Press.
Kinsley, David. 1988. *Hindu Goddesses: Visions of the Divine Feminine in the Hindu Religious Tradition*. Berkeley: University of California Press.
———. *Tantric Visions of the Divine Feminine: The Ten Mahavidyas*. Berkeley: University of California Press (Berkeley, 1997).
Kingsley, Peter. 1995. *Ancient Philosophy, Mystery, and Magic*. Oxford: Oxford University Press.
Konrad, Gyrogy and Szelenyi, Ivan. 1967. *Intellectuals on the Road to Class Power*. New York : Harcourt Brace Jovanovich.
Krause, Lawrence 2012. *A Universe from Nothing*. New York: Simon & Schusterp.
Krauss, Lawrence and Starkman, Glenn. 1999."The Fate of Life in the Universe," in *Scientific American*, November 1999.
———. forthcoming "Life, the Universe, and Nothing: Life and Death in an Ever-Expanding Universe," in *Astrophysical Journal*, available at xxx.lanl.gov/abs/astro-ph/9902189.
Krebs, Pierre. 2012. *Fighting for the Essence*. Arktos.
Kyrtatas, Dimitris. 1987. *The Social Structure of Early Christian Communities*. London: Verso.
Lai, W. 1977. "Reflections on *Esoteric Confucianism*," in *History of Religions* 17:1.
Lancaster, Roger. 1988 *Thanks to God and the Revolution*. Berkeley: University of California Press.
Lao Tzu. c. 500/1972. *The Tao Te Ching*. translated by Gia-fu Feng and Jane English. New York: Vintage.

Leaman, Olivier. 1997. *Averroes and His Philosophy*. New York: Routledge.
Laplace, Pierre Simon. 1819/1951 *A Philosophical Essay on Probabilities*. New York: Dover.
———. 1799–1825. *Treatise on Celestial Mechanics*. Paris.
Leff, Gordon. 1967. *Heresy in the Late Middle Ages*. New York: Barnes & Noble.
Lenin, V. I. 1902/1929. *What is to Be Done?* New York: International.
———. 1908/1970. *Materialism and Empiriocriticism*. Moscow: Progress.
———. 1916/1976. *Philosophical Notebooks* (Volume 38 of the Collected Works). Moscow: Progress.
Lenski, Gerhard and Jean. 1982. *Human Societies*. New York: McGraw Hill.
Li Ki. 1967. Translated by James Legge. Edited with an introduction and study guide by Ch'u Chai and Winberg Chai. New Hyde Park, NY: University Books.
Lindberg, David. 1978. *Science in the Middle Ages*. Chicago: University of Chicago Press (ed.).
———. 1992. *The Beginnings of Western Science*. Chicago: University of Chicago Press
Lockridge, Kenneth. 1970. *A New England Town: The First Hundred Years*. New York: Norton.
de Lubac, Henri. 1938/1988. *Catholicism: Christ and the Common Destiny of Man*, (San Francisco: Ignatius.
———. 1944/2007 *Corpus Mysticum: The Eucharist and the Church in the Middle Ages*, trans Gemma Simmonds with Richard Price and Christopher Stephens. Notre Dame: University of Notre Dame Press.
———. 1979. *La Postérité spirituelle de Joachim de Flore*. Paris: Lethielleux.
Luther, Marin. 1517/2015. *The Liberty of a Christian*, accessible at *The Modern History Sourcebook*, Fordham University, http://legacy.fordham.edu/halsall/mod/luther-freedomchristian.asp.
———. 1546/1914. *Martin Luther's Last Sermon in Wittenberg . . . Second Sunday in Epiphany, 17 January 1546.Dr. Martin Luthers Werke: Kritische Gesamtausgabe*. Weimar: Herman Boehlaus Nachfolger.
Lukacs, Georgi. 1922/1971. *History and Class Consciousness*. Cambridge: MIT Press.
———. 1953/1980. *The Destruction of Reason*. London: Merlin.
Lyotard, Jean Francois. 1979/1984. *The Postmodern Condition*, Minneapolis: University of Minnesota Press.
MacAleer, Graham. 1996."Saint Anselm: An Ethics of *Caritas* for a Relativist Agent," in *American Catholic Philosophical Quarterly* LXX.
Mannermaa, Tuomo. 2005. *The Christ Present in Faith*. Philadelphia: Fortress.
Maduro, Otto. 1982. *Religion and Social Conflict*. Maryknoll: Orbis.
Maistre, Joseph de. 1965. *Works*. New York: Macmillan.
Makdisi, George. 1989. "Scholasticism and Humanism in Classical Islam and the Christian West," in *Journal of the American Oriental Society* 109:2.
Malthus, Thomas. 1798. *An Essay on the Principle of Population*. Accessed at http://www.ac.wwu.edu/~stephan/malthus/malthus.o.html.
Mansueto, Anthony. 1985 "Blessed Are The Meek: Religion and Socialism in Italian American History," *Proceedings of the American Italian Historical Association*.
———. 1988. "Religion, Solidarity, and Class Struggle," in *Social Compass* XXXV:2
———. 1995. *Towards Synergism: The Cosmic Significance of the Human Civilizational Project*. Lanham, MD: University Press of America.
———. 2002a. *Religion and Dialectics*. Lanham, MD: University Press of America.

———. 2002b. *Knowing God: Restoring Reason in an Age of Doubt*. Aldershot, UK: Ashgate.

———. 2006. "A Question Centered Approach to Liberal Education," in *The Journal of Liberal Education*

———. 2010a. *The Death of Secular Messianisms*. Eugene, OR: Cascade

———. 2010b. *Knowing God: The Journey of the Dialectic*. Eugene, OR: Pickwick

———. 2011. *Knowing God: Doing Justice*. Eugene, OR: Pickwick

———. 2012 *Knowing God: The Ultimate Meaningfulness of the Universe*. Eugene, OR: Pickwick

———. 2013. "Religion and Ethnicity: The Case of Italian Americans," paper presented to the Loyola Conference on Italian American History, October 2013, Chicago, Illinois

Mansueto, Anthony and Maggie. 2005. *Spirituality and Dialectics*. Lanham, Maryland: Lexington Books.

Mao Zedong. 1938/1971."Combat Liberalism," in *Selected Works*. Peking: Foreign Languages Press.

Maritain, Jacques. 1937. *Degrees of Knowledge*. London: Bles.

———. 1951. *Man and the State*. Chicago: University of Chicago Press.

Marsden, George. 1980. *Fundamentalism in American Culture*. New York: Oxford

Marx, Karl. 1843a/1978. "For a Ruthless Criticism of Everything Existing," in *Marx-Engels Reader*, New York: Norton.

———. 1843b/1978. "Contribution to the Critique of Hegel's Philosophy of Right: Introduction," in *Marx-Engels Reader*, New York: Norton.

———. 1844/1978. *Economic and Philosophical Manuscripts*. New York: Norton.

———. 1846/1978. *The German Ideology*, in *Marx-Engels Reader*. New York: Norton.

———. 1848/1978. *The Communist Manifesto*, in *Marx-Engels Reader*. New York: Norton.

———. 1849/1978. *Wage Labor and Capital*, in *Marx-Engels Reader*. New York: Norton.

———. 1859/1961. *Contribution to the Critique of Political Economy: Preface* in Fromm, Erich. *Marx's Concept of Man*. New York: Continuum.

———. 1867/1977. *Capital*, Volume One. New York: Vintage.

———. 1881/1978. "Letter to Vera Zasulich," in *Marx-Engels Reader*. New York: Norton.

———. 1863/1963. *Theories of Surplus Value: Part One*. Moscow: Progress.

———. 1863/1971. *Theories of Surplus Value: Part Two*. Moscow: Progress.

Merton, Thomas. 1951/2002. *The Ascent to Truth*. New York: Harvest

———. 1968. *Zen and The Birds of Appetite*. New York: New Directions.

McGinn, Bernard. 1979 . *Apocalyptic Spirituality*. New York: Paulist

McGuire, Bill. 2003. "Will Global Warming Trigger a New Ice Age?" *The Guardian*, 13 November 2003

Milbank, John. 1990. *Theology and Social Theory*. London: Blackwell.

———. *The Word Made Strange*. Oxford: Blackwell.

———. 1999. "The Theological Critique of Philosophy in Hamman and Jacobi," in *Radical Orthodoxy*, edited by John Milbank, Catherine Pickstock and Graham Ward. London: Routledge.

———. 2006a "Geopolitical Theology," unpublished paper accessed at http://www.theologyphilosophycentre.co.uk/papers.php

———. 2006b "Only Theology saves Metaphysics: on the Modalities of Terror," unpublished paper accessed at http://www.theologyphilosophycentre.co.uk/papers.php

———. 2014. *Beyond Secular Order: The Representation of Being and the Representation of the People.*

Miller, Jon. 2012. "Spinoza and Natural Law," in *Reason, Religion, and Natural Law: From Plato to Spinoza*, Ed. Jonathan A. Jacobs, Oxford: Oxford University Press.

Millerman, Michael. 2013. "Heidegger, Left and Right: Differential Political Ontology and Fundamental Political Ontology Compared," in *The Fourth Theory*, accessed at http://www.4pt.su/en/content/heidegger-left-and-right.

Moore, Barrington. 1966. *Social Origins of Dictatorship and Democracy*. Boston: Beacon

Murdoch, John and Sylla, Edith. 1978. "The Science of Motion," in David Lindberg, editor, *Science in the Middle Ages*. Chicago: University of Chicago Press.

Nagarjuna, Siddha. c. 200/1970. *Madhyamakakarika*. Tokyo, Hokuseido Press. c. 200. *Mahaprajnaparamitasastra*. translated by the Tripi?akadharmacarya Kumarajiva, accessible at http://read.84000.co/resources/Indian%20Buddhist%20Classics/Lamotte,%20Vol.%203-%20Maha-prajnaparamita-sastra-%20by%20Nagarjuna%20%20(english%20translation).pdf.

Nasr, Seyyed Hussein. 1964. *Three Muslim Sages: Avicenna, Suhrawardi, Ibn-`Arabi*.

———. 1989, *Knowledge and the Sacred*. Albany: State University of New York.

Negri, Antonio. 1991. *The Savage Anomaly*, ed. and trans. Michael Hardt, Minneapolis: Minnesota University Press.

Neusner, Jacob. 1975/2003. *Invitation to the Talmud*. Eugene, OR: Wifp & Stock.

Nevin, John. 1846/2012. *The Mystical Presence: a Vindication of the Reformed or Calvinistic Doctrine of the Holy Eucharist*. Eugene. OR: Wipf & Stock.

Niebhur, Reinhold. 1932/2002. *Moral Man and Immoral Society: A Study of Ethics and Politics*. New York: Louisville: Westminster John Knox.

Newbigin, Lesslie. 1969. *The Finality of Christ*. London: SCM, 1969.

Newton, Isaac. 1687/1999 *The Philosophical Principles of Natural Philosophy*. Trans. I.B. Cohen. Berkeley: University of California Press.

———. 1700. *The Reasonableness and Certainty of the Christian Religion*. London

Nietzsche, Friedreich. 1889/1968. *The Will to Power*. New York: Random House.

Nylan, Michael. 2001. *The Five 'Confucian' Classics*. New Haven. Yale University Press.

Osthathios, Geevarghese Mar. 1979. *Theology of a Classless Society*. Maryknoll: Orbis

Paley, William. 1802/1986. *Natural Theology*. Charlottesville, VA: Ibis.

Pawlikowski, John. 1982. *Christ in the Light of Jewish-Christian Dialogue*. New York: Paulist.

Pedersen, Olaf. 1978. "Astronomy," in David Lindberg, editor, *Science in the Middle Ages*. Chicago: University of Chicago Press.

Persons, Claude. 2010. *The Deified Citizens of "The City of God,"* Dissertation prepared for Southeastern Baptist Theological Seminary, accessible at http://gradworks.umi.com/34/45/3445933.html.

Plato. c. 385 BCE/1968. *Republic*. trans. Alan Bloom, New York: Basic.

———. c. 385 BCE/1960. *Timaeus*. New York: Penguin.

Prajnaparamita-Hrdaya Sutra. 1st BCE. Accessible at http://kr.buddhism.org/zen/sutras/conze.htm.

Prokhovnik, Raia, 2004, *Spinoza and Republicanism*, London and New York: Palgrave Macmillan.

Pythagoras. c. 530 BCE/1996. *The Golden Verses*, in *Classical Greek Reader*. edited by Kenneth Atchity and Rosemary McKenna. New York: Henry Holt and Company.

Radhakrishnan, Sarvepalli and Moore, Charles. 1957. *A Sourcebook in Indian Philosophy*. Princeton: Princeton University Press.

Rahner, Karl. 1957/1968. *Spirit in the World*. New York: Herder.

———. 1976/1978. *Foundations of Christian Faith*. New York: Seabury.

Raschke, Carl . 2005 "Derrida and the Return of Religion: Religious Theory after Postmodernism," in *Journal of Religious and Cultural Theory* 6:2, 1–2.

Ratzinger, Joseph Cardinal. 1984. "Instruction Regarding Certain Aspects of the Theology of Liberation," United States Catholic Conference.

———. 1986. "Christian Freedom and Liberation," United States Catholic Conference

Reeves, Marjorie. 1969. *Prophecy in the Late Middle Ages*. New York: Oxford.

———. 1976. *The Prophetic Future in Joachim of Fiore*. New York: Oxford.

Reich, Robert. 1992. *The Work of Nations*. New York: Vintage.

Rohr, Richard. 2015. *Beyond the Birdbath: Richard Rohr Teaches the Franciscan Way*, online course accessible at http://cacbeta.org/bookstore-2/radicalgrace/itemlist/category/720-the-rohr-institute#.

Rose, Gillian. 1984. *The Dialectic of Nihilism*. London: Wiley-Blackwell.

Rosenthal, Michael, 1998, "Two Collective Action Problems in Spinoza's Social Contract Theory,"*History of Philosophy Quarterly*, 15 (4): 389–409.

———. 2001, "Tolerance as a Virtue in Spinoza's *Ethics*," *Journal of the History of Philosophy*, 39 (4): 535–57.

———. 2003, "Spinoza's Republican Argument for Toleration," *The Journal of Political Philosophy*, 11 (3): 320–37.

———. 2013, "The Siren Song of Revolution: Spinoza on the Art of Political Change," Eds. Erick Raphael Jimenez, Matthew Lampert, Christopher Roberts, and Rocío Zambrana, *Graduate Faculty Philosophy Journal*, 34 (1): 111–32.

Rousseau, Jean-Jacques. 1762/1962 *Le contrat social*. Paris: Freres.

Rowley, David. 1987. *Millenarian Bolshevism*. New York: Garland.

Richard L. Rubenstein. 1992. "God After the Death of God" in *After Auschwitz: History, Theology, and Contemporary Judaism*. 2nd. Ed. Baltimore: Johns Hopkins University Press.

———. 2003. *When Jesus Became God*. New York: Harcourt Brace.

Rumi, Jalal al-Din Mohammed. <1273/1914. „I Died as a Mineral", as translated in *The Mystics of Islam* (1914) edited by Reynold Alleyne Nicholson, 125.

Russell, James. 1994. *The Germanization of Early Medieval Christianity: A Sociohistorical Approach to Religious Transformation*. USA: Oxford University Press.

Samuel, Geoffrey. 2008. *The Origins of Yoga and Tantra*. Cambridge: Cambridge Univesity Press.

Ste. Croix, C. E. M de. 1982. *The Class Struggle in the Ancient Greek World: From the Archaic Age to the Arab Conquests*. London: Duckworth.

Sankara Acarya. 8th C CE/1890. *Vedanta Sutras with Commentary*. Trans. George Thibaut, in *Sacred Books of the East*, XXXIV and XXXVIII. Oxford: Clarendon.

———. 8th C CE/1929. *Sarvasiddhantasamgraha*. Trans. Prem Sundar Bose. Calcutta.

———. 8th C CE/2004. *Viveka-chudamani*, in in James Fieser and John Powers *Scriptures of the World's Religions*. New York: McGraw-Hill.

Sarkisyanz, E. 1965. *Buddhist Backgrounds of the Burmese Revolution*. The Hague: Nijhoff.

Sartre, Jean Paul. 1943/1993. *Being and Nothingness*. New York: Washington Square Press.
Schaff, Philip. 1844/2004, *The Principle of Protestantism*. Eugene, OR: Wipf & Stock.
Sereni, E. 1968 *Capitalismo nelle campagne*. Torino: Einaudi.
Sewell, William. 1980. *Work and Revolution in France*. New York: Cambridge University Press.
Siddhartha, Gautama (The Buddha). 6th C BCE/1915. *Anguttara-nikaya, Samyutta-nikaya, Visuddhi-maggi* in H.C Warren. *Buddhism in Translations*, Harvard Oriental Series 3, sixth issue. Cambridge: Harvard University Press.
Dharmchakrapravartansutra 3). acessible at http://www.budsas.org/ebud/ebsuto01.htm.
Silberman, Neil Asher. 1998. *Heavenly Powers*. New York: Grosset-Putnam.
———. ibn Sina. 11th C CE/2001 *Danishnamah* in Morewedge, Parwiz. *The Metaphysica of Avicenna*. Binghampton: Global.
———. 11th C CE/1996. *Isharat*. In Inati, Shams. *Ibn Sin and Mysticism*. London: Routledge & Kegan Paul
———. 11th C CE/2005. *al-Shifa'*, in Trans. Michael Marmura. *The Metaphysics of the Healing*. Salt Lake City: Bringham Young University.
Schmitt, Charles. 1966. *Perennial Philosophy: From Agostino Steuco to Leibniz*, Journal of the History of Ideas. 27:1.
Scholem, Gershon. 1941/1995. *Major Trends in Jewish Mysticism*. New York: Schoken
———. 1973. *Sabbatai Sevi: The Mystical Messiah*. Princeton: Princeton University Press.
Schuon, Frithjof. 1992. *Echoes of Perennial Wisdom*, Bloomington, IN: World Wisdom.
Smith, Adam. 1776. *The Wealth of Nations*. Accessed at http://www.econlib.org/LIBRARY/Smith/smWN.html.
Snellgrove, David. 2004. *Angkor: Before and After. A Cultural History of the Khmers*. London: Weatherhill.
Snodgrass, Anthony. 1980. *Archaic Greece: An Age of Experiment*. London: Dent.
Spinoza, Baruch. 1677/1955. *Ethics*. New York: Dover.
———. 1677/2007. *Theological Political Treatise*. Cambridge: Cambridge University Press.
Smith, Huston. 1995. *The World's Religions: Our Great Wisdom Traditions*. New York: HarperOne.
Stalin. Joseph. 1952/1972. *Economic Problems of Socialism in the U.S.S.R.* New York: International.
Stepheonson, Neal. 2009. *Anathem*. New York: Harper.
Stone, Merlin. 1976. *When God Was A Woman*. London: Dorset.
Tabor, James. 2006. *The Jesus Dynasty*. New York: Simon & Schuster.
Swimme, Brian and Berry, Thomas. 1992. *The Universe Story*. New York: HarperOne.
Tabor, James. 2006. *The Jesus Dynasty*. New York: Simon & Schuster.
Teilhard de Chardin, Pierre. 1955/1975. *The Phenomenon of Man*. New York: Harper & Row.
Ter Haar, B.J. 1992. *The White Lotus Teachings in Chinese Religious History*. Leiden: Brill.
Tertullian. 197/1914. *De praescriptione haereticorum*, translated by T.H. Bindley. London: SPCK, accessible at http://www.tertullian.org/articles/bindley_test/bindley_test_07prae.htm.

Theissen, Gerd. 1982. *The Social Setting of Pauline Christianity*. Philadelphia: Fortress
Thibault, Paul. 1972. *Savoir et pouvoir: philosophie thomiste et politique cléricale au XIXme siècle*. Quebec: Université de Laval.
Tipler, Frank. 1994. *The Physics of Immortality*, New York, Doubleday.
Thales of Miletus. c. 575 BCE/1996. *Water*, in *Classical Greek Reader*, edited by Kenneth Atchity and Rosemary McKenna. New York: Holt.
Thapar, Romila. 2002. *Early India: From the Origins to 1300*. Berkeley, California: University of California Press.
Tsung-mi. 828–835/1995. *Yuan jen lun*, in Peter Gregory, translator and editor *Inquiry in to the Origin of Humanity*. Honolulu: Kuroda Institute.
University of Hawaii Press.
Tracy, David. 1975. *Blessed Rage for Order*. Chicago: University of Chicago Press.
Unger, Roberto Mangabeira. 2014. *The Religion of the Future*. Cambrdige, MA: Harvard University Press.
Upanishads. ?/2007 *The Upanishads*. Tomales, CA: Blue Mountain.
Vahanian, Gabriel (1961). *The Death of God: The Culture of our Post-Christian Era*. New York: George Braziller.
van Shaik, Sam. 2011. *Tibet: A History*. London and New Haven: Yale University Press.
von Balthasar, Hans Urs. 1968. *Love Alone*. London: Allen & Unwin.
Wansbrough, John. 2004. *Quranic Studies*. New York: Prometheus.
Waters, Frank. 1963. *The Book of the Hopi*. New York: Viking Penguin.
Ware, Timothy. 1993. *The Orthodox Church*. New York: Penguin.
Waters, Frank. 1963. *The Book of the Hopi*. New York: Viking Penguin.
Weber, Max. 1918/2004. "Science as a Vocation," in *The Vocation Lectures*, trans. by Rodney Livingstone, New York: Hackett.
———. 1920/1958. *The Protestant Ethic and the Spirit of Capitalism*. New York Scribners.
———. 1921/1968. *Economy and Society*. New York: Bedminster.
Wetter, Gustav. 1952/1958. *Dialectical Materialism*, New York: Praeger.
Whitehead, Alfred North. 1929. *Process and Reality: An Essay in Cosmology*. New York: Macmillan.
Wilhelm, R. an d Baynes, C. F. 1967. *The I Ching or Book of Changes*. Princeton: Princeton University Press.
Williams. Paul. 1989. *Mahayana Buddhism*. New York: Routledge.
Wolf, Eric. 1969. *Peasant Wars of the Twentieth Century*. New York: Harper.
Wood, Ellen Meiksins, and Neal. 1978. *Class Ideology and Ancient Political Theory: Socrates, Plato, and Aristotle in Social Context*. Oxford: Basil Blackwell.
Xenophanes. c. 500/1996. *On Nature*, in *Classical Greek Reader*, edited by Kenneth Atchity and Rosemary McKenna. New York: Holt.
Yao Xinzhong. 2000. *An Introduction to Confucianism*. (Cambridge: Cambridge University Press.
Yao Wen-yuan. 1975. "The Social Basis of the Lin Biao Anti Party Clique." Chicago: Liberation.
Yovel, Yirmiyahu. 2001. *Spinoza and Other Heretics*. Princeton: Princeton University Press
Zhou Dunyi. 1017–73 *T'ai-chi t'u shuo* or *Explanation of the Diagram of the Great Ultimate*, Trans. Kurt Vall, in James Fieser and John Powers *Scriptures of the World's Religions*. New York: McGraw-Hill

Zhu Xi. 12th C CE/2004. *Xing qing xin yi deng mingyi*. Trans. Kurt Vall, in James Fieser and John Powers *Scriptures of the World's Religions*. New York: McGraw-Hill

Zimmermann, R.E. 1991. "The Anthropic Cosmological Principle" Philosophical Implications of Self-Reference," in Casti, John, and Karlqvist, Anders. Beyond Belief: Randomness, Prediction, and Explanation in Science. Boca Raton, FL: CRC Press

Zitara, Nicola. 1971 *L'unita d'Italia, Nascita di una colonia*. Milano: Jaca Book

Žižek, Slavoj. 2009. *The Monstrosity of Christ: Paradox or Dialectic?*. Cambridge, MA: The MIT Press.

———. 2012 *God in Pain: Inversions of Apocalypse*, with Boris Gunjević, New York: Seven Stories Press

www.ingramcontent.com/pod-product-compliance
Lightning Source LLC
Chambersburg PA
CBHW071238230426
43668CB00011B/1492